IFIP Advances in Information and Communication Technology

561

IFIP – The International Federation for Information Processing

IFIP was founded in 1960 under the auspices of UNESCO, following the first World Computer Congress held in Paris the previous year. A federation for societies working in information processing, IFIP's aim is two-fold: to support information processing in the countries of its members and to encourage technology transfer to developing nations. As its mission statement clearly states:

IFIP is the global non-profit federation of societies of ICT professionals that aims at achieving a worldwide professional and socially responsible development and application of information and communication technologies.

IFIP is a non-profit-making organization, run almost solely by 2500 volunteers. It operates through a number of technical committees and working groups, which organize events and publications. IFIP's events range from large international open conferences to working conferences and local seminars.

The flagship event is the IFIP World Computer Congress, at which both invited and contributed papers are presented. Contributed papers are rigorously refereed and the rejection rate is high.

As with the Congress, participation in the open conferences is open to all and papers may be invited or submitted. Again, submitted papers are stringently refereed.

The working conferences are structured differently. They are usually run by a working group and attendance is generally smaller and occasionally by invitation only. Their purpose is to create an atmosphere conducive to innovation and development. Refereeing is also rigorous and papers are subjected to extensive group discussion.

Publications arising from IFIP events vary. The papers presented at the IFIP World Computer Congress and at open conferences are published as conference proceedings, while the results of the working conferences are often published as collections of selected and edited papers.

IFIP distinguishes three types of institutional membership: Country Representative Members, Members at Large, and Associate Members. The type of organization that can apply for membership is a wide variety and includes national or international societies of individual computer scientists/ICT professionals, associations or federations of such societies, government institutions/government related organizations, national or international research institutes or consortia, universities, academies of sciences, companies, national or international associations or federations of companies.

More information about this series at http://www.springer.com/series/6102

Nicola Bombieri · Graziano Pravadelli ·
Masahiro Fujita · Todd Austin ·
Ricardo Reis (Eds.)

VLSI-SoC: Design and Engineering of Electronics Systems Based on New Computing Paradigms

26th IFIP WG 10.5/IEEE International Conference
on Very Large Scale Integration, VLSI-SoC 2018
Verona, Italy, October 8–10, 2018
Revised and Extended Selected Papers

 Springer

Editors
Nicola Bombieri
University of Verona
Verona, Italy

Masahiro Fujita
University of Tokyo
Tokyo, Japan

Ricardo Reis
Universidade Federal do Rio Grande
do Sul
Porto Alegre, Brazil

Graziano Pravadelli
University of Verona
Verona, Italy

Todd Austin
University of Michigan
Ann Arbor, MI, USA

ISSN 1868-4238   ISSN 1868-422X   (electronic)
IFIP Advances in Information and Communication Technology
ISBN 978-3-030-23427-0   ISBN 978-3-030-23425-6   (eBook)
https://doi.org/10.1007/978-3-030-23425-6

This Springer imprint is published by the registered company Springer Nature Switzerland AG
The registered company address is: Gewerbestrasse 11, 6330 Cham, Switzerland

Preface

This book contains extended and revised versions of the highest-quality papers presented during the 26th edition of the IFIP/IEEE WG10.5 International Conference on Very Large Scale Integration (VLSI-SoC), a global System-on-Chip Design and CAD conference. The 26th edition of the conference was held during October 8–10, 2018, at the Hotel Leon d'Oro, Verona, Italy. Previous conferences have taken place in Edinburgh, Scotland (1981); Trondheim, Norway (1983); Tokyo, Japan (1985); Vancouver, Canada (1987); Munich, Germany (1989); Edinburgh, Scotland (1991); Grenoble, France (1993); Chiba, Japan (1995); Gramado, Brazil (1997); Lisbon, Portugal (1999); Montpellier, France (2001); Darmstadt, Germany (2003); Perth, Australia (2005); Nice, France (2006); Atlanta, GA, USA (2007); Rhodes Island, Greece (2008); Florianopolis, Brazil (2009); Madrid, Spain (2010); Kowloon, Hong Kong, SAR China (2011), Santa Cruz, CA, USA (2012), Istanbul, Turkey (2013), Playa del Carmen, Mexico (2014), Daejeon, South Korea (2015), Tallin, Estonia (2016), and Abu Dhabi, United Arab Emirates (2017).

The purpose of this conference, sponsored by IFIP TC 10 Working Group 10.5, the IEEE Council on Electronic Design Automation (CEDA), and the IEEE Circuits and Systems Society, with the In-Cooperation of ACM SIGDA, is to provide a forum for the presentation and discussion of the latest academic and industrial results and developments as well as the future trends in the field of system-on-chip (SoC) design, considering the challenges of nano-scale, state-of-the-art and emerging manufacturing technologies. In particular, VLSI-SoC 2018 was held under the theme "Design and Engineering of Electronics Systems Based on New Computing Paradigms" by addressing cutting-edge research fields like heterogeneous, neuromorphic, and brain-inspired, biologically inspired, approximate computing systems. The chapters of this new book in the VLSI-SoC series continue its tradition of providing an internationally acknowledged platform for scientific contributions and industrial progress in this field.

For VLSI-SoC 2018, 27 papers out of 106 submissions were selected for presentation, and out of these 27 full papers presented at the conference, 13 papers were chosen by a special selection committee to have an extended and revised version included in this book. The selection process of these papers considered the evaluation scores during the review process as well as the review forms provided by members of the Technical Program Committee and the Session Chairs as a result of the presentations.

The chapters of this book have authors from Germany, India, Italy, Japan, Mexico, Singapore, The Netherlands, UAE, and USA. The Technical Program Committee for the regular tracks comprised 98 members from 25 countries.

VLSI-SoC 2018 was the culmination of the work of many dedicated volunteers: paper authors, reviewers, session chairs, invited speakers, and various committee chairs. We thank them all for their contributions.

This book is intended for the VLSI community at large, and in particular the many colleagues who did not have the chance to attend the conference. We hope you will enjoy reading this book and that you will find it useful in your professional life and for the development of the VLSI community as a whole.

June 2019

Nicola Bombieri
Graziano Pravadelli
Masahiro Fujita
Todd Austin
Ricardo Reis

Organization

The IFIP/IEEE International Conference on Very Large Scale Integration System-on-Chip (VLSI-SoC) 2018 took place during October 8–10, 2018, at the Hotel Leon d'Oro, Verona, Italy. VLSI-SoC 2018 was the 26th in a series of international conferences, sponsored by IFIP TC 10 Working Group 10.5 (VLSI), IEEE CEDA and ACM SIGDA.

General Chairs

Graziano Pravadelli   University of Verona, Italy
Todd Austin   University of Michigan, USA

Technical Program Chairs

Nicola Bombieri   University of Verona, Italy
Masahiro Fujita   University of Tokyo, Japan

Special Sessions Chairs

Sirnivas Katkoori   University of South Florida, USA
Katell Morin-Allory   TIMA Laboratory, France

PhD Forum Chairs

Kiyoung Choi   Seoul National University, South Korea
Sara Vinco   Politecnico di Torino, Italy

Local Chair

Franco Fummi   University of Verona, Italy

Industry Chair

Yervant Zorian   Synopsys, USA (TBC)

Publicity Chairs

Ricardo Reis   UFRGS, Brazil
Matteo Sonza Reorda   Politecnico di Torino, Italy

VLSI-SoC Steering Committee

Manfred Glesner	TU Darmstadt, Germany
Matthew Guthaus	UC Santa Cruz, USA
Luis Miguel Silveira	INESC ID, Portugal
Fatih Ugurdag	Ozyegin University, Turkey
Salvador Mir	TIMA, France
Ricardo Reis	UFRGS, Brazil
Chi-Ying Tsui	HKUST, Hong Kong, SAR China
Ian O'Connor	INL, France
Masahiro Fujita	The University of Tokyo, Japan

Publication Chairs

Davide Bertozzi	University of Ferrara, Italy
Mahdi Tala	University of Ferrara, Italy

Registration Chair

Michele Lora	Singapore University of Technology and Design, Singapore

Web Chair

Florenc Demrozi	University of Verona, Italy

Technical Program Committee

Analog, Mixed-Signal, and Sensor Architectures

Track Chairs

Piero Malcovati	University of Pavia, Italy
Tetsuya Iizuka	University of Tokyo, Japan

Digital Architectures: NoC, Multi- and Many-Core, Hybrid, and Reconfigurable

Track Chairs

Ian O'Connor	Lyon Institute of Nanotechnology, France
Michael Huebner	Ruhr-Universität Bochum, Germany

CAD, Synthesis, and Analysis

Track Chairs

Srinivas Katkoori   University of South Florida, USA
Ibrahim Elfadel   Masdar Institute, UAE

Prototyping, Verification, Modeling, and Simulation

Track Chairs

Tiziana Margaria   Lero, Ireland
Katell Morin-Allory   Grenoble Institute of Technology, France

Circuits and Systems for Signal Processing and Communications

Track Chairs

Fatih Ugurdag   Ozyegin University, Turkey
Luc Claesen   Hasselt University, Belgium

IoT, Embedded and Cyberphysical Systems: Architecture, Design, and Software

Track Chairs

Zebo Peng   Linkoping University, Sweden
Donatella Sciuto   Politecnico di Milano, Italy

Low-Power and Thermal-Aware IC Design

Track Chairs

Dimitrios Soudris   National Technical University of Athens NTUA,
                               Greece
Alberto Macii   Politecnico di Torino, Italy

Emerging Technologies and Computing Paradigms

Track Chairs

Andrea Calimera   Politecnico di Torino, Italy
Ricardo Reis   UFRGS, Brazil

Variability, Reliability, and Test

Track Chairs

Salvador Mir   University of Grenoble Alpes, France
Matteo Sonza Reorda   Politecnico di Torino, Italy

Hardware Security

Track Chairs

Mihalis Maniatakos	New York University Abu Dhabi, UAE
Lilian Bossuet	University of St. Etienne, France

Machine Learning for SoC Design and for Electronic Design Automation

Track Chairs

Mehdi Tahoori	Karlsruhe Institute of Technology, Germany
Manuel Barragan	TIMA, France

Technical Program Committee

Abdulkadir Akin	ETHZ, Switzerland
Aida Todri-Sanial	LIRMM, France
Alberto Bosio	LIRMM, France
Alberto Gola	AMS, Italy
Andrea Acquaviva	Politecnico di Torino, Italy
Anupam Chattopadhyay	Nanyang Technological University, Singapore
Arun Kanuparthi	Intel, USA
Bei Yu	University of Texas at Austin, USA
Brice Colombier	CEA, France
Carlos Silva Cardenas	Pontificia Universidad Catolica del Peru, Peru
Cecile Braunstein	PMC/LIP6, France
Chengmo Yang	University of Delaware, USA
Chun-Jen Tsai	National Chiao Tung University, Taiwan
Diana Goehringer	TU Dresden, Germany
Diego Barrettino	Ecole Polytechnique Federale de Lausanne, France
Donghwa Shin	Yeungnam University, South Korea
Edoardo Bonizzoni	University of Pavia, Italy
Elena Ioana Vatajelu	IMAG, France
Federico Tramarin	CNR-IEIIT, Italy
Franck Courbon	University of Cambridge, UK
Fynn Schwiegelshohn	Ruhr University Bochum, Germany
Georg Sigl	TU Munich, Germany
Gildas Leger	Inst. de Microelect. de Sevilla IMSE-CNM-CSIC, Spain
Giorgio Di Natale	LIRMM, France
Haluk Konuk	Broadcom, USA
Haris Javaid	Xilinx, Australia
Houman Homayoun	George Mason University, USA
Ippei Akita	Toyohashi University of Technology, Japan
Iraklis Anagnostopoulos	National Technical University of Athens, Greece

Jaan Raik	Tallin University, Estonia
Jones Yudi Mori	University of Brasilia, Brazil
Jinmyoung Kim	Samsung Advanced Institute of USA, Technology, South Korea
Johanna Sepulveda	Technical University of Munich, Germany
Jose Monteiro	INESC-ID, IST University of Lisbon, Portugal
Ke Huang	San Diego State University, USA
Kostas Siozios	Aristotle University of Thessaloniki, Greece
Lars Bauer	Karlsruhe Institute of Technology, Germany
Leandro Indrusiak	University of York, UK
Lionel Torres	LIRMM, France
Luciano Ost	University of Leicester, UK
Maksim Jenihhin	Tallinn University of Technology, Estonia
Maria Michael	University of Cyprus, Cyprus
Massimo Poncino	Politecnico di Torino, Italy
Matthias Sauer	University Freiburg, Germany
Mirko Loghi	Università di Udine, Italy
Nadine Azemard	LIRMM/CNRS, France
Nele Mentens	Katholieke Universiteit Leuven, Belgium
Nektarios Georgios Tsoutsos	New York University, USA
Ozgur Tasdizen	ARM, UK
Paolo Amato	Micron, Italy
Patri Sreehari	National Institute of Technology, Warangal, India
Peng Liu	Zhejiang University, China
Per Larsson-Edefors	Chalmers University, Sweden
Philippe Coussy	Université de Bretagne, France
Pierre-Emmanuel Gaillardon	University of Utah, USA
Po-Hung Chen	National Chiao Tung University, Taiwan
Raik Brinkmann	OneSpin Solutions, Germany
Rani S. Ghaida	Global Foundries, USA
Robert Wille	Johannes Kepler University Linz, Austria
Rouwaida Kanj	American University of Beirut, Lebanon
Said Hamdioui	Delft Technical University, The Netherlands
Salvatore Pennisi	University of Catania, Italy
Sezer Goren	Yeditepe University, Turkey
Shahar Kvatinsky	Technion - Israel Institute of Technology, Israel
Sicheng Li	HP, USA
Soheil Samii	General Motors, USA
Sri Parameswaran	University of New South Wales, Australia
Tetsuya Hirose	Kobe University, Japan
Theocharis Theocharides	University of Cyprus, Cyprus
Tolga Yalcin	NXP, UK
Valerio Tenace	Politecnico di Torino, Italy

Contents

A 65 nm CMOS Synthesizable Digital Low-Dropout Regulator Based on Voltage-to-Time Conversion with 99.6% Current Efficiency at 10-mA Load

Naoki Ojima[1(✉)], Toru Nakura[2], Tetsuya Iizuka[1,3], and Kunihiro Asada[1,3]

[1] Department of Electrical Engineering and Information Systems,
The University of Tokyo, Tokyo, Japan
ojima@silicon.u-tokyo.ac.jp
[2] Department of Electronics Engineering and Computer Science,
Fukuoka University, Fukuoka, Japan
[3] VLSI Design and Education Center, The University of Tokyo, Tokyo, Japan

Abstract. A synthesizable digital LDO implemented with standard-cell-based digital design flow is proposed. The difference between output and reference voltages is converted into delay difference using inverter chains as voltage-controlled delay lines, then compared in the time-domain. Since the time-domain difference is straightforwardly captured by a simple DFF-based phase detector, the proposed LDO does not need an analog voltage comparator, which requires careful manual design. All the components in the LDO can be described with Verilog codes based on their specifications, and placed-and-routed with a commercial EDA tool. This automated layout design relaxes the burden and time of implementation, and enhances process portability. The proposed LDO implemented in a 65 nm standard CMOS technology occupies 0.015 mm^2 area. With 10.4 MHz internal clock, the tracking response of the LDO to 200 mV switching in the reference voltage is ~4.5 µs and the transient response to 5 mA change in the load current is ~6.6 µs. At 10 mA load current, the quiescent current consumed by the LDO core is as low as 35.2 µA, which leads to 99.6% current efficiency.

1 Introduction

Along with the exponential advancement of process technologies, performance of LSI circuits rapidly improves and many functional building blocks such as analog, logic, RF, memory block, etc. can be integrated on a chip, which have brought system-on-a-chip (SoC) era. Meanwhile, in order to reduce power consumption as indicated by the scaling law, power supply voltages have been lowered. In addition, it is desirable that a power supply of each functional block is independently tuned according to the changing operating condition so as to have the

© IFIP International Federation for Information Processing 2019
Published by Springer Nature Switzerland AG 2019
N. Bombieri et al. (Eds.): VLSI-SoC 2018, IFIP AICT 561, pp. 1–13, 2019.
https://doi.org/10.1007/978-3-030-23425-6_1

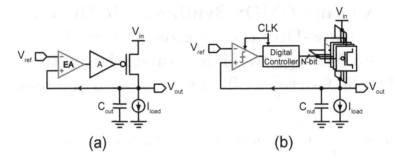

Fig. 1. LDO architectures. (a) Conventional analog LDO has a simple architecture, and includes an error amplifier, a driver amplifier and an analog pass transistor. (b) Digital LDO includes a comparator, a digital controller made of logic gates, and parallel pass transistors.

optimal power efficiency. The on-chip voltage regulation is essential for this purpose, because off-chip voltage regulators require large PCB area, which leads to increase in cost. For those reasons, efficient, tunable, fast-transient and on-chip power sources are in great demand for SoC, hence low-dropout (LDO) regulators are now widely used. As shown in Fig. 1(a), conventional LDOs have been designed with analog circuits and employed an error amplifier, a driver amplifier and an analog pass transistor to provide voltage regulation with negative feedback. When the supply voltage is high enough, they exhibit high current efficiency, fast transient response, high power supply rejection and small output ripple [1–4]. In addition, their area occupation could be smaller than other power management circuits such as switching regulators, because they do not require large inductors. However, they have difficulty in operating at low supply voltage, since amplifiers cannot sustain their dynamic range and high gain under such a situation. To solve this issue, the digital implementations of LDOs shown in Fig. 1(b) has been proposed [5–15]. A typical digital LDO has a digital controller made of logic gates that controls the number of turned-on PMOS switches at output stage, and employs an analog voltage comparator to detect the difference between reference and feedback voltages. Thus digital LDOs can eliminate amplifiers and operate under a low supply voltage. Moreover, since they are constructed mainly from digital logic gates, their performance can be easily improved by process downscaling and clock boosting.

A voltage comparator, however, often requires careful manual design so as to minimize the voltage offset between two inputs. Thus even digital LDOs also require sophisticated analog design flows, which is often time-consuming. A digital design flow, on the other hand, requires much less design effort, because its layout design is automated. Since circuit implementation in digital design flows is based on RTL source codes, the circuits that have the similar specification can be made easily even when the used process technologies are updated. Thus recently many analog circuits such as analog-to-digital converters (ADC) [16] or phase-locked loops (PLL) [17] are designed through digital automated flow, in order to take advantage of the relaxed design burden and process portability. Hence we have been motivated to implement LDOs, one of the indispensable blocks for SoCs, in digital design flows.

In order to relax the burden of manual analog designs, this paper proposes a synthesizable digital LDO, whose preliminary results have been presented in [18]. By utilizing voltage-to-time conversion, the proposed LDO has a suitable architecture for standard-cell-based automatic place and route (P&R).

2 Proposed Synthesizable LDO

2.1 Architecture

One of the design issues in constructing an LDO with standard cells is an implementation of a voltage comparison unit. Reference [16] reported that an analog voltage comparator can be implemented with 3-input NAND gates. Such comparators can be easily designed, but they suffer from the random systematic offset owing to the randomness of the automatic P&R. Thus the single comparator made of NAND gates is not suitable for precise voltage comparison. The PLL-like LDO in [6] employs voltage-controlled ring oscillators in order to convert the voltage difference into the phase difference. However, this architecture is not preferable because a voltage-controlled ring oscillator has an integral characteristic that adds a pole to the system, which deteriorates the stability of the loop. Moreover, voltage-controlled ring oscillators might be a cause to increase the current consumption of the voltage comparison unit. Some digital LDOs utilize voltage-to-time converters (VTC) and time-to-digital converters (TDC) [7,8], so that they exclude analog voltage comparators. Although a TDC can be composed of digital logic cells, its layout implementation actually requires manual design because its linearity is very sensitive to the parasitic capacitance of its layout pattern. Hence we propose to use a simple bang-bang detector, in order to relax the complexity of the layout and eliminate the systematic offset even when the layout is automatically placed and routed.

Our proposed LDO shown in Fig. 2 employs voltage-controlled delay lines (VCDL), and the difference between the reference and the output voltages are converted into the time-domain. The proposed LDO consists of two inverter chains, a bang-bang phase detector, a digital controller, a PMOS switch array, and an output capacitor. Though for this prototype a dedicated ring oscillator is used as an internal clock source and a pulse generator, these clock and pulse signals can be replaced by a clock for other blocks on the SoC. The digital controller generates 128-bit-width thermometer code from 1-bit output from the bang-bang phase detector to control the switches. The PMOS switch array has parallelly-aligned 128 PMOS transistors, all of which have the same size. Each gate of the switch is connected to each bit of the thermometer code from the digital controller. The two inverter chains have the same structure, which has a series connection of 128 inverters. As shown in Fig. 3, the bang-bang phase detector is simply composed of a D-FF and a buffer. The buffer is connected to the clock input of the D-FF to compensate the setup time of the D-FF. As shown

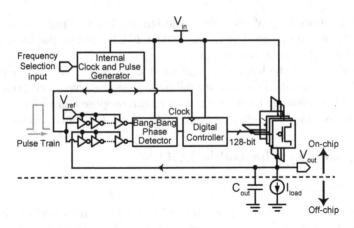

Fig. 2. Block diagram of the proposed LDO.

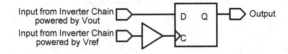

Fig. 3. Phase detector composed of standard cells.

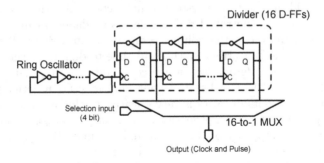

Fig. 4. Internal clock and pulse generator composed of a ring oscillator, a divider, and a multiplexer.

in Fig. 4, the internal clock and pulse generator is composed of inverters, D-FFs, and multiplexers for frequency tuning. The output capacitor is assembled off-chip. Once the switch PMOS transistor cell is added to a standard-cell library, all cells needed to compose the proposed LDO are included in the library and the LDO can be generated from Verilog gate-level netlists and synthesized with a P&R tool.

The layout of the PMOS switch has to follow the design rules for standard cells so that it can be placed and routed by the P&R tool. Figure 5 shows an outline of the PMOS switch cell layout. It is designed just by removing the

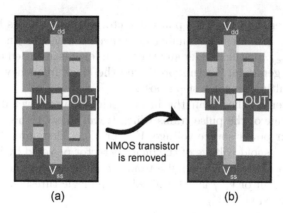

(a)   (b)

Fig. 5. (a) An inverter cell and (b) an additional PMOS transistor cell for the switch array.

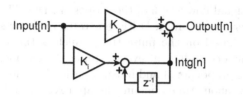

Fig. 6. Signal flow graph of the digital controller that includes proportional and integral paths.

NMOS transistor from the inverter cell for ease of the additional cell layout. Thus, the size of the PMOS switch cell is equal to that of the inverter cell.

The operation of the proposed LDO is described as follows. As shown in Fig. 2, the two inverter chains are powered by V_{ref} and V_{out}, respectively. An identical pulse train from the internal pulse generator enters into them at the same time. The inverter chains work as VCDLs. In other words, the inverter chains convert the voltage difference between V_{ref} and V_{out} into the delay difference that is compared by the phase detector. Based on the phase detector output, the digital controller changes the number of turned-on PMOS switches.

Figure 6 shows the signal flow graph of the digital controller. The operation of the digital controller is expressed by the following discrete-time difference equations.

$$\text{Intg}[n] = \text{Intg}[n-1] + K_i \times \text{Input}[n] \tag{1}$$

$$\text{Output}[n] = \text{Intg}[n] + K_p \times \text{Input}[n] \tag{2}$$

The digital controller includes proportional and integral paths. Output[n] is 7-bit binary. Then the binary output is decoded into thermometer code so that the number of turned-on PMOS switches can be controlled one by one. When V_{out} is higher than V_{ref}, the phase detector output becomes HIGH and the digital controller decreases the number of turned-on switches. On the contrary, when V_{out} is lower than V_{ref}, the phase detector output becomes LOW and the digital controller increases the number of turned-on switches. In this way V_{out} approaches to V_{ref}. As the divider and the multiplexer is attached to the internal clock and pulse generator, in this prototype the clock frequency can be easily tuned by the multiplexer for test purpose.

The components other than the inverter chains are powered by V_{in}. The HIGH-level voltage of the pulse trains which travel through the inverter chains are equal to their power source voltage, V_{ref} or V_{out}. Therefore, if V_{ref} is lower than the logic threshold voltage of the phase detector powered by V_{in}, the phase detector cannot be driven by the pulse from the inverter chain powered by V_{ref}. Thus, the lower limit of V_{ref} is determined by the logic threshold voltage of the standard cells powered by V_{in}.

2.2   Transfer Function of the Control Loop

Figure 7 shows the signal flow graph of the proposed LDO. The comparison unit composed of inverter chains and a D-FF generates an error sample. Since the comparison is done based on the pulse train which is the same signal as the clock, one clock delay occurs here at every sample. As previously described, the digital controller has proportional and integral paths. In order to investigate the loop stability in continuous-time domain, the approximation below is applied:

$$z \approx 1 + sT_s, \tag{3}$$

where T_s represents the sampling period. The transfer function of the digital controller is thus approximated as follows:

$$H_{ctrl} = K_p + \frac{1}{1 - z^{-1}} K_i \tag{4}$$

$$\approx K_p + \frac{1 + sT_s}{sT_s} K_i. \tag{5}$$

The output stage is composed of the switch array, the output capacitor, and the effective resistance. I_{pmos} is the current through a single PMOS switch. According to [9], the effective resistance R_l can be approximated as V_{out}/I_{load}. Using (3) and (5), the continuous-time open-loop transfer function $G(s)$ is given by

$$G(s) = \left(\frac{K_p}{1 + sT_s} + \frac{K_i}{sT_s} \right) \cdot \frac{I_{pmos}}{R_l^{-1} + sC_{out}}. \tag{6}$$

When I_{load} is small, R_l becomes big so that $R_l^{-1} \ll sC_{out}$. Then, $G(s)$ approximates

$$G(s) \approx \left(\frac{K_p}{1 + sT_s} + \frac{K_i}{sT_s} \right) \cdot \frac{I_{pmos}}{sC_{out}}. \tag{7}$$

If $K_p = 0$, the poles of the closed-loop transfer function are close to the imaginary axis, and thus the system tends to be unstable. To avoid oscillation, we add the proportional gain K_p to the digital controller. Figure 8 shows the bode plots

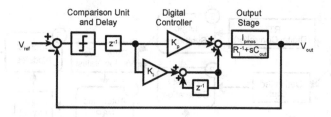

Fig. 7. Signal flow graph of the proposed LDO.

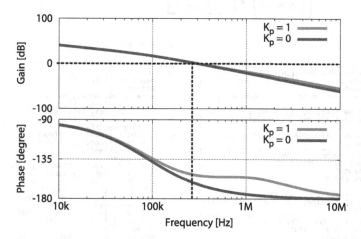

Fig. 8. Bode plots of the open loop system with the small I_{load} of 100 μA for $K_p = 0$ and $K_p = 1$.

of the open loop transfer function with small I_{load} of 100 μA for $K_p = 0$ and $K_p = 1$, respectively. When $K_p = 0$, the phase margin is 17°, whereas it is 27° when $K_p = 1$, which suppresses the abrupt phase change around 1 MHz.

2.3 Design Procedure of the Proposed LDO

This section explains the design procedure of the proposed LDO. Figure 9 shows the design flow diagram. The explanation follows the step numbers shown in Fig. 9. (0) The PMOS switch cell is designed in advance and added to the standard-cell library. (1) The specification of the circuit, such as maximum load current or reference voltage, is set. Based on this specification, the number of the PMOS switches in the switch array and the output bit width of the digital controller are determined. (2) The RTL Verilog code of the digital controller is prepared, then logically synthesized to have the gate-level Verilog netlist. (3) The gate-level Verilog netlists of other components, such as the inverter chain, the phase detector, the switch array, and the internal clock and pulse generator are generated by a dedicated script. Examples of the gate-level Verilog

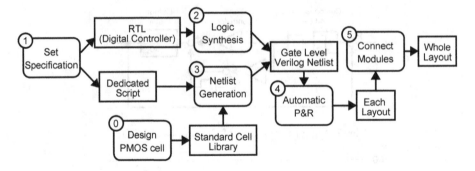

Fig. 9. Design flow of the proposed circuit.

(a)
```
module inverterChain(IN, OUT);
    input IN;
    output OUT;
    wire node0, node1, ..., node(K-1);

    inv U0 (.A(IN), .Y(node0));
    inv U1 (.A(node0), .Y(node1));
    ...
    inv UK (.A(node(K-1)), .Y(OUT));
endmodule
```

(b)
```
module phaseDetector(INP, INN, OUT);
    input INP, INN;
    output OUT;
    wire node0;

    buf U0 (.A(INN), .Y(node0));
    dff U1 (.D(INP), .C(node0), .Q(OUT));
endmodule
```

(c)
```
module switchArray(IN, OUT);
    input [N-1:0] IN;
    output OUT;

    pmos U0 (.A(IN[0]), .Y(OUT));
    pmos U1 (.A(IN[1]), .Y(OUT));
    ...
    pmos U(N-1) (.A(IN[N-1]), .Y(OUT));
endmodule
```

(d)
```
module clockAndPulseGenerator(SELECT, OUT);
    input [1:0] SELECT;
    output OUT;
    wire node0, node1, node2,
         q0, q1, q2, q3,
         xq0, xq1, xq2, xq3;

    // ring oscillator
    inv U0 (.A(node2), .Y(node0));
    inv U1 (.A(node0), .Y(node1));
    inv U2 (.A(node1), .Y(node2));
    // divider
    dff U3 (.D(xq0), .C(node2), .Q(q0));
    inv U4 (.A(q0), .Y(xq0));
    dff U5 (.D(xq1), .C(q0), .Q(q1));
    inv U6 (.A(q1), .Y(xq1));
    dff U7 (.D(xq2), .C(q1), .Q(q2));
    inv U8 (.A(q2), .Y(xq2));
    dff U9 (.D(xq3), .C(q2), .Q(q3));
    inv U10 (.A(q3), .Y(xq3));
    // multiplexer
    mul U11 (.A(q0), .B(q1), .C(q2), .D(q3),
             .S0(SELECT[0]), .S1(SELECT[1]),
             .Y(OUT));
endmodule
```

Fig. 10. Examples of the gate-level Verilog description: (a) inverter chain, (b) phase detector, (c) switch array, and (d) internal clock and pulse generator.

description is shown in Fig. 10. Since each building block has simple standard-cell-based structure, the gate-level netlist generation is simply implemented. For example, the switch array is constructed only by the parallel PMOS switch cells, and thus its gate-level netlist is generated easily by the script according to the specification. (4) The layout of each building block is individually placed and routed by a P&R tool. This is because they have different power supplies; the two inverter chains are powered by V_{out} or V_{ref} respectively, and the other blocks are powered by V_{in}. We use the same layout for both of the two inverter chains, so that there is little systematic offset in the voltage comparison unit. (5) All the layouts are connected together. It takes few hours to generate the whole layout of the proposed LDO from scratch, which is much less time than that in the case for the conventional LDO design with analog flows.

3   Prototype Implementation and Measurement Results

Based on the architecture described in the previous section, the prototype of the proposed LDO is fabricated in a 65 nm standard CMOS technology. Figure 11 shows the chip photo. The active area of the proposed LDO is $0.015\,\mu m^2$.

Figure 12 shows the measured tracking response of V_{out} with 10.4 MHz clock when V_{ref}, which is externally supplied in this measurement, switches between 600 mV and 800 mV. Here, I_{load} and C_{out} is 10 mA and 220 pF, respectively. When V_{ref} changes from 600 mV to 800 mV, the settling time is $4.5\,\mu s$, whereas it is $4.4\,\mu s$ when V_{ref} changes from 800 mV to 600 mV. Figure 13 shows the measured transient response of V_{out} with 10.4 MHz clock when I_{load} changes between 5 mA and 10 mA. V_{ref} of 800 mV and C_{out} of 220 pF are used in this experiment. When I_{load} changes from 5 mA to 10 mA, the settling time is $6.6\,\mu s$ and the undershoot is 303 mV. When I_{load} changes from 10 mA to 5 mA, the settling time is $6.0\,\mu s$ and the overshoot is 126 mV. Since the operation region of PMOS temporarily enters into saturation region when the undershoot occurs while it does not for the case of overshoot, the waveforms of V_{out} transient become different in these two cases.

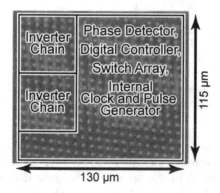

Fig. 11. Chip photo of the proposed LDO that occupies $115\,\mu m \times 130\,\mu m$ in 65 nm standard CMOS technology.

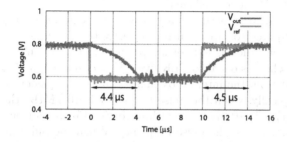

Fig. 12. Measured tracking response of V_{out} when V_{ref} switches between 600 mV and 800 mV with 10.4 MHz-clock, I_{load} of 10 mA and C_{out} of 220 pF.

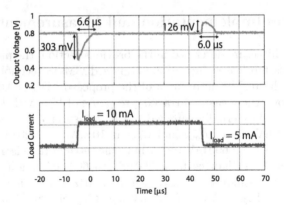

Fig. 13. Measured transient response of V_{out} when I_{load} changes between 5 mA and 10 mA with 10.4 MHz-clock, V_{ref} of 800 mV and C_{out} of 220 pF.

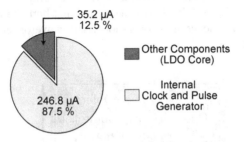

Fig. 14. Breakdown of the current consumption with I_{load} of 10 mA. Ratio of the current is calculated with circuit simulation.

The overall current consumption with 10.4 MHz clock and I_{load} of 10 mA is 282 μA including the current consumed at the internal clock and pulse generator, which is not essential in the actual use because it can be substituted by an internal clock for other functional blocks on the SoC. Based on the circuit simulation result, the LDO core consumes 12.5% of the total current as shown in Fig. 14. Thus, the quiescent current of the LDO core is assumed to be 35.2 μA, which leads to 99.6% current efficiency.

In the proposed architecture, V_{ref} is used as a power source of a VCDL. Hence, V_{ref} is required to supply current to drive the VCDL for voltage comparison. Figure 15 shows the current consumption from V_{ref} versus the frequency of the pulse train, which is equal to CLK, with V_{ref} of 800 mV and I_{load} of 10 mA. The pulse is sent from the internal oscillator, and its frequency is tuned by the multiplexer. Typically, when the pulse frequency is 10.4 MHz, the current consumption from V_{ref} is 10.6 μA. According to Fig. 15, the current consumption of V_{ref} is proportional to the pulse frequency. When the pulse frequency is set high in order to have the fast transient response, V_{ref} is required to supply more current.

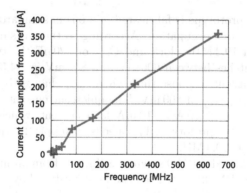

Fig. 15. Current consumption from V_{ref} versus the frequency of the pulse train.

Table 1 shows performance comparison to prior digital LDOs. This work realizes a competitive current efficiency and FOM_T with synthesizable architecture, while others cannot be fully synthesizable and need manual designs. Owing to the automated design flow of this work, if needed the maximum load current $I_{load,max}$ can be easily increased by adding more PMOS switches, at the expense of the increase in the area and the quiescent current.

Table 1. Comparison to prior arts

	This work	[5] CICC 2010	[6] JSSC 2014	[10] JSSC 2017	[11] JSSC 2018	[12] SSC-L 2018	[13] TPE 2018	[14] SSC-L 2018
Process	65 nm	65 nm	32 nm	65 nm	65 nm	65 nm	65 nm	28 nm
Active area [mm^2]	0.015	0.042	0.008	0.029	0.0023	0.012	0.014	0.019
V_{in} [V]	1.0	0.5	0.7–1.0	0.5–1.0	0.5–1.0	0.5–1.0	0.7–1.2	0.6–0.65
V_{out} [V]	0.8	0.45	0.5–0.9	0.45–0.95	0.3–0.45	0.35–0.95	0.6–1.1	0.55–0.6
$I_{load,max}$ [mA]	10	0.2	5	3.5	2	2.8	25	25
C_{out} [pF]	220	100000	100	400	400	100	1000	150
Quiescent I_q [μA]	35.2	2.7	92	12.5	14	45.2	6	28
Current efficiency [%]	99.6	98.7	98.2	96.3	99.8	98.4	99.97	99.96
Transient ΔV_{out} @ load step ΔI_{load}	300 mV @ 5 mA	40 mV @ 0.2 mA	150 mV @ 0.8 mA	40 mV @ 0.4 mA	40 mV @ 1.06 mA	46 mV @ 1.76 mA	200 mV @ 23.5 mA	56 mV @ 20 mA
FOM_T [ps][a]	93	270000	1150	1250	199	67.1	2.17	0.59

[a]$FOM_T = (C_{out} \times \Delta V_{out} \times I_q)/\Delta I_{load}^2$ [1]

4 Conclusion

This paper proposes a synthesizable digital LDO that is designed by a P&R tool. In the proposed LDO, by using inverter chains as VCDLs, the difference between the output and the reference voltages is converted into the delay difference that can be compared by a phase detector. The voltage control loop is all composed of standard cells and synthesizable, which drastically relaxes the design burden. The prototype is fabricated in a 65 nm standard CMOS technology with $0.015\,\text{mm}^2$ area occupation. According to the measurement results of the prototype, with 10.4 MHz clock and C_{out} of 220 pF the tracking response time when V_{ref} switches between 600 mV and 800 mV is $\sim4.5\,\mu\text{s}$ with I_{load} of 10 mA, and the transient response time when I_{load} changes between 5 mA and 10 mA is $\sim6.6\,\mu\text{s}$ with V_{ref} of 800 mV. The quiescent current consumed by the LDO core is as low as $35.2\,\mu\text{A}$ at 10 mA load current, which leads to 99.6% current efficiency. In our prototype, V_{ref} needs to supply $10.6\,\mu\text{A}$ current when the pulse frequency is 10.4 MHz.

In this paper, we used a PMOS switch cell made from an inverter cell. However, this customized PMOS switch cell can be substituted by a tri-state inverter cell [15] or a tri-state buffer cell. If the inputs of these cells are tied to LOW (in the case of tri-state inverters) or HIGH (in the case of tri-state buffers), the output PMOS transistors can be controlled by the tri-state control inputs. Thus, if these cells are included in the standard cell library, a fully standard-cell based synthesizable LDO can be realized and the design burden would be more relaxed.

Acknowledgment. This work is partly supported by JSPS KAKENHI Grant Number 17H03244, and is supported by VLSI Design and Education Center (VDEC), the University of Tokyo in collaboration with Synopsys, Inc., Cadence Design Systems, Inc., and Mentor Graphics, Inc.

References

1. Hazucha, P., Karnik, T., Bloechel, B.A., Parsons, C., Finan, D., Borkar, S.: Area-efficient linear regulator with ultra-fast load regulation. IEEE J. Solid State Circuits **40**(4), 933–940 (2005)
2. Lam, Y.H., Ki, W.H.: A 0.9 V 0.35 μm adaptively biased CMOS LDO regulator with fast transient response. In: Proceedings of IEEE International Solid-State Circuits Conference Digest of Technical Papers, pp. 442–626, February 2008
3. Milliken, R.J., Silva-Martinez, J., Sanchez-Sinencio, E.: Full on-chip CMOS low-dropout voltage regulator. IEEE Trans. Circuits Syst. I Regul. Pap. **54**(9), 1879–1890 (2007)
4. El-Nozahi, M., Amer, A., Torres, J., Entesari, K., Sanchez-Sinencio, E.: High PSR low drop-out regulator with feed-forward ripple cancellation technique. IEEE J. Solid State Circuits **45**(3), 565–577 (2010)
5. Okuma, Y., et al.: 0.5-V input digital LDO with 98.7% current efficiency and 2.7-μA quiescent current in 65 nm CMOS. In: Proceedings of IEEE Custom Integrated Circuits Conference, pp. 1–4, September 2010
6. Gangopadhyay, S., Somasekhar, D., Tschanz, J.W., Raychowdhury, A.: A 32 nm embedded, fully-digital, phase-locked low dropout regulator for fine grained power management in digital circuits. IEEE J. Solid State Circuits **49**(11), 2684–2693 (2014)
7. Otsuga, K., et al.: An on-chip 250 mA 40 nm CMOS digital LDO using dynamic sampling clock frequency scaling with offset-free TDC-based voltage sensor. In: Proceedings of IEEE International SOC Conference, pp. 11–14, September 2012

8. Oh, T., Hwang, I.: A 110-nm CMOS 0.7-V input transient-enhanced digital low-dropout regulator with 99.98% current efficiency at 80-mA load. IEEE Trans. Very Large Scale Integr. (VLSI) Syst. **23**(7), 1281–1286 (2015)

9. Nasir, S.B., Gangopadhyay, S., Raychowdhury, A.: All-digital low-dropout regulator with adaptive control and reduced dynamic stability for digital load circuits. IEEE Trans. Power Electron. **31**(12), 8293–8302 (2016)

10. Kim, D., Seok, M.: A fully integrated digital low-dropout regulator based on event-driven explicit time-coding architecture. IEEE J. Solid State Circuits **52**(11), 3071–3080 (2017)

11. Salem, L.G., Warchall, J., Mercier, P.P.: A successive approximation recursive digital low-dropout voltage regulator with PD compensation and sub-LSB duty control. IEEE J. Solid State Circuits **53**(1), 35–49 (2018)

12. Kim, S.J., Kim, D., Ham, H., Kim, J., Seok, M.: A 67.1-ps FOM, 0.5-V-hybrid digital LDO with asynchronous feedforward control via slope detection and synchronous PI with state-based hysteresis clock switching. IEEE Solid State Circuits Lett. **1**(5), 130–133 (2018)

13. Akram, M.A., Hong, W., Hwang, I.: Fast transient fully standard-cell-based all digital low-dropout regulator with 99.97% current efficiency. IEEE Trans. Power Electron. **33**(9), 8011–8019 (2018)

14. Zhao, L., Lu, Y., Martins, R.P.: A digital LDO with Co-SA logics and TSPC dynamic latches for fast transient response. IEEE Solid State Circuits Lett. **1**(6), 154–157 (2018)

15. Liu, J., Maghari, N.: A fully-synthesizable 0.6 V digital LDO with dual-loop control using digital standard cells. In: Proceedings of IEEE International New Circuits and Systems Conference (NEWCAS), pp. 1–4, June 2016

16. Weaver, S., Hershberg, B., Moon, U.: Digitally synthesized stochastic flash ADC using only standard digital cells. IEEE Trans. Circuits Syst. I Reg. Pap. **61**(1), 84–91 (2014)

17. Deng, W., et al.: A fully synthesizable all-digital PLL with interpolative phase coupled oscillator, current-output DAC, and fine-resolution digital varactor using gated edge injection technique. IEEE J. Solid State Circuits **50**(1), 68–80 (2015)

18. Ojima, N., Nakura, T., Iizuka, T., Asada, K.: A synthesizable digital low-dropout regulator based on voltage-to-time conversion. In: 26th IFIP/IEEE International Conference on Very Large Scale Integration (VLSI-SOC), October 2018

An Instruction Set Architecture for Secure, Low-Power, Dynamic IoT Communication

Shahzad Muzaffar and Ibrahim (Abe) M. Elfadel[✉]

Department of Electrical and Computer Engineering, Khalifa University,
P.O. Box 54224, Masdar City, Abu Dhabi, UAE
{shahzad.muzaffar,ibrahim.elfadel}@ku.ac.ae

Abstract. This chapter presents an instruction set architecture (ISA) dedicated to the rapid and efficient implementation of single-channel IoT communication interfaces. The architecture is meant to provide a programming interface for the implementation of signaling protocols based on the recently introduced pulsed-index schemes. In addition to the traditional aspects of ISA design such as addressing modes, instruction types, instruction formats, registers, interrupts, and external I/O, the ISA includes special-purpose instructions that facilitate bit stream encoding and decoding based on the pulsed-index techniques. Verilog HDL is used to synthesize a fully functional processor based on this ISA and provide both an FPGA implementation and a synthesised ASIC design in GLOBALFOUNDRIES 65 nm. The ASIC design confirms the low-power features of this ISA with consumed power around $31\,\mu W$ and energy efficiency of less than $10\,pJ/bit$. Finally, this chapter shows how the basic ISA can be extended to include cryptographic features in support of secure IoT communication.

Keywords: Dynamic signaling · Single-channel ·
Low-power communication · Clock and data recovery ·
Internet of things · Domain specific architecture ·
Pulsed-Index Communication · Instruction set architecture ·
Secure communication

1 Introduction

IoT nodes need to meet two conflicting requirements: high data-rate communication to support bursts of activity in sensing and communication, and low-power to improve energy autonomy. Unfortunately, existing protocols fail to meet these requirements simultaneously. Protocols providing high data rates, such as WiFi, WLAN, TCP/IP, USB, etc. [1–3], are power-hungry and involve complex controllers to handle two-way communications. On the other hand, low-power protocols such as 1-Wire [4] and UART [5] have low data rates.

© IFIP International Federation for Information Processing 2019
Published by Springer Nature Switzerland AG 2019
N. Bombieri et al. (Eds.): VLSI-SoC 2018, IFIP AICT 561, pp. 14–31, 2019.
https://doi.org/10.1007/978-3-030-23425-6_2

To fill up the gap and address these two requirements at once, a novel family of pulsed signaling techniques for single-channel, high-data-rate, low-power dynamic communication have been recently proposed under the name of Pulsed-Index Communication (PIC) [6,7]. The most important feature of this family of protocols is that they do not require any clock and data recovery (CDR). They are also highly tolerant of clocking differences between transmitter and receiver, and are fully adapted to the simple, low-power, area-efficient, and robust communication needs of IoT devices and sensors. These techniques are reviewed in Sect. 2 with their advantages and disadvantages clarified. The main issue that this chapter addresses is to provide a flexible framework that enables the implementation of the most suitable PIC technique for a given application. The issue of selecting and implementing a communication interface in a constrained IoT node is a prevalent one, and its solution should contribute to the streamlining of communication subsystem design in IoT devices.

One candidate solution is to program all the protocols on a microprocessor and control their selection and parameters through registers. This is a standard practice that is followed for data transfer protocols such as I^2C, I^2S, SPI, UART, and CAN. Another possible solution is to design ASIC for the newest generation of the protocol and make it backward compatible with older versions as in the case of USB 1.0 through 3.0 [8]. Such methods increase silicon area and power consumption, and do not provide any customization features. Yet another approach is to adopt the principles of hardware-software codesign and provide a special-purpose hardware supporting a tuned or extended Instruction Set Architecture that can be used to configure and implement the various communication protocols of a given family without changing or re-designing the on-chip hardware modules. An example of such approach can be found in Cisco's routers where the main CPU (e.g., MPC860 PowerQUICC processor from Motorala/NXP) includes an on-chip Communication Processor Module (CPM) [9]. The CPM is a RISC microcontroller dedicated to several special purpose tasks such as signal processing, communication interfaces, baud-rate generation, and direct memory access (DMA). The work described in this chapter is inspired with such a solution in that it proposes a flexible, fully programmable communication interface for the PIC family based on a full RISC-like ISA tailored for the efficient and seamless implementation of the PIC protocols.

Specifically, a set of special-purpose instructions and registers along with a compact assembly language is proposed to help perform the specific tasks needed for the generation of pulsed signals and to give access to all the hardware resources. The proposed ISA is called Pulsed-Index Communication Interface Architecture (PICIA) and is meant to help reduce the number of instructions required to implement a PIC family member without impacting the advantageous data rates or low-power operation of the PIC family. Verilog HDL is used to synthesize and verify a fully functional processor based on this ISA over the Spartan-6 FPGA platform. Furthermore, an ASIC design in the GLOBAL-FOUNDRIES 65 nm process confirms the low-power operation with $31.4\,\mu W$ and energy efficiency of less than $10\,pJ/bit$.

This chapter is an expanded version of an earlier publication of ours [10] and includes an entirely new section, Sect. 6, on secure IoT transmission using an extended ISA with cryptographic instructions. Other changes include improved figures and additional explanations that are spread throughout this chapter.

2 Pulsed-Signaling Techniques

Pulsed-signaling techniques are based on the basic concept of transmitting binary word attributes rather than modulated bits. The attributes are quantified, coded as pulse counts, and transmitted as streams of pulses. The key to the success of these techniques is the encoding step whose goal is to minimize the pulse count. At the receiver, the decoding is based on pulse counting by detecting the rising edge of each pulse. These techniques have the distinguished feature that they don't require any clock and data recovery (CDR), which significantly contributes to their low-power and small foot-print hardware implementations. Recently, three techniques based on this concept have been introduced, namely, Pulsed-Index Communication (PIC) [6], Pulsed-Decimal Communication (PDC) [7], and Pulsed-Index Communication Plus (PIC*plus*). With slight differences, these techniques apply an encoding scheme to a data word B to *minimize* the number of ON bits, and *move* them to the Least-Significant-Bit (LSB) end of the packet with the goal of lowering the number of pulses required to transmit the data bits. The encoding process includes a segmentation step where the data is broken into N independent segments of size l bits each (i.e. $N = B/l$). To maximize data rate, these use, on each segment, an encoding combination of bit inversion and/or segment reversion/flipping. For PIC and PIC*plus*, this combination is meant to reduce the number of ON bits and decrease their index values. For PDC, the same combination is meant to reduce the number of ON bits and decrease the decimal number represented by each segment. To facilitate decoding, flag pulses representing the type of encoding performed are added to each segment. Unlike PIC, the PDC segment flags of two consecutive segments and the PIC*plus* segment flags of four consecutive segments are combined in one data word flag and placed in the header. The PDC further applies a third segmentation step post-encoding whose goal is further reduce the number of pulses per segment and, therefore, further increase the data rate.

All the pieces of information including flags, the number of indices, and the indices themselves in the case of PIC and PIC*plus*, or the decimal numbers of each segment in the case of PDC, are transmitted in the form of pulse streams. Within a given packet, segment pulse streams are separated by an inter-symbol delay (α). The receiver counts the number of pulses for each pulse stream and applies the decoding according to the flags received.

3 Pulsed-Index Communication Interface Architecture (PICIA)

As described in Sect. 2, the PIC family members share many ideas, some of which are used in exactly the same way and others with few changes. Their packet formats are also quite similar. There could be a number of variations that could be introduced in these techniques as per needs and choice. The proposed PICIA can be used to generate not only these standard protocols with tune-able respective communication parameters (i.e. segment size, inter-symbol delay, pulse width etc.) but it can also be used to develop other customized communications techniques that use the same underlying idea of transmitting information in the form of pulses. The PICIA is described in detail in the next subsections.

Table 1. PICIA register set

	Register	Type	Organization
1	R0–R7	8 bit GP[a]	8-bit Value
2	Ctrl0	8 bit SP[b]	[0, Mode, 3-bit SegNum, 3-bit SegSize]
3	Ctrl1	8 bit SP	8-bit pulse width
4	LoadReg	16 bit SP	16-bit value

[a]General Purpose [b]Special Purpose

3.1 Register Set

The PICIA uses three types of registers. The first type includes a set of eight 8-bit registers, *R0 through R7*, which are programmer-accessible general-purpose registers. The second type is that of Control Registers *Ctrl0* and *Ctrl1* which are 8-bit registers used to store protocol configuration parameters such as mode of transaction (transmitter or receiver), segment number, segment size, and pulse width in terms of a number of clock cycles. These control registers are initially set by the programmer through specific instructions but, once set, they become accessible only to the system. The third type is the *LoadReg* register, which is a 16-bit, I/O-dedicated register used to read the I/O port, set the I/O port, and to store the updated results after an instruction is executed. Like the Control Registers, *LoadReg* is a privileged register accessible only to the system. These register types are summarized in Table 1. In the remainder of the text, the word register will always refer to a general-purpose register.

3.2 Instruction Formats

The PICIA instructions are all 16-bit long and are of three different types. The first type, *I-Type 1*, handles one operand at a time and is used in operations such as to read/write the I/O port, set/clear the *Load-Reg*, set various communication protocol parameters, and send/receive pulse streams. I-Type 1 is divided into five fragments, as shown in Fig. 1. The 5-bits *Opcode* represents the type of operation. *Type (R/C)* is used to set the type of operand (register or a constant) in an instruction. *Halt PC/WE* is used either to halt the PC during the transmission of pulse streams or to enable the store operation of received pulse-count to a specified register. The bit *E* sets

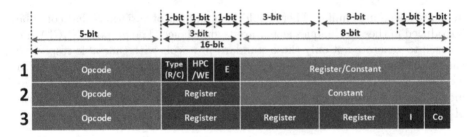

Fig. 1. PICIA instructions format

if an extra pulse should be added to the transmitted pulse stream and/or an extra pulse should be removed from the received pulse stream. The last 8-bits long fragment of I-Type 1 is used to indicate a register number or an immediate constant value.

The second type of instruction, *I-Type 2*, needs two operands and is used in operations such as updating a register with a given constant value, and jumping to a specified label in the code depending on the validity of a condition in a register. I-Type 2 is divided into three fragments, as shown in Fig. 1. The 5-bits *Opcode* represents the type of operation. The 3-bits *Register* field is used to indicate one of the general purpose registers and the 8-bits *Constant* field is used to provide a constant value or a label that is present in the code.

The third type of instruction, *I-Type 3*, handles two or three operands simultaneously. I-Type 3 is used in operations such as encoding (inversion and reversion with or without condition), combining and splitting encoding flags, and copying register contents or some other information to a specified register conditionally. I-Type 3 is divided into six fragments, as shown in Fig. 1. The 5-bits *Opcode* represents the type of operation. The 3-bits *Register* fields are used to indicate one of the general purpose registers. The combinations of 1-bit *I* and *Co* fields are used to select the source of information to be copied.

3.3 Addressing Modes

The PICIA employs three addressing modes: immediate, register, and auto-decrement. In the immediate mode, the source is either a constant or a label while the destination is one of the general-purpose, special-purpose, or program counter registers. In the register mode, the register contains the value of the operand. The auto-decrement mode is used only for jump operation where the branch to a label is taken and a specified register decrements by one if the register contains a non-zero number.

3.4 Interrupts

There are three interrupts in the PICIA supported processor. First, the I/O interrupt is generated when the data at the I/O port is available. The system remains in a halt state until the I/O interrupt is reached and the system starts the execution of instructions from the very start. Second, the transmitter interrupt is used to indicate the completion of the transmission of one pulse stream. The PICIA processor remains in a halt state, if activated, until transmitter interrupt is received and the execution continues from where it paused. Third, the receiver interrupt is generated when the reception of one pulse stream completes. The PICIA processor remains in a halt state until the receiver interrupt is received at which time, program execution is continued.

3.5   External I/O

Three external I/O ports are supported by the PICIA processor. One of these ports is the 16-bit data I/O port that is used to read from and write back to the external environment. To transmit and receive the packets in the form of pulse streams, a 1-bit signal I/O port is used. Another 1-bit data ready port is used to source the generation of I/O interrupts and start the execution of instructions.

4   PICIA Assembly Language

Before diving into the PICIA assembly language in detail, it is necessary to understand few relevant interpretations about the instructions and assembly language. These interpretations are shown in Table 2. The left part of the table shows the instruction interpretations where the values of the control bits are indicated along with the corresponding effect or representation. Similarly, the right part of the table does the same but for PICIA assembly language. The PICIA instructions are listed in Table 3 along with a brief description and an example for each. The instruction categories and types are given in Table 4. More details about the PICIA instructions are given in the next subsections.

Table 2. PICIA interpretation

Instruction interpretation		Assembly interpretation	
Control Bit	Value : Effect	Symbol	Meaning
Type (R/C)	0 : Register, 1 : Constant	R	Register Only
Halt PC	0 : No Halt, 1 : Halt	C	Constant Only
WE	0 : Register Write Disabled	RC	Register or Constant
	1 : Register Write Enabled		
E	0 : Extra Pulse Disabled	R, Rx, Ry, Rs	Register Number
	1 : Extra Pulse Enabled		
I	0 : No Indexing, 1 : Indexing	h	0 : No Halt, 1 : Halt
Co	0 : Copy Segment Disabled		
	1 : Copy Segment Enabled		

4.1   Type 1 Instructions (I-Type 1)

These instructions are concerned with configuration and transmission control operations and use only one operand. The first instruction towards this is *RP*, *read from port*, that collects the data from the I/O port and stores it in the *LoadReg*. *WP*, *write to port*, reads data from *LoadReg* and updates the I/O port. There is no operand to these instructions as the system accesses the special purpose register internally. *SSS* and *SSN* set the segment size and the segment number respectively in the *Ctrl0* register. The operand for both of these instructions is an immediate constant value. The operand to *SSS* can be any of 0, 1, or 2 that represents a segment size of 4, 8, or 16 bits respectively.

Segment size information helps the system break the data word into smaller independent segments. The operands to *SSN* can be the numbers 0, 1, 2, and 3. *SSN* is used to select the segment that is going to be processed by all the following instructions in the program until the segment number is changed again. *SM*, *set the mode*, also accesses the special purpose control register *Ctrl0* and sets or clears a bit representing the mode of operation. The operand to *SM* can either be 0 or 1 that represents the transmitter or receiver mode respectively. During transmitter mode, the signal port is used to send the pulses out and, during reception mode, the same port is used to receive the pulses from the external world. If the receiver mode is selected, the *LoadReg* is automatically cleared by the system to make it ready for reception. If the transmitter mode is selected, the *LoadReg* is updated automatically with the data present on I/O port. *SW*, *set pulse width*, sets the count of system-clock cycles for which the pulse remains high. The operand to *SW* is an 8-bit integer number.

The *SP*, *send pulses*, sends a pulse stream consists of a number of consecutive pulses equal in count specified by the operand that could either be a register or an immediate constant number. The argument h is used to decide if the system should halt during the transmission of a pulse stream or not. If 1, halt the system unless the pulse stream transmission is complete, or continue with the next instruction if 0. The argument E to *SP* instruction informs the system if the pulse stream should include the transmission of an additional pulse at the end of stream or not. This is helpful in representing the no-pulse or zero-index condition with only one pulse as it is in the case of PIC and PIC*plus* transmission, unlike PDC where all the pulse streams are transmitted with an additional pulse. If 1, include an extra pulse or send the exact number of pulses if 0. *SD* is a similar instruction but with minor differences. *SD*, *send the delay*, transmits an inter-symbol delay that is equal in length to the specified number of system-clock cycles. All the arguments and operands work in the same way as that of *SP* except that there is no choice of an extra pulse.

To set the expected number of clock cycles per inter-symbol delay during the process of reception, the instruction *SRD* is used which takes either a register number or a constant number as an operand to represent the number of clock cycles. During a reception, the system needs to wait for the incoming pulse stream so that the pulses can be counted to infer the sent information. To fulfil this task, the instruction *WRI*, *wait for receiver interrupt*, is used. The system

Table 3. PICIA assembly language

	Instruction	Description	Example
Configuration instructions			
1	RP	Load data from Input Pins to data register	RP
2	WP	Output the received data from data register to the Pins	WP
3	SSS C	Set segment size (C = 0, 1, 2 for 4 bit, 8 bit, 16 bit)	SSS 1
4	SSN C	Select segment number (C = 0, 1, 2, 3)	SSN 2
5	SM C	Set Mode (C = 0, 1 for Transmitter, Receiver). Setting RX mode clears LoadReg, setting TX loads input into LoadReg	SM 0
6	SW C	Set width of pulse (C = integer specifying cycle count)	SW 2
7	SRD RC	Set Receiver Inter-Symbol Delay equal to RC number of clock cycles	SRD R0
8	NOP	No operation	NOP
Encoding/Decoding instructions			
9	IV Rx,Ry	Inverse the selected segment. Rx = NOI & Ry = Flags (Rx/Ry = mR0, R1, ... R7)	IV R0, R1
10	IVC Rx, Ry	Inverse conditionally the selected segment if encoding condition satisfy (ON bits > Seg. Size/2). Rx = NOI & Ry = Flags (Rx/Ry = R0, R1,... R7)	IVC R0,R1
11	FL Rx, Ry	Flip selected segment bits. Rx = NOI & Ry = Flags (Rx/Ry = R0, R1, ... R7)	FL R0,R1
12	FLC Rx, Ry	Flip conditionally the selected segment bits if encoding condition satisfy (Seg. >Flip(Seg.)). Rx = NOI & Ry = Flags (Rx/Ry = R0, R1, ... R7)	FLC R0, R1
13	IVFL Rx, Ry	Invert and Flip selected segment bits. Rx = NOI & Ry = Flags (Rx/Ry = R0, R1, ... R7)	IVFL R0, R1
14	CRC R, Rs, I, Co	Copy register conditionally. R = Rs if I = 0. R = Rs , if I = 1 and LoadReg [Rs] = 1 and Co = 0. R = 0 otherwise. R = Selected Segment, if Co = 1. Rs is ignored. (R/Rs = R0, R1, ... R7). Can be used to clear the register	CRC R1, R2, 1, 1
15	CF R, Rx, Ry	Combine Flags. R = {Rx[1:0], Ry[1:0]}	CF R0,R1,R2
16	SF Rx, Ry, R	Split Flags. Rx = R[3:2], Ry = R[1:0]	SF R1, R2, R0

(*continued*)

Table 3. (*continued*)

	Instruction	Description	Example
		Transmission control instructions	
17	SP h, E, RC	Send RC number of pulses (RC = register number or constant value). Halt PC if h = 1 (h = 0, 1). (Type = 1 then it's a constant). Send one extra pulse if E = 1 (E = 0, 1)	SP 1, 1, 4
18	SD h, RC	Inter-Symbol delay of RC number of clock cycles. Halt PC if h = 1 (h = 0,1)	SD 1, 4
19	WRI WE, E, R	Wait for receiver pulse stream interrupt. PC halts till the interrupt arrives. Remove one extra pulse count if E = 1 (E = 0,1). Enable received pulse count write to register R (R = R0, R1, . . . R7) if WE = 1 (WE = 0,1)	WRI 1, 1, R0
20	SDB C	Sets the index bits or the data bits in the LoadReg as per the received pulse stream. (C=0,1 for indexing and data respectively)	SDB 1
		Register/Branch update instructions	
21	WR R, C	Write constant value to a register R (R = R0, R1, . . . R7)	WR R0,8
22	BNZD R, label	Branch to label and decrement R by 1 if the specified register R contains non-zero number. (R = R0,R1,. . . R7)	BNZD R0,loop

Table 4. I-Types Instructions

Instructions category	**I-Type**
Configuration	1
Transmission control	1
Register/Branch update	2
Encoding/Decoding	3

goes into the halt state when this instruction is executed and returns back to the normal state at the reception of receiver interrupt that is generated when a pulse stream is received completely. The incoming pulses are counted and the count decrements once if the argument E to *WRI* is set. The count is stored in a specified register R if the argument *WE* is set. Among different types of information chunks in a received packet, a pulse streams related to data could either represent the index number of an ON bit (as in PIC or PIC*plus*) or the decimal number for a segment (as in PDC or other custom techniques). The instruction *SDB*, *set data bits*, removes this confusion by informing the system if the received pulse count needs to be stored directly in the *LoadReg* as a segment's content (if $C = 1$) or a bit in the *LoadReg* needs to be set at the index number represented by the count (if $C = 0$). The last instruction in the category of I-Type 1 is *NOP*, *no operation*, that is used when there is a need to wait for some operation to complete, as in the case of instructions *SP* and *SD*, without halting the system. In this case, there should be enough number of *NOP*s (*PulsCount*+2) to wait for the completion of a pulse stream transmission. All or some of these *NOP*s can also be replaced by other instructions in order to perform useful tasks instead of waiting for transmission.

4.2   Type 2 Instructions (I-Type 2)

I-Type 2 is the smallest set of instructions. As mentioned earlier, these instructions handle two operands at a time and are concerned with register and/or branch update operations. One of the operands is a register and the other is an immediate constant. One of these instructions is *WR*, *write register*, that is used to store an immediate constant value to a specified general purpose register. The second instruction is the jump instruction *BNZD*, *branch and decrement if not zero*. The instruction takes two arguments, a register to check the condition and a label to jump to. If the content of the specified register is a non-zero value, the program counter jumps to the label and the register value decrements once. The *BNZD* is helpful in writing conditional loops.

4.3   Type 3 Instructions (I-Type 3)

These instructions are concerned with encoding and decoding and use either two or three operands, but all of these operands must be registers. The five instructions, described next, are used in encoding the selected segment. *IV*, *invert*, is used to complement the bits of the selected segment unconditionally and the resulting new segment replaces the corresponding segment in *LoadReg*. The operand register Rx stores the new number of ON bits (NOI) in the resulted segment and register Ry stores the corresponding flags to represent the encoding type, as per encoding description in PIC and PDC overview. The *IVC*, *invert conditionally*, works the same way as *IV* works but only if the condition of encoding is true. The condition, as mentioned earlier in the overview section, is that the number of ON bits in the selected segment should be greater than half the segment size. The Rx and Ry get updated with new NOI and Flags respectively. The *FL*, *flip*, and *FLC*, *flip conditionally*, work exactly the same way as *IV* and *IVC*, respectively, except for the base operation that is the bit wise reverse/flipping instead of inversion. The condition here for *FLC* is to check whether the content number of the selected segment is greater than the flipped content number of the same segment. If the condition is true, it means the ON bits are at the higher number of indices, hence, they represent a big decimal number and both of these can be reduced by relocating the ON bits to the lower index numbers. The fifth instruction that takes part in encoding is *IVFL*, *invert and flip*. The *IVFL* works in the same way as the other aforementioned four instructions work except it applies both the inversion and flipping together unconditionally.

The instructions *CF*, *combine the flags*, and *SF*, *split the flags*, are used for PDC, but can be used for any customized technique through PICIA. *CF* takes two operands, *Rx* and *Ry*, representing two flags to be combined and stores the result in the third operand register *R*. The first two LSBs of both *Rx* and *Ry*, in the same order, are combined to generate four LSBs in *R*. Similarly, *SF* splits the combined flags in a specified register *R* into two separate flags and stores these in registers *Rx* and *Ry*. The *Ry* takes the first two LSBs of *R* and *Rx* takes the next two LSBs of *R*.

The last and the most complex instruction of PICIA is *CRC*, *copy register conditionally*. Based on the given settings for *I* and *Co*, the instruction performs four different copy operations, as shown in Table 5 where *X* is the don't-care and [*Rs*] represents the index number of *LoadReg*. *CRC* can be used for a simple register to register copy because the instruction copies a register *Rs* to *R* if both *Co* and *I* are cleared. If *Co* is cleared and *I* is set, the source to be copied is decided by the bit of *LoadReg* located at the index number represented by the contents of register *Rs*. If the *LoadReg* bit at index *Rs* is cleared, 0 is copied to register *R*, or simply *Rs* is copied to *R* otherwise. This operation is helpful in generating PIC pulse streams. Remember, PIC selects the ON bits only in data and transmits their index numbers in the form of pulse streams. Therefore, *CRC* with such a configuration helps in finding if the target bit is ON or not. If the bit is ON, the index number of it needs to be transmitted that is present in register *Rs* and that is why it is copied to *R*. If the bit is OFF, nothing is there to transmit and that is why 0 is copied to register *R*. Hence, the index numbers of the ON bits can be transmitted in a loop. If *Co* is set, *I* becomes don't care and the contents of the selected segment are copied to register *R*. This is helpful in generating PDC pulse streams as, unlike PIC, it transmits the contents of the sub-segments in the form of pulse streams. Hence using such a configuration for *CRC*, all segments of the data word can be selected and transmitted one-by-one in a loop. All the configurations of *CRC* instruction can be used to generate any other customized transmission techniques based on the idea of transmitting the information in the form of pulse streams.

Table 5. CRC instruction functionality

Co	I	LoadReg[Rs]	Description
0	0	X	R = Rs
0	1	0	R = 0
		1	R = Rs
1	X	X	R = Selected Segment

5 Experimental Verification and Results

Verilog HDL is used to describe a fully functional processor based on the proposed ISA and a full experimental setup is implemented on the Xilinx Spartan-6 FPGA platform. The prototype platform is used to verify the functionality and performance of proposed PICIA. Extensive simulations and real-time hardware verification are performed to verify the results. A clock rate of 25 MHz is used for PICIA testing system. In the experimental flow, the PICIA processor's transmitter sends the 16-bit data starting at 0 with an increment of 1 at each transmission. The PICIA processor's receiver resends the same data back. The returned and original data words are compared to verify the complete round-trip chain.

In another experiment, the software aspects of two implementations are compared. In one implementation, the PIC family member techniques are developed for TI's MSP432X processor family. The reason for choosing the MSP432X in our experiments is that it is an ultra low-power RISC processor, and so it provides an appropriate off-the-shelf choice for comparing the PIC assembly programs using our PICIA processor vs. those of MSP432X. The second implementation used PICIA assembly language to develop the same techniques to run on the implemented processor. Both implementations use a 25 MHz clock. The number of instructions required to implement these techniques using MSP432X is approximately 1300 to 1400 on average whereas PICIA needs only 50 to 100 instructions. This is a notable reduction by a factor of 13 to 28, approximately. The data rates offered by the MSP432X implementation are also reduced significantly, approximately by a factor of 100. On the other hand, the data rates are preserved by the implementation of communication techniques using PICIA. The software implementation comparison is shown in Table 6 and Fig. 2.

An example showing how PICIA reduces the number of instructions is illustrated in Fig. 3. At the left side of the figure, an encoding example implemented in C for PDC is presented. If the encoding is implemented using a RISC ISA,

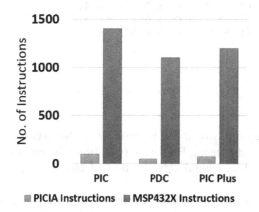

Fig. 2. PIC family implementation: PICIA vs. MSP432x

```
/* Segmentation */
seg0 = TxData & SEG_MASK;
seg1 = (TxData >> 8) & SEG_MASK;
/* Encoding */
seg0 = PDC_Encode(seg0, 0);
seg1 = PDC_Encode(seg1, 1);
/* Combine Flags */
CFlags = ((Flags1 << 2) & 0x0C) | Flags0;
/* Sub-Segmentation */
subSeg0 = seg0 & SUB_SEG_MASK;
subSeg1 = (seg0 >> 4) & SUB_SEG_MASK;
subSeg2 = seg1 & SUB_SEG_MASK;
subSeg3 = (seg1 >> 4) & SUB_SEG_MASK;


byte PDC_Encode(byte SegData, byte segNo) {
    byte countOfOnes = 0;
    byte SegDataFlipped = 0;
    byte Flags = 0x00;
    countOfOnes = ((SegData >> 7) & 1) + ((SegData >> 6) & 1)
                + ((SegData >> 5) & 1) + ((SegData >> 4) & 1)
                + ((SegData >> 3) & 1) + ((SegData >> 2) & 1)
                + ((SegData >> 1) & 1) + (SegData & 1);
    if (countOfOnes > ON_BITS_LIMIT) {
        SegData = ~SegData;
        Flags = 0x02;
    }
    SegDataFlipped = reverse(SegData);
    if (SegDataFlipped < SegData) {
        SegData = SegDataFlipped;
        Flags = Flags | 0x01;
    }
    if (segNo == 0) {
        Flags0 = Flags;
    } else {
        Flags1 = Flags;
    }
    return SegData;
}
char reverse(char b) {
    b = (b & 0xF0) >> 4 | (b & 0x0F) << 4;
    b = (b & 0xCC) >> 2 | (b & 0x33) << 2;
    b = (b & 0xAA) >> 1 | (b & 0x55) << 1;
    return b;
}
```

~150 RISC Instructions

~15 PICIA Instructions
1- SSS: Select Segment Size = 4
2- SSN: Select Segment Number 0
3- IVC: invert conditionally Seg0
4- FLC: flip conditionally Seg0
5-13: Repeat 2-to-4 steps 3 times
for Seg 1,2, & 3
14- CF: Combine Flags of Seg 0 & 1
15- CF: Combine Flags of Seg 2 & 3

Fig. 3. PICIA code reduction example

around 150 instructions would be required. On the other hand, if the same encoding is implemented using PICIA, only 15 instructions are required. A sample pseudo code in Fig. 3 highlights the flow of the program and the involved PICIA instructions.

We have also synthesized the PICIA processor system using GLOBALFOUNDRIES 65nm technology and estimated that PICIA hardware consumes around

Table 6. Results

	Implementation	
	PICIA	Stand-alone
Software implementation comparison		
Avg. no. of instructions	50–100	1300–1400
Avg. data rate (Mbps)	≈4.1–7.1	≈0.041-0.071
Hardware synthesis comparison		
Power (μW)	≈31.14	≈19–26.6
Avg. E_b (pJ/bit)	≈4.2–7.6	≈2.7-6.5
Area (gate count)	≈4700	≈2100–2400

$31.14\,\mu$W with a gate count of about 4700 gates. The power consumption results are promising as they remain well within the power budget of a full-hardware implementation of stand-alone pulsed-signaling techniques. Additionally, the consumption of hardware resources is comparable, data rates are preserved and the required number of instructions is reduced. Moreover, PICIA offers a customizable solution. The PICIA solution differs in that it offers a fully programmable communication interface that is specifically geared to the realization of pulsed-transmission techniques.

6   Securing PICIA

This section presents a possible extension of the PICIA to support of secure PIC communication [11]. An advantage of the proposed extension is that it does not require any modification in the PICIA instruction format as it employs the very same instruction types of Sect. 4 to add instructions dedicated to cryptographic functions. The security layer extension of PICIA offers a programmable environment to select not only a suitable encryption algorithm but also to choose among various execution options of the selected algorithm with the goal of trading off transmission security with data rate. Specifically, the PICIA security layer has the following features:

1. Support of multiple encryption algorithms such as simple XOR, MA5/1 [11] and AES.
2. Encryption gating in case the crypto function is not needed.
3. Configurable encryption hardware to tune the number of clock cycles used in data encryption. A tradeoff between the number of crypto clock cycles and the required crypto hardware resources is implemented through the iterative use of a smaller crypto unit. In such case, the unused crypto hardware units are gated.

In the following subsections, the security features of the extended PICIA architecture are highlighted.

Table 7. Security layer registers in addition to the regular registers of Table 1

5	Ctrl2	8 bit SP[a]	[Enable SL[b], 3-bit Enc.[c] Algorithm 4-bit Enc. Speed]
6	EncIniKey	16×16-bit SP	256-bit Initial Key Array of sixteen 16-bit registers

[a]Special Purpose [b]Security Layer [c]Encryption

6.1 Extended Register Set

Two new registers are added to the PICIA register set in support of the security layer extension, as shown in Table 7. The first register is the Control Register *Ctrl2* which is an 8-bit register used to store configuration parameters of the security layer such as enabling the security layer, selection of the encryption algorithm, and the speed of encryption in terms of number of clock cycles. The programmer initially sets the control register through a specific instruction but, once set, it becomes accessible only to the system. The second register is the 256-bit *EncIniKey* register, organized as an array of sixteen 16-bit registers, and used to store the initial encryption key. Like the Control Register, *EncIniKey* is a privileged register accessible only to the system.

6.2 Extended Instruction Set

Three new instructions are added to the PICIA assembly language in support of the security layer. They are shown in Table 8. These instructions deal with the configuration and control of the security layer. The first instruction is *ESL*, *enable security layer*, which activates the security layer and updates the *Ctrl2* register. The operand *En* is a one-bit modifier whose *ZERO* value signifies normal PIC transmission without encryption. Its *ONE* value enables encryption ahead of transmission. The second *ESL* operand, *Alg*, is a 3-bit operand that selects the encryption algorithm that should be used. There can be a maximum of eight hardware blocks in the PICIA processor system, each representing a particular encryption algorithm. In our current implementation, an *Alg* of 0 selects a simple XOR operation, while a value of 1 selects MA5/1, a modified, PIC-compatible version of the symmetric A5/1 encryption algorithm [11]. The third *ESL* operand, *ES*, is used to set the speed of the encryption process in terms of the number of clock cycles. This instruction assumes that the encryption techniques implemented within the PICIA processor support changing the number of clock cycles used to generate a full encrypted data word. For example, if MA5/1 is selected to use one clock cycle, the full encryption hardware would be utilized. If the same algorithm is chosen to use four clock cycles, then one-fourth of the hardware would be used, and the rest would be gated to save power. The *ES* operand takes an unsigned integer value in the range of 0 to 15. The number of encryption clock cycles is calculated as $n_C = 2^{ES}$. Through this operand, a trade-off between crypto latency and power can be easily programmed into the configuration of the security layer.

As described earlier, the length of the key register *EncIniKey* is 256 bits. The same register can also be used for initializing shorter keys, e.g, the 128-bit

Table 8. Security layer instructions in addition to those of Table 3

	Instruction	Description	Example
Security layer instructions			
23	ESL En,Alg,ES	Enable security layer. Enable if En=1, disable if En=0. Alg selects encryption algorithm (0:XOR, 1:MA5/1, ... 7:OtherAlgo7). ES sets encryption speed in terms of number of clock cycles/encryption-iteration. (Number of clock cycles $(n_C) = 2^{ES}$	ESL 1,0,1
24	LPI	Lock previously executed instruction. Unless unlocked, all the next instructions are considered as 16-bit constant values for the locked instruction	LPI
25	UPI	Unlock the locked instruction	UPI
Mapping			
Security layer instructions are mapped to I-Type 1			

initial key of MA5/1. There is therefore a need for introducing instructions for key-length setting and *EncIniKey* register initialization. Instructions *LPI*, *lock previous instruction*, and *UPI*, *unlock previous instruction*, are introduced for that very purpose. *LPI* locks the previously executed instruction in the control unit while keeping all the generated control signals active unless unlocked using *UPI*. In other words, these two instructions define the start and end of the user's key section in the assembly program and must follow the *ESL* instruction. All the 16-bit binary numbers between these two instructions are considered segments of the full initial key. These segments are stored in the *EncIniKey* register using an internal 4-bit offset register. The offset register defines the row index of a 16×16 array version of the *EncIniKey* register. The offset register is cleared when the *LPI* instruction is executed and is incremented when a 16-bit segment is stored successfully. An example of *EncIniKey* initialization is shown in Table 9, where the current offset represents the *EncIniKey* offset value before the execution of a given instruction and the updated offset represents the *EncIniKey* offset value after its execution.

6.3   Instruction Format

There is no change to the PICIA instructions format given in Fig. 1 as a result of adding of the crypto instructions. All the new assembly language instructions, described in previous subsections, are of the I-Type 1 instruction format. As shown in Fig. 4, the only change we need to account for is in terms of operand values. In particular, the *[Alg, ES]* operands are added to the field

Table 9. Key initialization examples

16-bit Key	64-bit Key	256-bit Key	Current Offset	Updated Offset
...	...	...	...	...
ESL 1, 1, 0	ESL 1, 1, 0	ESL 1, 1, 0	8	9
LPI	LPI	LPI	0	0
$0 \times$ F192	$0 \times$ F192	$0 \times$ F192	0	1
UPI	$0 \times$ 11AB	$0 \times$ 11AB	1	2
...	$0 \times$ A9F6	$0 \times$ A9F6	2	3
	$0 \times$ 3313	$0 \times$ 3313	3	4
	UPI	......	...	...
	...	......	...	...
		$0 \times$ 46F4	15	0
		UPI	15	0
		...	15	0

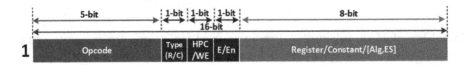

Fig. 4. Additional operand values in the PICIA I-Type 1 instructions

"Register/Constant" and the *En* operand, which controls the enabling of the security layer, is added to "E" field. The instruction opcode directs the instruction decoder to activate the control signals as per the issued assembly language command.

7   Conclusions

The Pulsed-Index Communication Interface Architecture (PICIA) is a RISC-style special purpose ISA for single-channel, low-power, high data rate, dynamic, and robust communication based on pulsed-signaling protocols. It is designed to facilitate the efficient generation of compact assembly code that is specific to such communication interfaces. This hardware/software co-design capability can be used to embed not only an existing PIC family member but also any custom nonstandard PIC protocol without changing the underlying hardware while greatly reducing the number of required instructions. Furthermore, such communication interface implementation will result in minimal to no impact on the data rates, power consumption, or the reliability of the protocols. The PICIA processor has been synthesized in GLOBALFUONDRIES 65 nm technology and has been found to consume only 31.14 µW, which translates into an energy efficiency of less than 10 pJ per transmitted bit. To support secure communication, the basic PICIA has been extended to provide a programmable environment for selecting a suitable encryption algorithm and controlling its latency at execution. PICIA's micro-architecture and the optimized hardware blocks that compactly implement its RISC-style ISA are the subject of a separate publication.

Acknowledgments. This work has been supported by the Semiconductor Research Corporation (SRC) under the Abu Dhabi SRC Center of Excellence on Energy-Efficient Electronic Systems (ACE^{4}S), Contract 2013 HJ2440, with customized funding from the Mubadala Development Company, Abu Dhabi, UAE.

References

1. Dayu, S., Huaiyu, X., Ruidan, S., Zhiqiang, Y.: A Geo-related IoT applications platform based on Google map. In: 7th International Conference on e-Business Engineering (ICEBE), Shanghai, China, pp. 380–384, November 2010
2. Byun, J., Kim, S.H., Kim, D.: Lilliput: ontology-based platform for IoT social networks. In: IEEE International Conference on Services Computing, Anchorage, AK, USA, pp. 139–146, June–July 2014
3. Hsu, J.M., Chen, C.Y.: A sensor information gateway based on thing interaction in IoT-IMS communication platform. In: 10th International Conference on Intelligent Information Hiding and Multimedia Signal Processing (IIH-MSP), Kitakyushu, Japan, pp. 835–838, August 2014
4. MAXIM: OneWireViewer User's Guide, Version 1.4 (2009)
5. dos Reis Filho, C., da Silva, E., de Azevedo, E., Seminario, J., Dibb, L.: Monolithic data circuit-terminating unit (DCU) for a one-wire vehicle network. In: Proceedings of the 24th European Solid-State Circuits Conference (ESSCIRC 1998), pp. 228–231, Hague, Netherlands, September 1998
6. Muzaffar, S., Shabra, A., Yoo, J., Elfadel, I.M.: A pulsed-index technique for single-channel, low power, dynamic signaling. In: Design, Automation and Test In Europe (DATE 2015), Grenoble, France, pp. 1485–1490, March 2015
7. Muzaffar, S., Elfadel, I.M.: A pulsed decimal technique for single-channel, dynamic signaling for IoT applications. In: 25th IFIP/IEEE International Conference on Very Large Scale Integration (VLSI-SoC 2017), Abu Dhabi, UAE, pp. 1–6, October 2017
8. Teja, R., Jammu, B.R., Adimulam, M., Ayi, M.: VLSI implementation of LTSSM. In: International conference of Electronics, Communication and Aerospace Technology (ICECA 2017), Coimbatore, India, pp. 129–134, April 2017
9. linux-mips.org: Cisco Systems Routers (2012). https://www.linux-mips.org/wiki/Cisco
10. Muzaffar, S., Elfadel, I.M.: An instruction set architecture for low-power, dynamic IoT communication. In: 26th IFIP/IEEE International Conference on Very Large Scale Integration (VLSI-SoC 2018), Verona, Italy, October 2018, To appear
11. Muzaffar, S., Waheed, O.T., Aung, Z., Elfadel, I.M.: Single-clock-cycle, multilayer encryption algorithm for single-channel IoT communications. In: IEEE Conference on Dependable and Secure Computing (DSC 2017), Taipei, Taiwan, pp. 153–158, August 2017

The Connection Layout in a Lattice of Four-Terminal Switches

Anna Bernasconi$^{(\boxtimes)}$, Antonio Boffa, Fabrizio Luccio, and Linda Pagli

Dipartimento di Informatica, Università di Pisa, Pisa, Italy
{anna.bernasconi,fabrizio.luccio,linda.pagli}@unipi.it

Abstract. A non classical approach to the logic synthesis of Boolean functions based on switching lattices is considered, for which deriving a feasible layout has not been previously studied. All switches controlled by the same literal must be connected together and to an input lead of the chip, and the layout of such connections must be realized in super-imposed layers. Inter-layer connections are realized with vias, with the overall goal of minimizing the number of layers needed. The problem shows new interesting combinatorial and algorithmic aspects. Since the specific lattice cell where each switch is placed can be decided with a certain amount of freedom, and one literal among several may be assigned for controlling a switch, we first study a lattice rearrangement (Problem 1) and a literal assignment (Problem 2), to place in adjacent cells as many switches controlled by the same literal as possible. Then we study how to build a feasible layout of connections onto different layers using a minimum number of such layers (Problem 3). We prove that Problem 2 is NP-hard, and Problems 1 and 3 appear also intractable. Therefore we propose heuristic algorithms for the three phases that show an encouraging performance on a set of standard benchmarks.

Keywords: Circuit layout · Switching lattices · Logic synthesis · Hard problems · Heuristics

1 Introduction

The logic synthesis of a Boolean function is the procedure for implementing the function into an electronic circuit. The literature on this subject is extremely vast and large part of it is devoted to *two-level* logic synthesis, where the function is implemented in a NAND or NOR circuit of maximal depth 2 [1]. In this paper, we focus on a different synthesis method based on a *switching lattice*, that is a two-dimensional array of four-terminal switches implemented in its cells. Each switch is linked to the four neighbors and is connected with them when the switch is ON, or is disconnected when the switch is OFF.

The idea of using regular two-dimensional arrays of switches to implement Boolean functions dates back to a seminal paper by Akers in 1972 [2]. Recently,

N. Bombieri et al. (Eds.): VLSI-SoC 2018, IFIP AICT 561, pp. 32–52, 2019.
https://doi.org/10.1007/978-3-030-23425-6_3

with the advent of a variety of emerging nanoscale technologies based on regular arrays of switches, synthesis methods targeting lattices of multi-terminal switches have found a renewed interest [3–5]. A Boolean function can be implemented in a lattice with the following rules:

- each switch is controlled by a Boolean literal, i.e. by one of the input variables or by its complement;
- if a literal takes the value 1 all corresponding switches are connected to their four neighbors, else they are not connected;
- the function evaluates to 1 for any input assignment that produces a connected path between two opposing edges of the lattice, e.g., the top and the bottom edges; the function evaluates to 0 for any input assignment that does not produce such a path.

For instance, the 3×3 lattice of switches and corresponding literals in Fig. 1a implements the function $f = x_1 x_2 x_3 + \overline{x}_1 \overline{x}_3 + \overline{x}_2 \overline{x}_3$. If we assign the values 1, 0, 0 to the variables x_1, x_2, x_3, respectively, we obtain paths of 1's connecting the top and the bottom edges of the lattices (Fig. 1b), and f evaluates to 1. On the contrary, the assignment $x_1 = 1, x_2 = 0, x_3 = 1$, on which f evaluates to 0, does not produce any path from the top to the bottom edge (Fig. 1c). All the other input assignments can be similarly checked.

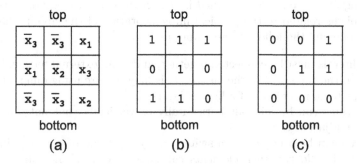

Fig. 1. A network of four terminal switches implementing the function $f = x_1 x_2 x_3 + \overline{x}_1 \overline{x}_3 + \overline{x}_2 \overline{x}_3$ (a); the lattice evaluated on the assignments 1, 0, 0 (b) and 1, 0, 1 (c), with 1's and 0's representing ON and OFF switches, respectively.

The synthesis of a function f on a lattice consists of finding an assignment of input literals to the switches, such that the top-bottom paths in the lattice implement f and the number of switches in the lattice is reduced as much as possible. Recalling that the *dual* f^D of a function f is such that $\overline{f^D}(\overline{x}_1, \ldots, \overline{x}_n) = f(x_1, \ldots, x_n)$, in [3,4] Altun and Riedel developed a synthesis method where the implicants (products) of the minimal irredundant SOP forms of the function f and of its dual f^D are respectively associated, in any order, to the columns and to the rows of the lattice. The literal assigned to a switch is chosen from the necessarily non-void intersection of the two subsets of literals appearing in the implicants corresponding to the intersecting column and row of the lattice. If several literals appear in the intersection anyone of them can be chosen. As an elementary example consider the function $f = x_1\overline{x}_3\overline{x}_4 + x_1x_2 + \overline{x}_1\overline{x}_3x_4$ and its dual $f^D = x_1\overline{x}_3 + x_1x_4 + x_2\overline{x}_3 + \overline{x}_1x_2\overline{x}_4$. Figure 2a shows the lattice for f where just one multiple assignment $x_1, \overline{x}_3$ occurs.

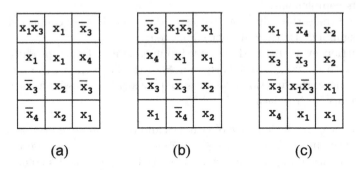

(a)   (b)   (c)

Fig. 2. A lattice implementing the function $x_1\overline{x}_3\overline{x}_4 + x_1x_2 + \overline{x}_1\overline{x}_3x_4$ (a), where a choice between x_1 and $\overline{x}_3$ must be performed in the first cell. The lattice after column permutation (b), and then row permutation (c), obtained with our method.

Starting from the lattice obtained by the Altun-Riedel method we consider three problems related to the physical implementation of the circuit, that must be solved obeying the following assumptions.

1. Equal literals must be connected together, and to an external terminal on one side (e.g. the top edge) of the lattice. This may require using different layers, and vias to connect cells of adjacent layers.
2. Connections can be laid out horizontally or vertically (but not diagonally) between adjacent cells.
3. Each cell can be occupied by a switch, or by a portion of a connecting wire, or by a via. No two such elements can share a cell on the same layer. In particular the connections cannot cross on the same layer.
4. The overall target is designing a layout with the minimum number of layers. Since the problem is computationally-hard, it will be relaxed to finding a reasonable layout by heuristic techniques.

The circuit will be built starting from the original $N \times M$ lattice (*level 0*), and superimposing to it a certain number H of layers (*levels 1 to H*), to give rise to a three-dimensional grid of size $N \times M \times (H+1)$. Note that the switches associated with the same literal cannot be generally connected all together on the same layer, so one or more subsets of these switches will be connected on a layer and then made available through vias on the next layers to be connected to other subsets.

Two degrees of freedom remain after the function has been synthesized, to be used to reduce the number of layers in the layout. One is the possibility of permuting lattice columns and rows arbitrarily, as exploited in the following Problem 1. The other is the possibility of selecting any literal from a multiple choice for each switch, as exploited in the following Problem 2. Problems 1 and 2 apply at level 0, preparing the lattice for the actual layout design which takes place in the next layers 1 to H, where the inputs of the switches associated with the same literal are connected together and to the corresponding external lead, as treated in the following Problem 3.

Problems 1, 2 and 3 are solved one after the other, each producing the input for the next one. Since all of them are computationally-hard, we solve them heuristically, then show experimentally that our solutions are efficient for standard benchmarks where the size of the lattice and the number of variables are reasonable. A preliminary version of this study limited to Problem 2 (without a proof on NP-hardness) and to Problem 3 has been presented in [6].

2   Rearranging the Lattice

In principle a lattice can be seen as an array $A[N \times M]$, or as a non-directed graph $G = (V, E)$ whose vertices correspond to the lattice cells (then $|V| = NM$) and whose edges correspond to the horizontal and vertical connections between adjacent cells (then $|E| = 2NM - N - M$). We shall refer indifferently to a lattice cell $A[i, j]$, $1 \leq i \leq N, 1 \leq j \leq M$, or to graph vertex v_k, $1 \leq k \leq NM$. Obviously the vertices have degree 2, 3, or 4 if they respectively correspond to corner, border, or internal cells of the lattice.

Let $x_1, x_2, \ldots, x_n$ be the variables of the function and L be the set of all literals, $|L| = 2n$. After the Altun-Rieder synthesis is completed, each cell $A[i, j]$ is associated with a non-void subset $L_{i,j} \in L$, from which one literal has to be eventually assigned to the corresponding graph vertex. We pose:

Definition 1. *If a single variable is associated to each vertex, an mc-area is a maximal connected subgraph S of G in which all variables hold the same literal. Equivalently an mc-area is the portion of the lattice corresponding to S.*

Note that if two mc-areas A_1, A_2 hold the same literal, no two cells $c_1 \in A_1$, $c_2 \in A_2$ may be adjacent since A_1 and A_2 are maximal.

A basic task is minimizing the number of mc-areas, or equivalently make them as large as possible, since this will imply reducing the number of layers. As shown below the core of this problem is NP-hard, so we study how to solve it heuristically. As already said we proceed in two consecutive phases. The first phase is aimed at permuting columns and rows in order to increase the number of adjacent cells holding common literals, even though subsets of two or more literals may still be associated to each cell. The second phase consists of the selection of one literal in each of the multiple assignments at the cells, so the mc-areas can be built according to Definition 1. To implement the first phase we pose:

Definition 2. *The weight of a pair of cells $A[r, s], A[u, v]$ is given by:* $w_{r,s}^{u,v} = |L_{r,s} \cap L_{u,v}|/(|L_{r,s}| \cdot |L_{u,v}|)$.

For example for $L_{r,s} = \{a, b, c\}, L_{u,v} = \{b, c, d, e\}$ we have $L_{r,s} \cap L_{u,v} = \{b, c\}$, then: $w_{r,s}^{u,v} = 2/(3 \cdot 4) = 1/6$. Note that $w_{r,s}^{u,v}$ is the probability for $A[r, s], A[u, v]$ to share the same literal if one literal is randomly chosen from $L_{r,s}$ and $L_{u,v}$.

The weight is relevant in our case for pairs of adjacent cells. As we are interested in building large mc-areas, we pose:

Problem 1. *Find a column permutation and a row permutation of A, to maximize the sum of weights of the pairs of adjacent cells.*

Once Problem 1 has been solved, one literal must be selected in each subset $L_{i,j}$ as stated in the following:

Problem 2. *Find a literal assignment for each cell $A[i, j]$ that minimizes the number of mc-areas.*

2.1   Solving Problem 1

To ease the task of Problem 1, an elementary observation is in order:

Observation 1. Two cells can be made adjacent by column or row permutation if and only if they lay on the same row or on the same column, respectively.

By Observation 1, column and row permutations can be independently performed since the result of one does not affect the result of the other. In fact the problem will be solved by a column permutation followed by a row permutation. We pose:

Definition 3. *The weight $C_{s,v}$ of a pair of columns s, v of the lattice is the sum of weights of all the pairs of cells lying in the columns s, v and in the same row, that is: $C_{s,v} = \sum_{i=1}^{N} w_{i,s}^{i,v}$.*

And, symmetrically:

Definition 4. *The weight $R_{r,u}$ of a pair of rows r, u of the lattice is the sum of weights of all the pairs of cells lying in the rows r, u and in the same column, that is: $R_{r,u} = \sum_{j=1}^{M} w_{r,j}^{u,j}$.*

For building large mc-areas we are interested in bringing adjacent pairs of columns and rows with higher weights, via permutations. To this end we adopt the following heuristic on the columns, then on the rows.

1. compute the weights $C_{s,v}$ of all pairs of columns;
2. build a stack S whose elements contain the pairs (s, v) with non-zero weights, ordered for decreasing value of such weights;
3. start with M subsets of adjacent columns, each containing exactly one of them;

4. pop one by one the pairs (s, v) from S: for the pair currently extracted decide a column re-arrangement (without actually performing it), merging two subsets of adjacent columns, one containing column s and the other containing column v, if the two columns can be made adjacent without breaking the subsets already built. The columns in each subset are kept ordered for increasing value of their index. This step 4 is performed according to the scheme COLUMN-PERM shown below;

5. once the stack S is empty, permute the groups of columns as indicated in the corresponding subsets previously determined. These groups can then be arranged in the lattice in any order.

COLUMN-PERMUTE

1. define a vector P of M elements, whose values are:

   $P[j] = 1$ if column j forms a subset of one column;

   $P[j] = 2$ if column j is the first one in a subset of more than one column;

   $P[j] = 3$ if column j is the last one in a subset of more than one column;

   $P[j] = 4$ if column j is neither the first one nor the last one in a subset of more than two columns;

2. initialize P as $P[j] = 1$ for $1 \leq j \leq M$;
   // all the initial subsets of columns contain one element:
   // recall that S is a stack of pairs of columns;

3. **while** S is not empty

   pop a pair (s, v) from S;

   if $(P[s] = 4$ OR $P[v] = 4)$ discard (s, v)

   else according to the values $P[s], P[v]$ the subsets
   of s and v are merged bringing s adjacent to v
   and the values of $P[s], P[v]$ are updated accordingly;

   // nine combinations of values $P[s], P[v]$ are possible:
   // for $P[s] = P[v] = 2$ and $P[s] = P[v] = 3$ the order
   // of the columns in one of the subsets must be inverted;

4. the process ends with one or more subsets each
   corresponding to the permutation of a group of columns.

After column permutation, the rows are permuted with a procedure perfectly symmetrical to the one given for columns, using row weights $R_{r,u}$.

In the lattice of Fig. 2(a), the pairs of columns in S with non-zero weights, ordered for decreasing values of the corresponding weights are:

$(1,2)$ $C_{1,2} = 3/2$, $(1,3)$ $C_{1,3} = 3/2$

producing the subsets of adjacent columns $\{1, 2\}, \{3\}$ and then $\{3, 1, 2\}$, from which the column permutation of Fig. 2(b) is built. The ordered pairs of rows in S with non-zero weights are:

(1,2) $R_{1,2} = 3/2$,   (1,3) $R_{1,3} = 3/2$,   (3,4) $R_{3,4} = 1$

producing the subsets of adjacent rows $\{1, 2\}, \{3\}, \{4\}, \{3, 1, 2\}, \{4\}$, and then $\{4, 3, 1, 2\}$, from which the final row permutation of Fig. 2(c) is built.

A global measure W of the amount of adjacent equal variables in the whole lattice, called the *lattice weight*, is naturally given by the sum of weights of all pairs of adjacent cells, or equivalently by the sum of weights of all the pairs of adjacent columns and rows, namely: $W = \sum_{j=1}^{M-1} C_{j,j+1} + \sum_{i=1}^{N-1} R_{i,i+1}$. In fact an increase of the value of W can be seen as an indicator of the advantage deriving from a column-row permutation. In the example of Fig. 2 the lattice weight increases from $W = 4$ (part (a)) to $W = 7$ (part (c) after column and row permutation). In the simulations discussed in the last section such value roughly doubles on the average after the heuristic for Problem 1 is applied.

Implemented with standard data structures, the time required by the above heuristic is $O(NM^2n + MN^2n)$ versus $O(NMn)$ of the input size (recall that n is the number of variables).

2.2   Hardness of Problem 1

Although our heuristic for Problem 1 shows an encouraging experimental value, a weakness derives from the decision of not restructuring a subset of columns/rows after it is built, aside from possibly inverting the order of its elements. Merging two subsets in a strictly optimal way would lead to an exponential explosion of the time needed with a possibly minor improvement of the result. Up to now we have not been able to decide the time complexity of the problem, although we believe that is NP-hard. We simply pose the question of its precise hardness as a challenging open problem.

2.3   Solving Problem 2

Problem 2 is of high computational interest for two reasons. The first is that the number of prime implicants in f and f^D strongly increases with the number of variables of the function, so that the elementary examples that we have given so far do not show the real entity of the phenomenon. In particular the possibility of having multiple assignments of many literals in the lattice cells is substantially high, making Problem 2 a crucial part of lattice rearrangement. The second reason is that Problem 2 is NP-hard as we will prove in the next subsection, so a clever heuristic must be devised for its solution. To this end a preliminary exam of the lattice is performed by applying the following Rule 1, with the attempt of reducing the number of literals contained in the subsets associated to the vertices.

Rule 1. Let v_j be a vertex; v_1, v_2, v_3, v_4 be the four vertices adjacent to v_j (if any); L_j, L_1, L_2, L_3, L_4 be the relative subsets of literals. Apply in sequence the following steps:

Step 1. Let $|L_j| > 1$. If a literal $x \in L_j$ does not appear in any of the sets L_i, for $1 \le i \le 4$, cancel x from L_j and repeat the step until at least one element remains in L_j.

Step 2. Let $|L_j| > 1$, and let $L_k \subset L_j$ with $k \in \{1,2,3,4\}$. If a literal $x \in L_j$ appears in exactly one set L_h with $h \in \{1,2,3,4\}$ and $h \ne k$, then cancel x from L_j and repeat the step until at least the literals of L_k remain in L_j.

We have:

Proposition 1. *The application of Rule 1 does not prevent finding a literal assignment that minimizes the number of mc-areas.*

Proof. Assume that a literal x canceled from v_j by Step 1 or Step 2 of the rule would instead be assigned to v_j in the final assignment.

Step 1. An mc-area containing only v_j with literal x would result. If, in a minimal solution, a different literal y is assigned to v_j and is not assigned to v_1, v_2, v_3, or v_4, the number of mc-areas remains the same. If instead y is assigned to one or more of these vertices the number of mc-areas decreases.

Step 2. If x is not assigned to v_h an mc-area containing only v_j with literal x would result, otherwise an mc-area containing v_j, v_h, and possibly other vertices with literal x would result. Since one of the literals $y \in L_k$ must be assigned to v_k in any minimal assignment, and $L_k \subset L_j$, then y could be assigned to v_j instead of x and the number of mc-areas would remain the same, or would decrease if y is assigned also to other neighbors of v_j. □

An example of application of step 2 of Rule 1 is shown in Fig. 3. A literal cancellation from L_j may induce a further cancellation in an adjacent cell. In the example of Fig. 3, if all the cells adjacent to v_h except for v_j do not contain the literal c, the cancellation of c from L_j induces the cancellation of c from L_h if step 1 of Rule 1 is subsequently applied to v_h.

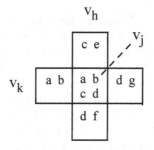

Fig. 3. Canceling a literal from a multiple choice using step 2 of Rule 1. Literals are denoted by a, b, c, d, e, f, g. Literal c in cells v_j, v_h is canceled from v_j.

Before running an algorithm for solving Problem 2, the sets L_i may be reduced using Rule 1 through a scanning of the lattice. This is a simple task, although a clever data structure must be devised for reducing the time required. Moreover several successive lattice scans may be applied for further reduction until no change occurs in a whole scan, although this is likely to produce much less cancellations than the first scan. These operations constitutes the first phase of any algorithm. Then, as the problem is computationally intractable, a heuristic must be applied. The following algorithm MC-AREAS proposed here, and already experimented in [7], builds each mc-area as a BFS tree, looking for a subset of adjacent vertices that share a same literal and assigning that literal to them. The lattice is treated as a tree.

MC-AREAS

1. start from a vertex v_i and reduce the associated set of literals L_i to just one of its elements l_i chosen at random; v_i will be the root of a tree T_i under construction for the current mc-area;

2. traverse the lattice from v_i in BFS form:
   forany vertex v_j encountered such that v_j does not belong to a BFS tree already built:
       if $(l_i \in L_j)$ assign l_i to v_j and insert v_j into T_i
       else insert v_j into a queue Q;
   continue the traversal for T_i;

3. **if** $(Q$ is not empy$)$ extract a new vertex v_i from Q and repeat steps 1 and 2 to build a new tree;

The experimental results discussed in the last section are derived following this approach. Better results would be possibly obtained with more skilled heuristics at the cost of a greater running time.

2.4   Hardness of Problem 2

To prove that Problem 2 is NP-hard we formulate it in graph form as done in [8] where the proof appeared. Let $G = (V, E)$ be an undirected graph and let C be a set of k colors such that each vertex $v_i \in V$ is associated to (or "contains") a non-void subset C_i of C. The graph problem equivalent to ours, indicated as *MPA* for *minimal partition (color) assignment*, is the one of assigning to each vertex v_i of G a single color from among the ones in C_i such that the number σ of maximal connected subgraphs of $G_1, \ldots, G_\sigma$ of G whose vertices have the same color is minimal. Dealing with a lattice, as required in our Problem 2, it is sufficient to start with *PMPA*, that is the MPA problem where G is planar. We have:

Proposition 2. *The PMPA Problem is NP-hard.*

Proof. Reduction from planar graph 3-coloring. Let H be an arbitrary planar graph to be 3-colored with colors $1, 2, 3$, and let G be a corresponding planar

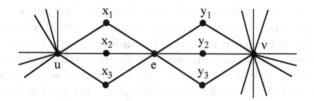

Fig. 4. Portion of graph G corresponding to the edge $e = (u, v)$ of graph H.

graph whose MPA must be built. The set of colors of G is $\{1, 2, 3, 4, 5, 6, 7, 8, 9\}$. For each edge $e = (u, v)$ of H there are nine vertices $u, e, v, x_1, x_2, x_3, y_1, y_2, y_3$ in G connected as shown in Fig. 4, with subsets of colors:

$$C_u = \{1, 2, 3\}, \ C_v = \{1, 2, 3\}, \ C_e = \{4, 5, 6, 7, 8, 9\},$$

$$C_{x_1} = \{1, 6, 7, 8, 9\}, \ C_{x_2} = \{2, 4, 5, 8, 9\}, \ C_{x_3} \{3, 4, 5, 6, 7\},$$

$$C_{y_1} = \{1, 4, 5, 6, 9\}, \ C_{y_2} = \{2, 5, 6, 7, 8\}, \ C_{y_3} \{3, 4, 7, 8, 9\}.$$

Consider a minimal collection of monochromatic connected subgraphs $G_1, \ldots,$ G_σ of G. We have: (1) the vertices u, v must belong to two distinct subgraphs G_i, G_j and the vertex e cannot belong to G_i or to G_j because $C_e \cap C_u = \emptyset$ and $C_e \cap C_v = \emptyset$; (2) at most one of the vertices x_1, x_2, x_3 may belong to G_i and at most one of the vertices y_1, y_2, y_3 may belong to G_j due to their colors; (3) at most two of the vertices x_1, x_2, x_3 and at most two of the vertices y_1, y_2, y_3 may belong to the same subgraph of e implying that the colors assigned to u and v must be different due to the colors of all the vertices involved. Letting $G = (V, E)$, from the points 1, 2, and 3 we have $\sigma \geq |V| + |E|$ and equality is met if and only if different colors can be assigned to u and v, depending on the color constraint imposed by the other vertices to which u and v are adjacent in H. That is, H can be 3-colored if and only if MPA can be solved on G with $\sigma = |V| + |E|$.   □

Starting from Theorem 2 we now prove that the result holds true even for planar grid-graphs *GMPA* as in the case of our lattice.

Proposition 3. *The GMPA Problem is NP-hard.*

Proof. We proceed in two steps. First we prove the result holds true for planar graphs of bounded vertex degree $d \geq 3$ by reduction from PMPA. Then we pass from bounded degree planar graphs to GMPA.

1. Reduction from PMPA, by insertion of new vertices to reduce all vertex degrees to at most 3. If edges $(a, b), (a, c), (a, d), (a, e)$ and possibly other edges (a, x) exist, i.e. $\deg(a) > 3$, insert a new vertex z with $C_z = C_a \cup C_b \cup C_c$, delete edges $(a, b), (a, c)$, and insert new edges $(a, z), (z, b), (z, c)$. Note that the degree of a decreases by 1, the degrees of b, c are unchanged, and z has degree 3. Continue until each vertex has degree ≤ 3. The solution for the new

graph, i.e. the connected mono-colored subgraphs, coincides with a solution for PMPA if the new vertices z are deleted and the original edges are restored. Note that the graph resulting after the transformation is planar.

2. A result of Leslie G. Valiant (Theorem 2 of [9]), states that a planar graph G of n vertices with degree at most four admits a planar embedding in an $O(n \times n)$ grid Γ. Of the $O(n^2)$ cells of Γ, obviously only n are used in the embedding for the vertices of G, while many of the others are used for embedding the edges of G as non intersecting sequences of cells in i, j directions. In [10] was then shown that one such embedding can be built where all edges are just straight line segments.

3. Build the embedding on Γ, and extend the grid to a new grid Γ' as follows. If two horizontal sequences of cells representing two edges of G lie in two rows $i, i+1$ and part of these sequences share the same columns (i.e. the two sequences are partly adjacent), insert a new empty row between i and $i+1$, using its cells where needed to fix vertical sequences possibly interrupted by the new row. Repeat the operation for any pair of partly adjacent sequences. Repeat the process on the columns, inserting new columns until no vertical sequences are partly adjacent. Note that the construction of Γ' has been done in time and space polynomial in n.

4. If two adjacent vertices a, b of G are embedded in two non adjacent cells of Γ', assign the set of colors $C_a \cap C_b$ to the cells of the sequence representing the edge (a, b). Repeat for all pairs of adjacent vertices. Assign a new color $c \notin C$ to all the grid cells not corresponding to the vertices and to the edges of G.

5. Solve GMPA on Γ' considering all the cells as vertices of a new larger graph. Discard the subsets of cells with color c, and in any other subset take only the cells corresponding to original vertices of G. These subsets constitute a solution for a bounded degree PMPA.   □

3   Solving Problem 3

After Problem 2 is solved, we have to choose how to connect the different mc-areas associated with the same literal and then connect them to the external input leads. To this end different layers are needed to attain all non-crossing connections. Formally we pose the following problem:

Problem 3. *Find a minimum number of layers allowing to connect together all the mc-areas with the same literal, and to connect them to the input leads, obeying the assumptions 1 to 4 of Sect. 1.*

The solution has to be constructive, that is, the actual layout must be shown.

In order to better understand the problem let us discuss an example. We start from a lattice of $N \times M$ cells each associated to one of the $2n$ input literals. Figure 5 shows a 5×6 lattice with 7 literals indicated for simplicity with the numbers 1 to 7. In practical applications we usually have $2n < N \times M$, hence there are cells assigned to the same literal that must be connected together to

1	1	5	5	2	2
1	4	2	1	5	5
3	3	2	1	5	7
3	3	2	4	6	6
5	6	6	3	3	7

Fig. 5. Example of starting lattice.

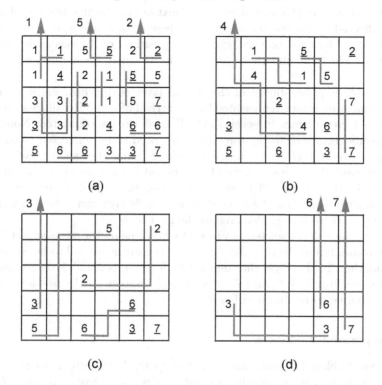

(a)　　　　　　　　(b)

(c)　　　　　　　　(d)

Fig. 6. (a) Layer 1 with the first connections. (b) Layer 2. (c) Layer 3. (d) Layer 4. Arrows indicate the connections to the input leads on the top edge. Underlined literals indicate the starting cells of the vias.

be reached in parallel from outside. Recall that these literals may be grouped in the mc-areas deriving from the previous lattice rearrangement. The starting lattice constitutes layer 0 of the layout, above which the connections are to be built in successive layers.

Suppose that the input leads to the circuit are in the top edge of the lattice. In layer 1 the only connections we can lay out are those of the mc-areas, and the mc-areas with cells in the top row may also be connected outside, see Fig. 6(a). Note that in layer 1 there is no room for other connections, hence a new layer

1	2	3
2	3	1
3	1	2

Fig. 7. A non solvable instance.

2 must be added. For each of the mc-areas connected in layer 1 and holding a literal that appears also in other mc-areas, or not yet connected to the outside, a single cell is connected through a *via* to the next layer. The final number of layers may be affected by the specific selection of these cells, however, in our heuristic we do not consider this point and choose the positions of the vias arbitrarily. In the layers of Fig. 6 the underlined literals indicate where the corresponding vias start.

A possible implementation of the second layer is shown in Fig. 6(b). Each surviving mc-area is now represented by the arrival of a via. Recall that connections cannot cross, hence in general not all areas can be connected. Note that areas already connected to the top edge don't need to be connected to the this edge again, even though they are not completely connected among each other. This is the case of the area associated with literal 1, while areas associated with literals 3, 6, and 7 have still to be connected to the top edge. Note also that all literals with label 4 can be connected in a single area and outside, therefore there is no need to connect this area to the next layer.

The next layer 3 is depicted in Fig. 6(c) where one on the two areas of literal 3 can be connected to the top edge, but these two areas are still to be connected to one another. In this layer the connections for literals 2 and 5 are completed, while vias for literals 3, 6, and 7 are arbitrarily chosen. In the last layer 4 the layout is completed as shown in Fig. 6(d).

3.1 Impossible Instances

To address Problem 3 formally we must start with a crucial observation, namely not all instances of it are solvable no matter how many layers are used. As an introduction consider the lattice of Fig. 7 where each row contains a cyclic shift of the literals in the previous row and all these shift are different. It is easy to see that no cells with the same literal can be connected together independently of any column/row permutation. We now show that the vast majority of problem instances are theoretically solvable, although some may require an exceedingly high number of layers to be practically solved. We have:

Proposition 4. *A problem instance cannot be solved if and only if in the initial literal assignment no two adjacent cells share a same literal after any column/row permutation (Problem 1) and, no matter how the multiple assignments are resolved (Problem 2), each cell in row zero contains a literal that occurs also in another cell.*

Proof. If part. Assume that no two adjacent cells share a same literal after any solution of Problems 1 and 2. Although the cells of row zero can be connected to the output, there will be no way to connect them to the other cells with the same literal since all cells will be occupied by a via in all layers.

Only-if part. If at least one of the conditions stated in the proposition does not hold, at least one cell in layer 2 is made available (or "free") for routing due to an area built in layer 1, or to a connection to the output in that layer. Once a free cell arises, it can be "moved" to any cell of the array by consecutive movements of adjacent literals as in the well known *15-slide game*, and any literal adjacent to the free cell can similarly be moved around to be brought adjacent to a cell with the same literal. Proceeding with this strategy all cells with a same literal can be linked together and brought to the output.   □

Note that the strategy indicated in the only-if part of the above proof may require a very large number of layers if only a small number ν of free cells exists in a layer, as only ν movements can be done in that layer. In particular, if only a few cells are made free by the solution of Problems 1 and 2, i.e. if layer 1 contains a large number of small mc-areas, the routing mechanism could require so many layers not to apply in practice. A decision on building or not such a layout must be taken after the simulation on significant examples.

3.2 Hardness of Problem 3

In the solution of Problem 3, the cells containing the same literal in any layer are connected, in the best case, as trees (and not as general subgraphs) to minimize the occupation of free cells, see next Sect. 3.3. The problem of minimizing the number of layers is related to the one of building the maximum number of such trees in any layer whose edges do not intersect. If a 15-slide movement of free cells is required the problem is NP-hard [11]. If such movements are not required the problem has strong similarities with other known NP-hard problems dealing with grid embedding of graphs, as for example determining the Steiner tree among k vertices on a grid [12], or determining the rectilinear crossing number of a graph [13], etc.

We have not been able to prove that Problem 3 is NP-hard, and leave it as a challenging open problem. For its solution we rely on a heuristic algorithm that produces satisfying results on a large class of benchmark instances as shown in the last section. If no tree can be directly built in a layer, as discussed in the previous subsection, the heuristic stops declaring that routing is impossible. Otherwise we have:

Proposition 5. *Let α be the number of mc-areas generated by Problems 1 and 2, h be the number of literals involved in the lattice, and k be the number of literals appearing in the cells of the top edge. An upper and a lower bound to the number H of layers are given by $\alpha + \lceil (h - k)/M \rceil$ and $\lceil h/M \rceil$, respectively.*

Proof. Upper bound. First note that in layer 1 all the cells of any mc-area are connected together, and in each of the successive layers at least one pair of cells having a via from the previous layer, and holding the same literal, are connected. Then at most α layers are needed to connect all the cells holding the same literal. In addition all the h literals must be connected to the corresponding inputs leads on the top edge of the lattice. For the k literals already in this edge the connections can take place in layer 1. The remaining $h - k$ literals, in the worst case, may be brought to a further layer $\alpha + 1$ by vias and connected to the input leads in $\lceil (h - k)/M \rceil$ layers.

Lower bound. Observe that h external leads must be displayed on the top edge of the lattice, possibly in different layers, and this edge contains M cells.   □

In the example of Fig. 6 we have $\alpha = 15$ (there are 15 mc-areas in layer 0), $h = 7, k = 3$, and $M = 6$. The proposed layout with $H = 4$ layers is far from approaching the upper bound $15 + \lceil 4/6 \rceil = 16$, while is closer to the lower bound $\lceil 7/6 \rceil = 2$.

3.3 Heuristics for Problem 3

Let us now discuss possible greedy heuristics to solve Problem 3 in a reasonable amount of time.

Independently of the lattices that cannot be solved according to the conditions stated in Proposition 4, other cases may require an exceedingly large number of layers if the "15-slide game" moves are required, as indicated in the proof of the same Proposition 4. We do not accept such moves, treating a lattice requiring them as unsolvable. This limitation shows a minor importance in practice since our algorithms failed very rarely to find a layout for a theoretically solvable lattice, out of a very large number of cases, see Sect. 4.

The general structure of our heuristics consists of the following two main steps:

1. Starting with layer 0 resulting from a re-arrangement of the lattice done in Problems 1 and 2, build the connecting trees for all mc-areas in layer 1, and connect the literals of the top side to the external leads.
2. While there are trees with the same literals still to be connected between them and/or to the outside:
   (a) place a via on a cell chosen at random of each such a tree;
   (b) add a new layer to receive the vias;
   (c) try to connect together as many vias as possible, associated to the same literal;
   (d) try to connect each group of cells containing a literal to the corresponding external lead, if not already done.

Step 1 can be implemented in a standard way, in a lattice traversal. Note that this initial step is optimal, i.e., no algorithm for the minimization of the number of layers can do better on the first layer.

To implement the second and main step of the heuristics we introduce the concept of *free area* where a connection between cells with the same literal can be displayed, namely:

Definition 5. *In the layers from 2 on, a free cell is one not containing a via; a free area is a maximal connected subset of free cells; the boundary cells of a free area are the ones surrounding it.*

For example layer 2 in Fig. 6(b) contains seven free areas, as shown in Fig. 8. Using proper coding and data structures, free areas and their boundary cells can be easily computed through a scanning of the lattice in optimal time $O(N \times M)$. We have:

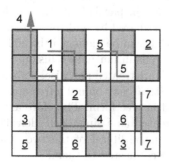

Fig. 8. Layer 2 of Fig. 6(b) with the seven free areas shown in grey.

Proposition 6. *In any given layer from 2 on, cells holding the same literal can be connected together through free cells if and only if they are boundary cells of the same free area.*

Proof. If part. Any subset of cells holding the same literal and bounding the same free area can be connected by a tree of connections laid out inside the area.

Only if part. Cells not bounding any free area are completely surrounded by vias holding different literals and cannot be connected to any other cell in that layer. For cells holding the same literal but not bounding the same area, any connecting path would inevitably meet another via.   □

Some considerations are in order. If a set of cells holding the same literal and facing the same free area are connected using free cells inside the area, other boundary cells of the same area can be connected only if the required connections do not cross those already laid out on that area. If two cells holding the same literal bound different areas they can still be connected in the layer through a path that meets only vias with their same literal, if any. If these conditions are not met, the cells must be connected in a next layer.

In the example of Fig. 8 four free areas can be used to connect the two 1's in cells (1,2), (2,4); the two 5's in cells (1,4), (2,5); the two 7's in cells (3,6), (5,6); and the two 4's in cells (2,2), (4,4), the latter also connected to the external lead, as already shown in Fig. 6(b). The two 5's in cells (1,4) and (5,1) cannot be connected in this layer since they do not bound the same free area. However, if literal 2 in cell (3,3) were a 5, that connection would have been possible passing through cell (3,3), thus merging connections laid out in two different free areas. The still missing connections among different 5's, 2's, 6's, and 3's, will be done in the free areas of layers 3 and 4 as shown in Fig. 6.

On these grounds we execute the crucial points c, d in step 2 of our heuristic first computing all the free areas in the layer, then trying to connect all boundary cells assigned to the same literal and facing the same free area. A relevant feature of this process is that free areas are mutually disjoint, then the searches for connections can be performed in parallel creating a thread for each free area. The only portion of the layer shared by multiple threads are the boundary cells facing different free areas, that can be managed through lock variables that force the threads to access those cells in mutual exclusion.

The cells to be connected are treated pairwise, however, a subset of more than two cells holding the same literal may bound a free area and as many as possible of them must be connected in tree form. Therefore as soon as two of them are connected, the couple is treated as a single cell identified as the central cell of the connecting path holding the literal of the two, and the process continues looking for other cells to be connected to them.

Clearly a connecting path cuts the free area in two parts and other cells facing this same area may become unreachable from one another. We could solve this issue by recomputing the free areas after a new connection is done, but this approach is computationally very heavy. Therefore, we compute free areas only once in each layer, and then apply a proper *non-exhaustive search algorithm* to limit the search for non-existing connections, still guaranteeing that mutually reachable cells will be connected with high probability.

Let us now briefly discuss the possible implementations of this search within each free area. The main point is considering a boundary cell c_1 that must be connected to a target cell c_2 through a path of distinct free cells in a free area. This can be formalized as a state space search, where the state space is of size $O(4^{N \times M})$ as the number of cells in the area is $O(N \times M)$ and there are at most four possible moves from each cell. As a search in this space would be prohibitively expensive, we use heuristics to find solutions of high quality as quickly as possible. We have tested several heuristics proposed in the literature, while for space reasons the results reported in Sect. 4 are limited to *Best-first* and *Greedy-beam* (see [14,15]) that select the next cell to visit according to an estimate of the Manhattan distance from the target cell. The first heuristic provides better results but its time complexity $O(4^{N \times M})$ is very high and can be applied only to small size lattices. The time complexity of *Greedy-beam* is instead linear in the lattice size, but produce worse quality results. In fact it may fail in connecting some mutually reachable cells on a given layer, so the final layout may contain a high number of layers. Depending on the lattice size and on the specific application, we can therefore select one of the two heuristics (or, for that matter, other known ones), trading quality of results vs. scalability.

4   Experimental Results

In this section we report the experimental results related to the physical implementation of switching lattices $N \times M$ according to the assumptions 1 to 4 reported in Sect. 1. The physical implementation of a lattice is a 3-dimensional grid $N \times M \times (H + 1)$, where H is the number of layers needed to route all the connections among switches controlled by the same input literal. The aim of our experimentation is to determine whether the proposed implementation can be considered technologically feasible. To this ends we have considered the lattices obtained applying the Altun-Riedel method to the benchmark functions taken from LGSynth93 [16], where each output has been treated as a separate Boolean function. For space reasons, in the following Table 1 we report only a significant subset of these functions as representative indicators of our experiments.[1]

The experiments have been run on a IntelCore i7-4710HQ 2.50 GHz CPU with 8 GB of main memory, running Linux Ubuntu 17.10. The algorithms have been implemented in C according to the lines indicated in the paper for the solution of Problems 1, 2 and 3.

Table 1 is organized as follows. The first column reports the name and the number of the separate output functions of the benchmark circuit. The following two columns report the number of different literals occurring in the lattice and its dimension $N \times M$. The last four columns report the number H of layers computed with the *Best-first* and the *Greedy-beam* heuristics, together with the

Table 1. Number of layers for the lattice layout of a subset of standard benchmark circuits, built along the lines indicated in Problems 1, 2 and 3.

Bench	lit	N×M	Best-first		Greedy Beam	
			H	Time(s)	H	Time(s)
add6(5)	24	156×156	7	733.21	8	0.43
adr4(1)	16	36×36	6	0.19	8	0.02
alu2(2)	16	10×11	4	0.01	4	0.01
alu2(5)	20	13×14	4	0.01	4	0.01
alu3(0)	8	4×5	3	0.01	3	0.01
alu3(1)	12	7×8	4	0.01	4	0.01
b12(0)	7	6×4	4	0.01	4	0.01
b12(1)	9	5×7	4	0.01	4	0.01
b12(2)	10	6×7	3	0.01	3	0.01
bcc(5)	28	27×9	10	0.02	9	0.01
bcc(7)	29	31×11	10	0.03	11	0.01
bcc(8)	29	31×12	10	0.04	9	0.01
bcc(27)	28	39×19	10	0.13	12	0.02
bcc(43)	28	20×10	6	0.02	6	0.01
bench1(2)	18	45×24	10	0.26	11	0.04

---

[1] Experimental results on a much larger set of benchmark functions may be requested to the present authors.

Table 1. (*continued*)

Bench	lit	N×M	Best-first		Greedy Beam	
			H	Time(s)	H	Time(s)
bench1(3)	18	31×16	8	0.03	9	0.01
bench1(5)	18	50×27	9	0.31	9	0.04
bench1(6)	18	35×21	9	0.09	12	0.03
bench1(7)	18	43×21	9	0.12	12	0.02
bench1(8)	18	44×24	9	0.19	10	0.04
bench(6)	10	8×4	5	0.01	5	0.01
br2(4)	18	18×8	6	0.01	6	0.01
br2(5)	19	14×4	6	0.01	6	0.01
br2(6)	19	16×5	6	0.01	6	0.01
clpl(3)	11	6×6	3	0.01	3	0.01
clpl(4)	9	5×5	3	0.01	3	0.01
co14(0)	28	92×14	11	0.29	12	0.04
dc1(4)	7	5×4	–	0.01	–	0.01
dc2(4)	11	10×9	5	0.01	5	0.01
dc2(5)	9	6×6	4	0.01	4	0.01
dk17(1)	10	8×2	6	0.01	6	0.01
dk17(3)	11	11×3	–	0.01	–	0.01
dk17(4)	12	9×3	5	0.01	5	0.01
ex1010(0)	20	91×46	11	8.42	13	0.24
ex4(4)	13	17×6	7	0.01	7	0.01
ex4(5)	27	35×45	7	0.51	8	0.02
ex5(32)	14	4×10	3	0.01	3	0.01
ex5(36)	11	2×8	2	0.01	2	0.01
ex5(38)	13	4×9	3	0.01	3	0.01
ex5(40)	15	6×12	5	0.01	5	0.01
ex5(43)	15	8×14	6	0.01	6	0.01
exam(5)	13	11×6	4	0.01	4	0.01
exam(9)	20	59×30	9	0.75	12	0.04
max128(5)	14	14×17	6	0.01	6	0.01
max128(8)	13	5×10	5	0.01	5	0.01
max128(17)	14	26×25	7	0.06	8	0.01
max1024(5)	20	117×122	10	191.33	14	0.89
mp2d(6)	14	10×6	5	0.01	5	0.01
mp2d(9)	14	6×8	3	0.01	3	0.01
mp2d(10)	10	6×3	4	0.01	4	0.01
sym10(0)	20	130 × 210	9	1571.93	10	2.14
tial(5)	28	181×181	10	1491.45	12	1.19
z4(0)	7	15×15	5	0.01	6	0.01
z4(1)	14	28×28	7	0.08	7	0.01
Z5xp1(2)	14	12×11	4	0.01	4	0.01
Z5xp1(3)	14	18×18	5	0.01	7	0.01
			336	3999,8	367	5,61

corresponding running time. The last row reports the sum of the values of the corresponding column. The cases where the algorithm failed in finding a layout (see Sect. 3.3) are marked with a hyphen.

As expected, we have obtained layouts with a smaller number of layers using the *Best-first* heuristic at the expense of a higher computation time. However we note that the increase in the number of layers computed with the faster *Greedy-beam* heuristic appears quite limited.

Finally, these simulations have shown the effectiveness of the heuristic for Problem 1: indeed, the number of layers computed applying only the heuristics for Problems 2 and 3, without first permuting rows and columns, increases on average of about 35% using *Best-first*, and of about 43% using *Greedy-beam*. Moreover, running both the heuristic for Problem 1 and the algorithm MC-AREAS for Problem 2, we have obtained a considerable reduction of the number of layers, when compared with the results published in [6].

5 Concluding Remarks

We have presented the first study on connection layout for two-dimensional switching lattices referring to the network implementation proposed by Altun and Riedel [4]. We have shown how to build a stack of consecutive layers where the connections between switches driven by the same variable can be laid without crossings, with the aim of minimizing the number H of layers. Since the problem is computationally intractable we have designed a family of heuristics for finding satisfactory solutions, then applied to a very large set of standard Boolean functions to validate our approach. For space reasons we have presented only the results obtained with the fastest and the slowest heuristics, and only for a subset of the functions analyzed taken as representative of the work done.

The overall design consists of three main phases, studied as Problems 1, 2 and 3. The first two are aimed at rearranging the switch positions and their literal assignment of the starting lattice, in order to place in adjacent cells as many switches controlled by the same literal as possible. The third phase then builds the actual connections on the different layers of the chip.

Countless improvements are open. While the NP-hardness of Problem 2 has been proved, for theoretical completeness also the NP-hardness of Problems 1 and 3 has to be proved to fully justify the use of heuristics. Better algorithms could be studied, and tested on larger data samples. The layout for other switching lattices should be considered. The layout rules should possibly be changed, in particular allowing more than one wire traversing a switch area in the higher layers. We are presently working on all these issues.

References

1. Micheli, G.D.: Synthesis and Optimization of Switching Theory. McGrow Hill, New York (1994)
2. Akers, S.B.: A rectangular logic array. IEEE Trans. Comput. **21**(8), 848–857 (1972)

3. Altun, M., Riedel, M.D.: Lattice-based computation of Boolean functions. In: Proceedings of the 47th Design Automation Conference, DAC 2010, pp. 609–612, Anaheim, California, USA, 13–18 July 2010
4. Altun, M., Riedel, M.D.: Logic synthesis for switching lattices. IEEE Trans. Comput. **61**(11), 1588–1600 (2012)
5. Gange, G., Søndergaard, H., Stuckey, P.J.: Synthesizing optimal switching lattices. ACM Trans. Des. Autom. Electron. Syst. **20**(1), 6:1–6:14 (2014)
6. Bernasconi, A., Boffa, A., Luccio, F., Pagli, L.: Two combinatorial problems on the layout of switching lattices. In: IFIP/IEEE International Conference on Very Large Scale Integration (VLSI-SoC) (2018)
7. Bernasconi, A., Luccio, F., Pagli, L., Rucci, D.: Literal selection in switching lattice design. In: Proceedings of the 13th International Workshop on Boolean Problems (IWSBP 2018), pp. 205–220 (2018)
8. Luccio, F., Xia, M.: The MPA graph problem: definition and basic properties. Technical report, University of Pisa, Department of Informatics (2018)
9. Valiant, L.G.: Universality considerations in VLSI circuits. IEEE Trans. Comput. **30**(2), 135–140 (1981)
10. de Fraysseix, H., Pach, J., Pollack, R.: Small sets supporting fáry embeddings of planar graphs. In: Proceedings of the 20th Annual ACM Symposium on Theory of Computing, pp. 426–433, Chicago, Illinois, USA, 2–4 May 1988
11. Ratner, D., Warmuth, M.K.: Finding a shortest solution for the N × N extension of the 15-puzzle is intractable. In: Proceedings of the 5th National Conference on Artificial Intelligence, Volume 1: Science, pp. 168–172, Philadelphia, PA, 11–15 August 1986
12. Chu, C.C.N., Wong, Y.: FLUTE: fast lookup table based rectilinear steiner minimal tree algorithm for VLSI design. IEEE Trans. CAD Integr. Circ. Syst. **27**(1), 70–83 (2008)
13. Fox, J., Pach, J., Suk, A.: Approximating the rectilinear crossing number. In: Hu, Y., Nöllenburg, M. (eds.) GD 2016. LNCS, vol. 9801, pp. 413–426. Springer, Cham (2016). https://doi.org/10.1007/978-3-319-50106-2_32
14. Hart, P.E., Nilsson, N.J., Raphael, B.: A formal basis for the heuristic determination of minimum cost paths. IEEE Trans. Syst. Sci. Cybern. **4**(2), 100–107 (1968)
15. Russell, S.J., Norvig, P.: Artificial Intelligence - A Modern Approach. Prentice Hall Series in Artificial Intelligence, 2nd edn. Prentice Hall, Upper Saddle River (2003)
16. Yang, S.: Logic synthesis and optimization benchmarks user guide version 3.0. user guide, Microelectronic Center (1991)

Building High-Performance, Easy-to-Use Polymorphic Parallel Memories with HLS

L. Stornaiuolo[1(✉)], M. Rabozzi[1(✉)], M. D. Santambrogio[1(✉)], D. Sciuto[1(✉)], C. B. Ciobanu[2,3(✉)], G. Stramondo[3(✉)], and A. L. Varbanescu[3(✉)]

[1] Politecnico di Milano, Milan, Italy
{luca.stornaiuolo,marco.rabozzi,marco.santambrogio,
donatella.sciuto}@polimi.it
[2] Technische Universiteit Delft, Delft, The Netherlands
c.b.ciobanu@tudelft.nl
[3] Universiteit van Amsterdam, Amsterdam, The Netherlands
{c.b.ciobanu,g.stramondo,a.l.varbanescu}@uva.nl

Abstract. With the increased interest in energy efficiency, a lot of application domains experiment with Field Programmable Gate Arrays (FPGAs), which promise customized hardware accelerators with high-performance and low power consumption. These experiments possible due to the development of High-Level Languages (HLLs) for FPGAs, which permit non-experts in hardware design languages (HDLs) to program reconfigurable hardware for general purpose computing.

However, some of the expert knowledge remains difficult to integrate in HLLs, eventually leading to performance loss for HLL-based applications. One example of such a missing feature is the efficient exploitation of the local memories on FPGAs. A solution to address this challenge is PolyMem, an easy-to-use polymorphic parallel memory that uses BRAMs. In this work, we present HLS-PolyMem, the first complete implementation and in-depth evaluation of PolyMem optimized for the Xilinx Design Suite. Our evaluation demonstrates that HLS-PolyMem is a viable alternative to HLS memory partitioning, the current approach for memory parallelism in Vivado HLS. Specifically, we show that PolyMem offers the same performance as HLS partitioning for simple access patterns, and outperforms partitioning as much as 13x when combining multiple access patterns for the same data structure. We further demonstrate the use of PolyMem for two different case studies, highlighting the superior capabilities of HLS-PolyMem in terms of performance, resource utilization, flexibility, and usability.

Based on all the evidence provided in this work, we conclude that HLS-PolyMem enables the efficient use of BRAMs as parallel memories, without compromising the HLS level or the achievable performance.

Keywords: Polymorphic Parallel Memory · High-Level Synthesis · FPGA

© IFIP International Federation for Information Processing 2019
Published by Springer Nature Switzerland AG 2019
N. Bombieri et al. (Eds.): VLSI-SoC 2018, IFIP AICT 561, pp. 53–78, 2019.
https://doi.org/10.1007/978-3-030-23425-6_4

1   Introduction

The success of High-Level Languages (HLLs) for non-traditional computing systems, like Field Programmable Gate Arrays (FPGAs), has accelerated the adoption of these platforms for general purpose computing. In particular, the main hardware vendors released tools and frameworks to support their products by allowing the design of optimized kernels using HLLs. This is the case, for example, for Xilinx, which allows using C++ or OpenCL within the Vivado Design Suite [1] to target FPGAs. Moreover, FPGAs are increasingly used for data-intensive applications, because they enable users to create custom hardware accelerators, and achieve high-performance implementations with low power consumption. Combining this trend with the fast-paced development of HLLs, more and more users and applications aim to experiment with FPGA accelerators.

In the effort of providing HLL tools for FPGA design, some of the features used by hardware design experts are difficult to transparently integrate. One such feature is the efficient use of BRAMs, the FPGA distributed, high-bandwidth, on-chip memories [2]. BRAMs can provide memory-system parallelism, but their use remains challenging due to the many different ways in which data can be partitioned in order to achieve efficient parallel data accesses. Typical HLL solutions allow easy-to-use mechanisms for basic data partitioning. These mechanisms work well for simple data access patterns, but can significantly limit the patterns for which parallelism (and thus, increased performance) can be achieved. Changing data access patterns on the application side is the current state-of-the-art approach: by matching the application patterns with the simplistic partitioning models of the HLL, one can achieve parallel operations and reduce the kernel execution time. However, if at all possible, this transformation also requires extensive modification of the application code, which is cumbersome and error-prone to the point of canceling the productivity benefits of HLLs.

To address the challenges related to the design and practical use of parallel memory systems for FPGA-based applications, PolyMem, a Polymorphic Parallel Memory, was proposed [3]. PolyMem is envisioned as a high-bandwidth, two-dimensional (2D) memory *used to cache performance-critical data on the FPGA chip*, making use of the distributed memory banks (the BRAMs). PolyMem is inspired by the Polymorphic Register File (PRF) [4], a runtime customizable register file for Single Instruction, Multiple Data (SIMD) co-processors. PolyMem is suitable for FPGA accelerators requiring high bandwidth, even if they do not implement full-blown SIMD co-processors on the reconfigurable fabric.

The first hardware implementation of the Polymorphic Register File was designed in System Verilog [5]. MAX-PolyMem is the first prototype of PolyMem written entirely in MaxJ, and targeted at Maxeler Data Flow Engines (DFEs) [3,6]. Our new HLS PolyMem is an alternative HLL solution, proven to be easily integrated with the Xilinx toolchains. The current work is an extension of our previous implementation presented in [7].

Figure 1 depicts the architecture of a system using (HLS-)PolyMem. The FPGA board (with a high-capacity DRAM memory), is connected to the host CPU through a PCI Express link. PolyMem acts as a high-bandwidth, 2D parallel software cache, able to feed an on-chip application kernel with multiple data elements every clock cycle. The focus of this work is to provide an efficient implementation of PolyMem in Vivado HLS, and employ it to maximize memory-accesses parallelism by exploiting BRAMs; we empirically demonstrate the gains we get from PolyMem by comparison against the partitioning of BRAMs, as provided by Xilinx tools, for three case-studies.

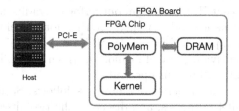

Fig. 1. System organization using PolyMem as a parallel cache.

In this work, we provide empirical evidence that HLS-PolyMem provides significant improvements in terms of both performance and usability when compared with the current memory partitioning approach present in Vivado HLS. To this end, we highlight the following novel aspects of this work:

- We provide a new, complete, open-source implementation [45] of PolyMem for Vivado HLS. This new implementation contains all the memory access schemes supported by the original PRF, as well as its multiview feature. Our implementation can be easily integrated within the Xilinx Hardware-Software Co-Design Workflow;
- We present a basic, high-level PolyMem interface (i.e., a rudimentary API for using PolyMem). The API includes basic parallel read and write operations. Furthermore, our API was further extended to support masked writes, avoiding overwrites and further reduce latency. For example, when PolyMem supports wide parallel access (e.g., 8 elements), but the user requires less data to be stored (e.g., 5 elements), and wants to avoid overwriting existing data (e.g., the remaining 3 elements). We demonstrate the use of the API in all the applications discussed in this paper (synthetic and real-life examples alike);
- We design and prototype a synthetic, parameterized microbenchmarking framework to thoroughly evaluate the performance of HLS-PolyMem. Our microbenchmarking strategy is based on chains of operations using one or several parallel access patterns, thus stressing both the performance and flexibility of the proposed parallel memory. The framework is extended to enable the comparison against existing HLS memory partitioning schemes. Finally, we show how to use these microbenchmarks to provide an extensive analysis of HLS-PolyMem's performance.

- We design, implement, and analyze in detail two case-study applications which demonstrate the ability of our HLS-PolyMem to cope with real applications and data, multiple memory access patterns, and tiling. Our experiments for these case-studies focus on performance, resource-utilization, and productivity, and contrast our HLS PolyMem with standard memory partitioning techniques.

Our results, collected for both synthetic and real-life case-studies, thoroughly demonstrate that HLS PolyMem outperforms traditional HLS partitioning schemes in performance and usability. We therefore conclude that our HLS-PolyMem is the first approach that enables HLS programmers to use BRAMs to construct flexible, multiview parallel memories, which can still be easily embedded in the traditional HLS modus operandi.

The remainder of this paper is organized as follows. Section 2 provides an introduction to parallel memories, and discusses the two alternative implementations presented in this work: the PRF-inspired PolyMem and the HLS partitioning schemes. Section 3 presents the HLS PolyMem class for Vivado, together with the proposed optimizations. In Sect. 4 we present our microbenchmarking framework, as well as the our in-depth evaluation using this synthetic workload. Section 5 describes our experience with designing, implementing, and evaluating the two case studies. Section 6 highlights relevant related work and, finally, our conclusion and future work directions are discussed in Sect. 7.

2   Parallel Memories: Challenges and Solutions

2.1   Parallel Memories

Definition 1 (Parallel Memory). *A Parallel Memory (PM) is a memory that enables the access to multiple data elements in parallel.*

A parallel memory can be realized by combining a set of independent memories, referred to as *banks* or *lanes*. The *width of the parallel memory*, i.e., the number of banks used in the implementation, represents the maximum number of elements that can be read in parallel. The *capacity* of the parallel memory refers to the amount of data that it can store. A specific element contained in a PM is identified by its *location*, a combination of a *memory module identifier* (to specify which one of the sequential memories hosts the data) and an *in-memory address* (to specify where within that memory the element is stored).

Depending on how the information is stored and/or retrieved from the memory, we distinguish three types of parallel memories: redundant, non-redundant, and hybrid.

Redundant PMs. The simplest implementation of a PM is a fully redundant one, where all M sequential memory blocks contain fully replicated information. The benefit of such a memory is that it allows an application to access any combination of M data elements in parallel. However, such a solution has two major drawbacks: first, the total capacity of a redundant PM is M times lower than the combined capacities of all its banks, and, second, parallel writes are very expensive in order to maintain information consistency.

To use such a memory, the application requires minimal changes, and the architecture is relatively simple to manage.

Non-redundant PMs. Non-redundant PMs completely avoid data duplication: each data item is stored in only one of the M banks. The one-to-one mapping between the coordinate of an element in the application space and a memory location is part of the memory configuration. These memories can use the full capacity of all the memory resources available, and data consistency is guaranteed by avoiding data replication, making parallel writes feasible as well. The main drawback of non-redundant parallel memories is that they require additional logic - compared to redundant memories - to perform the mapping, and they restrict the possible parallel accesses: if two elements are stored in the same bank, they cannot be accessed in parallel.

There are two major approaches used to implement non-redundant PM: (1) use a set of predefined mapping functions that enable parallel accesses in a set of predefined shapes [4,8–10], or, (2) derive an application-specific mapping function [11,12]. For the first approach, the application requires additional analysis and potential changes, while the architecture is relatively fixed. For the second approach, however, a new memory architecture needs to be implemented for every application, potentially a more challenging task when the parallel memory is to be implemented in hardware.

Hybrid PMs. Besides the two extremes discussed above, there are also hybrid implementations of parallel memories, which combine the advantages of the two previous approaches by using partial data redundancy [13]. Of course, in this case, the challenge is to determine which data should be replicated and where. In turn, this solution requires both application and architecture customization.

2.2 The Polymorphic Register File and PolyMem

A PRF is a parameterizable register file, which can be logically reorganized by the programmer or a runtime system to support multiple register dimensions and sizes simultaneously [4]. The simultaneous support for multiple conflict-free access patterns, called *multiview*, is crucial, providing flexibility and improved performance for target applications. The *polymorphism* aspect refers to the support for adjusting the sizes and shapes of the registers at runtime. Table 1 presents the PRF *multiview* schemes (ReRo, ReCo, RoCo and ReTr), each supporting a combination of at least two conflict-free access patterns. A scheme is used to store data within the memory banks of the PRF, such that it allows different parallel *access types*. The different *access types* refer to the actual data elements that can be accessed in parallel. PolyMem reuses the PRF conflict-free parallel storage techniques and patterns, as well as the polymorphism idea. Figure 2(a) illustrates the access patterns supported by the PRF and PolyMem.

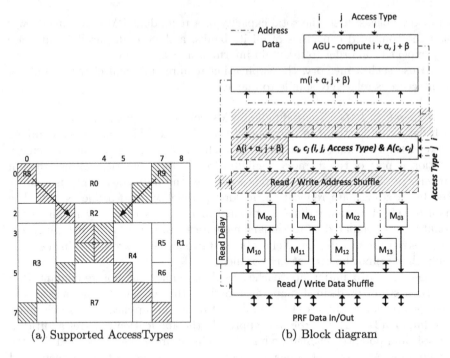

(a) Supported AccessTypes   (b) Block diagram

Fig. 2. PRF [4] design. The inputs are the matrix indexes (i, j) pointing to the first cell of the block of data the user wants to read/write in parallel, and the AccessType to select the shape of the parallel access.

Table 1. The PRF memory access schemes

PRF schemes	Available access types
ReO	Rectangle
ReRo	Rectangle, row, main/secondary diagonals
ReCo	Rectangle, column, main/secondary diagonals
RoCo	Row, column, rectangle
ReTr	Rectangle, transposed rectangle

In this example, a 2D logical address space of 8×9 elements contains 10 memory Regions (R), each with different size and location: matrix, transposed matrix, row, column, main and secondary diagonals. In a hardware implementation with eight memory banks, each of these regions can be read using one (R1–R9) or several (R0) parallel accesses.

By design, the PRF optimizes the memory throughput for a set of predefined memory access patterns. For PolyMem, we consider $p \times q$ memory modules and the five parallel access schemes presented in Table 1. Each scheme supports dense, conflict-free access to $p \cdot q$ elements. When implemented in reconfigurable technology, PolyMem allows application-driven customization: its capacity, number of read/write ports, and the number of lanes can be configured to best support the application needs.

The block diagram in Fig. 2(b) shows, at high level, the PRF architecture. The multi-bank memory is composed of a bi-dimensional matrix containing $p \times q$ memory modules. This enables parallel access to $p \cdot q$ elements in one memory operation. The inputs of the PRF are shown at the top of the diagram. AccessType represents the parallel access pattern. (i, j) are the top-left coordinates of the parallel access. The list of elements to access is generated by the AGU module and is sent to the A and m modules: the A module generates one in-memory address for each memory bank in the PRF, while the m module applies the mapping function of the selected scheme and computes, for each accessed element, the memory bank where it is stored. The Data Shuffle block reorders the Data In/Out, ensuring the PEF user obtains the accessed data in their original order.

2.3 Matrix Storage in a Parallel Memory

Figure 3 compares two ways for a 6×6 matrix to be mapped in BRAMs to enable parallel accesses. Thus, the default Vivado HLS partitioning techniques with a factor of 3 is compared against a PolyMem with 3 memory banks, organized exploiting the PolyMem RoCo scheme.

The memory banks, in this case, are organized in a 1×3 structure, allowing parallel access to rows and columns of three, eventually unaligned, elements. The left side of Fig. 3 shows an example of a matrix to be stored in the partitioned

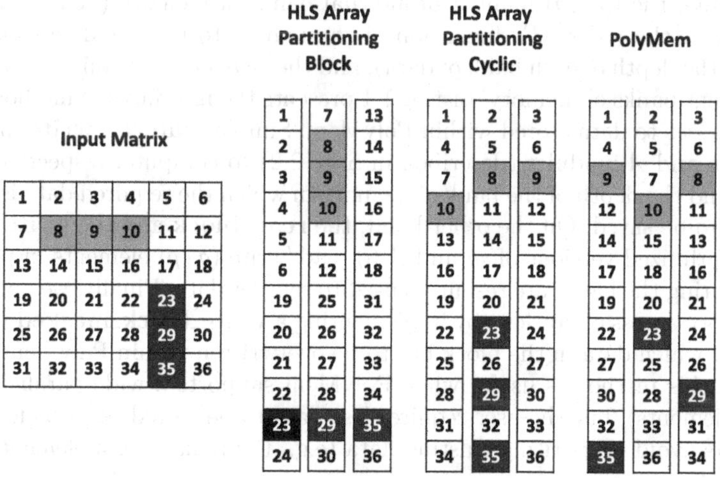

Fig. 3. Comparison between different partitioning techniques offered by Vivado HLS (facto = 3) and the RoCo scheme of PolyMem, with 3 memory banks, for data stored in a 6×6 matrix. PolyMem allows 3 parallel data reads/writes, from the rows and the columns of the original matrix. Unaligned blocks are also supported.

BRAMs, aiming to achieve read/write parallelism. The right side illustrates three techniques used to partition the matrix, using two unaligned, parallel accesses of 3 elements (gray and black in the figure), starting respectively from the cells containing elements 8 and 23. The HLS Array Partitioning techniques enable either the black or the gray access to be performed in parallel (for Block and Cyclic, respectively). Using PolyMem with a RoCo scheme, each element of each access is mapped on a different memory bank; in turn, this organization enables *both* the gray and the black access to happen in a single (parallel) operation[1].

3   Implementation Details

This section describes the main components of our PolyMem implementation for Vivado HLS. The goal of integrating PolyMem in the Xilinx workflow is to provide users with an easy-to-use solution to exploit parallelism when accessing data stored on the on-chip memory with different access patterns.

Our Vivado HLS PolyMem implementation exploits all the presented five schemes (ReO, ReRo, ReCo, RoCo, ReTr) to store on the FPGA BRAMs the data required to perform the application operations. Compared to the default Vivado memory partitioning techniques, which allow hardware parallelism with a single access pattern, a PolyMem employing a multiview scheme allows multiple types of access simultaneously for unaligned data with conservative hardware resources usage.

We implemented a template-based class *polymem* that exploits loop unrolling to parallelize memory accesses. When HLS PolyMem is instantiated within the user application code, it is possible to specify $DATA\_T$, i.e., the type of data to be stored, the $(p \times q)$ number of internal banks of memory (i.e., the level of parallelism), the $(N \times M)$ dimension of the matrix to be stored (also used to compute the depth of each bank of data), and the *scheme* to organize data within the different banks of memory. Listing 1.1 presents the interfaces of methods that allow accesses to data stored within PolyMem. Simple **read** and **write** methods use the m and A modules (described in Sect. 2.2) to compute, respectively, the address and the depth of the bank of memory in which the required data is stored or needs to be saved. On the other hand, the **read_block** and the **write_block** exploit optimized versions of m and A to read/write $(q \cdot p)$ elements in parallel, while limiting the hardware resources used to reorder data. Finally, we optimized the memory access operations by implementing a **write_block_masked** method to specify which data in the block has to be overwritten within PolyMem. As an example, this method is useful when PolyMem supports a wide parallel access (e.g., 8 elements), but the user requires less data to be stored (e.g., 5 elements), and wants avoid overwriting existing data (e.g., the remaining 3 elements).

---

[1] This small-scale example is included for visualization purposes only. Real-applications are likely to use more memory banks, allowing parallel accesses to larger data blocks.

Listing 1.1. List of the methods interfaces to allow user read/write data by used sequential or parallel accesses

```
DATA_T read(int i, int j);

void write(DATA_T data, int i, int j);

void read_block(int i, int j, DATA_T out[p * q],
                int PRF_ACCESS_TYPE);

void write_block(DATA_T in[p * q], int i, int j,
                 int PRF_ACCESS_TYPE);

void write_block_masked(DATA_T in[p * q],
                        ap_uint<p * q> mask,
                        int i, int j,
                        int PRF_ACCESS_TYPE);
```

4   Evaluation and Results

In this Section, we focus on the evaluation of HLS PolyMem. The evaluation is based on a synthetic benchmark, where we demonstrate that PolyMem offers a high-performance, high-productivity alternative to partitioned memories in HLS.

4.1   Experimental Setup

We present the design and implementation of our microbenchmarking suite, and detail the way all our measurements are performed. All the experiments in this section are validated and executed on a Xilinx Virtex-7 VC707 board (part xc7vx485tffg1761-2), with the following hardware resources: 303600 LUTs, 607200 FFs, 1030 BRAMs, and 2800 DSPs. We instantiate a Microblaze processor on the FPGA to control the DMA that transfers data between the FPGA board DRAM memory and the on-chip BRAMs where the computational kernel performs memory accesses. The Microblaze also starts and stops an AXI Timer to measure the execution time of each experiment. The data transfers to and from the computational kernel employ the AXI Stream technology.

Microbenchmark Design. To provide an in-depth evaluation of our Polymorphic memory, we designed a specific microbenchmark which tests the performance of PolyMem together with its flexibility - i.e., its ability to cope with applications that require different parallel access types *to the same data structure*. Moreover, we compare the results of the Polymem-augmented design with the ones achievable by partitioning the memory with the default techniques available in Vivado HLS. To ensure a fair comparison, we utilize a Vivado HLS Cyclic array partition with a factor equal to the number of PolyMem lanes (both designs can access at most $p \cdot q$ data elements in parallel from the BRAMs).

The requirements we state for such a microbenchmark are:

1. Focus on the reading performance of the memory, in terms of bandwidth;
2. Support all access types presented in Sect. 2.2;
3. Test a combination of more access types, to further demonstrate the flexibility of polymorphism;
4. Measure the overall bandwidth achieved by these memory transfers.

To achieve these requirements, we designed different computational kernels (IP Cores) that perform a (configurable) number of parallel memory reads, from various locations inside the memory, using different parallel access patterns. Each combination of parallel reads is performed in two different scenarios. The accessed on-chip FPGA memory (BRAMs) M, where the input data are stored, is partitioned by using (1) the default techniques available in Vivado HLS, and (2) the HLS PolyMem technology.

A high-level description of the operations executed by the computational kernels and measured by the timer is presented in Listing 1.2. Memory M is used to store the input data and it is physically implemented in partitioned BRAMs. The kernel receives the data to fill the memory M and N_READS matrix coordinates to perform parallel accesses with different access types - i.e., *given an access type and the matrix coordinates (i, j), the computational kernel reads a block of data starting from (i, j) and following the access type.* When the memory reads are done, the kernel sends sampled results on the output stream.

Listing 1.2. The structure of the proposed microbenchmark

```
stream in data to fill memory M
stream in N_READS read_coordinates

synchronize // wait for streaming to complete

// process reads
foreach ACCESS_TYPE in POLYMEM_SCHEME_SUPPORTED_ACCESS_TYPES:
    chunk_size = N_READS / N_SUPPORTED_ACCESS_TYPES
    foreach (i,j) in chunk_of_read_coordinates:
        current_results_block = M.read_block(i, j, ACCESS_TYPE)
// done processing reads

foreach k in range(N_RESULTS_BLOCKS):
    stream out the k^th results_block

synchronize // wait for streaming to complete
```

By comparing the performance results of HLS-partitioning and PolyMem, we are able to assess which scheme provides both performance and flexibility, and, moreover, provide a quantitative analysis of the performance gap between the two. We provide more details on how the measurements are performed in the following paragraphs.

The complete code used for all the experiments described in this section is available in our code repository [45].

Measurement Setup. In order to measure the performance of the two different parallel memory microbenchmaks, we propose a setup as presented in Fig. 4. Specifically, in this diagram, "Memory" is either an HLS-partitioned memory, or an instance of PolyMem (as described in the previous paragraph).

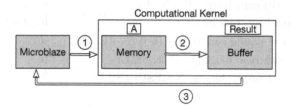

Fig. 4. The measurement setup used for microbenchmarks. The measured bandwidth corresponds to phase 2, where reading the data from the parallel memory happens.

In order to measure the performance of the two memories, we propose an approach based on the following steps.

1. Measure, on the Microblaze processor, the overhead of phases 1 and 3. We note that phases 1 and 3 are implemented using the basic streaming constructs provided by the AXI Stream technology. We achieve this by a one-time measurement where no memory reads or only one memory read are performed.
2. Measure, on the Microblaze processor, the execution time of the complete setup, from the beginning of phase 1 to the end of phase 3. Due to the explicit synchronization between phases 1, 2, and 3, we can guarantee that no overlap happens between them.
3. Determine, by subtraction, the absolute execution time of phase 2 alone, which is a measure of the parallel memory's reading performance.
4. Present the absolute performance of the two memories in terms of achieved bandwidth. For the case of PolyMem, we can also assess the efficiency of the implementation by comparing the achieved bandwidth with that predicted by the theoretical performance model [14].
5. Present the relative performance of the two parallel memories as **speedup**. We calculate speedup as the ratio of the execution time of HLS-based partitioning solution over the execution of the PolyMem-based solution. We chose to use the entire execution time, including the copy overhead, as an estimate of a realistic benchmark when the same architecture is used for real-life applications. We note that this choice is pessimistic, as the overhead of phases 1 and 3 can be quite large.

4.2   Results

All the results presented in this section are from experiments performed using the settings in Table 2.

The input data stream employs double precision (64-bit) numbers, and the computational kernel receives an amount of data (equal for all the experiments), that includes the input matrix and the list of coordinates (i, j):

Table 2. Microbenchmark settings

Clock frequency (ClkFr)	200 MHz
Data type (DType)	64-bit double
Input matrix size ($DIM \times DIM$)	96×96
HLS partitioning factor (FACTOR)	16
PolyMem lanes ($p \times q$)	16 (2×8)
Number of passed coordinates (i, j) (N_READS)	3072
Size of each read block (BLOCK_SIZE)	16
Number of output blocks (N_RESULTS_BLOCKS)	50

$$\text{N\_IN\_DATA} = (\text{DIM} \cdot \text{DIM}) + (\text{N\_READS} \cdot 2) = 15360 \text{ 64-bit elements}$$

The number of data that the computational kernel reads from the memory is computed as follow:

$$\text{N\_READ\_DATA} = (\text{N\_READS} \cdot \text{BLOCK\_SIZE}) = 49152 \text{ 64-bit elements}$$

The output data stream employs double precision 64-bit numbers, and the computational kernel sends back to the microblaze a sample of the results (data read), equal for all the experiments, amounting to:

$$\text{N\_OUT\_DATA} = (\text{N\_RESULTS\_BLOCKS} \cdot \text{BLOCK\_SIZE}) = 80064\text{-bit elements}$$

To measure the overheads introduced by the data transfers in terms of hardware resources utilization and execution time, we implemented two computational kernels: the first one does not perform any memory accesses (the BRAMs are not even partitioned) and the second one performs only one memory access (the added execution time of this one access is negligible). The second kernel was executed for both memory configurations (HLS Cyclic and PolyMem). The results are shown in Table 3. The consistent execution time indicates that the overhead is systematic and constant.

Table 3. Hardware resources utilization and execution time spent in phases 1 and 3 of the proposed architecture

Memory	Access	LUT	FF	BRAM	DSP	Runtime [μs]
-	-	41400	34064	21	0	265
HLS Cyclic	Row	43194	35302	172	0	265
PolyMem	Row	46375	36444	172	0	265

Table 4. Hardware resources utilizations, execution times and bandwidths for microbenchmark experiments with different memory configurations and access schemes

Memory	Scheme	LUT	FF	BRAM	DSP	Runtime [µs]	BW [GB/s]
HLS Cyclic	ReO	45800	36121	172	0	503	1.54
PolyMem	ReO	45590	36364	172	0	283	20.35
HLS Cyclic	ReRo	90197	65993	174	224	503	1.54
PolyMem	ReRo	59082	40661	172	0	283	20.35
HLS Cyclic	ReCo	85055	64679	174	164	503	1.54
PolyMem	ReCo	62549	40434	172	0	283	20.35
HLS Cyclic	RoCo	67066	54217	174	100	503	1.54
PolyMem	RoCo	55025	38944	172	0	283	20.35
HLS Cyclic	ReTr	62259	54244	174	40	503	1.54
PolyMem	ReTr	51282	37744	172	0	283	20.35

Given the data transfers execution time overhead equal to 265 ns, we can compute the bandwidth (BW) in GB/s for each new experiment with the following formula:

$$BW[B/s] = \frac{\text{N\_READS} * \text{BLOCK\_SIZE} * 8}{(\text{Exec. time} - \text{overhead})}$$

In Table 4, we report the detailed results of our microbenchmarking experiments, in terms of hardware resource utilization, execution time, and bandwidth. We provide results for the two different memory configurations and all PolyMem access schemes. As shown in Listing 1.2, the memory accesses are equally divided among the access patterns supported by the selected scheme. We further note that, for all the schemes, the speedup of the end-to-end computation (i.e., phases 1, 2 and 3 from Fig. 4) is 1.78x. For the actual computation, using the parallel memory (i.e., without the data transfer overhead), the PolyMem outperforms HLS partitioning by as much as 13.22x times. Moreover, in terms of hardware resources, (1) the BRAM utilization is similar for both parallel memories, which indicates no overhead for PolyMem, (2) PolyMem is more economical in terms of "consumed" LUT and FF (up to 20% less), and (3) HLS partitioning makes use of DSPs, while PolyMem does not. The following paragraph contains an evaluation of these results.

Unaligned Accesses and Final Evaluation. The results suggest that the Vivado HLS default partitioning techniques are not able to exploit parallel reads for the described access patterns. This is due to the fact that, even if the data are correctly distributed among the BRAMs to perform at least one access type, parallel accesses unaligned with respect to the partitioning factor are not supported. To prove that, we perform experiments where *the memory reads are forced to be aligned with respect to the partitioning factor*, for one of the access type - e.g. having a cyclic partitioned factor of 4 on the Ro access, it is possible to read 4 data in parallel at the coordinates {(i, j), (i, j+1), (i, j+2), (i, j+3)}, only if j is a multiple of 4. This is possible, at compile time, by using the *integer division* on the reading coordinates (i, j) as follows:

$$\text{aligned-j} = \left\lfloor \frac{j}{\text{BLOCK\_SIZE}} \right\rfloor * \text{BLOCK\_SIZE}$$

This ensures that aligned-j is a multiple of the number of memory banks - i.e. BLOCK_SIZE. Using aligned-j for the data access allows the HLS compiler to perform more aggressive optimizations parallelizing the access to the partitioned memory. Table 5 shows the results for the RoCo scheme with different combinations of access types, where forced aligned accesses are performed or not. The cases where the memory reads are aligned with respect to the partitioning factor are the only ones where the default Vivado HLS partitioning is able to achieve the same performance of PolyMem, while using fewer hardware resources. However, even in this cases, the default Vivado HLS partitioning is not able to perform all the memory accesses with the right amount of parallelism if the application requires multiple access patterns. Practical examples showing the advantages of using PolyMem are provided in the following section.

5   Application Case-Studies

In this Section, we analyze two case-study applications, i.e., matrix multiplication and Markov chain, that exploit our HLS PolyMem to parallelize accesses to matrix data.

Each application demonstrates different HLS PolyMem features. In the matrix multiplication case-study, we show how our approach outperforms implementations that use the default partitioning of Vivado HLS. For the Markov Chain application, we show how HLS PolyMem enables performance gains with minimal changes to the original software code.

Table 5. Hardware resources utilizations, execution times and bandwidths for the RoCo scheme with different combinations of access types with and without forced aligned accesses (**FA**)

Memory	Access types	LUT	FF	BRAM	DSP	Runtime [μs]	BW [GB/s]
HLS Cyclic	Ro	60127	52552	174	64	503	1.54
PolyMem	Ro	45641	36432	172	0	283	20.35
HLS Cyclic	**FA Ro**	43048	35316	173	0	283	20.35
PolyMem	**FA Ro**	45175	36391	173	0	283	20.35
HLS Cyclic	Ro, Co, Re	67066	54217	174	100	503	1.54
PolyMem	Ro, Co, Re	55025	38944	172	0	283	20.35
HLS Cyclic	Ro, Co, **FA Re**	47812	38003	173	0	429	2.23
PolyMem	Ro, Co, **FA Re**	55328	38975	173	0	283	20.35

5.1   Matrix Multiplication (MM)

With this case study, we aim to demonstrate the usefulness of the multiview property of HLS-PolyMem. Specifically, we investigate, in the context of a real application, two aspects: (1) if there is any performance loss or overhead between the two parallel memories for a single matrix multiplication, and (2) what is the performance gap between the two types of parallel memories in the case where multiple parallel access shapes are needed, on the same data structure, in the same application.

Single Matrix Multiplication. For our first experiment, the application performs one multiplication of two square matrices, B and C, of size DIM, that are stored by using either the default HLS array partitioning techniques or the HLS PolyMem implementation. Since the multiplication $B \times C$ is performed by accessing the rows of B and multiply-accumulating the data with the columns of C, it is convenient, when using HLS default partitioning, to partition B on the second dimension and C on the first one. Indeed, this allows to achieve parallel accesses to the rows of B and columns of C in the innermost loop of the computation.

On the other hand, for the HLS PolyMem implementation, we store both B and C in the HLS PolyMem, configured with a RoCo scheme, because it allows parallel accesses to both rows and columns.

Listings 1.3 and 1.4 show the declaration of the matrices and their partitioning using the HLS default partitioning and the HLS PolyMem, respectively. Both parallel memories use 16 lanes (i.e., data is partitioned onto 16 memory banks): the HLS partitioned scheme uses a parallel factor of 16, while the B and C HLS PolyMem instances are initialized with $p = 4$ and $q = 4$.

Listing 1.3. Declaration and partitioning of matrices to parallelize accesses to rows (dim=2) of B and to columns (dim=1) of C with a parallel factor of 16.

```
float B[DIM][DIM];
#pragma HLS array_partition variable=B block factor=16 dim=2
float C[DIM][DIM];
#pragma HLS array_partition variable=C block factor=16 dim=1
```

Listing 1.4. Declaration of the matrices stored by using the HLS PolyMem with the RoCo scheme with a parallel factor of $4 \cdot 4 = 16$.

```
#include "hls_prf.h"
hls::prf<float, 4, 4, DIM, DIM, SCHEME_RoCo> B;
hls::prf<float, 4, 4, DIM, DIM, SCHEME_RoCo> C;
```

Listings 1.5 and 1.6 show the matrix multiplication code when using the HLS default partitioning and the HLS PolyMem, respectively.

Listing 1.5. Matrix multiplication code that leverages default HLS partitioning to perform parallel accesses.

```
// B*C matrix multiplication
for (int i = 0; i < DIM; ++i)
  for (int j = 0; j < DIM; ++j) {
#pragma HLS PIPELINE II=1
    float sum = 0;
    for (int k = 0; k < DIM; ++k)
      sum += B[i][k] * C[k][j];
    OUT[i][j] = sum;
  }
```

Listing 1.6. Matrix multiplication code that exploits the HLS PolyMem with RoCo scheme to perform parallel accesses.

```
// B*C matrix multiplication
for (int i = 0; i < DIM; ++i)
  for (int j = 0; j < DIM; ++j) {
#pragma HLS PIPELINE II=1
    float sum = 0;
    for (int k = 0; k < DIM; k += 16) {
      B.read_block(i, k, temp_row, ACCESS_Ro);
      C.read_block(k, j, temp_col, ACCESS_Co);
      for (int t = 0; t < 16; t++)
        sum += temp_row[t] * temp_col[t];
    }
    OUT[i][j] = sum;
  }
```

Double (Mirrored) Matrix Multiplication. Even though both approaches achieve the goal of computing the matrix multiplication by accessing 16 matrix elements in parallel, the HLS PolyMem solution provides more flexibility when additional data access patterns are required, which is often the case for larger kernels. In order to highlight this aspect, we also consider a second kernel function, in which both the $B \times C$ and the $C \times B$ products need to be computed. This effectively means that the new kernel can only enable 16 parallel accesses for both multiplications if the matrices allow parallel reads in using both row- and column-patterns.

Results and Analysis. Table 6 reports the latency and resource utilization estimated by Vivado HLS when computing the single matrix multiplication kernel (1MM), $B \times C$ (rows 1, 2), and when computing the double multiplication (2MM's), $B \times C$ followed by $C \times B$ (rows 3, 4 and 5, 6) for the two parallel memories under consideration.

As expected, when using the default Vivado HLS partitioning techniques, the second multiplication ($C \times B$) cannot be computed efficiently due to the way in which the matrix data is partitioned into the memory banks, as described in Sect. 2. Indeed, C can only be accessed in parallel by rows and B by columns.

Table 6. Latency and hardware resources for matrix multiplication with different memory configurations and matrix dimensions

Memory	Matrix size	Parallel factor	Latency		Hardware resources			
			1 MM	2 MM's	BRAM	DSP	FF	LUT
HLS	32	4	4227	n.a	18	40	6162	6485
PolyMem	32	4 (2 × 2)	4227	n.a	18	40	6153	6018
HLS	32	4	4227	16503	18	40	7444	9197
PolyMem	32	4 (2 × 2)	4227	4227	18	40	7367	7364
HLS	96	16	28033	442722	96	164	28554	40474
PolyMem	96	16 (4 × 4)	28033	28033	96	160	30969	43636

On the other hand, the implementation based on HLS PolyMem is perfectly capable of performing both matrix products ($B \times C$ and $C \times B$) efficiently. The performance data reflects this very well: the estimated latency reported in Table 6 is the same for both products in the PolyMem case, and drastically different in the case of HLS partitioning.

It is also worth noting that for a matrix size of 32 × 32, the two approaches have similar resource consumption, while for matrices with larger dimensions and a parallel factor of 16, the HLS PolyMem has a resource consumption overhead in terms of FF and LUT of at most 8.5% compared to the HLS default partitioning schemes. Finally, in order to empirically validate the designs, we implemented the kernel module performing both $B \times C$ and $C \times B$ with matrix size of 96 and a parallel factor of 16 on a Xilinx Virtex-7 VC707 with a target frequency of 100 MHz. The benchmarking system is similar to that presented in Sect. 4: a soft Microblaze core is used to manage the experiment, the input/output data (matrices B and C, and the result) are streamed into parallel memory, and the actual multiplication operations are performed using the parallel memory. For the kernel with a single multiplication, the performance of the two solutions is the same. However, for the kernel with the double multiplication, the HLS PolyMem version achieves an overall speedup of 5x compared to the implementation based on HLS memory partitioning.

5.2 Markov Chain and the Matrix Power Operation

With this case study, which has at its core the matrix power operation, we aim to reinforce the need for multiview accesses to the same data structure, and further demonstrate how tiling can be easily achieved and used in conjuction with HLS-PolyMem, to further alleviate its resource overhead.

A Markov Chain is a stochastic model used to describe real-world processes. Some of its most relevant applications are found in queuing theory, the study of population growths [15], and in stochastic simulation methods such as Gibbs sampling [16] and Markov Chain Monte Carlo [17]. Moreover, Page Rank [18], an algorithm used to rank websites by search engines, leverages a time-continuous variant of this model. A Markov Chain can also describe a system composed of multiple discrete states, where the probability of being in a state depends only on the previous state of the system.

A Markov Transition Matrix A, which is a variant of an adjacency matrix, can be used to represent a Markov Chain. In this matrix, each row contains the probability to move from the current state to any other state of the system. More specifically, given two states i and j, the probability to transition from i to j is $a_{i,j}$, where $a_{i,j}$ is the element at row i and column j of the transition matrix A.

Computing the h-th power of the Markov Transition Matrix is a way to determine what is the probability to transition from an initial state to a final state in h steps. Furthermore, when the number of steps h tends to infinity, the result of A^h can be used to recover the stationary distribution of the Markov Chain, if it exists.

From a computational perspective, an approximate value for the result of $lim_{x \to \infty} A^x$ is obtained for large enough values of x. In our implementation, matrix A is stored in a HLS PolyMem, so that both rows and columns can be accessed in parallel. We then compute A^2 and save the result into a support matrix A_temp, partitioned on the second dimension. After A^2 is computed, we can easily compute A^{2^h} by copying back results to the HLS PolyMem and iterating the overall computation h times.

Listing 1.7 shows an HLS PolyMem-based algorithm that can be used to compute A^{2^h}. The implementation consists of an outermost loop repeated h times in which we compute the product $A \times A$ whose result is stored in $A_t emp$ and copied back to the PolyMem for A before the next iteration.

Implementing the same algorithm by using the HLS partitioning techniques, as presented in the previous case study, results in poor exploitation of the available parallelism, or in duplicated data, since A needs to be accessed both by rows and columns.

Listing 1.7. HLS PolyMem implementation of A^{2^h}

```
hls::prf<float, p, q, DIM, DIM, SCHEME_RoCo> A;

for(int iter=0; iter<h; iter ++){
  // A*A matrix multiplication
  for (int i = 0; i < DIM; ++i){
    for (int j = 0; j < DIM; ++j) {
#pragma HLS PIPELINE II=1
      float sum = 0;
      for (int k = 0; k < DIM; k += p*q) {
        A.read_block(i, k, temp_row, ACCESS_Ro);
        A.read_block(k, j, temp_col, ACCESS_Co);
        for (int t = 0; t < p*q; t++)
          sum += temp_row[t] * temp_col[t];
      }
      A_temp[i][j] = sum;
    }
  }
}
```

```
// Copy back results to PolyMem
for (int i = 0; i < DIM; ++i){
    for (int t = 0; t < DIM; t += p*q) {
#pragma HLS PIPELINE II=1
        A.write_block(&A_temp[i][t], i, t, ACCESS_Ro);
    }
}
}
```

The HLS PolyMem enables parallel accesses to matrix A for both rows and columns, but adds some overhead in terms of hardware resources and complexity of the logic to shuffle data within the right memory banks. The resources overhead has a quadratic growth with respect to the number $p \cdot q$ of parallel memories used to store data [4].

A possible solution to this problem is a simple form of tiling, were we reduce the dimension of PolyMem by dividing the input matrix A and storing its values in a grid of multiple PolyMem s. If A has $DIM \times DIM$ elements, it is possible to organize the on-chip memory to store data in a grid of $b \times b$ square blocks, each having size $\frac{DIM}{b} \times \frac{DIM}{b}$. In order to preserve the same level of parallelism, we can re-engineer the original computation to work in parallel on the data stored in each memory within the grid. Instead of computing a single vectorized row-column product, it is possible to perform the computation on multiple row-column products in parallel and reduce the final results.

Figure 5 shows how the input matrix is divided in multiple memories according to the choice of the parameters p, q and b. Moreover, the figure also shows which is the data accessed concurrently at each step of the computation. As an example, for the case $p = q = b = 2$ there are 4 row-column products performed in parallel (b^2) and for each of them 4 values are processed in parallel ($p \cdot q$).

It is important to notice that when $p = q = 1$ the PolyMem reduces to memories in which a single element is accessed in parallel. In this case, each PolyMem can be removed and substituted by a single memory bank.

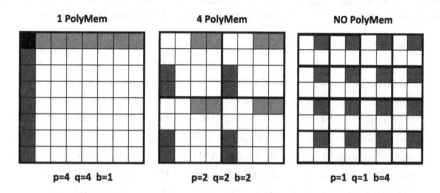

Fig. 5. Comparison between different partitioning of the input matrix in a grid of b^2 components implemented by PolyMem with a level of parallelism of $p \times q$. When both p and q are set to 1, it is possible to remove the HLS PolyMem logic.

In Table 7 we report the latency and the resource utilization estimated by Vivado HLS together with the number of lines of code (LOC) for different configurations of the parameters p, q and b on 8 iterations of the power operation for a 384×384 matrix. The numbers demonstrate that by re-engineering the code and the access patterns ($b > 1$), it is possible to achieve a smaller overall latency. However, this comes at the cost of a more convoluted code which is approximately twice as long, in terms of lines of code, as the original version. On the contrary, by using a single PolyMem ($b = 1$) we can still obtain higher performance than using the default HLS array partitioning techniques, with a much smaller and simpler code base. Indeed, PolyMem allows to reduce the time to develop an optimized FPGA-based implementation of the algorithm with minor modifications to the original software code. Thanks to HLS PolyMem we raise the level of abstraction of parallel memory accesses, thus enhancing the overall design experience and productivity.

Finally, to validate the flexibility the HLS PolyMem library, we implemented and tested the application by using Xilinx SDx tool, that enables OpenCL integration and automatically generates the PCIe drivers for communication. In this case, the benchmarking follows a similar method as the one presented in Sect. 4.1 and Fig. 4, with two amendments: (1) instead of using the Microblaze softcore, we manage the experiment directly from the CPU of the host system where the FPGA board acts as an accelerator, and (2) the transfers from stages (1) and (3) are performed in blocks over the PCIe bus. We synthesized a design for a matrix size of 256 and parameters $p = q = b = 2$ at 200 MHz, and we benchmarked its performance on the Xilinx Kintex Ultrascale ADM-PCIE-KU3 platform. The obtained throughput is 1.6 GB/s. We note that this number is significantly lower than the expected performance of the HLS-PolyMem itself because it also includes the PCIe overhead. Without this overhead, the performance of the computation using the parallel memory alone is expected to be similar to the performance of a single PolyMem block with $p \times q$ lanes, running

Table 7. Latency, hardware resources and lines of code, for 8 iterations of the matrix power operation with different memory configurations and a matrix size of 384

Memory	p	q	b	Latency	Hardware resources				LOC
					BRAM	DSP	FF	LUT	
PolyMem	2	2	1	1557835871	1036	14	9936	11071	98
PolyMem	2	4	1	840333407	1044	17	19678	28855	98
PolyMem	4	4	1	488632423	1060	31	36138	53621	98
multi PolyMem	1	1	2	758085955	1036	14	6967	5572	188
multi PolyMem	1	2	2	394149976	1044	28	14709	12934	188
multi PolyMem	2	2	2	214032480	1060	45	24845	22418	188
NO PolyMem	1	1	4	101848419	1124	76	32852	13706	188

at 200 MHz, which should be in the same order as that presented in Table 1 (i.e., 21 GB/s for a 16-lane HLS-PolyMem).

6 Related Work

The concept of parallel memory is fairly old, and has been widely discussed in scientific literature. As early as 1971, Kuck et al. discuss the advantages and disadvantages of using memory systems with power of two memory banks [19], based on results collected from a study on performed on the Illiac IV machine.

One of the earliest design methodologies and general designs of a parallel memory system suitable, dedicated to image processing applications, are presented in [20]. The memory space is already organized as a 2D structure, while the parameters p, q are the parameters of the parallel region to be accessed; the authors discuss three different mapping functions, and ultimately demonstrate the benefits parallel accesses bring to image processing.

In the 90s, more work has been devoted to investigating various addressing schemes and their implementation. For example, [9] investigates schemes based on linear addressing transformation (i.e., XOR schemes), and the use of these schemes for accessing memory in conflict-free manner using multiple strides, blocks, and FFT access patterns. In [21], another memory system design, enabling different parallel accesses to a 2D parallel memory is presented; their design is different in that it focuses on 2D memories to be accessed by arrays of 2D processing units, and thus their mapping and addressing functions are specialized.

SIMD processors have fueled more research in building and using parallel memories efficiently. For example, the use of memory systems that leverage a prime number of memory modules to provide parallel accesses for rectangles, rows, columns, and diagonals is investigated in [22]; the authors prove the advantages in building fast mapping/addressing functions for such particular memories, an idea already envisioned and analyzed in [23]. In the same work [22], Park also introduces a Multi Access Memory System, which provides access to multiple sub-array types, although it uses memory modules in a redundant manner. Research proposing an addressing function for 2D rectangular accesses, suitable for multimedia applications, is presented in [10]; the aim of this work is to minimize the number of required memory modules for efficient (i.e., full utilization) parallel accesses. The work in [24] also aims at the full utilization of the memory modules, introducing a memory system based on linear skewing (the same idea from 1971 [19]) that support accesses to block and diagonal conflict-free accesses in a 2D space. [25] proposes a memory system with power of 2 memory modules able to perform strided access with a power of two interval in horizontal and vertical directions. The analysis of parallel memories is also refined - for example, the effect of using a parallel memory to the dynamic instruction count of an application is explored in [8].

The PRF multiview access schemes - which are fundamental for this work - are explained in detail in [4], together with the hardware design and implementation requirements. This work introduces an efficient HLS implementation of the PRF addressing schemes, greatly simplifying the deployment of PolyMem on FPGAs. Alternative schemes also exist. For example, the Linear-Transformation-Based (LTB) algorithm for automatic generation of memory partitions of multi-dimensional arrays, which is suitable for being used during FPGA HLS loop pipelining, is described in [11]. The Local Binary Pattern (LBP) algorithm from [12] considers the case of multi-pattern and multi-array memory partitioning. [26] discusses the advantages of a hierarchical memory structures generated on tree-based network, as well as different methods for their automatic generation.

Building a memory hierarchy for FPGA kernels is recognized as a difficult, error-prone task [27,28]. For example, [28–32] focus on the design of generic, traditional caches. Moreover, the recently released High-Level Synthesis (HLS) tools for FPGAs [33] provide a simple set of parallel access patterns to on-chip memory starting from high-level languages implementations. More recently, work has been done on using the Polyhedral Model to automatically determine the module assignment and addressing functions [34]. By comparison, our work proposes a parallel, polymorphic memory which can be exploited from HLS tools and *acts as a caching mechanism* between the DRAM and the processing logic; instead of supporting placement and replacement policies, our memory is configured for the application at hand, and it is directly accessible for reading and writing. Moreover, PolyMem includes a *multiView feature*, enabling multiple conflict-free access types, a capability not present in other approaches [34].

Application-specific caches have also been investigated for FPGAs [26,29,35], though none of these are polymorphic or parallel. For example, in [36], the authors demonstrate why and how different caches can be instantiated for specific data structures with different access patterns. PolyMem starts from a similar idea, but, benefiting from its multi-view, polymorphic design, it improves on it by using a single large memory for all these data structures. Many of PolyMem's advantages arise from its PRF-based design [4], which is more flexible and performs better than alternative memory systems [37–40]; its high performance in scientific applications has also been proven for practical applications [41–43]. As stated before, the first hardware implementation of the Polymorphic Register File was designed in System Verilog [5]. MAX-PolyMem was the first prototype of PolyMem written entirely in MaxJ, and targeted at Maxeler DFEs [3,6]. Our new HLS PolyMem is an alternative HLL solution, proven to be easily integrated with the Xilinx toolchains.

In summary, compared to previous work on enabling easy-to-use memory hierarchies and/or caching mechanisms for FPGAs, PolyMem proposes a PRF-based design that supports polymorphic parallel accesses through a single, multi-view, application-specific software cache. The previous HLS implementation [3] has demonstrated good performance, but was specifically designed to be used on Maxeler-based systems. Our current HLS-PolyMem is the most generic implementation to date, it preserves the advantages of the previous incarnations of the system in terms of performance and flexibility, and adds the ease-of-use of an HLS library that can be easily integrated in the design flow of modern tools like Vivado HLx and Vivado SDx.

7   Conclusion and Future Work

In this paper, we presented a C++ implementation of PolyMem optimized for Vivado HLS, ready-to-use as a library for applications requiring parallel memories. Compared to the naive optimizations using HLS array partitioning techniques, the HLS PolyMem implementation is better in terms of performance, provides high flexibility in terms of supported parallel access patterns, and requires virtually zero implementation effort in terms of code re-engineering. Our design exposes an easy-to-use interface to enhance design productivity for FGPA-based applications. This interface provides methods for both the basic parallel read/write operations, and it is extended with to support masked on-chip parallel accesses. Furthermore, we provide a full, open-source implementation of HLS-PolyMem, supporting all the original PolyMem schemes [45]. Our evaluation, based on comprehensive microbenchmarking, demonstrates sustained high-performance for all these schemes. Our results demonstrate HLS-PolyMem achieves the same level of performance as HLS-partitioning for simple access patterns (i.e., rows and columns), and significant performance benefits compared with HLS-partitioning for more complex access patterns. We observe bandwidth improvement as high as 13x for complex access patterns combinations, which HLS partitioning simply cannot support.

We also proved the flexibility of the library among the Xilinx Design Tools, by implementing the kernels for *both* the Vivado workflow with a Virtex-7 VC707 and the SDx workflow with a Kintex Ultrascale 3 ADM-PCIE. Our empirical analysis of our library on two case studies (Matrix multiplication and Markov Chains) demonstrated competitive results in terms of latency, low code complexity, but also a small overhead in terms of hardware resource utilization.

Our future work focuses on three different directions. First, we aim to provide the usability of HLS for more case-studies, and further develop the API to better support end-users. Second, we aim to further improve the implementation of the HLS-PolyMem backend. For example, we consider improving the HLS PolyMem shuffle module by exploiting a Butterfly Network [44] for the memory banks connections, and enhance our HLS implementation to support both standard and customized addressing. Third, we envision a wizard-like framework to automatically analyze the user application code, estimate the potential benefits of using HLS-PolyMem, and suggest how to actually embed the parallel memory in the code to reach the best possible performance.

References

1. White Paper: Vivado Design Suite: "Vivado Design Suite" (2012). https://www.xilinx.com/support/documentation/white_papers/wp416-Vivado-Design-Suite.pdf
2. Weinhardt, M., Luk, W.: Memory access optimisation for reconfigurable systems. IEE Proc. Comput. Digit. Tech. **148**(3), 105–112 (2001)
3. Ciobanu, C.B., Stramondo, G., de Laat, C., Varbanescu, A.L.: MAX-PolyMem: high-bandwidth polymorphic parallel memories for DFEs. In: IEEE IPDPSW - RAW 2018, pp. 107–114, May 2018

4. Ciobanu, C.: Customizable register files for multidimensional SIMD architectures. Ph.D. thesis, TU Delft, The Netherlands (2013)
5. Ciobanu, C., Kuzmanov, G.K., Gaydadjiev, G.N.: Scalability study of polymorphic register files. In: Proceedings of DSD, pp. 803–808 (2012)
6. Ciobanu, C.B., et al.: EXTRA: an open platform for reconfigurable architectures. In: SAMOS XVIII, pp. 220–229 (2018)
7. Stornaiuolo, L., et al.: HLS support for polymorphic parallel memories. In: 2018 IFIP/IEEE International Conference on Very Large Scale Integration (VLSI-SoC), pp. 143–148. IEEE (2018)
8. Gou, C., Kuzmanov, G., Gaydadjiev, G.N.: SAMS multi-layout memory: providing multiple views of data to boost SIMD performance. In: ICS, pp. 179–188. ACM (2010)
9. Harper, D.T.: Block, multistride vector, and FFT accesses in parallel memory systems. IEEE Trans. Parallel Distrib. Syst. **2**(1), 43–51 (1991)
10. Kuzmanov, G., Gaydadjiev, G., Vassiliadis, S.: Multimedia rectangularly addressable memory. IEEE Trans. Multimedia **8**, 315–322 (2006)
11. Wang, Y., Li, P., Zhang, P., Zhang, C., Cong, J.: Memory partitioning for multidimensional arrays in high-level synthesis. In: DAC, p. 12. ACM (2013)
12. Yin, S., Xie, Z., Meng, C., Liu, L., Wei, S.: Multibank memory optimization for parallel data access in multiple data arrays. In: Proceedings of ICCAD, pp. 1–8. IEEE (2016)
13. auf der Heide, F.M., Scheideler, C., Stemann, V.: Exploiting storage redundancy to speed up randomized shared memory simulations. Theor. Comput. Sci. **162**(2), 245–281 (1996)
14. Stramondo, G., Ciobanu, C.B., Varbanescu, A.L., de Laat, C.: Towards application-centric parallel memories. In: Mencagli, G., et al. (eds.) Euro-Par 2018. LNCS, vol. 11339, pp. 481–493. Springer, Cham (2019). https://doi.org/10.1007/978-3-030-10549-5_38
15. Arsanjani, J.J., Helbich, M., Kainz, W., Boloorani, A.D.: Integration of logistic regression, Markov chain and cellular automata models to simulate urban expansion. Int. J. Appl. Earth Obs. Geoinformation **21**, 265–275 (2013)
16. Smith, A.F., Roberts, G.O.: Bayesian computation via the Gibbs sampler and related Markov chain Monte Carlo methods. J. R. Stat. Society. Ser. B (Methodol.) **55**, 3–23 (1993)
17. Gilks, W.R., Richardson, S., Spiegelhalter, D.: Markov Chain Monte Carlo in Practice. CRC Press, Boca Raton (1995)
18. Kamvar, S.D., Haveliwala, T.H., Manning, C.D., Golub, G.H.: Extrapolation methods for accelerating PageRank computations. In: Proceedings of the 12th International Conference on World Wide Web, pp. 261–270. ACM (2003)
19. Budnik, P., Kuck, D.: The organization and use of parallel memories. IEEE Trans. Comput. **C–20**(12), 1566–1569 (1971)
20. Van Voorhis, D.C., Morrin, T.: Memory systems for image processing. IEEE Trans. Comput. **C–27**(2), 113–125 (1978)
21. Kumagai, T., Sugai, N., Takakuwa, M.: Access methods of a two-dimensional access memory by two-dimensional inverse omega network. Syst. Comput. Jpn. **22**(7), 22–31 (1991)
22. Park, J.W.: Multiaccess memory system for attached SIMD computer. IEEE Trans. Comput. **53**(4), 439–452 (2004)
23. Lawrie, D.H., Vora, C.R.: The prime memory system for array access. IEEE Trans. Comput. **31**(5), 435–442 (1982)

24. Liu, C., Yan, X., Qin, X.: An optimized linear skewing interleave scheme for on-chip multi-access memory systems. In: Proceedings of the 17th ACM Great Lakes Symposium on VLSI, GLSVLSI 2007, pp. 8–13 (2007)
25. Peng, J.y., Yan, X.l., Li, D.x., Chen, L.z.: A parallel memory architecture for video coding. J. Zhejiang Univ. Sci. A **9**, 1644–1655 (2008). https://doi.org/10.1631/jzus.A0820052
26. Yang, H.J., Fleming, K., Winterstein, F., Chen, A.I., Adler, M., Emer, J.: Automatic construction of program-optimized FPGA memory networks. In: FPGA 2017, pp. 125–134 (2017)
27. Putnam, A., et al.: Performance and power of cache-based reconfigurable computing. In: ISCA 2009, pp. 395–405 (2009)
28. Adler, M., Fleming, K.E., Parashar, A., Pellauer, M., Emer, J.: Leap scratchpads: automatic memory and cache management for reconfigurable logic. In: FPGA 2011, pp. 25–28 (2011)
29. Chung, E.S., Hoe, J.C., Mai, K.: CoRAM: an in-fabric memory architecture for FPGA-based computing. In: FPGA 2011, pp. 97–106 (2011)
30. Yiannacouras, P., Rose, J.: A parameterized automatic cache generator for FPGAs. In: FPT 2003 (2003)
31. Gil, A.S., Benitez, J.B., Calvino, M.H., Gomez, E.H.: Reconfigurable cache implemented on an FPGA. In: ReConFig 2010 (2010)
32. Mirian, V., Chow, P.: FCache: a system for cache coherent processing on FPGAs. In: FPGA 2012, pp. 233–236 (2012)
33. Cong, J., Liu, B., Neuendorffer, S., Noguera, J., Vissers, K., Zhang, Z.: High-level synthesis for FPGAs: from prototyping to deployment. IEEE Trans. Comput. Aided Des. Integr. Circuits Syst. **30**(4), 473–491 (2011)
34. Wang, Y., Li, P., Cong, J.: Theory and algorithm for generalized memory partitioning in high-level synthesis. In: Proceedings of the 2014 ACM/SIGDA International Symposium on Field-programmable Gate Arrays, FPGA 2014, pp. 199–208. ACM, New York (2014)
35. Putnam, A.R., Bennett, D., Dellinger, E., Mason, J., Sundararajan, P.: CHiMPS: a high-level compilation flow for hybrid CPU-FPGA architectures. In: FPGA 2008, p. 261 (2008)
36. Nalabalapu, P., Sass, R.: Bandwidth management with a reconfigurable data cache. In: IPDPS 2005. IEEE (2005)
37. Kuck, D., Stokes, R.: The Burroughs scientific processor (BSP). IEEE Trans. Comput. **C–31**(5), 363–376 (1982)
38. Panda, D., Hwang, K.: Reconfigurable vector register windows for fast matrix computation on the orthogonal multiprocessor. In: Proceedings of ASAP, pp. 202–213, May–July 1990
39. Corbal, J., Espasa, R., Valero, M.: MOM: a matrix SIMD instruction set architecture for multimedia applications. In: Proceedings of the SC 1999 Conference, pp. 1–12 (1999)
40. Park, J., Park, S.B., Balfour, J.D., Black-Schaffer, D., Kozyrakis, C., Dally, W.J.: Register pointer architecture for efficient embedded processors. In: Proceedings of DATE, pp. 600–605 (2007)
41. Ramirez, A., et al.: The SARC architecture. IEEE Micro **30**(5), 16–29 (2010)
42. Ciobanu, C., Martorell, X., Kuzmanov, G.K., Ramirez, A., Gaydadjiev, G.N.: Scalability evaluation of a polymorphic register file: a CG case study. In: Proceedings of ARCS, pp. 13–25 (2011)
43. Ciobanu, C., Gaydadjiev, G., Pilato, C., Sciuto, D.: The case for polymorphic registers in dataflow computing. Int. J. Parallel Program. **46**, 1185–1219 (2018)

44. Avior, A., Calamoneri, T., Even, S., Litman, A., Rosenberg, A.L.: A tight layout of the butterfly network. Theory Comput. Syst. **31**(4), 475–488 (1998)
45. https://github.com/storna/hls_polymem

Rectification of Arithmetic Circuits
with Craig Interpolants in Finite Fields

Utkarsh Gupta[1]([✉]), Irina Ilioaea[2], Vikas Rao[1], Arpitha Srinath[1],
Priyank Kalla[1], and Florian Enescu[2]

[1] Electrical and Computer Engineering, University of Utah,
Salt Lake City, UT, USA
{utkarsh.gupta,vikas.k.rao,arpitha.srinath}@utah.edu, kalla@ece.utah.edu
[2] Mathematics and Statistics, Georgia State University, Atlanta, GA, USA
iilioaea1@student.gsu.edu, fenescu@gsu.edu

Abstract. When formal verification of arithmetic circuits identifies the presence of a bug in the design, the task of rectification needs to be performed to correct the function implemented by the circuit so that it matches the given specification. In our recent work [26], we addressed the problem of rectification of buggy finite field arithmetic circuits. The problems are formulated by means of a set of polynomials (ideals) and solutions are proposed using concepts from computational algebraic geometry. Single-fix rectification is addressed – i.e. the case where any set of bugs can be rectified at a single net (gate output). We determine if single-fix rectification is possible at a particular net, formulated as the Weak Nullstellensatz test and solved using Gröbner bases. Subsequently, we introduce the concept of Craig interpolants in polynomial algebra over finite fields and show that the rectification function can be computed using algebraic interpolants. This article serves as an extension to our previous work, provides a formal definition of Craig interpolants in finite fields using algebraic geometry and proves their existence. We also describe the computation of interpolants using elimination ideals with Gröbner bases and prove that our procedure computes the smallest interpolant. As the Gröbner basis algorithm exhibits high computational complexity, we further propose an efficient approach to compute interpolants. Experiments are conducted over a variety of finite field arithmetic circuits which demonstrate the superiority of our approach against SAT-based approaches.

Keywords: Rectification · Arithmetic circuits · Gröbner bases ·
Craig interpolants

1 Introduction

The past decade has witnessed extensive investigations into formal verification of arithmetic circuits. Circuits that implement polynomial computations over

This research is funded in part by the US National Science Foundation grants CCF-1619370 and CCF-1320385.

N. Bombieri et al. (Eds.): VLSI-SoC 2018, IFIP AICT 561, pp. 79–106, 2019.
https://doi.org/10.1007/978-3-030-23425-6_5

large bit-vector operands are hard to verify automatically using methods such as SAT/SMT-solvers, decision diagrams, etc. Recent techniques have investigated the use of polynomial algebra and algebraic geometry techniques for their verification. These include verification of integer arithmetic circuits [1–3], integer modulo-arithmetic circuits [4], word-level RTL models of polynomial datapaths [5,6], finite field combinational circuits [7–9], and also sequential designs [10]. A common theme among the above approaches is that designs are modeled as sets of polynomials in rings with coefficients from integers $\mathbb{Z}$, finite integer rings $\mathbb{Z}_{2^k}$, finite fields $\mathbb{F}_{2^k}$, and more recently also from the field of fractions $\mathbb{Q}$. Subsequently, the verification checks are formulated using algebraic geometry [11] (e.g., the Nullstellensatz), and *Gröbner basis (GB)* theory and technology [12] are used as decision procedures (ideal membership test) for formal verification.

While these techniques are successful in proving correctness or detecting the presence of bugs, *the task of post-verification debugging, error diagnosis and rectification of arithmetic circuits has not been satisfactorily addressed.* Debugging and rectification of arithmetic circuits is of utmost importance. Arithmetic circuits are mostly custom designed; this raises the potential for errors in the implementation, which have to be eventually rectified. Instead of redesigning the whole circuit, it is desirable to synthesize rectification sub-functions with minimal topological changes to the existing design – a problem often termed as *partial synthesis.* Moreover, the debug, rectification and partial synthesis problem is analogous to that of synthesis for Engineering Change Orders (ECO), where the current circuit implementation should be minimally modified (rectified) to match the ECO-modified specification. The partial synthesis approach also applies here to generate ECO-patches for rectification.

The problem of debug, rectification and ECO synthesis has been addressed for control-dominated applications and random-logic circuits, where the early developments of [13–15] were extended by [16] by formulating as CNF-SAT, and computing rectification functions using *Craig Interpolants* [17] in propositional logic.

Craig Interpolation (CI) is a method in automated reasoning to construct and refine abstractions of functions. It is a logical tool to extract concise explanations for the infeasibility of a set of mutually inconsistent statements. As an alternative to quantifier elimination, CI finds application in verification as well as in partial synthesis – and therefore, in rectification. In propositional logic, they are defined as follows.

Definition 1.1 (Craig Interpolants). Let (A, B) be a pair of CNF formulas (sets of clauses) such that $A \wedge B$ is unsatisfiable. Then there exists a formula I such that: (i) $A \implies I$; (ii) $I \wedge B$ is unsatisfiable; and (iii) I refers only to the common variables of A and B, i.e. $Var(I) \subseteq Var(A) \cap Var(B)$. The formula I is called the **interpolant** of (A, B).

Despite these advancements in automated debugging and rectification of control and random logic circuits, the aforementioned SAT and CI-based approaches are infeasible for rectification of arithmetic circuits.

1.1 Problem Description, Objectives, and Contributions

We address the problem of rectification of buggy finite field arithmetic circuits. Our problem setup is as follows:

- A specification model (*Spec*) is given either as a polynomial description f_{spec} over a finite field, or as a golden model of a finite field arithmetic circuit. The finite field considered is the field of 2^k elements (denoted by $\mathbb{F}_{2^k}$), where k is the operand-width (bit-vector word length). An implementation (*Impl*) circuit C is also given.
- Equivalence checking is performed between the *Spec* and the *Impl* circuit C, and the presence of a bug is detected. No restrictions on the number, type, or locations of the bugs are assumed.
- We assume that error-diagnosis has been performed, and a subset X of the nets of the circuit is identified as *potential rectification locations*, called target nets.

Given the *Spec*, the buggy *Impl* circuit C, the set X of potential rectifiable locations, our objective is to determine whether or not the buggy circuit can be rectified at *one particular net (location) $x_i \in X$*. This is called **single-fix rectification** in literature [16]. If a single-fix rectification does exist at net x_i in the buggy circuit, then our subsequent objective is to derive a polynomial function $U(X_{PI})$ in terms of the set of primary input variables X_{PI}. This polynomial needs to be further translated (synthesized) into a logic sub-circuit such that $x_i = U(X_{PI})$ acts as the rectification function for the buggy *Impl* circuit C so that this modified C matches the specification.

Given the above objective, this article makes the following specific contributions to solve the debug and rectification problem.

1. We formulate the test for single-fix rectifiability at a net x_i using concepts and techniques from algebraic geometry [12].
   - The problem is modeled in polynomial rings of the form $\mathbb{F}_{2^k}[x_1, \ldots, x_n]$, where k corresponds to the operand-width and the variables $x_1, \ldots, x_n$ are the nets of the circuit.
   - The rectification test is formulated using elimination ideals and the Weak Nullstellensatz, and solved using Gröbner basis as a decision procedure.
2. If rectification is feasible at x_i, then we compute a rectification function $x_i = U(X_{PI})$.
   - We show that the rectification function $U(X_{PI})$ can be determined based on the concept of Craig interpolants in algebraic geometry. While Craig interpolation is a well-studied concept in propositional and first-order logic theories, to the best of our knowledge, it has not been investigated in algebraic geometry.
   - We define Craig interpolants in polynomial algebra in finite fields and prove their existence. We also show how to compute such an interpolant using Gröbner bases.

3. The rectification function $U(X_{PI})$ obtained using Craig interpolants is a polynomial in $\mathbb{F}_{2^k}[x_1, \ldots, x_n]$. We subsequently show how a logic circuit can be obtained from this polynomial.
4. We use Gröbner basis not only as a decision procedure for the rectification test, but also as a quantification procedure for computing the rectification function. Computation of Gröbner bases exhibits very high complexity. To make our approach scalable, we further show how to exploit the topological structure of the given circuit to improve this computation.

We demonstrate the application of our techniques to rectify finite field arithmetic circuits with large operand sizes, where conventional SAT-solver based rectification approaches are infeasible.

The paper is organized as follows. The following section reviews previous work in automated diagnosis and rectification, and recent applications of Craig interpolants. Section 3 describes concepts from computer algebra and algebraic geometry. Section 4 describes an equivalence checking framework using the Weak Nullstellensatz over finite fields. Section 5 presents results that ascertain the single-fix rectifiability of the circuit. Section 6 introduces Craig interpolants in finite fields using Gröbner basis methods, and gives a procedure for obtaining the rectification function through algebraic interpolants. Section 7 addresses improvements to the Gröbner basis computation. Section 8 presents our experimental results and Sect. 9 concludes the paper.

2   Review of Previous Work

Automated diagnosis and rectification of digital circuits has been addressed in [13,18]. The paper [14] presents algorithms for synthesizing Engineering Change Order (ECO) patches. The partial equivalence checking problem has been addressed in [15,19] that checks whether a partial implementation can be extended to a complete design so that it becomes equivalent to a given specification. The partial implementation comprises black-boxes for which some functions f_i's need to be computed. The problem is formulated as Quantified Boolean Formula (QBF) solving: does there exist a function f_i, such that for all primary input assignments, the *Impl* circuit is equivalent to the *Spec* circuit. Incremental SAT-solving based approach has been presented in [20] in lieu of solving the QBF problem. This approach has been extended in [21,22] to generate rectification functions when the *Impl* circuit topology is fixed. The use of Craig interpolation as an alternative to quantifier elimination has been presented in [16,23,24] for ECO applications. The single-fix rectification function approach in [23] has been extended in [16] to generate multiple partial-fix functions. Recently, an efficient approach on resource aware ECO patch generation has been presented in [25].

As these approaches are SAT based, they work well for random logic circuits but are not efficient for arithmetic circuits. In contrast, this article presents a word-level formulation for single-fix rectification using algebraic geometry techniques. Computer algebra has been utilized for circuit debugging and rectification in [27–29]. These approaches rely heavily on the structure of the circuit for debugging, and in general, are incomplete. If the arithmetic circuit contains redundancies, the approach may not identify the buggy gate, nor compute the rectification function. On the other hand, our approach is complete, as it can always compute a single-fix rectification function, if one exists. Although our polynomial algebra based approach is applicable to any circuit in general, it is more efficient and practical for finite field arithmetic circuits.

The concept of Craig interpolants has been extensively investigated in many first order theories for various applications in synthesis and verification. Given the pair (A, B) of two mutually inconsistent formulas (cf. Definition 1.1) and a proof of their unsatisfiability, a procedure called the *interpolation system* constructs the interpolant in linear time and space in the size of the proof [30]. As the abilities of SAT solvers for proof refutation have improved, interpolants have been exploited as abstractions in various problems that can be formulated as unsatisfiable instances, e.g. model checking [30], logic synthesis [31], etc. Their use as abstractions have also been replicated in other (combinations of) theories [32–35], etc. However, the problem has been insufficiently investigated over polynomial ideals in finite fields from an algebraic geometry perspective. In that regard, the works that come closest to ours are by Gao *et al.* [36] and [37]. While they do not address the interpolation problem per se, they do describe important results of Nullstellensatz, projections of varieties and quantifier elimination over finite fields that we utilize to develop the theory and algorithms for our approach. Moreover, prior to debugging, our approach requires that verification be performed to detect the presence of a bug. For this purpose, we make use of techniques presented in [7,8,38].

We have described the notion of Craig interpolants in finite fields in our work [26]. This article is an extended version of that work where we formally define Craig interpolants in finite fields and prove their existence. Moreover, we describe a procedure for computing an interpolant and prove that the computed interpolant is the smallest. The computation of interpolants uses Gröbner basis based algorithms which have high computational complexity. In contrast to [26], we further propose an efficient approach to compute interpolants based on the given circuit topology.

3   Preliminaries: Notation and Background Results

Let $\mathbb{F}_q$ denote the finite field of q elements where $q = 2^k$, $\overline{\mathbb{F}}_q$ be its algebraic closure, and k is the operand width. The field $\mathbb{F}_{2^k}$ is constructed as $\mathbb{F}_{2^k} \equiv \mathbb{F}_2[x] \pmod{P(x)}$, where $\mathbb{F}_2 = \{0, 1\}$, and $P(x)$ is a primitive polynomial of degree k. Let α be a primitive element of $\mathbb{F}_{2^k}$, so that $P(\alpha) = 0$. Let $R = \mathbb{F}_q[x_1, \ldots, x_n]$ be the polynomial ring in n variables $x_1, \ldots, x_n$, with coefficients from $\mathbb{F}_q$. A monomial is a power product of variables $x_1^{e_1} \cdot x_2^{e_2} \cdots x_n^{e_n}$, where $e_i \in \mathbb{Z}_{\geq 0}, i \in \{1, \ldots, n\}$. A *polynomial* $f \in R$ is written as a finite sum of terms $f = c_1 X_1 + c_2 X_2 + \cdots + c_t X_t$, where $c_1, \ldots, c_t$ are coefficients and $X_1, \ldots, X_t$ are monomials. A monomial order $>$ (or a term order) is imposed on the ring – i.e. a total order and a well-order on all the monomials of R s.t. multiplication with another monomial preserves the order. Then the monomials of all polynomials $f = c_1 X_1 + c_2 X_2 + \cdots + c_t X_t$ are ordered w.r.t. $>$, such that $X_1 > X_2 > \cdots > X_t$, where $lm(f) = X_1$, $lt(f) = c_1 X_1$, and $lc(f) = c_1$ are called the *leading monomial*, *leading term*, and *leading coefficient* of f, respectively. In this work, we employ lexicographic (lex) term orders (see Definition 1.4.3 in [12]).

Polynomial Reduction via Division: Let f, g be polynomials. If $lm(f)$ is divisible by $lm(g)$, then we say that f *is reducible to* r modulo g, denoted $f \xrightarrow{g} r$, where $r = f - \frac{lt(f)}{lt(g)} \cdot g$. This operation forms the core operation of polynomial division algorithms and it has the effect of canceling the leading term of f. Similarly, f can be *reduced w.r.t. a set of polynomials* $F = \{f_1, \ldots, f_s\}$ to obtain a remainder r. This reduction is denoted as $f \xrightarrow{F}_+ r$, and the remainder r has the property that no term in r is divisible (i.e. cannot be canceled) by the leading term of any polynomial f_i in F.

We model the given circuit C by a set of multivariate polynomials $f_1, \ldots, f_s \in \mathbb{F}_{2^k}[x_1, \ldots, x_n]$; here $x_1, \ldots, x_n$ denote the nets (signals) of the circuit. Every Boolean logic gate of C is represented by a polynomial in $\mathbb{F}_2$, as $\mathbb{F}_2 \subset \mathbb{F}_{2^k}$. This is shown below. Note that in $\mathbb{F}_{2^k}$, $-1 = +1$.

$$
\begin{aligned}
z &= \neg a &\to\; & z + a + 1 \quad (\mathrm{mod}\ 2) \\
z &= a \wedge b &\to\; & z + a \cdot b \quad (\mathrm{mod}\ 2) \\
z &= a \vee b &\to\; & z + a + b + a \cdot b \quad (\mathrm{mod}\ 2) \\
z &= a \oplus b &\to\; & z + a + b \quad (\mathrm{mod}\ 2)
\end{aligned}
\tag{1}
$$

Definition 3.1 (Ideal of polynomials). *Given a set of polynomials* $F = \{f_1, \ldots, f_s\}$ *in* $\mathbb{F}_q[x_1, \ldots, x_n]$, *the ideal* $J \subseteq R$ *generated by* F *is,*

$$
J = \langle f_1, \ldots, f_s \rangle = \{ \sum_{i=1}^{s} h_i \cdot f_i : h_i \in \mathbb{F}_q[x_1, \ldots, x_n] \}.
$$

The polynomials $f_1, \ldots, f_s$ *form the basis or the generators of* J.

Let $\boldsymbol{a} = (a_1, \ldots, a_n) \in \mathbb{F}_q^n$ be a point in the affine space, and f a polynomial in R. If $f(\boldsymbol{a}) = 0$, we say that f *vanishes* on $\boldsymbol{a}$. In verification, we have to analyze the *set of all common zeros* of the polynomials of F that lie within the field $\mathbb{F}_q$. In other words, we need to analyze solutions to the system of polynomial equations $f_1 = f_2 = \cdots = f_s = 0$. This zero set is called the *variety*. It depends not just on the given set of polynomials but rather on the ideal generated by them. We denote it by $V(J) = V(f_1, \ldots, f_s)$, and it is defined as follows:

Definition 3.2 (Variety of an ideal). *Given a set of polynomials* $F = \{f_1, \ldots, f_s\}$ *in* $\mathbb{F}_q[x_1, \ldots, x_n]$, *their variety*

$$
V(J) = V(f_1, \ldots, f_s) = \{ \boldsymbol{a} \in \mathbb{F}_q^n : \forall f \in J, f(\boldsymbol{a}) = 0 \}
$$

We denote the complement of a variety, $\mathbb{F}_q^n \setminus V(J)$, by $\overline{V(J)}$.

The Weak Nullstellensatz: To ascertain whether $V(J) = \emptyset$, we employ the Weak Nullstellensatz over $\mathbb{F}_q$, for which we use the following notations.

Definition 3.3 (Sum and Product of Ideals). *Given two ideals $J_1 = \langle f_1, \ldots, f_s \rangle, J_2 = \langle h_1, \ldots, h_r \rangle$, their sum and product are*

$$J_1 + J_2 = \langle f_1, \ldots, f_s, h_1 \ldots, h_r \rangle$$
$$J_1 \cdot J_2 = \langle f_i \cdot h_j : 1 \leq i \leq s, 1 \leq j \leq r \rangle$$

Ideals and varieties are dual concepts: $V(J_1 + J_2) = V(J_1) \cap V(J_2)$, *and* $V(J_1 \cdot J_2) = V(J_1) \cup V(J_2)$. *Moreover, if $J_1 \subseteq J_2$ then $V(J_1) \supseteq V(J_2)$.*

For all elements $\alpha \in \mathbb{F}_q, \alpha^q = \alpha$. Therefore, the polynomial $x^q - x$ vanishes everywhere in $\mathbb{F}_q$, and is called the vanishing polynomial of the field. Let $J_0 = \langle x_1^q - x_1, \ldots, x_n^q - x_n \rangle$ be the ideal of all vanishing polynomials in R. Then the variety of ideal J_0 is the entire affine space, i.e. $V(J_0) = \mathbb{F}_q^n$. Moreover, by extending any ideal $J \in R = \mathbb{F}_q[x_1, \ldots, x_n]$ by the ideal of all vanishing polynomials in R, the variety is restricted to points within $\mathbb{F}_q^n$, i.e. $V(J + J_0) \subset \mathbb{F}_q^n$.

Theorem 3.1 (The Weak Nullstellensatz over finite fields (from Theorem 3.3 in [37])). *For a finite field $\mathbb{F}_q$ and the ring $R = \mathbb{F}_q[x_1, \ldots, x_n]$, let $J = \langle f_1, \ldots, f_s \rangle \subseteq R$, and let $J_0 = \langle x_1^q - x_1, \ldots, x_n^q - x_n \rangle$ be the ideal of vanishing polynomials. Then $V(J) = \emptyset \iff 1 \in J + J_0$.*

To determine whether $V(J) = \emptyset$, we need to test whether or not the unit element 1 is a member of the ideal $J + J_0$. For this *ideal membership test, we need to compute a Gröbner basis of $J + J_0$.*

Gröbner Basis of Ideals: An ideal may have many different sets of generators: $J = \langle f_1, \ldots, f_s \rangle = \cdots = \langle g_1, \ldots, g_t \rangle$. Given a non-zero ideal J, a *Gröbner basis* (GB) for J is one such set $G = \{g_1, \ldots, g_t\}$ that possesses important properties that allow to solve many polynomial decision problems.

Definition 3.4 (Gröbner basis [12]). *For a monomial ordering $>$, a set of non-zero polynomials $G = \{g_1, g_2, \ldots, g_t\}$ contained in an ideal J, is called a Gröbner basis of J iff $\forall f \in J, f \neq 0$, there exists $g_i \in \{g_1, \ldots, g_t\}$ such that $lm(g_i)$ divides $lm(f)$; i.e., $G = GB(J) \Leftrightarrow \forall f \in J : f \neq 0, \exists g_i \in G : lm(g_i) \mid lm(f)$.*

Then $J = \langle G \rangle$ holds and so $G = GB(J)$ forms a basis for J. Buchberger's algorithm [39] is used to compute a Gröbner basis. The algorithm, shown in Algorithm 1, takes as input the set of polynomial $F = \{f_1, \ldots, f_s\}$ and computes their Gröbner basis $G = \{g_1, \ldots, g_t\}$ such that $J = \langle F \rangle = \langle G \rangle$, where the variety $V(\langle F \rangle) = V(\langle G \rangle) = V(J)$. In the algorithm,

$$Spoly(f_i, f_j) = \frac{L}{lt(f_i)} \cdot f_i - \frac{L}{lt(f_j)} \cdot f_j \qquad (2)$$

where $L = LCM(lm(f_i), lm(f_j))$.

Algorithm 1. Buchberger's Algorithm

Require: $F = \{f_1, \ldots, f_s\}$
Ensure: $G = \{g_1, \ldots, g_t\}$
1: $G := F$;
2: **while** $G' \neq G$ **do**
3:      $G' := G$
4:      **for** each pair $\{f_i, f_j\}, i \neq j$ in G' **do**
5:          $Spoly(f_i, f_j) \xrightarrow{G'}_+ h$
6:          **if** $h \neq 0$ **then**
7:              $G := G \cup \{h\}$

A GB may contain redundant polynomials, and it can be *reduced* to eliminate these redundant polynomials from the basis. A reduced GB is a canonical representation of the ideal. Moreover, when $1 \in J$, then $G = reduced\_GB(J) = \{1\}$. Therefore, to check if $V(J) = \emptyset$, from Theorem 3.1 we compute a reduced GB G of $J + J_0$ and see if $G = GB(J + J_0) = \{1\}$. If so, the generators of ideal J do not have any common zeros in $\mathbb{F}_q^n$.

Craig Interpolation: The Weak Nullstellensatz is the polynomial analog of SAT checking. For UNSAT problems, the formal logic and verification communities have explored the notion of abstraction of functions by means of Craig interpolants, which has been applied to circuit rectification [16].

Given the pair (A, B) and their refutation proof, a procedure called the *interpolation system* constructs the interpolant in linear time and space in the size of the proof [30]. We introduce the notion of Craig interpolants in polynomial algebra over finite fields, based on the results of the Nullstellensatz. We make use of the following definitions and theorems for describing the results on Craig interpolants in finite fields.

Definition 3.5. Given an ideal $J \subset R$ and $V(J) \subseteq \mathbb{F}_q^n$, the *ideal of polynomials that vanish on* $V(J)$ is $I(V(J)) = \{f \in R : \forall \boldsymbol{a} \in V(J), f(\boldsymbol{a}) = 0\}$.

If $I_1 \subset I_2$ are ideals then $V(I_1) \supset V(I_2)$, and similarly if $V_1 \subset V_2$ are varieties, then $I(V_1) \supset I(V_2)$.

Definition 3.6. For any ideal $J \subset R$, the **radical** of J is defined as $\sqrt{J} = \{f \in R : \exists m \in \mathbb{N} \; s.t. f^m \in J\}$.

When $J = \sqrt{J}$, then J is called a radical ideal. Over algebraically closed fields, the *Strong Nullstellensatz* establishes the correspondence between radical ideals and varieties. Over finite fields, it has a special form.

Lemma 3.1 (From [36]). For an arbitrary ideal $J \subset \mathbb{F}_q[x_1, \ldots, x_n]$, and $J_0 = \langle x_1^q - x_1, \ldots, x_n^q - x_n \rangle$, the ideal $J + J_0$ is radical; i.e. $\sqrt{J + J_0} = J + J_0$.

Theorem 3.2 (*The Strong Nullstellensatz over finite fields (Theorem 3.2 in [36])*). For any ideal $J \subset \mathbb{F}_q[x_1, \ldots, x_n]$, $I(V(J)) = J + J_0$.

Definition 3.7. *Given an ideal $J \subset \mathbb{F}_q[x_1, \ldots, x_n]$, the l-th elimination ideal J_l is an ideal in R defined as $J_l = J \cap \mathbb{F}_q[x_{l+1}, \ldots, x_n]$.*

Theorem 3.3 *(Elimination Theorem (from Theorem 2.3.4 [12])).* Given an ideal $J \subset R$ and its GB G w.r.t. the lexicographical (lex) order on the variables where $x_1 > x_2 > \cdots > x_n$, then for every $0 \leq l \leq n$ we denote by G_l the GB of l-th elimination ideal of J and compute it as:

$$G_l = G \cap \mathbb{F}_q[x_{l+1}, \ldots, x_n].$$

J_l is called the l-th elimination ideal as it eliminates the first l variables from J.

Example 3.1 (from [11]). *Consider polynomials $f_1 : x^2 - y - z - 1$, $f_2 : x - y^2 - z - 1$, and $f_3 : x - y - z^2 - 1$ and the ideal $J = \langle f_1, f_2, f_3 \rangle \subset \mathbb{C}[x, y, z]$. $GB(J)$ with lex term order $x > y > z$ equals to $\{g_1 : x - y - z^2 - 1, g_2 : y^2 - y - z^2 - z, g_3 : 2yz^2 - z^4 - z^2, g_4 : z^6 - 4z^4 - 4z^3 - z^2\}$. Then, the GB of 2nd elimination ideal of J is $G_2 = GB(J) \cap \mathbb{C}[z] = \{g_4\}$ and GB of 1st elimination ideal is $G_1 = GB(J) \cap \mathbb{C}[y, z] = \{g_2, g_3, g_4\}$.*

Definition 3.8. Given an ideal $J = \langle f_1, \ldots, f_s \rangle \subset R$ and its variety $V(J) \subset \mathbb{F}_q^n$, the l-th projection of $V(J)$ denoted as $Pr_l(V(J))$ is the mapping

$$Pr_l(V(J)) : \mathbb{F}_q^n \to \mathbb{F}_q^{n-l}, \ Pr_l(a_1, \ldots, a_n) = (a_{l+1}, \ldots, a_n),$$

for every $\mathbf{a} = (a_1, \ldots, a_n) \in V(J)$.

In a general setting, the projection of a variety is a subset of the variety of an elimination ideal: $Pr_l(V(J)) \subseteq V(J_l)$. However, operating over finite fields, when the ideals contain the vanishing polynomials, then the above set inclusion turns into an equality.

Lemma 3.2 (Lemma 3.4 in [36]). Given an ideal $J \subset R$ that contains the vanishing polynomials of the field, then $Pr_l(V(J)) = V(J_l)$, i.e. the l-th projection of the variety of ideal J is equal to the variety of its l-th elimination ideal.

4 Algebraic Miter for Equivalence Checking

Given f_{spec} as the *Spec* polynomial and an *Impl* circuit C, we need to construct an *algebraic miter* between f_{spec} and C. For equivalence checking, we need to prove that the miter is infeasible. Figure 1 depicts how a word-level algebraic miter is setup. Suppose that $A = \{a_0, \ldots, a_{k-1}\}$ and $Z = \{z_0 \ldots, z_{k-1}\}$ denote the k-bit primary inputs and outputs of the finite field circuit, respectively. Then $A = \sum_{i=0}^{k-1} a_i \alpha^i, Z = \sum_{i=0}^{k-1} z_i \alpha^i$ correspond to polynomials that relate the word-level and bit-level inputs and outputs of C. Here α is the primitive element of $\mathbb{F}_{2^k}$. Let Z_S be the word-level output for f_{spec}, which computes some polynomial function $\mathcal{F}(A)$ of A, so that $f_{spec} : Z_S + \mathcal{F}(A)$. The word-level outputs Z, Z_S are mitered to check if for all inputs, $Z \neq Z_S$ is infeasible.

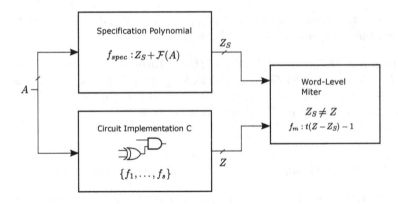

Fig. 1. Word-level miter

The logic gates of C are modeled as the set of polynomials $F = \{f_1, \ldots, f_s\}$ according to Eq. (1). In finite fields, the disequality $Z \neq Z_S$ can be modeled as a single polynomial f_m, called the miter polynomial, where $f_m = t \cdot (Z - Z_S) - 1$, and t is introduced as a free variable. If $Z = Z_S$, then $Z - Z_S = 0$. So $f_m : t \cdot 0 + 1 = 0$ has no solutions (miter is infeasible). Whereas if for some input A, $Z \neq Z_S$, then $Z - Z_S \neq 0$. Let $t^{-1} = (Z - Z_S) \neq 0$. Then $f_m : t \cdot t^{-1} - 1 = 0$ has a solution as (t, t^{-1}) are multiplicative inverses of each other. Thus the miter becomes feasible.

Corresponding to the miter, we construct the ideal $J = \langle f_{spec}, f_1, \ldots, f_s, f_m \rangle$. In our formulation, we need to also include the ideal J_0 corresponding to the vanishing polynomials in variables $Z, Z_s, A, t,$ and x_i; here Z, Z_s, A, t are the word-level variables that take values in $\mathbb{F}_{2^k}$, and x_i corresponds to the bit level (Boolean) variables in the miter. In fact, it was shown in [7] that in J_0 it is sufficient to include vanishing polynomials for only the primary input bits ($x_i \in X_{PI}$). Therefore, $J_0 = \langle x_i^2 - x_i : x_i \in X_{PI} \rangle$.

In this way, equivalence checking using the algebraic model is solved as follows: Construct an ideal $J = \langle f_{spec}, f_1, \ldots, f_s, f_m \rangle$, as described above. Add to it the ideal $J_0 = \langle x_i^2 - x_i : x_i \in X_{PI} \rangle$. Determine if the variety $V(J + J_0) = \emptyset$, i.e. if *reduced* $GB(J + J_0) = \{1\}$? If $V(J + J_0) = \emptyset$, the miter is infeasible, and

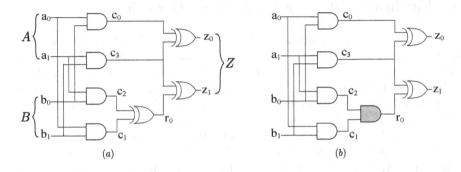

Fig. 2. Correct (a) and buggy (b) 2-bit modulo multiplier circuit implementations

C implements f_{spec}. If $V(J + J_0) \neq \emptyset$, the miter is feasible, and there exists a bug in the design.

Example 4.1. *Consider a modulo multiplier with output Z and inputs A, B. The Spec polynomial is given as $f_{spec} : Z + A \cdot B \pmod{P(X)}$, where $P(X)$ is a primitive polynomial of the field. An implementation of such a multiplier with operand (Z, A, B) bit-width $= 2$ is shown in Fig. 2(a).*

Now let's say that the designer has introduced a bug, and the XOR gate with output net r_0 has been replaced with an AND gate in the actual implementation in the circuit of Fig. 2(b). The polynomials for the gates of the correct circuit implementation are,

$$f_1 : c_0 + a_0 \cdot b_0, \quad f_2 : c_1 + a_0 \cdot b_1, \quad f_3 : c_2 + a_1 \cdot b_0, \quad f_4 : c_3 + a_1 \cdot b_1,$$
$$f_5 : r_0 + c_1 + c_2, \quad f_6 : z_0 + c_0 + c_3, \quad f_7 : z_1 + r_0 + c_3,$$

whereas for the buggy implementation, the polynomial f_5 is $f_5' : r_0 + c_1 c_2$. The problem is modeled over $\mathbb{F}_4$ and let α be a primitive element of $\mathbb{F}_4$. The word-level polynomials are $f_8 : Z + z_0 + z_1 \alpha$, $f_9 : A + a_0 + a_1 \alpha$, and $f_{10} : B + b_0 + b_1 \alpha$. The specification polynomial is $f_{spec} : Z_s + AB$. We create a miter polynomial against this specification as $f_m : t(Z - Z_s) - 1$.

To perform equivalence checking of the correct implementation and the specification polynomial, we construct ideal $J = \langle f_{spec}, f_1, \ldots, f_5, \ldots, f_{10}, f_m \rangle$. Computing GB of $J + J_0$ (J_0 is the ideal of vanishing polynomials) results in $\{1\}$, implying the the circuit in Fig. 2(a) is equivalent to the specification. However, computing GB of the ideal $J' + J_0$ where $J' = \langle f_{spec}, f_1, \ldots, f_5', \ldots, f_{10}, f_m \rangle$ results in a set of polynomials $G = \{g_1, \ldots, g_t\} \neq \{1\}$, implying the presence of a bug(s) in the design.

5   Formulating the Rectification Check

Equivalence checking is performed between the *Spec* and *Impl* circuit C, and it reveals the presence of a bug in the design. Post-verification, we assume that error diagnosis has been performed, and a set of nets X has been identified as potential single-fix rectifiable locations. While the nets in X might be target nets for single-fix, the circuit may or may not be rectifiable at any $x_i \in X$. We have to first ascertain that the circuit is indeed single-fix rectifiable at some $x_i \in X$, and subsequently compute a rectification function $U(X_{PI})$, so that $x_i = U(X_{PI})$ rectifies the circuit at that net.

5.1   Single Fix Rectification

Using the Weak Nullstellensatz (Theorem 3.1), we formulate the test for rectifiability of C at a net x_i in the circuit. For this purpose, we state and prove the following result, which is utilized later.

Proposition 5.1. Given two ideals J_1 and J_2 over some finite field such that $V(J_1) \cap V(J_2) = \emptyset$, there exists a polynomial U which satisfies $V(J_1) \subseteq V(U) \subseteq \overline{V(J_2)}$.

Proof. Over finite fields $\mathbb{F}_q$, $V(J_1)$ and $V(J_2)$ are finite sets of points. Every finite set of points is a variety of some ideal. Therefore, given $V(J_1) \cap V(J_2) = \emptyset$, there exists a set of points (a variety) which contains $V(J_1)$, and which does not intersect with $V(J_2)$. Let this variety be denoted by $V(J_I)$, where J_I is the corresponding ideal. Then $V(J_1) \subseteq V(J_I) \subseteq \overline{V(J_2)}$. In addition, we can construct a polynomial U that vanishes exactly on the points in $V(J_I)$ by means of the Lagrange's interpolation formula. $\qquad \square$

We now present the result that ascertains the circuit's rectifiability at a target net. Let the net $x_i \in X$ (*i.e.* i^{th} gate) be the rectification target, and a possible rectification function be $x_i = U(X_{PI})$. Then the ith gate is represented by a polynomial $f_i : x_i + U(X_{PI})$. Consider the ideal J corresponding to the algebraic miter – the polynomials $f_1, \ldots, f_i, \ldots, f_s$ representing the gates of the circuit, the specification polynomial f_{spec}, and the miter polynomial f_m:

$$ J = \langle f_{spec}, f_1, \ldots, f_i : x_i + U(X_{PI}), \ldots, f_s, f_m \rangle. $$

The following theorem checks whether the circuit is indeed single-fix rectifiable at the net x_i.

Theorem 5.1. Construct two ideals:

- $J_L = \langle f_{spec}, f_1, \ldots, f_i : x_i + 1, \ldots, f_s, f_m \rangle$ where $f_i : x_i + U(X_{PI})$ in J is replaced with $f_i : x_i + 1$.
- $J_H = \langle f_{spec}, f_1, \ldots, f_i : x_i, \ldots, f_s, f_m \rangle$ where $f_i : x_i + U(X_{PI})$ in J is replaced with $f_i : x_i$.

Compute $E_L = (J_L + J_0) \cap \mathbb{F}_{2^k}[X_{PI}]$ and $E_H = (J_H + J_0) \cap \mathbb{F}_{2^k}[X_{PI}]$ to be the respective elimination ideals, where all the non-primary input variables have been eliminated. Then the circuit can be single-fix rectified at net x_i with the polynomial function $f_i : x_i + U(X_{PI})$ to implement the specification iff $1 \in E_L + E_H$.

Proof. We will first prove the *if* case of the theorem. Assume $1 \in E_L + E_H$, or equivalently $V_{X_{PI}}(E_L) \cap V_{X_{PI}}(E_H) = \emptyset$. The subscript X_{PI} in $V_{X_{PI}}$ denotes that the variety is being considered over X_{PI} variables, as the non-primary inputs have been eliminated from E_L and E_H. Using Proposition 5.1, we can find a polynomial $U(X_{PI})$ such that,

$$ V_{X_{PI}}(E_L) \subseteq V_{X_{PI}}(U(X_{PI})) \subseteq \overline{V_{X_{PI}}(E_H)}. \qquad (3) $$

Note, however, that since $V_{X_{PI}}(E_L), V_{X_{PI}}(E_H)$ are considered over only primary input bits, they contain points from $\mathbb{F}_2^{|X_{PI}|}$. Therefore, there exists a polynomial $U(X_{PI})$ as in Eq. (3) with coefficients only in $\mathbb{F}_2$.

Let us consider a point p in $V(J)$. Point p is an assignment to every variable in J such that all the generators of J are satisfied. We denote by a, the projection of p on the primary inputs (i.e. the primary input assignments under p). There are only two possibilities for $U(X_{PI})$,

1. $U(a) = 1$, or in other words $a \notin V_{X_{PI}}(U(X_{PI}))$. It also implies that the value of x_i under p must be 1 because $x_i + U(X_{PI}) = 0$ needs to be satisfied. Since the generator f_i of J_L also forces x_i to be 1 and all other generators are exactly the same as those of J, p is also a point in $V(J_L)$. Moreover, E_L is the elimination ideal of J_L, and therefore, $a \in V_{X_{PI}}(E_L)$. But this a contradiction to our assumption that $V_{X_{PI}}(E_L) \subseteq V_{X_{PI}}(U(X_{PI}))$ and such a point a (and p) does not exist.

2. $U(a) = 0$, or in other words $a \in V_{X_{PI}}(U(X_{PI}))$. Using similar argument as the previous case, we can show that $a \in V_{X_{PI}}(E_H)$. This is again a contradiction to our assumption $V_{X_{PI}}(U(X_{PI})) \subseteq \overline{V_{X_{PI}}(E_H)}$.

In conclusion, there exists no point in $V(J)$ (or the miter is infeasible) when $U(X_{PI})$ satisfies Eq. 3, and therefore, circuit can be rectified at x_i.

Now we will prove the *only if* direction of the proof. We show that if $1 \notin E_L + E_H$, then there exists no polynomial $U(X_{PI})$ that can rectify the circuit. If $1 \notin E_L + E_H$, then E_L and E_H have a common zero. Let a be a point in $V_{X_{PI}}(E_L)$ and $V_{X_{PI}}(E_H)$. This point can be extended to some points p' and p'' in $V(J_L)$ and $V(J_H)$, respectively. Notice that in point p' the value of x_i will be 1, and in p'' x_i will be 0. Any polynomial $U(X_{PI})$ will either evaluate to 0 or 1 for the assignment a to the primary inputs. If it evaluates to 1, then we can say that p' is in $V(J)$ as f_i in J forces $x_i = 1$ and all other generators of J and J_L are same. This implies that $f_m(p') = 0$ (f_m: miter polynomial is feasible) and this choice of $U(X_{PI})$ will not rectify the circuit. If $U(X_{PI})$ evaluates to 0, then p'' is a point in $V(J)$.

Therefore, no choice of $U(X_{PI})$ can rectify the circuit if $1 \notin E_L + E_H$.   □

Example 5.1. *Consider the buggy modulo multiplier circuit of Fig. 2(b) (reproduced in Fig. 3), where the gate output r_0 should have been the output of an XOR gate, but an AND gate is incorrectly implemented. We apply Theorem 5.1 to check for single-fix rectifiability at r_0. The polynomials for the gates of the correct circuit implementation are,*

$$f_1 : c_0 + a_0 \cdot b_0, \quad f_2 : c_1 + a_0 \cdot b_1, \quad f_3 : c_2 + a_1 \cdot b_0, \quad f_4 : c_3 + a_1 \cdot b_1,$$
$$f_5 : r_0 + c_1 + c_2, \quad f_6 : z_0 + c_0 + c_3, \quad f_7 : z_1 + r_0 + c_3$$

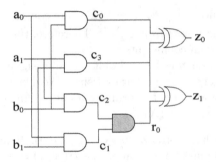

Fig. 3. A buggy 2-bit modulo multiplier circuit

The problem is modeled over $\mathbb{F}_4$ and let α be a primitive element of $\mathbb{F}_4$. The word-level polynomials are $f_8 : Z + z_0 + z_1\alpha$, $f_9 : A + a_0 + a_1\alpha$, and $f_{10} : B + b_0 + b_1\alpha$. The specification polynomial is $f_{spec} : Z_s + AB$. We create a miter polynomial against this specification as $f_m : t(Z - Z_s) - 1$.

The ideals J_L and J_H are constructed as:

$$J_L = \langle f_{spec}, f_1, \ldots, f_4, r_0 + 1, f_6, \ldots, f_{10}, f_m \rangle$$
$$J_H = \langle f_{spec}, f_1, \ldots, f_4, r_0, f_6, \ldots, f_{10}, f_m \rangle$$

The ideal J_0 is:

$$J_0 = \langle b_1^2 - b_1, b_0^2 - b_0, a_1^2 - a_1, a_0^2 - a_0 \rangle,$$

and the corresponding ideals E_L and E_H are computed to be:

$$E_L = \langle a_0b_1 + a_1b_0, a_1b_0b_1 + a_1b_0, a_0a_1b_0 + a_1b_0 \rangle$$
$$E_H = \langle b_0b_1 + b_0 + b_1 + 1, a_1b_1 + a_1 + b_1 + 1, a_0b_1 + a_1b_0 + 1,$$
$$a_0b_0 + a_0 + b_0 + 1, a_0a_1 + a_0 + a_1 + 1 \rangle$$

Computing a Gröbner basis G of $E_L + E_H$ results in $G = \{1\}$. Therefore, we can rectify this circuit at r_0.

On the other hand, if we apply the rectification theorem at net c_2, the respective ideals E_L and E_H are as follows,

$$E_L = \langle a_0^2 + a_0, a_1^2 + a_1, b_0^2 + b_0, b_1^2 + b_1, a_1b_0 + b_0, a_0b_1b_0 + a_0b_1 + a_0b_0 + a_0, a_0a_1 + a_0 \rangle$$
$$E_H = \langle a_0^2 + a_0, b_0^2 + b_0, b_1^2 + b_1, b_1b_0 + b_1 + b_0 + 1, a_1 + 1, a_0b_0 + a_0 + b_0 + 1 \rangle$$

When we compute $G = GB(E_L + E_H)$, we obtain $G \neq \{1\}$ indicating that single-fix rectification is not possible at net c_2, for the given bug.

6   Craig Interpolants in Finite Fields

Once it is ascertained that a net x_i admits single-fix rectification, the subsequent task is to compute a rectification polynomial function $x_i = U(X_{PI})$ in terms of the primary inputs of the circuit. In this section, we describe how such a rectification polynomial function can be computed. For this purpose, we introduce the concept of Craig interpolants using algebraic geometry in finite fields.

We describe the setup for Craig interpolation in the ring $R = \mathbb{F}_q[x_1, \ldots, x_n]$. Partition the variables $\{x_1, \ldots, x_n\}$ into disjoint subsets A, B, C. We are given two ideals $J_A \subset \mathbb{F}_q[A, C]$, $J_B \subset \mathbb{F}_q[B, C]$ such that the C-variables are common to the generators of both J_A, J_B. *From here on, we will assume that all ideals include the corresponding vanishing polynomials.* For example, generators of J_A include $\boldsymbol{A^q - A, C^q - C}$, where $\boldsymbol{A^q - A} = \{x_i^q - x_i : x_i \in A\}$, and so on. Then these ideals become radicals and we can apply Lemmas 3.1 and 3.2. We use $V_{A,C}(J_A)$ to denote the variety of J_A over the $\mathbb{F}_q$-space spanned by A and C variables, i.e. $V_{A,C}(J_A) \subset \mathbb{F}_q^A \times \mathbb{F}_q^C$. Similarly, $V_{B,C}(J_B) \subset \mathbb{F}_q^B \times \mathbb{F}_q^C$.

Now let $J = J_A + J_B \subseteq \mathbb{F}_q[A, B, C]$, and suppose that it is found by application of the Weak Nullstellensatz (Theorem 3.1) that $V_{A,B,C}(J) = \emptyset$. When we compare the varieties of J_A and J_B, then we can consider the varieties in $\mathbb{F}_q^A \times \mathbb{F}_q^B \times \mathbb{F}_q^C$, as $V_{A,B,C}(J_A) = V_{A,C}(J_A) \times \mathbb{F}_q^B \subset \mathbb{F}_q^A \times \mathbb{F}_q^B \times \mathbb{F}_q^C$. With this setup, we define the interpolants as follows.

Definition 6.1 (*Interpolants in finite fields*). Given two ideals $J_A \subset \mathbb{F}_q[A, C]$ and $J_B \subset \mathbb{F}_q[B, C]$ where A, B, C denote the three disjoint sets of variables such that $V_{A,B,C}(J_A) \cap V_{A,B,C}(J_B) = \emptyset$. Then there exists an ideal J_I satisfying the following properties:

1. $V_{A,B,C}(J_I) \supseteq V_{A,B,C}(J_A)$
2. $V_{A,B,C}(J_I) \cap V_{A,B,C}(J_B) = \emptyset$
3. Generators of J_I contain only the C-variables; or $J_I \subseteq \mathbb{F}_q[C]$.

We call $V_{A,B,C}(J_I)$ the **interpolant** in finite fields of the pair $(V_{A,B,C}(J_A), V_{A,B,C}(J_B))$, and the corresponding ideal J_I the **ideal-interpolant**.

As the generators of J_I contain only the C-variables, the interpolant $V_{A,B,C}(J_I)$ is of the form $V_{A,B,C}(J_I) = \mathbb{F}_q^A \times \mathbb{F}_q^B \times V_C(J_I)$. Therefore, the subscripts A, B for the interpolant $V_{A,B,C}(J_I)$ may be dropped for the ease of readability.

Example 6.1 Consider the ring $R = \mathbb{F}_2[a, b, c, d, e]$, partition the variables as $A = \{a\}, B = \{e\}, C = \{b, c, d\}$. Let ideals

$$J_A = \langle ab, bd, bc + c, cd, bd + b + d + 1 \rangle + J_{0,A,C}$$
$$J_B = \langle b, d, ec + e + c + 1, ec \rangle + J_{0,B,C}$$

where $J_{0,A,C}$ and $J_{0,B,C}$ are the corresponding ideals of vanishing polynomials. Then,

$$V_{A,B,C}(J_A) = \mathbb{F}_q^B \times V_{A,C}(J_A) =$$
$$(abcde) : \{01000, 00010, 01100, 10010, 01001, 00011, 01101, 10011\}$$
$$V_{A,B,C}(J_B) = \mathbb{F}_q^A \times V_{B,C}(J_B) =$$
$$(abcde) : \{00001, 00100, 10001, 10100\}$$

Ideals J_A, J_B have no common zeros as $V_{A,B,C}(J_A) \cap V_{A,B,C}(J_B) = \emptyset$. The pair (J_A, J_B) admits a total of 8 interpolants:

1. $V(J_S) = (bcd) : \{001, 100, 110\}$
   $J_S = \langle cd, b + d + 1 \rangle$
2. $V_C(J_1) = (bcd) : \{001, 100, 110, 101\}$
   $J_1 = \langle cd, bd + b + d + 1, bc + cd + c \rangle$
3. $V_C(J_2) = (bcd) : \{001, 100, 110, 011\}$
   $J_2 = \langle b + d + 1 \rangle$
4. $V_C(J_3) = (bcd) : \{001, 100, 110, 111\}$
   $J_3 = \langle b + cd + d + 1 \rangle$
5. $V_C(J_4) = (bcd) : \{001, 100, 110, 011, 111\}$
   $J_4 = \langle bd + b + d + 1, bc + b + cd + c + d + 1 \rangle$
6. $V_C(J_5) = (bcd) : \{001, 100, 110, 101, 111\}$
   $J_5 = \langle bc + c, bd + b + d + 1 \rangle$
7. $V_C(J_6) = (bcd) : \{001, 100, 110, 101, 011\}$
   $J_6 = \langle bd + b + d + 1, bc + cd + c \rangle$
8. $V_C(J_L) = (bcd) :$
   $\{001, 011, 100, 101, 110, 111\}$
   $J_L = \langle bd + b + d + 1 \rangle$.

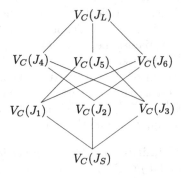

Fig. 4. The Interpolant lattice for Example 6.1

It is easy to check that all $V(J_I)$ satisfy the 3 conditions of Definition 6.1. Note also that $V(J_S)$ is the smallest interpolant, contained in every other interpolant. Likewise, $V(J_L)$ contains all other interpolants and it is the largest. The other containment relationships are shown in the corresponding interpolant lattice in Fig. 4; $V_C(J_1) \subset V_C(J_5), V_C(J_1) \subset V_C(J_6)$, etc.

Theorem 6.1 (Existence of Craig Interpolants). An ideal-interpolant J_I, and correspondingly the interpolant $V_{A,B,C}(J_I)$, as given in Definition 6.1, always exists.

Proof. Consider the elimination ideal $J_I = J_A \cap \mathbb{F}_q[C]$. We show J_I satisfies the three conditions for the interpolant.

Condition 1: $V_{A,B,C}(J_I) \supseteq V_{A,B,C}(J_A)$. This condition is trivially satisfied due to construction of elimination ideals. As $J_I \subseteq J_A$, $V_{A,B,C}(J_I) \supseteq V_{A,B,C}(J_A)$.

Condition 2: $V_{A,B,C}(J_I) \cap V_{A,B,C}(J_B) = \emptyset$. This condition can be equivalently stated as $V_{B,C}(J_I) \cap V_{B,C}(J_B) = \emptyset$ as neither J_I nor J_B contain any variables from the set A. We prove this condition by contradiction. Let's assume that there exists a common point $(\mathbf{b}, \mathbf{c})$ in $V_{B,C}(J_I)$ and $V_{B,C}(J_B)$. We know that the projection of the variety $Pr_A(V_{A,C}(J_A))$ is equal to the variety of the elimination ideal $V_C(J_I)$, where $J_I = J_A \cap \mathbb{F}_q[C]$, due to Lemma 3.2. Therefore, the point $(\mathbf{c})$ in the variety of J_I can be extended to a point $(\mathbf{a}, \mathbf{c})$ in the variety of J_A. This implies that the ideals J_A and J_B vanish at $(\mathbf{a}, \mathbf{b}, \mathbf{c})$. This is a contradiction to our initial assumption that the intersection of the varieties of J_A and J_B is empty. Thus J_I, J_B have no common zeros.

Condition 3: The generators of J_I contain only the C-variables. This condition is trivially satisfied as J_I is the elimination ideal obtained by eliminating A-variables in J_A.   □

The above theorem not only proves the existence of an interpolant, but also gives a procedure to construct its ideal: $J_I = J_A \cap \mathbb{F}_q[C]$. In other words, compute a reduced Gröbner basis G of J_A w.r.t. the elimination order $A > B > C$ and take $G_I = G \cap \mathbb{F}_q[C]$. Then G_I gives the generators for the ideal-interpolant J_I.

Example 6.2. *The elimination ideal J_I computed for J_A from Example 6.1 is $J_I = J_S = \langle cd, b + d + 1 \rangle$ with variety $V_C(J_I) = (bcd) : \{001, 100, 110\}$. This variety over the variable set A and C is $V_{A,C}(J_I) = (abcd) : \{0001, 0100, 0110, 1001, 1100, 1110\}$, and it contains $V_{A,C}(J_A)$. Moreover, $V_{A,B,C}(J_I)$ also has an empty intersection with $V_{A,B,C}(J_B)$.*

Theorem 6.2 (Smallest interpolant). *The interpolant $V_{A,B,C}(J_S)$ corresponding to the ideal $J_S = J_A \cap \mathbb{F}_q[C]$ is the smallest interpolant.*

Proof. Let $J_I \subseteq \mathbb{F}_q[C]$ be any another ideal-interpolant $\neq J_S$. We show that $V_C(J_S) \subseteq V_C(J_I)$. For $V_C(J_I)$ to be an interpolant it must satisfy

$$V_{A,B,C}(J_A) \subseteq V_{A,B,C}(J_I)$$

which, due to Theorem 3.2, is equivalent to

$$I(V_{A,B,C}(J_A)) \supseteq I(V_{A,B,C}(J_I)) \implies J_A \supseteq J_I$$

As the generators of J_I only contain polynomials in C-variables, this relation also holds for the following

$$J_A \cap \mathbb{F}_q[C] \supseteq J_I \implies J_S \supseteq J_I \implies V_C(J_S) \subseteq V_C(J_I).$$ □

6.1 Computing a Rectification Function from Craig Interpolants

Back to our formulation of single-fix rectification, from Theorem 5.1 we have $1 \in E_L + E_H$ or $V(E_L) \cap V(E_H) = \emptyset$. Therefore, we can consider the pair (E_L, E_H) for Craig interpolation. In other words, based on the notation from Definition 6.1, $J_A = E_L$ and $J_B = E_H$. Moreover, E_L and E_H are elimination ideals containing only X_{PI} variables. As a result, the partitioned set of variables for Craig interpolation A, B, and C all correspond to primary inputs. Furthermore, we want to compute an ideal J_I in X_{PI} such that

$V_{X_{PI}}(E_L) \subseteq V_{X_{PI}}(J_I)$ and $V_{X_{PI}}(J_I) \cap V_{X_{PI}}(E_H) = \emptyset$. The *smallest ideal-interpolant* $J_I = E_L \cap \mathbb{F}_{2^k}[X_{PI}] = E_L$ itself. Therefore, we use E_L to compute the correction function $U(X_{PI})$.

Obtaining $U(X_{PI})$ from E_L: In finite fields, given an ideal J, it always possible to find a polynomial U such that $V(U) = V(J)$. The reason is that every ideal in a finite field has a finite variety, and a polynomial with those points as its roots can always be constructed using the Lagrangian interpolation formula. We construct the rectification polynomial U from the ideal-interpolant E_L as shown below, such that $V(E_L) = V(U)$.

Let the generators of E_L be denoted by $g_1, \ldots, g_t$. We can compute U as,

$$U = (1 + g_1)(1 + g_2) \cdots (1 + g_t) + 1 \tag{4}$$

It is easy to assert that $V(U) = V(E_L)$. Consider a point $\boldsymbol{a}$ in $V(E_L)$. As all of $g_1, \ldots, g_t$ vanish $(= 0)$ at $\boldsymbol{a}$,

$$U(\boldsymbol{a}) = (1 + g_1(\boldsymbol{a}))(1 + g_2(\boldsymbol{a})) \cdots (1 + g_t(\boldsymbol{a})) + 1$$
$$= (1 + 0)(1 + 0) \cdots (1 + 0) + 1 = 0$$

Conversely, for a point $\boldsymbol{a}' \notin V(E_L)$, at least one of $g_1, \ldots, g_t$ will evaluate to 1. Without loss of generality, if g_1 evaluates to 1 at $\boldsymbol{a}'$, then $U = (1 + 1)(1 + 0) \cdots (1 + 0) + 1 \neq 0$.

Using Eq. (4), a recursive procedure is derived to compute U, and it is depicted in Algorithm 2. At every recursive step, we also reduce the intermediate results by $(\bmod\ J_0)$ (line 7) so as to avoid terms of high degree. In this fashion, from the ideal-interpolant E_L, we compute the single-fix rectification polynomial function $U(X_{PI})$, and synthesize a sub-circuit at net x_i such that $x_i = U(X_{PI})$ rectifies the circuit.

Algorithm 2. Compute U from J such that $V(U) = V(J)$

1: $U = compute\_U(J, J_0) + 1$
2: **procedure** $compute\_U(J, J_0)$ /*$J = \langle g_1, \ldots, g_t \rangle$*/
3:      **if** $size(J) = 1$ **then**
4:          **return** $(1 + J[1])$
5:      $subset J = \{J[1], J[2], \ldots, J[size(J) - 1]\}$
6:      $poly\ S_1 = compute\_U(subset J, J_0)$
7:      $Perform\ S_1 \cdot J[size(J)] \xrightarrow{J_0}_+ S_2$
8:      **return** $S_1 + S_2$

Example 6.3. *Example 5.1 showed that the buggy circuit of Fig. 3 can be rectified at net r_0. This rectification check required the computation of the (Gröbner basis of) ideal E_L. Using Algorithm 2, we compute $U(X_{PI})$ from E_L to be $a_0 b_1 + a_1 b_0$, and the rectification polynomial as $r_0 + a_0 b_1 + a_1 b_0$. This can be synthesized into a sub-circuit as $r_0 = (a_0 \wedge b_1) \oplus (a_1 \wedge b_0)$, by replacing the modulo 2 product and sum in the polynomial with the Boolean AND and XOR operators, respectively.*

7 Efficient Gröbner Basis Computations for E_L and E_H

The proposed rectification approach requires the computation of (generators of) elimination ideals E_L and E_H. This is achieved by computing a Gröbner basis each for $GB(J_L + J_0) \cap \mathbb{F}_{2^k}[X_{PI}]$ and $GB(J_H + J_0) \cap \mathbb{F}_{2^k}[X_{PI}]$, respectively. The rectification polynomial function $x_i = U(X_{PI})$ is subsequently derived from the generators of E_L. As the generators of J_L and J_H comprise polynomials derived from the entire circuit, these GB-computations become infeasible for larger circuits due to its high complexity. In [37], it was shown that the time and space complexity of computing $GB(J + J_0)$ over $\mathbb{F}_q[x_1, \ldots, x_n]$ is bounded by $q^{O(n)}$. In the context of our work, as $q = 2^k$ where k is the operand-width, and n the number of variables (nets) in the miter, we have to overcome this complexity to make our approach practical for large circuits.

Prior work [8] has shown that the GB-computation can be significantly improved when the polynomials are derived from circuits. By analyzing the topology of the given circuit, a specialized term order can be derived that can significantly reduce the number of *Spoly* computations in the GB-algorithm. We present a similar approach to improve the GB-computation for ideals E_L, E_H.

Lemma 7.1 (Product Criterion [40]). *For two polynomials f_i, f_j in any polynomial ring R, if the equality $lm(f_i) \cdot lm(f_j) = LCM(lm(f_i), lm(f_j))$ holds, i.e. if $lm(f_i)$ and $lm(f_j)$ are relatively prime, then $Spoly(f_i, f_j) \xrightarrow{G}_+ 0$.*

Buchberger's algorithm therefore does not pair those polynomials f_i, f_j (Algorithm 1, line 4) whose leading monomials are relatively prime, as they do not produce any new information in the basis. Moreover, based on the above criterion, when the leading monomials of *all polynomials in the basis* $F = \{f_1, \ldots, f_s\}$ are relatively prime, then all $Spoly(f_i, f_j) \xrightarrow{G}_+ 0$. As no new polynomials are generated in Buchberger's algorithm, F already constitutes a Gröbner basis $(F = GB(J))$. For a combinational circuit C, a specialized term order $>$ can always be derived by analyzing the circuit topology which ensures such a property [4, 7]:

Proposition 7.1 (From [7]). Let C be an arbitrary combinational circuit. Let $\{x_1, \ldots, x_n\}$ denote the set of all variables (signals) in C. Starting from the primary outputs, perform a *reverse topological traversal* of the circuit and order the variables such that $x_i > x_j$ if x_i appears earlier in the reverse topological order. Impose a *lex* term order $>$ to represent each gate as a polynomial f_i, s.t. $f_i = x_i + tail(f_i)$. Then the set of all polynomials $\{f_1, \ldots, f_s\}$ forms a Gröbner basis G, as $lt(f_i) = x_i$ and $lt(f_j) = x_j$ for $i \neq j$ are relatively prime. This term order $>$ is called the **Reverse Topological Term Order (RTTO)**.

RTTO ensures that the set of all polynomials $\{f_1, \ldots, f_s\}$ of the given circuit C have relatively prime leading terms. However, the model of the algebraic miter (Fig. 1, with the *Spec* and the miter polynomial, in addition to the given circuit) is such that under RTTO $>$, not all polynomials have relatively prime leading terms. However, we show that imposition of RTTO on the miter still significantly reduces the amount of computation required for Gröbner bases. We demonstrate the technique on the GB computation for the ideal $J_L + J_0$ (analogously also for $J_H + J_0$), corresponding to the miter, as per Theorem 5.1.

Given the word-level miter of Fig. 1, impose a lexicographic (*lex*) monomial order on the ring R, with the following variable order:

$$t > Z > Z_S > A > \text{nets of } C \text{ in RTTO order} > \text{Primary input variables} \quad (5)$$

Here t is the free variable used in the miter polynomial, and Z, Z_s are the word-level outputs of *Impl* and *Spec*, respectively, and A is the word-level input. Corresponding to the circuit in Fig. 3 (Example 5.1), we use a *lex* term order with variable order:

$$t > Z > Z_S > A > B > z_1 > z_0 > r_0 > c_0 > c_1 > c_2 > c_3 > b_1 > b_0 > a_1 > a_0 \quad (6)$$

The polynomials $\{f_1, \ldots, f_{10}, f_{spec}, f_m\}$ in Example 5.1 are already written according to the term order of Eq. (6). Note also that the leading terms of the generators of the ideal J_L are the same as the leading terms of polynomials in $\{f_1, \ldots, f_{10}, f_{spec}, f_m\}$. From among these, the only pair of polynomials that *do not have relatively prime leading* terms are f_8 and f_m. This condition also holds when considering the ideal $J_L + J_0$ (instead of only J_L) as J_0 is composed of only bit-level primary input variables.

In general, modeling an algebraic miter with RTTO $>$ will ensure that we have *exactly one pair of polynomials with leading monomials that are not relatively prime*. This pair includes: (i) the miter polynomial $f_m : tZ - tZ_s - 1$, with $lm(f_m) = tZ$; and (ii) the polynomial (hereafter denoted by f_o) that relates the word-level and bit-level variables of the circuit, $f_o : Z + z_0 + z_1\alpha + \cdots + z_{k-1}\alpha^{k-1}$, with $lm(f_o) = Z$. Therefore, in the first iteration of Algorithm 1 for computing $GB(J_L + J_0)$, the only critical pair to compute is $Spoly(f_m, f_o)$, as all other pairs reduce to 0, due to Lemma 7.1. Moreover, computing $Spoly(f_m, f_o)$ results in $Spoly(f_m, f_o) = t(Z_S + z_0 + \cdots + z_{k-1}\alpha^{k-1}) + 1$. Once again, RTTO $>$ ensures the following:

Lemma 7.2. $Spoly(f_m, f_o) \xrightarrow{J_L + J_0}_+ h = t \cdot r + 1$, where r is a polynomial in bit-level primary input variables.

Proof. Consider the polynomial reduction of $Spoly(f_m, f_o) \xrightarrow{J_L + J_0}_+ h$:

$$t(Z_S + z_0 + \cdots + z_{k-1}\alpha^{k-1}) + 1 \xrightarrow{f_{spec}}_+$$

where $f_{spec} = Z_S + \mathcal{F}(A)$. The remainder for this reduction will be

$$t(\mathcal{F}(A) + z_0 + \cdots + z_{k-1}\alpha^{k-1}) + 1,$$

where $\mathcal{F}(A)$ is the polynomial specification in word-level input variable(s). This remainder is then reduced by the polynomial relating the word-level and bit-level primary input variables, i.e. by $A + a_0 + \cdots + a_{k-1}\alpha^{k-1}$. The subsequent remainder is

$$
\begin{aligned}
t(\mathcal{F}(A) + z_0 + \cdots + z_{k-1}\alpha^{k-1}) + 1 \xrightarrow{A+a_0+\cdots+a_{k-1}\alpha^{k-1}}_{+} \\
t(z_0 + \cdots + z_{k-1}\alpha^{k-1} + \mathcal{G}(a_0, \cdots, a_{k-1})) + 1,
\end{aligned}
\tag{7}
$$

where the word-level specification polynomial $\mathcal{F}(A)$ gets reduced to a polynomial expression $\mathcal{G}(a_0, \ldots, a_{k-1})$ in primary input bits. Due to RTTO $>$, subsequent divisions of the above remainder in Eq. (7) by $\{f_1, \ldots, f_s\}$ will successively cancel the terms in variables $z_i, i = 0, \ldots, k-1$, and express them in terms of the primary input bits. Since primary input bits are last in RTTO $>$, they never appear as leading terms in any of the polynomials in J_L; so the terms in primary input bits cannot be canceled. As a result, after complete reduction of $Spoly(f_m, f_o)$ by $J_L + J_0$, the remainder will be a polynomial expression of the form $Spoly(f_m, f_o) \xrightarrow{J_L+J_0}_{+} h = t \cdot r + 1$, where r is a polynomial only in bit-level primary input variables.   □

Coming back to the computation $GB(J_L+J_0)$, the polynomial h is now added to the current basis, i.e. $G = \{J_L+J_0\} \cup \{h\}$ in Buchberger's algorithm (Line 7 in Algorithm 1). This polynomial h now needs to be paired with other polynomials in the basis. There are only two sets of possibilities for subsequent critical pairings: (i) the pair $Spoly(f_m, h)$; and (ii) to pair h with corresponding vanishing polynomials from the ideal J_0. For all other polynomials $f_i \in \{f_1, \ldots, f_s\}$, $lm(h)$ and $lm(f_i)$ have relatively prime leading terms, so $Spoly(h, f_i)_{i=1,\ldots,s} \xrightarrow{J_L+J_0}_{+} 0$; so the pairs (h, f_i) need not be considered in $GB(J_L + J_0)$. We now show that $Spoly(f_m, h) \xrightarrow{G=\{J_L+J_0\}\cup\{h\}}_{+} 0$, so the pair (f_m, h) also need not be considered.

From Lemma 7.2 and its proof, we have that $h = t \cdot r + 1$ and $Z + Z_S \xrightarrow{G=\{J_L+J_0\}}_{+} = r$, with r composed of primary input bits. Let $r = e+r'$, where $e = lt(r)$ is the leading term and $r' = r - e$ is $tail(r)$, both expressed in primary input bits. With this notation, $h = te+tr'+1$ and $lt(h) = te$. The LCM L of leading monomials of f_m and h is $L = LCM(lm(f_m), lm(h)) = LCM(tZ, te) = tZe$. Consider the computation $Spoly(f_m, h)$:

$$
\begin{aligned}
Spoly(f_m, h) &= \frac{L}{lt(f_m)} \cdot f_m - \frac{L}{lt(h)} \cdot h \\
&= ef_m + Zh = e(tZ + tZ_S + 1) + Z(te + tr' + 1) \\
&= tr'Z + teZ_S + Z + e
\end{aligned}
\tag{8}
$$

Next consider the reduction of $Spoly(f_m, h)$ by $\{J_L + J_0\} \cup \{h\}$, where h itself is used in the division. The reduction $Spoly(f_m, h) \xrightarrow{h}_+$ is computed as,

$$tr'Z + teZ_S + Z + e \xrightarrow{h}_+ tr'Z + (tr' + 1)Z_S + Z + e$$
$$= tr'(Z + Z_S) + Z + Z_S + e$$
$$= (tr' + 1)(Z + Z_S) + e \tag{9}$$

Reducing the intermediate remainder of Eq. (9) by the polynomials in $J_L + J_0$ results in $(tr'+1)(r)+e$. This reduction process is similar to the one in the proof of Lemma 7.2. Now consider the polynomial $(tr' + 1)(r) + e$

$$(tr' + 1)(r) + e = (tr' + 1)(e + r') + e$$
$$= ter' + tr'^2 + e + r' + e$$
$$= ter' + tr'^2 + r' \tag{10}$$

The polynomial in Eq. (10) can be further reduced by h which results in 0 implying that $Spoly(f_m, h) \xrightarrow{\{J_L + J_0\} \cup \{h\}}_+ 0$.

$$ter' + tr'^2 + r' \xrightarrow{h}_+ (tr' + 1)r' + tr'^2 + r'$$
$$= tr'^2 + r' + tr'^2 + r' = 0$$

In summary, we have shown that to compute E_L as $GB(J_L + J_0) \cap \mathbb{F}_{2^k}[X_{PI}]$, we only need to compute $Spoly(f_m, f_o) \xrightarrow{J_L + J_0}_+ h$, and pair h with polynomials of J_0, as all other $Spoly(h, f_i)$ reduce to 0. This gives us the following procedure to compute the Gröbner basis of E_L (respectively E_H):

1. Compute $Spoly(f_o, f_m) \xrightarrow{J_L + J_0}_+ h$, where (f_m, f_o) is the only pair of polynomials in $J_L + J_0$ that do not have relatively prime leading monomials.
2. Use Buchberger's algorithm to compute GB of the set of vanishing polynomials and h, i.e. compute $G = GB(J_0 = \{x_i^2 - x_i : x_i \in X_{PI}\}, h)$.
3. From G, collect the polynomials *not containing* t; i.e $E_L = G \cap \mathbb{F}_{2^k}[X_{PI}]$. These polynomials generate the ideal E_L.

The same technique is also used to compute E_H by replacing J_L with J_H in the above procedure. In our approach, we use the above procedures to compute E_L, E_H for Theorem 5.1 and then compute $U(X_{PI})$ from E_L using Algorithm 2.

8   Experimental Results

We have performed rectification experiments on finite field arithmetic circuits that are used in cryptography, where the implementation is different from the specification due to exactly one gate. This is to ensure that single-fix rectification is feasible for such bugs, so that a rectification function can be computed. We have implemented the procedures described in the previous sections—i.e.

the concepts of Theorem 5.1, Sect. 7 and Algorithm 2—using the SINGULAR symbolic algebra computation system [ver. 4-1-0] [41]. Given a *Spec*, a buggy *Impl* circuit C, and the set X of rectification targets, our approach checks for each net $x_i \in X$ if single-fix rectification is feasible, and if so, computes a rectification function $x_i = U(X_{PI})$. The experiments were conducted on a desktop computer with a 3.5 GHz Intel Core^{TM} i7-4770K Quad-core CPU, 16 GB RAM, running 64-bit Linux OS.

Experiments are performed with three different types of finite field circuit benchmarks. Two of these are the Mastrovito and the Montgomery multiplier circuit architectures used for modular multiplication. Mastrovito multipliers compute $Z = A \times B \pmod{P(x)}$ where $P(x)$ is a given primitive polynomial for the datapath size k. Montgomery multipliers are instead preferred for exponentiation operations (often required in cryptosystems). The last set of benchmarks are circuits implementing point addition over elliptic curves used for encryption, decryption and authentication in elliptic curve cryptography (ECC).

Table 1. Mastrovito multiplier rectification against Montgomery multiplier specification. Time in seconds; Time-out = 5400 s; k: Operand width

k	# of Gates		SAT	Theorem 5.1	Algorithm 2	Mem
	Mas	Mont				
4	48	96	0.09	0.03	0.001	8.16 MB
8	292	319	158.34	0.41	0.006	20.36 MB
9	237	396	4,507	0.47	0.001	18.95 MB
10	285	480	TO	0.84	0.001	28.2 MB
16	1,836	1,152	TO	73.63	0.024	0.32 GB
32	5,482	4,352	TO	3621	0.043	2.4 GB

First we present the results for the case where the reference *Spec* is given as a Montgomery multiplier, and the buggy implementation is given as a Mastrovito multiplier, which is to be rectified. Theorem 5.1, along with efficient GB-computation of the ideals E_L, E_H, is applied at a net $x_i \in X$, such that the circuit is rectifiable at x_i. Table 1 compares the execution time for the SAT-based approach of [16] against ours (Theorem 5.1) for checking whether a buggy Mastrovito multiplier can be rectified at a certain location in the circuit against a Montgomery multiplier specification. The SAT procedure is implemented using the *abc* tool [42]. We execute the command *inter* on the ON set and OFF set as described in [16]. The SAT-based procedure is unable to perform the necessary unsatisfiability check for circuits beyond 9-bit operand word-lengths, whereas our approach easily scales to 32-bit circuits. Using our approach, the polynomial $U(X_{PI})$ needed for rectification is computed from E_L and the time is reported in Table 1 in the Algorithm 2 column. The last column in the table shows the memory usage of our approach.

We also perform the rectification when the *Spec* is given as a polynomial expression instead of a circuit. Table 2 shows the results for checking whether the incorrect Mastrovito implementation can be single-fix rectified against the word-level specification polynomial $f_{spec} : Z_S + A \cdot B$.

Table 2. Mastrovito multiplier rectification against polynomial specification $Z_S = AB$. Time in seconds; Time-out = 5400 s; k: Operand width

k	# of Gates	Theorem 5.1	Algorithm 2	Mem
4	48	0.01	0.001	7.24 MB
8	292	0.08	0.006	14.95 MB
16	1,836	4.83	0.038	0.2 GB
32	5,482	100.52	0.015	1.42 GB
64	21,813	4,989	0.117	12.25 GB

Point addition is an important operation required for the task of encryption, decryption and authentication in ECC. Modern approaches represent the points in projective coordinate systems, *e.g.*, the López-Dahab (LD) projective coordinate [43], due to which the operations can be implemented as polynomials in the field.

Table 3. Point Addition circuit rectification against polynomial specification $D = B^2 \cdot (C + aZ_1^2)$. Time in seconds; Time-out = 5400 s; k: Operand width

k	# of Gates	Theorem 5.1	Algorithm 2	Mem
8	243	0.05	0.022	9.73 MB
16	1,277	3.48	0.019	88.78 MB
32	3,918	86.75	0.028	0.47 GB
64	1,5305	4,923	0.053	7.13 GB

Example 8.1. *Consider point addition in López-Dahab (LD) projective coordinate. Given an elliptic curve:* $Y^2 + XYZ = X^3 Z + aX^2 Z^2 + bZ^4$ *over* $\mathbb{F}_{2^k}$, *where* X, Y, Z *are* k-*bit vectors that are elements in* $\mathbb{F}_{2^k}$ *and similarly,* a, b *are constants from the field. We represent point addition over the elliptic curve as* $(X_3, Y_3, Z_3) = (X_1, Y_1, Z_1) + (X_2, Y_2, 1)$. *Then* X_3, Y_3, Z_3 *can be computed as follows:*

$$A = Y_2 \cdot Z_1^2 + Y_1 \qquad\qquad B = X_2 \cdot Z_1 + X_1$$
$$C = Z_1 \cdot B \qquad\qquad D = B^2 \cdot (C + aZ_1^2)$$
$$Z_3 = C^2 \qquad\qquad E = A \cdot C$$
$$X_3 = A^2 + D + E \qquad\qquad F = X_3 + X_2 \cdot Z_3$$
$$G = X_3 + Y_2 \cdot Z_3 \qquad\qquad Y_3 = E \cdot F + Z_3 \cdot G$$

Each of the polynomials in the above design are implemented as (gate-level) logic blocks and are interconnected to obtain final outputs X_3, Y_3 and Z_3. Table 3 shows the results for the block that computes $D = B^2 \cdot (C + aZ_1^2)$. Our approach can rectify up to 64-bit circuits.

Limitations of Our Approach: We also performed experiments where we apply Theorem 5.1 at a gate output which *cannot* rectify the circuit. We used the Montgomery multiplier as the specification and a Mastrovito multiplier as the implementation. For 4- and 8-bit word-lengths, the execution time of our approach was comparable to that of the SAT-based approach, and was ~ 0.1 s. For the 16-bit multipliers, the SAT-based approach completed in 0.11 s. On the other hand, application of Theorem 5.1 resulted in a memory explosion and consumed ~ 30 GB of memory within 5–6 min. This is due to the fact that when $1 \notin E_L + E_H$, then $GB(E_L + E_H)$ is not equal to $\{1\}$ and the Gröbner basis algorithm produces a very large output. To improve our approach we are working on term ordering heuristics so that our approach can perform efficiently in both cases. We also wish to employ other data-structures better suited to circuits, as SINGULAR's data structure is not very memory efficient. SINGULAR also has an upper limit on the number of variables (32,768) that can be accommodated in the system, limiting application to larger circuits.

9   Conclusion

This paper considers single-fix rectification of arithmetic circuits. The approach is applied after formal verification detects the presence of a bug in the design. We assume that post-verification debugging has been performed a set (X) of nets is provided as rectification targets. The paper presents necessary and sufficient conditions that ascertains whether a buggy circuit can be single-fix rectified at a net $x_i \in X$. When single-fix rectification is feasible, we compute a rectification polynomial function $x_i = U(X_{PI})$, which can be synthesized into a circuit. For this purpose, the paper introduces the notion of Craig interpolants in algebraic geometry in finite fields, proves their existence, and gives an effective procedure for their computation. Furthermore, we show how the rectification polynomial can be computed from algebraic interpolants. Experiments are performed over various finite field arithmetic circuits that show the efficiency of our approach as against SAT-based approaches. Limitations of our approach are also analyzed. We are currently investigating the extension of our approach to multi-fix rectification.

References

1. Ritirc, D., Biere, A., Kauers, M.: Column-wise verification of multipliers using computer algebra. In: Formal Methods in Computer-Aided Design (FMCAD), pp. 23–30 (2017)
2. Ciesielski, M., Yu, C., Brown, W., Liu, D., Rossi, A.: Verification of gate-level arithmetic circuits by function extraction. In: 52nd ACM/EDAC/IEEE Design Automation Conference (DAC), pp. 1–6 (2015)

3. Sayed-Ahmed, A., Große, D., Kühne, U., Soeken, M., Drechsler, R.: Formal verification of integer multipliers by combining Gröbner basis with logic reduction. In: Design, Automation Test in Europe Conference Exhibition (DATE), pp. 1048–1053 (2016)
4. Wienand, O., Wedler, M., Stoffel, D., Kunz, W., Greuel, G.-M.: An algebraic approach for proving data correctness in arithmetic data paths. In: Gupta, A., Malik, S. (eds.) CAV 2008. LNCS, vol. 5123, pp. 473–486. Springer, Heidelberg (2008). https://doi.org/10.1007/978-3-540-70545-1_45
5. Shekhar, N., Kalla, P., Enescu, F.: Equivalence verification of polynomial datapaths using ideal membership testing. IEEE Trans. CAD 26(7), 1320–1330 (2007)
6. Tew, N., Kalla, P., Shekhar, N., Gopalakrishnan, S.: Verification of arithmetic datapaths using polynomial function models and congruence solving. In: Proceedings of International Conference on Computer-Aided Design (ICCAD), pp. 122–128 (2008)
7. Lv, J., Kalla, P., Enescu, F.: Efficient Gröbner basis reductions for formal verification of Galois field arithmetic circuits. IEEE Trans. CAD 32(9), 1409–1420 (2013)
8. Pruss, T., Kalla, P., Enescu, F.: Efficient symbolic computation for word-level abstraction from combinational circuits for verification over finite fields. IEEE Trans. CAD 35(7), 1206–1218 (2016)
9. Lvov, A., Lastras-Montano, L., Trager, B., Paruthi, V., Shadowen, R., El-Zein, A.: Verification of Galois field based circuits by formal reasoning based on computational algebraic geometry. Form. Methods Syst. Des. 45(2), 189–212 (2014)
10. Sun, X., Kalla, P., Pruss, T., Enescu, F.: Formal verification of sequential Galois field arithmetic circuits using algebraic geometry. In: Proceedings of Design, Automation and Test in Europe (2015)
11. Cox, D., Little, J., O'Shea, D.: Ideals, Varieties, and Algorithms: An Introduction to Computational Algebraic Geometry and Commutative Algebra. Springer, New York (2007). https://doi.org/10.1007/978-0-387-35651-8
12. Adams, W.W., Loustaunau, P.: An Introduction to Gröbner Bases. American Mathematical Society, Providence (1994)
13. Madre, J.C., Coudert, O., Billon, J.P.: Automating the diagnosis and the rectification of design errors with PRIAM. In: Kuehlmann, A. (ed.) The Best of ICCAD. Springer, Boston (2003). https://doi.org/10.1007/978-1-4615-0292-0_2
14. Lin, C.C., Chen, K.C., Chang, S.C., Marek-Sadowska, M.: Logic synthesis for engineering change. In: Proceedings of Design Automation Conference (DAC), pp. 647–652 (1995)
15. Scholl, C., Becker, B.: Checking equivalence for partial implementations. In: Equivalence Checking of Digital Circuits. Springer, Boston (2004)
16. Tang, K.F., Wu, C.A., Huang, P.K., Huang, C.Y.: Interpolation-based incremental ECO synthesis for multi-error logic rectification. In: Proceedings of Design Automation Conference (DAC), pp. 146–151 (2011)
17. Craig, W.: Linear reasoning: a new form of the Herbrand-Gentzen theorem. J. Symb. Log. 22(3), 250–268 (1957)
18. Liaw, H.T., Tsaih, J.H., Lin, C.S.: Efficient automatic diagnosis of digital circuits. In: Proceedings of ICCAD, pp. 464–467 (1990)
19. Gitina, K., Reimer, S., Sauer, M., Wimmer, R., Scholl, C., Becker, B.: Equivalence checking of partial designs using dependency quantified Boolean formulae. In: IEEE International Conference on Computer Design (ICCD) (2013)

20. Jo, S., Matsumoto, T., Fujita, M.: SAT-based automatic rectification and debugging of combinational circuits with LUT insertions. In: IEEE 21st Asian Test Symposium (2012)
21. Fujita, M., Mishchenko, A.: Logic synthesis and verification on fixed topology. In: 22nd International Conference on Very Large Scale Integration (VLSI-SoC) (2014)
22. Fujita, M.: Toward unification of synthesis and verification in topologically constrained logic design. Proc. IEEE **103**, 2052–2060 (2015)
23. Wu, B.H., Yang, C.J., Huang, C.Y., Jiang, J.H.R.: A robust functional ECO engine by SAT proof minimization and interpolation techniques. In: International Conference on Computer Aided Design, pp. 729–734 (2010)
24. Ling, A.C., Brown, S.D., Safarpour, S., Zhu, J.: Toward automated ECOs in FPGAs. IEEE Trans. CAD **30**(1), 18–30 (2011)
25. Dao, A.Q., et al.: Efficient computation of ECO patch functions. In: 55th Design Automation Conference (DAC), pp. 51:1–51:6, June 2018
26. Gupta, U., Ilioaea, I., Rao, V., Srinath, A., Kalla, P., Enescu, F.: On the rectifiability of arithmetic circuits using Craig interpolants in finite fields. In: International Conference on Very Large Scale Integration (VLSI-SoC), pp. 49–54 (2018)
27. Ghandali, S., Yu, C., Liu, D., Brown, W., Ciesielski, M.: Logic debugging of arithmetic circuits. In: IEEE Computer Society Annual Symposium on VLSI (2015)
28. Farahmandi, F., Mishra, P.: Automated debugging of arithmetic circuits using incremental Gröbner basis reduction. In: IEEE International Conference on Computer Design (ICCD) (2017)
29. Farahmandi, F., Mishra, P.: Automated test generation for debugging arithmetic circuits. In: Proceedings of the 2016 Conference on Design, Automation & Test in Europe, DATE (2016)
30. McMillan, K.L.: Interpolation and SAT-based model checking. In: Hunt, W.A., Somenzi, F. (eds.) CAV 2003. LNCS, vol. 2725, pp. 1–13. Springer, Heidelberg (2003). https://doi.org/10.1007/978-3-540-45069-6_1
31. Lee, R.-R., Jiang, J.-H.R., Hung, W.-L.: Bi-decomposing large Boolean functions via interpolation and satisfiability solving. In: Proceedings of Design Automation Conference (DAC), pp. 636–641 (2008)
32. McMillan, K.: An interpolating theorem prover, theoretical computer science. In: Tools and Algorithms for the Construction and Analysis of Systems (TACAS 2004), vol. 345, no. 1, pp. 101–121 (2005)
33. Kapur, D., Majumdar, R., Zarba, G.: Interpolation for data-structures. In: Proceedings of ACM SIGSOFT International Symposium on Foundation of Software Engineering, pp. 105–116 (2006)
34. Cimatti, A., Griggio, A., Sebastiani, R.: Efficient interpolant generation in satisfiability modulo theories. In: Ramakrishnan, C.R., Rehof, J. (eds.) TACAS 2008. LNCS, vol. 4963, pp. 397–412. Springer, Heidelberg (2008). https://doi.org/10.1007/978-3-540-78800-3_30
35. Griggio, A.: Effective word-level interpolation for software verification. In: Formal Methods in Computer-Aided Design (FMCAD), pp. 28–36 (2011)
36. Gao, S., Platzer, A., Clarke, E.: Quantifier elimination over finite fields with Gröbner bases. In: Algebraic Informatics: 4th International Conference, CAI, pp. 140–157 (2011)
37. Gao, S.: Counting zeros over finite fields with Gröbner bases. Master's thesis, Carnegie Mellon University (2009)
38. Lv, J.: Scalable formal verification of finite field arithmetic circuits using computer algebra techniques. Ph.D. dissertation, Univ. of Utah, August 2012

39. Buchberger, B.: Ein Algorithmus zum Auffinden der Basiselemente des Restk-lassenringes nach einem nulldimensionalen Polynomideal. Ph.D. dissertation, University of Innsbruck (1965)
40. Buchberger, B.: A criterion for detecting unnecessary reductions in the construction of Gröbner-bases. In: Ng, E.W. (ed.) Symbolic and Algebraic Computation. LNCS, vol. 72, pp. 3–21. Springer, Heidelberg (1979). https://doi.org/10.1007/3-540-09519-5_52
41. Decker, W., Greuel, G.-M., Pfister, G., Schönemann, H.: Singular 4-1-0 – a computer algebra system for polynomial computations (2016). http://www.singular.uni-kl.de
42. Brayton, R., Mishchenko, A.: ABC: an academic industrial-strength verification tool. In: Touili, T., Cook, B., Jackson, P. (eds.) CAV 2010. LNCS, vol. 6174, pp. 24–40. Springer, Heidelberg (2010). https://doi.org/10.1007/978-3-642-14295-6_5
43. López, J., Dahab, R.: Improved algorithms for elliptic curve arithmetic in $GF(2^n)$. In: Tavares, S., Meijer, H. (eds.) SAC 1998. LNCS, vol. 1556, pp. 201–212. Springer, Heidelberg (1999). https://doi.org/10.1007/3-540-48892-8_16

Energy-Accuracy Scalable Deep Convolutional Neural Networks: A Pareto Analysis

Valentino Peluso and Andrea Calimera[✉]

Department of Control and Computer Engineering, Politecnico di Torino,
10129 Turin, Italy
{valentino.peluso,andrea.calimera}@polito.it

Abstract. This work deals with the optimization of Deep Convolutional Neural Networks (ConvNets). It elaborates on the concept of *Adaptive Energy-Accuracy Scaling* through *multi-precision* arithmetic, a solution that allows ConvNets to be adapted at run-time and meet different energy budgets and accuracy constraints. The strategy is particularly suited for embedded applications made run at the "edge" on resource-constrained platforms. After the very basics that distinguish the proposed adaptive strategy, the paper recalls the software-to-hardware vertical implementation of precision scalable arithmetic for ConvNets, then it focuses on the energy-driven per-layer precision assignment problem describing a meta-heuristic that searches for the most suited representation of both weights and activations of the neural network. The same heuristic is then used to explore the optimal trade-off providing the Pareto points in the energy-accuracy space. Experiments conducted on three different ConvNets deployed in real-life applications, i.e. Image Classification, Keyword Spotting, and Facial Expression Recognition, show adaptive ConvNets reach better energy-accuracy trade-off w.r.t. conventional static fixed-point quantization methods.

1 Introduction

Deep Neural Networks (DNNs) are computational models that emulate the activity of the human brain during pattern recognition. They consist of deep chains of neural layers that apply non-linear transformations on the input data [1]. The projection on the new feature-space enables a more efficient classification, achieving accuracies that are close, and in some cases even above, those scored by the human brain. Convolutional Neural Networks [2] (ConvNets hereafter) are the first example of DNNs applied to problems of human-level complexity. They have brought about breakthroughs in computer vision [3] and voice recognition [4], improving the state-of-the-art in many application domains. From a practical viewpoint, the forward pass through a ConvNet is nothing more than matrix multiplications between pre-trained parameters (the synaptic weights of the hidden neurons) and the input data.

© IFIP International Federation for Information Processing 2019
Published by Springer Nature Switzerland AG 2019
N. Bombieri et al. (Eds.): VLSI-SoC 2018, IFIP AICT 561, pp. 107–127, 2019.
https://doi.org/10.1007/978-3-030-23425-6_6

The most common use-case for ConvNets is image classification where a multi-channel image (e.g. RGB) is processed producing as output the probability that the subject depicted in the picture belongs to a specific class of objects or concepts (e.g. car, dog, airplane, etc.). One can see this end-to-end inference process as a kind of data compression: high-volume raw-data (the pixels of the image) are compressed into a highly informative tag (the resulting class). In this regard, the adoption on the Internet-of-Things (IoT) is disruptive: distributed smart-objects with embedded ConvNets may implement data-analytics at the edge, near the source of data [5], with advantages in terms of predictability of the service response time, energy efficiency, privacy and, in general, scalability of the IoT infrastructure.

The design of embedded ConvNets encompasses a training stage during which the synaptic weights of the hidden neurons are learned using a back-propagation algorithm (e.g. the Stochastic Gradient Descent [6]). The learning is supervised and accuracy-driven, namely, it adjusts the weights such that an accuracy loss function evaluated over a set of labeled samples is minimized. Once trained, the ConvNet can be flashed on the smart-object and deployed at the edge, where it runs inference on never occurred samples. To notice that ConvNets presented in the literature show different depth (number of layers) and size (number of neurons per layer); also the topology may change due to optional layers used to reduce the cardinality of the intermediate activations, e.g., local pooling layers, or their sparsity, e.g. Rectified Linear Units (ReLU). Regardless of the internal structure, ConvNets show a common characteristic, complexity. Even the most simple model, e.g. AlexNet [2] or the more compact MobileNets [7], show millions of synaptic weights to be stored and tens of thousands of matrix convolutions to be run [5]. This prevents their use on low-power embedded platforms which offer low storage capacity, low compute power, and limited energy budget. How to design ConvNets that fit the stringent resource constraints while preserving classification accuracy is the new challenge indeed.

Recent works introduced several optimization strategies, both at the software level and hardware level [8]. They mainly exploit the intrinsic redundancy of ConvNets in order to reduce (*i*) the number of weights/neurons (the so-called *pruning* methods) or (*ii*) the arithmetic precision (*quantization* methods) or (*iii*) both [9]. Precision scaling is of practical interest due to its simplicity and the solid theories developed in the past for DSP applications. It concurrently reduces the memory footprint (the lower the bit-width, the lower the memory footprint) and the execution latency (the lower the bit-width, the faster the execution). The use of fixed-point arithmetic with 16- and 8-bit [10] instead of the 32-bit floating-point, or even below, e.g. 6 and 4-bit [11], has shown remarkable savings with no, or very marginal accuracy drop. Aggressive binarization [12] is an alternative approach provided that large accuracy loss is acceptable. Obviously, the implementation of quantized ConvNets asks for integer units that can process data with reduced representations; recent hardware designs, both from industry and academia, follow this trend [13–15].

Most of the existing optimizations, both pruning and quantization, were originally conceived as static methods. Let's consider quantization. For a given ConvNet the numeric precision of the weights is defined at design-time and then kept constant during run-time. Therefore, the design effort is that of finding the proper bit-width such that accuracy losses are minimized [16]. Although effective, this approach is very conservative as inference always operates at full speed and hence under maximum resource usage. Adaptive strategies that speculate on the quality of results to reach higher energy efficiency are a more interesting option for portable devices deployed on non-critical missions [17]. There exist applications or use-cases for which the classification accuracy can be relaxed without affecting much the user perception, or, alternatively, conditions under which other extra-functional properties of the system, e.g. energy budget or latency, get higher priority. For such cases, one may use the arithmetic precision as a control knob to manage the resources. This concept of energy-accuracy scaling is a well-established technique for VLSI designs [18], while it represents a less explored option for ConvNets (and DNNs in general).

The idea of energy-accuracy scalable ConvNets through dynamic precision scaling was first introduced in [19] and then elaborated in [20] with the introduction of an energy-driven optimization framework. The method applies to software-programmable arithmetic accelerators where precision scaling is achieved through variable-latency Multiply & Accumulate (MAC) instructions. This implementation applies for any general purposes MCUs (e.g. [21]) or application-specific processors with a multi-precision instruction-set (e.g. Google TPU [22]); it can also be extended to dedicated architecture (both ASIC or FPGA accelerators [23]). This chapter further investigates on this strategy introducing a Pareto analysis of the energy-accuracy space. An optimization engine is used to identify the arithmetic precision that minimizes energy and accuracy loss concurrently. The obtained precision settings can be loaded at run-time with minimal overhead thus to allow ConvNets to reach the operating conditions that satisfy the requirements imposed at the system-level. As test-benches we used three real-life applications built upon state-of-the-art ConvNets, i.e. Image Classification [24], Keyword Spotting [25], and Facial Expression Recognition [26]. Experimental results suggest the proposed strategy is a practical solution for the development of flexible, yet efficient IoT applications.

The remaining sections are organized as follows. Section 2 gives an overview of related works in the field. Section 3 describes the implementation details for the single weight-set multi-precision arithmetic used in scalable ConvNets. Section 4 recalls the optimization engine and the energy-accuracy models adopted. Finally, Sect. 5 shows the Pareto analysis over the three benchmarks and the performance of the optimization heuristic.

2   Related Works

With the emerging of the edge-computing paradigm, the reduction of ConvNets complexity has become the new challenge for the IoT segment. The problem is being addressed from different perspectives: with the design of custom hardware that improves the execution of data-intensive loops achieving energy efficiencies of few pico-Joules/operation [11,27]; with new learning strategies that generate less complex networks [28]; with iso-accuracy compression techniques aimed at squeezing the model complexity. A thorough review is reported in [29]. To notice that while many existing techniques are conceived as static methods, the dynamic management of ConvNets is a less explored field. This work deals with this latter aspect.

2.1 Adaptive ConvNets

Following the recent literature, the concept of adaptive ConvNets may have multiple interpretations and hence different implementations. On the one hand, there are solutions that adapt to the complexity of the input data. On the other hand, solutions that adapt to external conditions or triggers, regardless of data complexity.

The former class is mainly represented by techniques that implement the general principle of coarse-to-fine computation [30]. These methods make use of branches in the internal network topology generating *conditional* deep neural nets [31]. In its most simple implementation, a conditional ConvNet is made up of a chain of two classifiers, a *coarse* classifier (for "easy" inputs) and a *fine* classifier (for "hard" inputs) [32]; the *coarse* classifier is always-on, while the *fine* classifier is occasionally activated for "hard" inputs (statistically less frequent). As a result, ConvNets can adapt to the complexity of data at run-time. An extension with deeper chains of quantized micro-classifiers is proposed in [33], while in [34] authors propose the use of Dynamic Voltage Accuracy Frequency Scaling (DVAFS) for the recognition of objects of different complexity.

Concerning the second class, that is the main target of this work, adaptivity is achieved by tuning the computational effort of the ConvNet depending on the desired accuracy. The control knob is the arithmetic precision of the convolutional layers. The work described in [19] is along this direction as it introduces an HW-SW co-design to implement multi-precision arithmetic at run-time. Depending on the parallelism of the HW integer units (e.g. 16- or 8-bits), weights can be loaded and processed using different bit-widths thus to achieve different degrees of accuracy under different energy budgets. This is the enabler for accuracy-energy scaling adaptive ConvNets. To notice that unlike static quantization methods where different accuracy levels could be achieved using multiple pre-trained weight-sets stored as separate entities, here the precision scaling is achieved using a single set of weights and incomplete arithmetic operations. The same strategy is adopted in this work.

Hybrid solutions may jointly exploit the complexity of the input problem with the accuracy imposed at the application level. For instance, the authors of [35] introduce the concept of multi-level classification where the classification task can be performed at different levels of semantic abstraction: the higher the abstraction, the easier the classification problem. Then, depending on the abstraction level and the desired accuracy, the ConvNet is tuned to achieve the maximum energy efficiency.

2.2 Fixed-Point Quantization

Since the multi-precision strategy adopted in this work encompasses the quantization to fixed-point, this subsection gives a brief taxonomy of the existing literature on the subject.

Complexity reduction through fixed-point quantization exploits the characteristics of the weight distributions across different convolutional layers in order to find the most efficient data representation [36]. Two main stages are involved: the definition of the *bit-width*, i.e. the data parallelism, and the *radix-point scaling*, i.e. the position of the radix point. A common practice is to define the bit-width depending on hardware availability (e.g. 16-, 8-bit for most of the architectures), then find the radix-point position that minimizes the quantization error. The existing techniques, mainly from the DSP theory, differ in the radix-point scaling scheme. A complete review is out of the scope of this work and the interested reader can refer to [8]. It is worth emphasizing that a one-size-fits-all solution does not exist as efficiency is affected by the kind of neural networks under analysis and the characteristics of the adopted hardware.

A more relevant discriminant factor is the spatial granularity at which the fixed-point format is applied, *per-net* or *per-layer*. In the former case all the layers share the same representation; in the latter case, each layer has its own representation. Since the weights distribution may substantially differ from layer to layer, a finer, i.e. per-layer, approach achieves lower accuracy loss [36].

Whatever the granularity is, existing works from the machine-learning community, e.g. [36,37], focused on accuracy-driven optimal precision scaling. Only a few papers take hardware resources into account, which is paramount when dealing with embedded systems. The authors of [16] briefly describe a greedy approach where low precision is assigned starting from the first layer of the net (topological order) without considering the complexity of the layer. In [10] authors describe the design of embedded ConvNets for FPGAs and propose a per-layer precision scaling that is aware of the number of memory accesses. Only very few works, e.g. [20,29], bring energy consumption as a direct variable in the optimization loop.

3 Energy-Accuracy Scalable Convolution

The proposed adaptive ConvNet strategy leverages precision scalable arithmetic. This section introduces a possible implementation of matrix convolution using software-programmable multi-precision Multiply & Accumulate (MAC) instructions. It first describes the algorithmic details, then it presents a custom processing element that accelerates the variable-latency MAC with minimal design overhead.

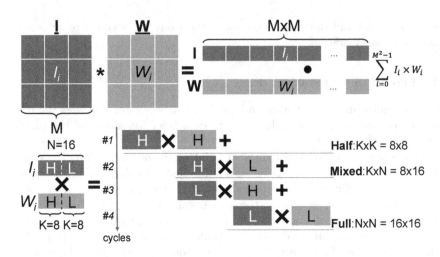

Fig. 1. Iterative multiply-accumulate algorithm.

3.1 SW: Multiprecision Convolution

For a given layer in a ConvNet, the convolution between the $M \times M$ input map matrix $\underline{I}$ and the $M \times M$ weight matrix of a kernel $\underline{W}$ is the dot-product of the two unrolled vectors I and W of length $(M \times M)$. The dot-product between I and W is the sum of the $(M \times M)$ products $I_i \times W_i$, as shown in Fig. 1.

Assuming a N-bit fixed-point representation ($N = 16$ in this work), I_i and W_i can be seen as two concatenated halfwords of $K = N/2$ bits ($K = 8$); the most significant parts I_i^H and W_i^H and the least significant parts I_i^L and W_i^L. As pictorially described in Fig. 1, each single product $I_i \times W_i$ is implemented by means of a four-cycles procedure where the most significant and least significant halfwords are iteratively multiplied, shifted and accumulated. To notice that I_i^H and W_i^H are signed integers, I_i^L and W_i^L are unsigned. Different precision options can be reached by stopping the execution at earlier cycles: *half* $(K \times K)$ 1 cycle, *mixed* $(K \times N)$ 2 cycles and *full* $(N \times N$-bit$)$ 4 cycles; an additional *mixed* precision option $(N \times K)$ is also obtained by swapping the second and the third cycle (2 cycles).

The same four options can be extended to the dot-product procedure as described in Algorithm 1. At *half*-precision, both the operands I_i and W_i are reduced to K bits. The first loop (lines 1–2) operates on the most significant parts I_i^H, W_i^H. The result is then returned (line 3). At *mixed*-precision, only one operand, the input I_i (or the weight W_i, not shown in the pseudo-code), is reduced to K bits. First, the partial result r is shifted of K-bits (line 4), then the second loop (lines 5–6) iterates on I_i^H and W_i^L (I_i^L and W_i^H) and the result is returned (line 7). At *full*-precision, both W_i and I_i are taken as N bit operands. In this case the last two loops (lines 8–12) come into play and they iterate on the least significant parts W_i^L and I_i (both H and L) thus to complete the remaining part of the product. To summarize, with $N = 16$, the available precision options

---

Algorithm 1. Iterative multiply-accumulate algorithm

    Input: I, W, *precision*
    Output: Dot-Product r
1 **for** $i = 0$; $i < M$; $i = i + 1$ **do**
2 | $r = r + I_i^H \times W_i^H$
3 **if** $(precision{=}{=}half)$ **then return** r ;   `// half:KxK`
4 $r = r \ll K$
5 **for** $i = 0$; $i < M$; $i = i + 1$ **do**
6 | $r = r + I_i^H \times W_i^L$
7 **if** $(precision{=}{=}mixed)$ **then return** r ;   `// mixed:KxN`
8 **for** $i = 0$; $i < M$; $i = i + 1$ **do**
9 | $r = r + I_i^L \times W_i^H$
10 $r = r \ll K$
11 **for** $i = 0$; $i < M$; $i = i + 1$ **do**
12 | $r = r + I_i^L \times W_i^L$
13 **return** r ;   `// full:NxN`

---

are: *half* ($K \times K$, i.e. 8×8), *mixed* ($N \times K$, i.e. 16×8 or $K \times N$, i.e. 8×16), *full* ($N \times N$, i.e. 16×16). Given the regular structure of the algorithm, all them can be implemented on the same $K \times K$ MAC unit.

    This straightforward algorithm offers a simple way to adjust the precision of the results and the resource usage. Firstly, it allows the computational effort, and hence the energy consumption, to scale with the arithmetic precision; secondly, it alleviates the memory bandwidth as less bits need to be moved from/to the memory banks at lower precisions[1].

3.2 HW: Variable-Latency Processing Element

Figure 2 gives the RTL-view of the proposed processing element (PE) for $N = 16$. The PE is composed by 9×9 multiplier, where the 9th bit is used for the sign extension of the operands. As described in the previous subsection, the most significant parts (I_i^H, W_i^H) are signed, while the least significant parts (I_i^L, W_i^L) are unsigned. Therefore, the MSB of (I_i^L, W_i^L) belongs to the module, while that of (I_i^H, W_i^H) is the sign. In order to account for this issue we implemented the following mechanism: when (I_i^H, W_i^H) are processed, the sign is extended to the 9th by concatenating the MSB (i.e. the sign) of I and W; when (I_i^L, W_i^L) are processed a 0 is concatenated. The selection is done through the control signals *signed-I* and *signed-W* driven by the local control unit (omitted in the picture for the sake of space). The same control unit is in charge of feeding the MAC with the right sequence of data (H or L) fetched from a local memory.

    The accumulator has 16 guard bits and an embedded saturation logic to handle underflow and overflow. The role of the programmable shifter is two-fold. First, to shift the partial results when needed (see Algorithm 1). Second,

---

[1] We assume the availability of memories that support both word (N-bit) and halfword (K-bit) accesses [38].

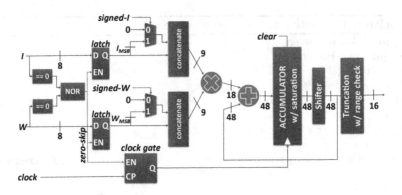

Fig. 2. 8 × 8 HW unit for multi-precision MAC.

to implement the dynamic fixed point arithmetic by moving the radix point of the final accumulation result depending on the desired fractional length [39]. A *range check* logic drives bit saturation if the result does not fit the word-length.

In order to minimize the dynamic power consumption, a *zero-skipping* strategy [34] is implemented by means of latch-based operand isolation and clock-gating. If one of the operands is zero, then the latches prevent the propagation of inputs minimizing the switching activity, while the clock-gating cell disables the clock signal thus reducing the equivalent load capacitance of the clock signal.

3.3   Hardware Characterization

The proposed SW-HW precision scaling strategy can be implemented using both FPGA and ASIC technologies. In this work we designed and characterized the 8 × 8 MAC unit using a commercial 28 nm UTBB FDSOI technology and the Synopsys Galaxy Platform, versions L-2016.03. The frequency constraint is set to 1 GHz at 0.90 V in a typical process corner (compliant with recent works that used the same technology [40]). Power consumption is extracted using Synopsys PrimeTime L-2016.06 with SAIF back-annotation. Collected results show a standard cell area of 1443 μm² and total average power consumption of 0.95 mW. Compared to a traditional 8×8 MAC unit, the proposed architecture shows 3.7% area penalty.

Table 1. Energy/MAC vs precision

Precision ($I \times W$)	N_{cycles}	E_{MAC} (pJ)
16 × 16	4	3.80
16 × 8	2	1.90
8 × 16	2	1.90
8 × 8	1	0.95

Table 1 shows the latency (N_{cycles}) and the energy consumption per MAC operation (E_{MAC}) for the four precisions available. As one can see, each row in the table corresponds to a different implementation point in the precision-energy space. If one of the two operands is zero, energy E_{zero} reduces substantially due to the zero-skipping logic: $E_{\mathrm{zero}} = 0.103 E_{\mathrm{MAC}}$.

4   Energy-Driven Precision Assignment

4.1   Fixed-Point Quantization

The shift from floating-point to fixed-point is a well-known problem in the DSP domain. In this sub-section, we review the basic theory and the main aspects involving this work.

A floating-point value V can be represented with a binary word Q of N bits using the following mapping function:

$$V = Q \cdot 2^{-FL} \tag{1}$$

FL indicates the fraction length, i.e. the position of the radix-point in Q. Given a set of real values, the choice of N and FL affects the information loss due to quantization. Since the bit-width N is usually given as a design constraint (e.g. 16-bit in this work), the problem reduces to searching the optimal FL (the integer length IL is then given by N-IL). The choice of FL affects the maximum representable value $|V_{\mathrm{max}}|$ and the minimum quantization error Q_{step}. Concerning $|V_{\mathrm{max}}|$, the relationship is described in the following equation:

$$FL = \left\lfloor \log_2 \left(\frac{2^{BW-1} - 1}{|V_{\mathrm{max}}|} \right) \right\rfloor \tag{2}$$

A trade-off does exit: the lower the FL the lower the V_{max}; the larger the FL the lower the Q_{step}. The decision of which constraint to guard more ($|V_{\mathrm{max}}|$ or Q_{step}) mainly depends on the distribution of the original floating-point weights and their importance in the neural model under quantization.

A dynamic fixed-point scheme is implemented where the fraction length is defined layer-by-layer. The FL_{opt} that minimizes the L2 distance between the original 32-bit floating point values and the quantized values is searched among $N - 1$ possible values. The search is done over a calibration set built by randomly picking 100 samples from the training set. To be noted that our problem formulation applies a symmetric linear quantization using a binary radix-point scaling.

As an additional piece of information, it is important to underline that quantization is not followed by retraining, a very time-consuming procedure even for small ConvNets.

4.2   Multiprecision Fixed-Point ConvNets

Problem Formulation. For a ConvNet of L layers, the classification accuracy can be scaled to different values by optimally selecting the arithmetic precision of each layer. The choice of such optimal precision should be done for the *input map* (**I**) and the *weight* (**W**) matrices of each layer each layer i, and for the *output map* matrix (**O**) of the last layer[2].

Assuming the availability of the four accuracy options described in Sect. 3, i.e. *full* (16 × 16), *mixed* (16 × 8 or 8 × 16), *half* (8 × 8), the precision for **I** and **W** of each layer, and that of **O** for last layer, can be assigned to 8-bit or 16-bit. We encode the unknown of the problem as a vector X of $(2 \times L + 1)$ Boolean variables x_i, where the variable $x_{2 \times L + 1}$ refers to **O**. The encoding map is: $x = 0 \rightarrow$ 8-bit, $x = 1 \rightarrow$ 16-bit. The optimal assignment is the one that minimizes the total energy consumption $E(X)$ while ensuring an accuracy loss $\lambda(X)$ lower than a user-defined constraint $\lambda_{\max}$.

Energy-Driven Precision Assignment. The optimal precision assignment to each layer is carried out using a custom meta-heuristic based on Simulated Annealing (SA). Algorithm 2 shows the pseudo-code of the SA. It gets as inputs the parameters listed in Table 2.

Table 2. Simulated annealing hyper-parameters

T_0	Initial temperature
T_f	Final temperature
X_0	Starting solution
cooling	Temperature derating factor (*geometric* in our case)
K_b	Normalization factor of the acceptance probability
iter	Number of iterations for each temperature T
$\lambda_{\max}$	User-defined accuracy drop (percentage)
cal_set	Calibration set size

In all the experiments, the starting solution X_0 is the full-precision (16-bit) to all the L layers (both **I** and **W**, and **O**. The estimation of the accuracy drop is done on a subset of images randomly picked from the training set, referred to as the calibration set. Its size is defined by the *cal_set* parameter.

At each iteration, the next state is generated as a random perturbation of the current state (line 6). For those states that satisfy the accuracy constraint (line 7), the energy cost function E is evaluated (line 8) through the function *energy*. If ΔE (line 9) reduces (line 10), the new state is accepted (lines 11–12).

---

[2] The precision of **O** does not impact computation as it only affects the number of memory accesses.

Algorithm 2. Simulated Annealing

Input: T_0, T_f, X_0, cooling, K_b, iter, $\lambda_t extrmmax$, cal_set

Output: X

1 $T = T_0$
2 $E = $ energy(X_0)
3 $E_{max} = $ energy $(ones\ (2L+1))$; $E_{min} = $ energy $(zeros\ (2L+1))$
4 **while** $(T \geq T_f)$ **do**
5   **for** $i = 0$; $i < $ iter; $i = i+1$ **do**
6          $next\_state = move\ (current\_state)$
7   **if** $accuracy\_drop(next\_state, cal\_set, tested) < \lambda_{max}$ **then**
8              $E\_next = energy\ (next\_state)$
9              $\Delta E = (E\_next - E\_current)\ /\ (E_{max} - E_{min})$
10   **if** $(dE < 0)$ or $(exp[-\Delta E / K_b \cdot T] > random(0,\ 1))$ **then**
11   current_state = next_state
12   E_current = E_new
13   **if** $E\_current < E\_best$ **then**
14   E_best = E_current
15   best_state = current_state
16         $update(tested)$
17     $T = T \cdot cooling$
18 **return** $best\_state$

If not, the new state is accepted following a Boltzmann probability function (lines 10–12); the acceptance ratio gets smaller as T reduces. States that show minimum energy are iteratively saved as best solutions (lines 13–15). Once the total number of iterations is reached (line 5), the temperature T is cooled down (line 17). The process iterates till the minimum temperature T_f is reached (line 4).

The bottleneck of the algorithm is the call to the function *accuracy_drop*. For this reason, the algorithm takes trace of already processed states; this information is fed to the *accuracy_drop* function which can eventually by-pass accuracy estimation (line 16).

Energy. The system-level architecture depicted in Fig. 3 serves as a general template to describe Application-Specific Processors for ConvNets computing, e.g. [11]. It consists of a planar array of processing elements (PE), in our case the MAC units described in Sect. 3, a set of SRAM buffers for storing temporal data (Input Buffer, Weight Buffer, and Output Buffer), an off-chip memory (DRAM) and its DMA, a control unit (RISC) that schedules the operations.

The total energy consumption E is the sum of two main contributions: $E = E^{comp} + E^{mem}$. E^{comp} is the energy consumed by the PE array, E^{mem} is the energy consumed due to data movement through the memory hierarchy.

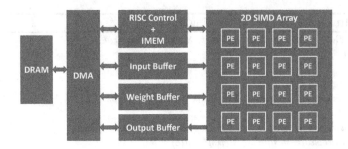

Fig. 3. Architectural template of ConvNet accelerators.

The first term is defined as:

$$E^{\text{comp}} = \sum_{i=1}^{L} E^{\text{MAC}} \cdot N_{\text{cycles}}(x_i) \cdot N_i^{\text{MAC}} + E^{\text{zero}} \cdot N_i^{\text{zero}} \quad (3)$$

L is the number of layers of the ConvNet. E^{MAC} is the energy consumption of the *half*-precision MAC (row 8×8 in Table 1). N_{cycles} is the latency of a single MAC operation of the i-th layer; it is given as multiple of the latency of the *half*-precision MAC (row 8×8 in Table 1) and it is function of the precision x_i. N_i^{MAC} is the number of non-zero MAC operations of the i-th layer. E_i^{zero} is the energy consumed under zero-skipping (mostly due to leakage). N_i^{zero} is the number of zero MAC.

The second term is defined as:

$$E^{\text{mem}} = \sum_{i=1}^{2 \cdot L + 1} E^{\text{MAC}} \cdot [\alpha_i(x_i) + \beta_i(x_i) + \gamma_i(x_i)] \quad (4)$$

E^{MAC} is the same as in Eq. 3, while α_i, β_i and γ_i are three parameters that describe the energy consumed by the i-th layer due to reading/writing the *input map* (α_i), the *weights* (β_i), the *output map* (γ_i). More specifically they represent the ratio between the energy consumption of the memory and the energy consumption of the PE array; here again, the energy unit is the *half*-precision MAC (row 8×8 in Table 1) [11]. Obviously, α and β do not contribute for the final output layer: $\alpha_{L+1} = 0$ and $\beta_{L+1} = 0$.

All the three parameters are function of the layer precision x_i: both fetch and write-back operations depend on (i) the accuracy of the MAC algorithm, and (ii) the number of zero-multiplications (switching activity to/from memory may change substantially). Moreover α_i, β_i, γ_i change depending on the ConvNet model: number and size of weights/channels per layer, stride and padding. Finally, they also differ depending on the size of the hardware components (PE array, and global buffers). Since the target of this work is not the energy model per se, not even the evaluation of different architectural solutions, α_i, β_i, γ_i are extracted for the architecture proposed in [11] and then scaled to our precision reduction strategy. The same E^{mem} model applies to different architectures by proper tuning of the three parameters.

Accuracy Drop. The accuracy drop is computed as the ratio between the number of miss-classified images and the total number of images in the calibration set (*cal_set*), hence its estimation implies the execution of S feed-forward inferences using the quantized fixed-point model (S as the cardinality of *cal_set*).

Unfortunately, common GPUs do not have integer units. To address this issue we implemented the *fake* quantization proposed in [37]. It is a SW strategy that emulates the loss of information due to fixed-point arithmetic still using floating-point data-type. Each layer is wrapped with a software module that converts its input data and weights (32-bit floating-point) into a *fake* integer, namely, still a 32-bit floating-point number subtracted of an amount equal to the error that the fixed-point representation would have brought. The advantage is that all the fixed-point operations are physically run by the high-performance FP units.

5 Results

5.1 Experimental Set-up

The objective of this work is to provide a Pareto analysis of adaptive ConvNets implemented with the proposed energy-accuracy scaling strategy. As benchmarks we adopted three different applications which are reaching widespread use in several domains: Image Classification (IC), Keyword Spotting (KWS), Facial Expression Recognition (FER). Additional details provided in the next subsection. The exploration in the energy-accuracy space is conducted using the SA engine introduced in Sect. 4. More specifically, the algorithm is made run under different accuracy loss constraints, from 1% to 15% with step 1%, and collecting the energy consumption reached by the optimal precision settings.

Table 3 summarizes the SA parameters used in the experiments. For all the networks we selected the same hyper-parameters, except for the number of iterations *iter* at a given temperature T. As described in the next sub-section, the three ConvNets have different number of layers, hence different complexity; as the cardinality of the search space increases, more iterations are needed to explore the cost function.

Table 3. Simulated annealing hyper-parameters values

	IC	KWS	FER
T_0	512		
T_f	2.5		
K_b	1e$-$2		
cooling	2.5		
iter	10	10^2	10^3
λ_{max}	1%–15%, step 1%		
cal_set	2000		

5.2   Benchmarks

Image Classification (IC): the typical image recognition on the popular *CIFAR-10* dataset. The dataset collects 60000 32×32 RGB images [24] evenly split in 10 classes, with 50000 and 10000 samples for the train-set and test-set respectively. The adopted ConvNet is taken from the Caffe framework [41], which consists of three convolutional layers interleaved with max-pooling and one fully-connected layer.

The three benchmarks under analysis serve very different purposes; their functionality and main characteristics, as well as their training set, are described separately therefore.

Keyword Spotting (KWS): a standard problem in the field of speech recognition. We considered a simplified version of the problem[3]. The reference dataset is the Speech Commands Dataset [25]; it counts of $65k$ 1 s-long audio samples collected during the repetition of 30 different words by thousands of different people. The goal is to recognize 10 specific keywords, i.e. "Yes", "No", "Up", "Down","Left", "Right", "On", "Off", "Stop", "Go", out of the 30 available words; samples that do not fall in these 10 categories are labeled as "unknown".

Table 4. Benchmarks overview. Considering that each convolutional layer with shape (ch, k_h, k_w), fully-connected with shape (ch), and max-pooling layer with shape (k_h, k_w). Where k_h and k_w are respectively the kernel height and width, while ch denotes the number of output channels.

Application	IC		KWS		FER	
Dataset	CIFAR-10 [24]		Speech Commands [25]		FER2013 [26]	
Input Shape	$3 \times 32 \times 32$		$1 \times 32 \times 40$		$1 \times 48 \times 48$	
Model Architecture	Conv2d	(32,5,5)	Conv2d	(186,32,8)	Conv2d	(32,3,3)
	MaxPool2d	(3,3)	MaxPool2d	(1,1)	Conv2d	(32,3,3)
	Conv2d	(32,5,5)	Conv2d	(64,10,4)	Conv2d	(32,3,3)
	MaxPool2d	(3,3)	Linear	(32)	MaxPool2d	(2,2)
	Conv2d	(64,5,5)	Linear	(128)	Conv2d	(64,3,3)
	MaxPool2d	(3,3)	Linear	(128)	Conv2d	(64,3,3)
	Linear	(10)	Linear	(12)	Conv2d	(64,3,3)
					MaxPool2d	(2,2)
					Conv2d	(128,3,3)
					Conv2d	(128,3,3)
					Conv2d	(128,3,3)
					MaxPool2d	(2,2)
					Linear	(7)
Top-1 Acc	83.04%		80.94%		65.67%	
#MACs	12 298 240		504 128		149 331 456	
#Op. Points	512		8 192		2 097 152	

---

[3] https://www.tensorflow.org/tutorials/sequences/audio_recognition.

There is also an additional "silence" class made up of background noise samples (pink noise, white noise, and human-made sounds). The training set and test set collect 56196 and 7518, respectively. The adopted ConvNet is the *cnn-one-fstride4* described in [42]; it has two convolutional layers, one max-pooling layer and four fully-connected layers. The ConvNet is fed with the spectrogram of the recorded signal which is obtained through the pre-processing pipeline introduced in [42] (extraction of $time \times frequency = 32 \times 40$ inputs w/o any data augmentation).

Facial Expression Recognition (FER): it is about inferring the emotional state of people from their facial expression. Quite popular in the field of vision reasoning, this task is very challenging as many face images might convey multiple emotions. The reference dataset is the *Fer2013* dataset given by the Kaggle competition [26]. It collects 32297 48×48 gray-scale facial images split into 7 categories, i.e. "Angry", "Disgust", "Fear", "Happy", "Sad", "Surprise", "Neutral". The training set counts of 28708 examples, while the remaining 3589 are in the test set. The adopted ConvNet[4] consists of nine convolutional layers evenly spaced by three max-polling layers, and one fully-connected layer.

Each benchmark is powered by a different model whose topology is described in Table 4. Within the same table we also collected additional information: the top-1 classification accuracy achieved with the original 32-bit floating-point model (Top-1 Acc.) training w/o any optimization; the overall number of MAC instructions for one inference run using 32-bit floating-point representations (#MAC); the number of possible precision configurations, namely the number of possible operating points in the parameters space (#Op. Points).

Concerning the Top-1 accuracy reported in Table 4, the results are consistent with the state-of-the-art. They were obtained with a dedicated training and testing framework integrated into PyTorch, version 0.4.1, with the following settings: 150 training epochs using the Adam algorithm [43]; learning rate 1e−3; linear decay 0.1 every 50 epochs; batch size of 128 samples randomly picked from the training set; non-overlapping testing set and training set.

5.3   Results

Table 5 shows the top-1 prediction accuracy achieved with a coarse *per-net* precision scaling scheme in which all the layers share the same precision.

The table collects the results for the original 32-bit floating-point model and the four fixed-point precision options made available with the multi-precision arithmetic described in Sect. 3. To notice that we do not run any retraining after quantization. This allows storing a single set of weights for any desired precision. Previous works suggest a re-training stage to recover the loss due to quantization and this would imply that each precision is coupled with a different fine-tuned model. What we propose instead is the use of a unique set of weights trained at full-precision (i.e. 16-bit for both weights and activations), then, at

---

[4] Inspired by https://github.com/JostineHo/mememoji.

Table 5. Per-net precision scaling: top-1 accuracy

	32-bit FP	*full* 16×16 Fix	*mixed* 8×16 Fix	*mixed* 16×8 Fix	*half* 8×8 Fix
IC	83.04%	83.04%	82.27%	73.07%	73.93%
KWS	80.94%	80.92%	79.99%	77.26%	76.97%
FER	65.67%	65.70%	64.31%	62.78%	59.04%

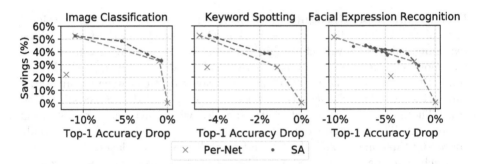

Fig. 4. Operating points. Accuracy drop normalized w.r.t. full precision (16 × 16). (Color figure online)

run-time, data are fetched and processed with the right precision. This is the key advantage of the proposed multi-precision scheme and the main enabler for adaptive ConvNets.

As reported in the table, the full-precision fixed-point ConvNets (column 16×16 Fix) keeps almost the same accuracy of the original floating-point model (the maximum relative drop is 0.02% for KWS). The results are in line with previous works and motivate the choice of 16 × 16 as the baseline for comparison. Concerning the mixed-precision options, 8×16 assigns 8-bit to input maps (I) and 16-bit to the weights (W); 16×8 does the opposite. The 8×16 option is by far more accurate than 16×8: minimum drop of 0.93% for **IC**; maximum drop of 2.07% for **FER**. The half-precision (column 8×8) shows larger loss: minimum drop of 4.90% for **KWS**; maximum drop 10.97% for **IC**. These numbers suggest the per-net granularity is too weak for effective deployment of adaptive ConvNets. Among the four available precision options, a very small set per se, only three are of practical use, i.e. 16×16, 8×16, 16×8. Indeed, when precision is reduced to 8 × 8 all the three benchmarks show a dramatic quality degradation. For instance, when shifted from 8 × 16 to 8 × 8, the **IC** shows a 10× drop (from 0.93% to 10.97%). This calls for a finer precision assignment policy, which is the technique proposed in this work.

A detailed analysis of the results is provided by means of a Pareto analysis, Fig. 4. The plots show the possible operating points in the energy-accuracy space achieved with a per-net precision scaling (blue ×) and the proposed per-layer precision scaling (red •). Each point comes with a different precision setting.

Table 6. Comparison between the per-net precision scaling and the per-layer precision scaling with the proposed SA optimization: the collected statistics refer to the Pareto curves of the two solutions (full-precision excluded).

	Optimization	# Op. Points	Av. Drop	Av. Savings	Av. Exec. Time
IC	Per-Net	2	−5.95	42.56	-
	SA	4	−4.84	42.83	8 s
KWS	Per-Net	2	−3.52	40.09	-
	SA	4	−2.93	44.95	13 s
FER	Per-Net	2	−6.13	41.41	-
	SA	8	−4.60	39.83	66 min 18 s

The accuracy drop and the energy savings are normalized with respect to full-precision (rightmost × marker with 0% accuracy drop). The dotted lines connect the points at the Pareto frontier. As aforementioned, with the per-net granularity only three among four points are Pareto. Moreover, the shift from one operating point to another is very coarse with substantial accuracy drop. The advantage of the per-layer is twofold. First, the Pareto curve is more dense and hence it gives more options for a finer control; this aspect is evident in larger ConvNets (e.g. **FER**). Second, the Pareto curve is dominating the per-net solutions, thus enabling larger (or comparable) average energy savings.

Table 6 reports some statistics over the subset of Pareto points, both per-net and per-layer. The column *#Op. Points* gives the number of Pareto Points; column *Av. Drop* refer to the accuracy drop averaged over the Pareto points; column *Av. Savings* does the same for the energy savings. For all the three benchmarks the energy-accuracy scaling operated with an optimal per-layer multi-precision assignment ensures optimality and usability on several context scenarios. Table 6 also shows the average execution time taken by the SA engine to draw a Pareto point, column *Av. Exec. Time*. Results are collected on a workstation powered by an Intel i7-8700K CPU and an NVIDIA GTX-1080 GPU with CUDA 9.0. As expected, time gets larger with network complexity. For the largest benchmark (**FER**) the tool consumes 66 min and 18 s.

A viable option to improve performance is to reduce the granularity at which the SA explores the parameters space. This can be achieved by constraining the number of iterations for each explored temperature T (parameter *iter* in Table 2). A quantitative comparison is given in Fig. 5, whose plot shows the Pareto curves obtained with *iter* = 1000 (the original value), 500 and 250 for the **FER** benchmark. The execution time reduces linearly, i.e. (66 min, 18 s) with *iter* = 1000, (33 min, 35 s) with *iter* = 500, (16 min, 36 s) with *iter* = 250, while the quality of results reveal more interesting trends. Whereas it is generally true that a larger *iter* leads to better absolute numbers, the gain practically fades when considering the relative distance between the obtained curves. With *iter* = 1000 the average savings across the Pareto points (39.3%) is just 5% larger than that obtained

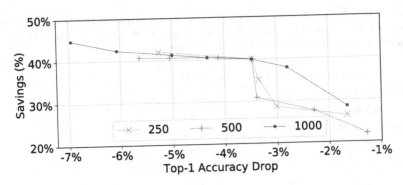

Fig. 5. Pareto analysis for **FER** benchmark using different number of iterations during the SA evolution: 1000, 500, 250.

using $iter = 500$ (34.6%) and $iter = 250$ (34.4%); both $iter = 1000$ and $iter = 500$ collects the same number of Pareto points, 7 overall; only with $iter = 250$ the number of Pareto points reduces from 7 to 5. This analysis suggests that for larger ConvNets there's a margin for tuning the SA to reasonable execution time w/o degrading much the quality.

6   Conclusions

The evolution of ConvNets has been driven by accuracy improvement. High accuracy reflected on large-scale network topologies which turned the inference into a too expensive task for low-power, energy-constrained embedded systems. ConvNets compression is therefore an urgent need for the growth of neural computing at the edge. While most of the existing techniques mainly focus on static optimizations, dynamic resource management represents a viable option to further improve energy efficiency. This chapter introduced a practical implementation of adaptive ConvNets. The proposed strategy allows ConvNets to relax their computational effort, and hence their energy consumption, leveraging the accuracy margin typical of non-critical applications. The technique is built upon a low overhead implementation of dynamic multi-precision arithmetic. The resulting ConvNets are free to move in the energy-accuracy space achieving better trade-offs. A Pareto analysis conducted on three representative applications (Image Recognition, Keyword Spotting, Facial Expression Recognition) quantified the energy savings suggesting potential improvement for the Simulated Annealing (SA) optimization engine. Future works will bring this adaptive strategy to larger ConvNets deployed on real HW implementations.

References

1. LeCun, Y., Bengio, Y., Hinton, G.: Deep learning. Nature **521**(7553), 436–444 (2015)
2. Krizhevsky, A., Sutskever, I., Hinton, G.E.: ImageNet classification with deep convolutional neural networks. In: Advances in Neural Information Processing Systems, pp. 1097–1105 (2012)
3. Russakovsky, O., Deng, J., Su, H., Krause, J., Satheesh, S., et al.: Imagenet large scale visual recognition challenge. Int. J. Comput. Vis. **115**(3), 211–252 (2015)
4. Hinton, G., Deng, L., Yu, D., Dahl, G.E., Mohamed, A.-R., et al.: Deep neural networks for acoustic modeling in speech recognition: the shared views of four research groups. IEEE Signal Process. Mag. **29**(6), 82–97 (2012)
5. Xu, X., Ding, Y., Hu, S.X., Niemier, M., Cong, J., et al.: Scaling for edge inference of deep neural networks. Nat. Electron. **1**(4), 216 (2018)
6. Bottou, L.: Large-scale machine learning with stochastic gradient descent. In: Lechevallier, Y., Saporta, G. (eds.) Proceedings of COMPSTAT'2010, pp. 177–186. Springer, Heidelberg (2010). https://doi.org/10.1007/978-3-7908-2604-3_16
7. Howard, A.G., Zhu, M., Chen, B., Kalenichenko, D., Wang, W., et al.: MobileNets: efficient convolutional neural networks for mobile vision applications. arXiv preprint arXiv:1704.04861 (2017)
8. Sze, V., Chen, Y.-H., Yang, T.-J., Emer, J.: Efficient processing of deep neural networks: a tutorial and survey. arXiv preprint arXiv:1703.09039 (2017)
9. Grimaldi, M., Tenace, V., Calimera, A.: Layer-wise compressive training for convolutional neural networks. Future Internet **11**(1) (2018). http://www.mdpi.com/1999-5903/11/1/7
10. Szegedy, C., Liu, C., Jia, Y., Sermanet, P., Reed, S., et al.: Going deeper with convolutions. In: Proceedings of the IEEE Conference on Computer Vision and Pattern Recognition, pp. 1–9 (2015)
11. Chen, Y.-H., Krishna, T., Emer, J.S., Sze, V.: Eyeriss: an energy-efficient reconfigurable accelerator for deep convolutional neural networks. IEEE J. Solid State Circ. **52**(1), 127–138 (2017)
12. Courbariaux, M., Bengio, Y., David, J.-P.: BinaryConnect: training deep neural networks with binary weights during propagations. In: Advances in Neural Information Processing Systems, pp. 3123–3131 (2015)
13. Flamand, E., Rossi, D., Conti, F., Loi, I., Pullini, A., et al.: Gap-8: a RISC-V SoC for AI at the edge of the IoT. In: 2018 IEEE 29th International Conference on Application-Specific Systems, Architectures and Processors (ASAP), pp. 1–4. IEEE (2018)
14. Moons, B., Verhelst, M.: A 0.3-2.6 TOPS, W precision-scalable processor for real-time large-scale ConvNets. In: IEEE Symposium on VLSI Circuits (VLSI-Circuits), pp. 1–2. IEEE (2016)
15. Albericio, J., Delmás, A., Judd, P., Sharify, S., O'Leary, G., et al.: Bit-pragmatic deep neural network computing. In: Proceedings of the 50th Annual IEEE/ACM International Symposium on Microarchitecture, pp. 382–394. ACM (2017)
16. Moons, B., De Brabandere, B., Van Gool, L., Verhelst, M.: Energy-efficient ConvNets through approximate computing. In: 2016 IEEE Winter Conference on Applications of Computer Vision (WACV), pp. 1–8. IEEE (2016)
17. Shafique, M., Hafiz, R., Javed, M.U., Abbas, S., Sekanina, L.: Adaptive and energy-efficient architectures for machine learning: challenges, opportunities, and research roadmap. In: 2017 IEEE Computer Society Annual Symposium on VLSI (ISVLSI), pp. 627–632. IEEE (2017)

18. Alioto, M., De, V., Marongiu, A.: Energy-quality scalable integrated circuits and systems: continuing energy scaling in the twilight of moore's law. IEEE J. Emerg. Sel. Top. Circuits Syst. **8**(4), 653–678 (2018)
19. Peluso, V., Calimera, A.: Weak-MAC: arithmetic relaxation for dynamic energy-accuracy scaling in ConvNets. In: IEEE International Symposium on Circuits and Systems (ISCAS), pp. 1–5. IEEE (2018)
20. Peluso, V., Calimera, A.: Energy-driven precision scaling for fixed-point ConvNets. In: 2018 IFIP/IEEE International Conference on Very Large Scale Integration (VLSI-SoC), pp. 1–6. IEEE (2018)
21. Lai, L., Suda, N.: Enabling deep learning at the IoT edge. In: Proceedings of the International Conference on Computer-Aided Design, p. 135. ACM (2018)
22. Jouppi, N.P., Young, C., Patil, N., Patterson, D., Agrawal, G., et al.: In-datacenter performance analysis of a tensor processing unit. In: Proceedings of the 44th Annual International Symposium on Computer Architecture, ISCA 2017, pp. 1–12. ACM, New York (2017). http://doi.acm.org/10.1145/3079856.3080246
23. Moons, B., Verhelst, M.: An energy-efficient precision-scalable ConvNet processor in 40-nm CMOS. IEEE J. Solid State Circuits **52**(4), 903–914 (2017)
24. Krizhevsky, A., Hinton, G.: Learning multiple layers of features from tiny images. Technical report, Citeseer (2009)
25. Warden, P.: Speech commands: a dataset for limited-vocabulary speech recognition. arXiv preprint arXiv:1804.03209 (2018)
26. Challenges in representation learning: facial expression recognition challenge. http://www.kaggle.com/c/challenges-in-representation-learning-facial-expression-recognition-challenge
27. Andri, R., Cavigelli, L., Rossi, D., Benini, L.: YodaNN: an architecture for ultra-low power binary-weight CNN acceleration. IEEE Trans. Comput. Aided Des. Integr. Circuits Syst. **37**, 48–60 (2017)
28. Gu, J., Wang, Z., Kuen, J., Ma, L., Shahroudy, A., et al.: Recent advances in convolutional neural networks. Pattern Recogn. (2017). http://www.sciencedirect.com/science/article/pii/S0031320317304120
29. Yang, T.J., Chen, Y.H., Sze, V.: Designing energy-efficient convolutional neural networks using energy-aware pruning. In: 2017 IEEE Conference on Computer Vision and Pattern Recognition (CVPR), pp. 6071–6079, July 2017
30. Fleuret, F., Geman, D.: Coarse-to-fine face detection. Int. J. Comput. Vis. **41**(1), 85–107 (2001)
31. Panda, P., Sengupta, A., Roy, K.: Conditional deep learning for energy-efficient and enhanced pattern recognition. In: Proceedings of the 2016 Conference on Design, Automation & Test in Europe, DATE 2016, pp. 475–480. EDA Consortium, San Jose (2016). http://dl.acm.org/citation.cfm?id=2971808.2971918
32. Yan, Z., Zhang, H., Piramuthu, R., Jagadeesh, V., DeCoste, D., et al.: HD-CNN: hierarchical deep convolutional neural networks for large scale visual recognition. In: Proceedings of the IEEE International Conference on Computer Vision, pp. 2740–2748 (2015)
33. Neshatpour, K., Behnia, F., Homayoun, H., Sasan, A.: ICNN: an iterative implementation of convolutional neural networks to enable energy and computational complexity aware dynamic approximation. In: Design, Automation & Test in Europe Conference & Exhibition (DATE), pp. 551–556. IEEE (2018)
34. Moons, B., Uytterhoeven, R., Dehaene, W., Verhelst, M.: 14.5 envision: A 0.26-to-10TOPS, W subword-parallel dynamic-voltage-accuracy-frequency-scalable convolutional neural network processor in 28 nm FDSOI. In: IEEE International Solid-State Circuits Conference (ISSCC), pp. 246–247. IEEE (2017)

35. Peluso, V., Calimera, A.: Scalable-effort ConvNets for multilevel classification. In: 2018 IEEE/ACM International Conference on Computer-Aided Design (ICCAD), pp. 1–8. IEEE (2018)
36. Lin, D., Talathi, S., Annapureddy, S.: Fixed point quantization of deep convolutional networks. In: International Conference on Machine Learning, pp. 2849–2858 (2016)
37. Shan, L., Zhang, M., Deng, L., Gong, G.: A dynamic multi-precision fixed-point data quantization strategy for convolutional neural network. In: Xu, W., Xiao, L., Li, J., Zhang, C., Zhu, Z. (eds.) NCCET 2016. CCIS, vol. 666, pp. 102–111. Springer, Singapore (2016). https://doi.org/10.1007/978-981-10-3159-5_10
38. Jahnke, S.R., Hamakawa, H.: Micro-controller direct memory access (DMA) operation with adjustable word size transfers and address alignment/incrementing. US Patent 6,816,921, 9 November 2004
39. Courbariaux, M., Bengio, Y., David, J.-P.: Training deep neural networks with low precision multiplications. arXiv preprint arXiv:1412.7024 (2014)
40. Desoli, G., Chawla, N., Boesch, T., Singh, S.-P., Guidetti, E.: 14.1 A 2.9 TOPS, W deep convolutional neural network SoC in FD-SOI 28 nm for intelligent embedded systems. In: 2017 IEEE International Solid-State Circuits Conference (ISSCC), pp. 238–239. IEEE (2017)
41. Jia, Y., Shelhamer, E., Donahue, J., Karayev, S., Long, J., et al.: Caffe: convolutional architecture for fast feature embedding. In: Proceedings of the 22nd ACM International Conference on Multimedia, pp. 675–678. ACM (2014)
42. Sainath, T.N., Vinyals, O., Senior, A., Sak, H.: Convolutional, long short-term memory, fully connected deep neural networks. In: 2015 IEEE International Conference on Acoustics, Speech and Signal Processing (ICASSP), pp. 4580–4584. IEEE (2015)
43. Kingma, D., Ba, J.: Adam: a method for stochastic optimization. arXiv preprint arXiv:1412.6980 (2014)

ReRAM Based In-Memory Computation of Single Bit Error Correcting BCH Code

Swagata Mandal[1]([⊠]), Yaswanth Tavva[2], Debjyoti Bhattacharjee[2],
and Anupam Chattopadhyay[2]

[1] Department of Electronics and Communication Engineering,
Jalpaiguri Government Engineering College (Autonomous), Jalpaiguri, India
swaga89@gmail.com
[2] School of Computer Science Engineering, Nanyang Technological University,
Singapore, Singapore

Abstract. Error resilient high speed robust data communication is the primary need in the age of big data and Internet-of-things (IoT), where multiple connected devices exchange huge amount of information. Different multi-bit error detecting and correcting codes are used for error mitigation in the high speed data communication though it introduces delay and their decoding structures are quite complex. Here we have discussed the implementation of single bit error correcting Bose, Chaudhuri, Hocquenghem (BCH) code with simple decoding structure on a state-of-the art ReRAM based in-memory computing platform. ReRAM devices offer low leakage power, high endurance and non-volatile storage capabilities, coupled with stateful logic operations. The proposed lightweight library presents the mapping for generation of elements on Galois field (GF) for computation of BCH code, along with encoding and decoding operations on input data stream using BCH code. We have verified the results for BCH code with different dimensions using SPICE simulation. For (15,11) BCH code, the number of clock cycles required for element generation, decoding and encoding of BCH code are 103, 230 and 251 respectively, which demonstrates the efficacy of the mapping.

Keywords: Error correcting code · BCH code ·
In memory computing · ReRAM

1 Introduction

In the age of big data and IoT, error resilient data storage, analysis and transmission are very crucial in different fields like social media, health care, deep space exploration and underwater surveillance etc. Even though the chances of data corruption in the silicon based semiconductor memory has grown with the shrinking of technology node, semiconductor based storage devices like random access memory (RAM), read only memory (ROM) and flash memory popularly

© IFIP International Federation for Information Processing 2019
Published by Springer Nature Switzerland AG 2019
N. Bombieri et al. (Eds.): VLSI-SoC 2018, IFIP AICT 561, pp. 128–146, 2019.
https://doi.org/10.1007/978-3-030-23425-6_7

used in the memory industry still have large footprint [1]. In order to prevent data corruption in the semiconductor memories, various traditional error mitigation techniques like triple modular redundancy (TMR), concurrent error detection (CED) [2] and readback with scrubbing [3] are generally used. The above mentioned methods consume large area, power and are not suitable for real time applications. Sometimes interleaving is used for error mitigation in memory but it increases the complexity of the memory and is not useful for small memory devices.

In order to alleviate the drawbacks of TMR, CED or scrubbing, various error detecting and correcting (EDAC) codes are used for error mitigation in the data memory as well as in the communication channels. In general, single bit errors in the memory are corrected by using single bit error correcting code such as Hamming or Hisao code. In order to correct multiple erroneous bits, multi-bit error correcting block codes like Bose, Chaudhuri, Hocquenghem (BCH) code [4], Reed-Solomon code [5] are used. They have greater decoding complexity and large overhead due to the presence of more number of redundant bits compared to single bit error correcting code. Data in the memory is arranged as a matrix. Hence, different product codes are used for error mitigation in the memory where two low complexity block codes are used as component codes. Product codes formed using only Hamming codes as component codes [6] or Hamming code and parity code as component codes [6], are used to correct multi-bit upset in the SRAM based semiconductor memory. Error detection capability of different complex EDAC codes can be concatenated with Hamming code to generate low complexity multi-bit error correcting code, such as RS code concatenated with Hamming code [7] and BCH code concatenated with Hamming code [8]. In addition to block code, memory based convolutional codes [9] are also used for error mitigation in the storage devices.

Error detection and correction methods discussed so far are implemented separately that read data from memory, perform encoding and decoding operation and finally write back data into the memory. With the rise of emerging technologies, computing can be performed in the memory itself, alongside storage of data unlike traditional von Neumann computing models [10]. Redox based Random Access Memory (ReRAM) is one of the non-volatile storage technology which supports such in memory computing [11]. Due to high circuit density, high retention capability and low power consumption, ReRAM technology is capable of being used as an alternative of NAND or NOR flash in the industry. Unlike CMOS or TTL based semiconductor memory technology, ReRAM uses different dielectric materials to develop its crossbar structure. ReRAM demonstrates good switching characteristics between high and low resistance state compared to other emerging memories like magnetic random access memory (MRAM), ferroelectric random access memory (FRAM) [12], etc. ReRAM based memory technology is compatible with conventional CMOS based design flow and provides inherent parallelism due to its crossbar structure. The working principle of ReRAM technology involves formation of low resistance conducting path through dielectric material by applying a high voltage across it. The conducting path arises due to multiple mechanisms like metal defect, vacancy, etc. [13]. The conducting tunnel through insulator can be controlled by an external voltage source for performing SET or RESET operations on the device.

Several in-memory computation platforms have already been proposed using ReRAMs, such as, general purpose in memory arithmetic circuit implementations [14], neuromorphic computing platforms [15] and general purpose Programmable Logic-in-Memory (PLiM) [16]. Apart from these general purpose applications, ReRAM based computation platforms are also used to implement different domain specific algorithms like machine learning [17,18], encryption [19] or compression algorithm [20].

Authors in [21] proposed efficient hardware implementation of BCH code. Further, hardware implementation of non-binary BCH code or RS code is also proposed by authors in [22]. The basic building blocks of error correcting code is the finite field arithmetic. The hardware implementation of high throughput finite field multiplier circuit on field programmable gate array (FPGA) and application specific integrated circuit (ASIC) are discussed by authors in [23]. Recently, ReRAM based in memory computation of Galois field (GF) arithmetic is described by authors in [24]. In this work, we propose the first in-memory BCH encoding and decoding operation library. Specifically, our contributions are as follows:-

- This work presents the first in-memory implementation of encoding and decoding operation of BCH code using ReRAM crossbar array.
- The proposed mapping harnesses the bit-level parallelism offered by ReRAM crossbar arrays and supports a wide variety of crossbar dimensions.
- In order to perform matrix multiplication during encoding and decoding operations, we have proposed a new method of implementation of binary matrix multiplication using ReRAM crossbar array. We refer the method as BiBLAS-3, since it is a level-3 binary basic linear algebra subprogram.
- The proposed implementation has a very low footprint in terms of devices required as well as energy, which makes it suitable for use as building blocks for different applications.

The rest of the paper is organized as follows. Section 2 presents the fundamentals of GF arithmetic, basics of encoding and decoding operations using BCH code along with a succinct introduction to ReVAMP, a state-of-the-art ReRAM based in-memory computing platform. Section 3 presents detailed implementation of element generation of GF, encoding and decoding operations for the ReVAMP platform using BiBLAS-3. Experimental results are described in Sect. 4, followed by conclusion in Sect. 5.

2 Preliminaries

In this section, we present the fundamentals of encoding and decoding operation using BCH code. We introduce the preliminaries of logic operation using ReVAMP architecture. The encoding and decoding operations of the BCH code will be performed on binary GF, that we describe briefly.

2.1 Galois Field Arithmetic

A field is a set of elements on which basic mathematical operations like addition and multiplication can be performed without leaving the set. Hence, these basic operations must satisfy *distributive, associative* and *commutative* laws [25]. The order of a field is the number of elements in the field. A field with finite number of elements is known as GF. The order of the GF is always a prime number or the power of a prime number. If p be a prime number and m be a positive integer, then GF will contain p^m elements and can be represented as $GF(p^m)$.

For $m = 1, p = 2$, the elements in GF will be $\{0,1\}$ and this is known as binary field. Here, we will consider GF of 2^m elements from the binary field $GF(2)$ where $m > 1$. If U be the set of the elements of the field and α be an element of $GF(2^m)$, then U can be represented by Eq. (1).

$$U = [0, \alpha^0, \alpha^1, \alpha^2, \alpha^3, \ldots\ldots, \alpha^{2^m-1}] \tag{1}$$

Let $f(x)$ be a polynomial over $GF(2^m)$ and it is said to be irreducible if $f(x)$ is not divisible by any other polynomial in $GF(2^m)$ with degree less than m, but greater than zero [26]. The irreducible polynomial is a primitive polynomial, if the smallest positive integer q for which $f(x)$ divides $x^q + 1$, where $q = 2^m - 1$. For each value of m, there can be multiple primitive polynomials, but we will use the primitive polynomial with least number of terms for computation over GF.

(a)	
$GF(2^m)$	**Primitive Polynomial**
2^2	$x^2 + x + 1$
2^3	$x^3 + x + 1$
2^4	$x^4 + x + 1$
2^5	$x^5 + x^2 + 1$
2^6	$x^6 + x + 1$
2^7	$x^7 + x^3 + 1$

(b)		
Power Repr.	**Polynomial Repr.**	**4-Tuple Repr.**
0	0	(0,0,0,0)
1	α^0	(0,0,0,1)
α	α^1	(0,0,1,0)
α^2	α^2	(0,1,0,0)
α^3	α^3	(1,0,0,0)
α^4	$\alpha + 1$	(0,0,1,1)
α^5	$\alpha^2 + \alpha$	(0,1,1,0)
α^6	$\alpha^3 + \alpha^2$	(1,1,0,0)
α^7	$\alpha^3 + \alpha + 1$	(1,0,1,1)
α^8	$\alpha^2 + 1$	(0,1,0,1)
α^9	$\alpha^3 + \alpha$	(1,0,1,0)
α^{10}	$\alpha^2 + \alpha + 1$	(0,1,1,1)
α^{11}	$\alpha^3 + \alpha^2 + \alpha$	(1,1,1,0)
α^{12}	$\alpha^3 + \alpha^2 + \alpha + 1$	(1,1,1,1)
α^{13}	$\alpha^3 + \alpha^2 + 1$	(1,1,0,1)
α^{14}	$\alpha^3 + 1$	(1,0,0,1)

Fig. 1. (a) Primitive polynomial for various order GF. (b) Representation of elements in $GF(2^4)$.

Table 1. Variation of dimension of single bit error correcting BCH code with the order of GF.

Order of $GF(m)$	Dimension of BCH code	α^k
3	(7, 4)	$\alpha^k = \alpha^{k-2} + \alpha^{k-3}$
4	(15, 11)	$\alpha^k = \alpha^{k-3} + \alpha^{k-4}$
5	(31, 26)	$\alpha^k = \alpha^{k-3} + \alpha^{k-5}$
6	(63, 57)	$\alpha^k = \alpha^{k-5} + \alpha^{k-6}$
7	(127, 120)	$\alpha^k = \alpha^{k-4} + \alpha^{k-7}$

The list of primitive polynomials for different values of m is shown in Fig. 1a. These primitive polynomials are the basis of computation using the elements of GF. For the generation of elements of GF, we will start from two basic elements 0, 1 and another new element α.

In this paper, we have discussed encoding and decoding operation of single bit error correcting BCH code on $GF(2^m)$ where m varies from 3 to 7. As α is an element of $GF(2^m)$, it must satisfy the primitive polynomial corresponding to $GF(2^m)$. With the variation of m, not only primitive polynomial changes but also dimension of BCH code changes as shown in Table 1. If α be an element in $GF(2^m)$, α^k (where k is an positive integer and $k > 2$) is also be an element of $GF(2^m)$ and the recursive expression that will be used to calculate α^k for different values m in $GF(2^m)$ are shown in Table 1. Here in Fig. 1b we have illustrated the power, polynomial and 4-Tuple representation of all the elements of $GF(2^4)$ are shown in Fig. 1b. Based on the elements of GF, the encoding and decoding operations of BCH code will be performed.

2.2   Basics of BCH Encoding and Decoding Operation

BCH is a powerful random error correcting cyclic code which is basically general purpose multi-bit error correcting Hamming code. Given two integers m and t such that $m > 3$ and $t < 2^m - 1$, then there exists a binary BCH code whose block length will be $n = 2^m - 1$ with the number of parity check bits equal to $(n - k) \leq mt$ and the minimum distance will be $d_{min} \geq (2t + 1)$. This will represent t error correcting BCH code. If α be a primitive element in $GF(2^m)$, then generator polynomial $g(x)$ of t error correcting BCH code of length $2^m - 1$ will be lowest degree polynomial over $GF(2)$ and $\alpha, \alpha^2, \ldots, \alpha^{2t}$ will be its root. Hence, the Eq. (2) must satisfy.

$$g(\alpha^i) = 0 \quad \forall i \in \{1, 2, \ldots, t\} \tag{2}$$

If $\phi_i(x)$ be the minimal polynomial of α^i, then $g(x)$ will be formed using the Eq. (3).

$$g(x) = LCM\{\phi_1(x), \phi_2(x), \ldots, \phi_{2t}(x)\} \tag{3}$$

As α^i and $\alpha^{i'}$ (where $i = i'2^l$, i' is odd and $l > 1$) are conjugate to each other $\phi_i(x) = \phi_{i'}(x)$. Hence, $g(x)$ will be formed using the Eq. (4).

$$g(x) = LCM\{\phi_1(x), \phi_3(x), \ldots, \phi_{2t-1}(x)\} \tag{4}$$

Since we will use single bit error correcting BCH code, the generator polynomial $g(x)$ for $GF(2^4)$ is given by

$$g(x) = \phi_1(x) = x^4 + x + 1$$

The degree of $g(x)$ will be at most mt and the number of parity bits will be $(n-k)$. After the generation $g(x)$, the encoding operation will involve multiplication of input data $D(x)$ with $g(x)$, i.e, $C(x) = D(x) \times g(x)$.

The decoding operation of BCH code will involve the following steps:

1. Syndrome computation.
2. Determine the error locater polynomial λ from the syndrome components S_1, $S_2, \ldots, S_{2t}$.
3. Find the error location by solving the error locater polynomial $\lambda(x)$.

Let $r(x) = r_0 + r_1 x + r_2 x^2 + \ldots + r_{n-1} x^{n-1}$ be the received data and $e(x)$ be the error pattern, then $r(x) = D(x) + e(x)$. For t error correcting BCH code, the parity check matrix will be

$$H = \begin{bmatrix} 1 & \alpha & \alpha^2 & \alpha^3 & \cdots & \alpha^{(n-1)} \\ 1 & \alpha^3 & (\alpha^3)^2 & (\alpha^3)^3 & \cdots & (\alpha^3)^{(n-1)} \\ 1 & \alpha^5 & (\alpha^5)^2 & (\alpha^5)^3 & \cdots & (\alpha^5)^{(n-1)} \\ \vdots & \vdots & \vdots & \vdots & \ddots & \vdots \\ 1 & \alpha^{(2t-1)} & (\alpha^{(2t-1)})^2 & (\alpha^{(2t-1)})^3 & \cdots & (\alpha^{(2t-1)})^{(n-1)} \end{bmatrix}$$

The syndrome is a $2t$-tuple $S = (S_1, S_2, \ldots, S_{2t}) = r \times H^T$ where H is the parity check matrix. Since we are considering single bit error correcting BCH code, t will be equal to 1 and $S = S_1 = r \times H^T$.

In the next step, from the syndrome values $2t$ nonlinear equations are formed which will be solved using either Berlekamp-Massey or Euclid's algorithm [27] and an error locater polynomial is formed using the roots obtained by solving the $2t$ nonlinear equations. Finally, the roots of the error locater polynomial is solved using Chien search algorithm [27]. Single bit error correcting BCH code generate only one syndrome whose value can directly locate the position of the erroneous bit and hence, we have not discussed the detailed implementation of step 2 and step 3 of the decoding of BCH code.

2.3   In-Memory Computing Using ReRAM

In this subsection, we describe the ReRAM-based in-memory computing platform—ReVAMP, introduced in [28]. The architecture, presented in Fig. 2 utilizes ReRAM crossbar with lightweight peripheral circuitry for in-memory

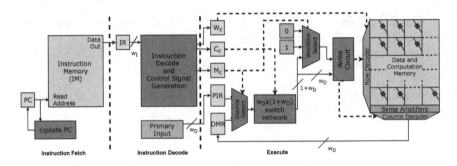

Fig. 2. ReVAMP architecture.

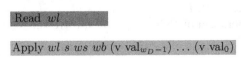

Fig. 3. ReVAMP instruction format.

computing. The ReRAM crossbar memory is used as data storage and computation memory (DCM). This is where in-memory computation using ReRAM devices takes place. A ReRAM crossbar memory consists of multiple 1-Select 1-Resistance (1S1R) ReRAM devices [29], arranged in the form of a crossbar [30]. A V/2 scheme is used for programming the ReRAM array. Unselected lines are kept to ground. In a readout phase, the presence of a high current (≈ 5 μA) is considered as logic '1' while presence of a low current (<2 μA) is interpreted as logic '0'. Like conventional RAM arrays, ReRAM memories are accessed as w_D-bit wide words. Each ReRAM device has two input terminals, namely the wordline wl and bitline bl. The internal resistive state Z of the ReRAM acts as a third input and stored bit. The next state of the device Z^n can be expressed as Boolean majority function with three inputs, where the bitline input is inverted.

$$Z^n = M_3(Z, wl, \overline{bl}) \tag{5}$$

This forms the fundamental logic operation that can be realized using ReRAM devices. Using the intrinsic function Z^n, inversion operation can be realized. Since majority and inversion operation form a functionally complete set, any Boolean function can be realized using the Z^n.

The ReVAMP architecture has a three-stage pipeline with Instruction Fetch, Instruction Decode and Execution stages, as shown in Fig. 2. The instruction memory (IM) can be a regular memory or a ReRAM memory, with the program counter being used to address and fetch the stored instructions in the Instruction Fetch stage.

The architecture supports two instructions—*Read* and *Apply*, as presented in Fig. 3. *Read* instruction reads a specified word, wl from the DCM and stores it in the Data Memory Register (DMR). The read out word, available in the

DMR, can be used as input by the following instructions. The *Apply* instruction is used for computation in the DCM. The address wl specifies the word in the DCM that will be computed upon. A bit flag s chooses whether the inputs will be from primary input register (PIR) or DMR. Two-bit flag ws is used to select the wordline input – 11 selects '1', 10 selects '0', 00 selects wb bit within the chosen data source for use as wordline input while 01 is an invalid value for ws. The pairs (v, val) are used to specify individual bitline inputs. The bit flag v indicates if the input is NOP or a valid input. Similar to wb, the bits val specify the bit within the chosen data source for use as bitline input.

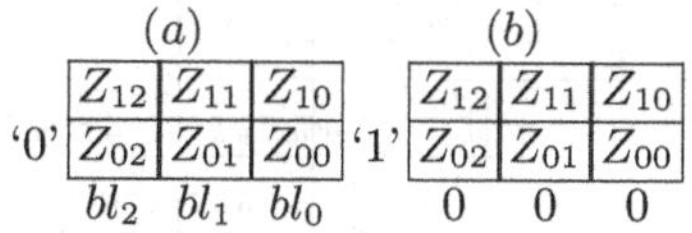

$$
\begin{array}{ccccc}
& (a) & & & (b) \\
& \begin{array}{|c|c|c|}
\hline Z_{12} & Z_{11} & Z_{10} \\
\hline
\end{array} & & & \begin{array}{|c|c|c|}
\hline Z_{12} & Z_{11} & Z_{10} \\
\hline
\end{array} \\
\text{`0'} & \begin{array}{|c|c|c|}
\hline Z_{02} & Z_{01} & Z_{00} \\
\hline
\end{array} & & \text{`1'} & \begin{array}{|c|c|c|}
\hline Z_{02} & Z_{01} & Z_{00} \\
\hline
\end{array} \\
& \begin{array}{ccc} bl_2 & bl_1 & bl_0 \end{array} & & & \begin{array}{ccc} 0 & 0 & 0 \end{array}
\end{array}
$$

Fig. 4. A 2×3 ReRAM crossbar, i.e., a crossbar with two rows and three bitlines. Z_{ij} represents the state of device at wordline i and bitline j. (a) Computation on 0th row with '0' and $\{bl_0, bl_1, bl_2\}$ as the wordline and bitline inputs respectively. Valid inputs can be either $\{$'1' $(+2.4\,\mathrm{V})$ or '0' $(-2.4\,\mathrm{V})$ $\}$. (b) 0th row is being read out, by setting wordline to '1' $(+2.4\,\mathrm{V})$ and the bitlines to 0 $(0\,\mathrm{V})$.

Figure 4 shows a 2×3 ReRAM crossbar array, which can act as the DCM. The operation in Fig. 4(a) can be expressed as an *Apply* instruction,

$$\text{Apply 0 00 00 00 1 00 1 01 1 10}$$

and the PIR contents are set to $bl_0 \; bl_1 \; bl_2$. The operation in Fig. 4(b) can be expressed as Read 0. From here on, we express the in-memory compute operations in the crossbar representation.

3   Methodology

The ReVAMP architecture performs in-memory computing operation using ReRAM devices capable of computing three-input Boolean majority with a single input inverted. Boolean majority with inverter is a functionally complete set. Therefore, it can be used for computation of arbitrary Boolean functions. The ReVAMP allows simultaneous computation on all devices that share a common wordline. A signal is required to read out the contents of a word. A recent work demonstrated multiple mathematical operation on the elements of GF using ReVAMP architecture [24]. In this section, we present the mapping of encoding and decoding operation of BCH code using these mathematical operation on the ReVAMP architecture. It involves three steps: generation of GF elements, encoding using BCH code and decoding using BCH code. The encoding and decoding operation using BCH code basically involves matrix multiplication which we will implement using ReRAM crossbar with the help of the BiBLAS operations proposed in [31]. We use the terms wordline and rows interchangeably. Similarly, the terms bitline and columns are used interchangeably.

Table 2. Generation operation for elements in $GF(2^3)$ using 8×3 DCM.

Step 1

'1'	0	0	0
	0	0	0
	0	0	0
	0	0	0
	0	0	0
	...		
	0	0	0
	$\overline{a_{00}}$	$\overline{a_{01}}$	$\overline{a_{02}}$

Step 2

	a_{00}	a_{01}	a_{02}
'1'	0	0	0
	0	0	0
	0	0	0
	0	0	0
	...		
	0	0	0
	$\overline{a_{10}}$	$\overline{a_{11}}$	$\overline{a_{12}}$

Step 3

	a_{00}	a_{01}	a_{02}
	a_{10}	a_{11}	a_{12}
'1'	0	0	0
	0	0	0
	0	0	0
	...		
	0	0	0
	$\overline{a_{20}}$	$\overline{a_{21}}$	$\overline{a_{22}}$

Step 4...

	a_{00}	a_{01}	a_{02}
	a_{10}	a_{11}	a_{12}
	a_{20}	a_{21}	a_{22}
'1'	0	0	0
	0	0	0
	...		
	0	0	0
	$\overline{a_{00}}$	$\overline{a_{01}}$	$\overline{a_{02}}$

Step 6

	a_{00}	a_{01}	a_{02}
'1'	a_{10}	a_{11}	a_{12}
	a_{20}	a_{21}	a_{22}
'0'	a_{00}	a_{01}	a_{02}
	a_{00}	a_{01}	a_{02}
	...		
	0	0	0
	0	0	0

Step 7...

	a_{00}	a_{01}	a_{02}
	a_{10}	a_{11}	a_{12}
	a_{20}	a_{21}	a_{22}
	a_{00}	a_{01}	a_{02}
	a_{00}	a_{01}	a_{02}
	...		
	0	0	0
	a_{10}	a_{11}	a_{12}

Step 9

	a_{00}	a_{01}	a_{02}
	a_{10}	a_{11}	a_{12}
	a_{20}	a_{21}	a_{22}
	$a_{00}.\overline{a_{10}}$	$a_{01}.\overline{a_{11}}$	$a_{02}.\overline{a_{12}}$
'1'	$a_{00}+\overline{a_{10}}$	$a_{01}+\overline{a_{11}}$	$a_{02}+\overline{a_{12}}$
	...		
	0	0	0
	0	0	0

Step 10

	a_{00}	a_{01}	a_{02}
	a_{10}	a_{11}	a_{12}
	a_{20}	a_{21}	a_{22}
'1'	$a_{00}.\overline{a_{10}}$	$a_{01}.\overline{a_{11}}$	$a_{12}.\overline{a_{22}}$
	$a_{00}+\overline{a_{10}}$	$a_{01}+\overline{a_{11}}$	$a_{02}+\overline{a_{12}}$
	...		
	0	0	0
	$a_{00}+\overline{a_{10}}$	$a_{01}+\overline{a_{11}}$	$a_{02}+\overline{a_{12}}$

Step 11

	a_{00}	a_{01}	a_{02}
	a_{10}	a_{11}	a_{12}
	a_{20}	a_{21}	a_{22}
	$a_{00}\oplus a_{10}$	$a_{01}\oplus a_{11}$	$a_{02}\oplus a_{12}$
'0'	$a_{00}+\overline{a_{10}}$	$a_{01}+\overline{a_{11}}$	$a_{02}+\overline{a_{12}}$
	...		
	0	0	0
	'1'	'1'	'1'

Step 12

	a_{00}	a_{01}	a_{02}
'1'	a_{10}	a_{11}	a_{12}
	a_{20}	a_{21}	a_{22}
	$a_{00}\oplus a_{10}$	$a_{01}\oplus a_{11}$	$a_{02}\oplus a_{12}$
	0	0	0
	...		
	0	0	0
	0	0	0

Step 13

	a_{00}	a_{01}	a_{02}
	a_{10}	a_{11}	a_{12}
	a_{20}	a_{21}	a_{22}
	a_{30}	a_{31}	a_{32}
'1'	0	0	0
	...		
	0	0	0
	0	0	0
	a_{10}	a_{11}	a_{12}

Step 14

	a_{00}	a_{01}	a_{02}
	a_{10}	a_{11}	a_{12}
	a_{20}	a_{21}	a_{22}
	a_{30}	a_{31}	a_{32}
'1'	$\overline{a_{10}}$	$\overline{a_{11}}$	$\overline{a_{12}}$
	...		
	0	0	0
	0	0	0

Step 15...

	a_{00}	a_{01}	a_{02}
	a_{10}	a_{11}	a_{12}
	a_{20}	a_{21}	a_{22}
	a_{30}	a_{31}	a_{32}
'1'	$\overline{a_{10}}$	$\overline{a_{11}}$	$\overline{a_{12}}$
	...		
	0	0	0
'1'	0	0	0
	$\overline{a_{10}}$	$\overline{a_{11}}$	$\overline{a_{12}}$

Step 41

	a_{00}	a_{01}	a_{02}
	a_{10}	a_{11}	a_{12}
	a_{20}	a_{21}	a_{22}
	a_{30}	a_{31}	a_{32}
	a_{40}	a_{41}	a_{42}
'1'	a_{50}	a_{51}	a_{52}
	a_{40}	a_{41}	a_{42}
	a_{40}	a_{41}	a_{42}
	0	0	0

Step 42

	a_{00}	a_{01}	a_{02}
	a_{10}	a_{11}	a_{12}
	a_{20}	a_{21}	a_{22}
	a_{30}	a_{31}	a_{32}
	a_{40}	a_{41}	a_{42}
	a_{50}	a_{51}	a_{52}
'0'	a_{40}	a_{41}	a_{42}
	a_{40}	a_{41}	a_{42}
	0	0	0

Step 43...

	a_{00}	a_{01}	a_{02}
	a_{10}	a_{11}	a_{12}
	a_{20}	a_{21}	a_{22}
	a_{30}	a_{31}	a_{32}
	a_{40}	a_{41}	a_{42}
	a_{50}	a_{51}	a_{52}
	a_{40}	a_{41}	a_{42}
	0	0	0
	a_{50}	a_{51}	a_{52}

Step 45

	a_{00}	a_{01}	a_{02}
	a_{10}	a_{11}	a_{12}
	a_{20}	a_{21}	a_{22}
	a_{30}	a_{31}	a_{32}
	a_{40}	a_{41}	a_{42}
	a_{50}	a_{51}	a_{52}
	$a_{40}.\overline{a_{50}}$	$a_{41}.\overline{a_{51}}$	$a_{42}.\overline{a_{52}}$
'1'	$a_{40}+\overline{a_{50}}$	$a_{41}+\overline{a_{51}}$	$a_{42}+\overline{a_{52}}$
	0	0	0

Step 46

	a_{00}	a_{01}	a_{02}
	a_{10}	a_{11}	a_{12}
	a_{20}	a_{21}	a_{22}
	a_{30}	a_{31}	a_{32}
	a_{40}	a_{41}	a_{42}
	a_{50}	a_{51}	a_{52}
	$a_{40}.\overline{a_{50}}$	$a_{41}.\overline{a_{51}}$	$a_{42}.\overline{a_{52}}$
'0'	$a_{40}+\overline{a_{50}}$	$a_{41}+\overline{a_{51}}$	$a_{42}+\overline{a_{52}}$
	$a_{40}+\overline{a_{50}}$	$a_{41}+\overline{a_{51}}$	$a_{42}+\overline{a_{52}}$

Step 47

	a_{00}	a_{01}	a_{02}
	a_{10}	a_{11}	a_{12}
	a_{20}	a_{21}	a_{22}
	a_{30}	a_{31}	a_{32}
	a_{40}	a_{41}	a_{42}
	a_{50}	a_{51}	a_{52}
	a_{60}	a_{61}	a_{62}
	$a_{40}+\overline{a_{50}}$	$a_{41}+\overline{a_{51}}$	$a_{42}+\overline{a_{52}}$
	'1'	'1'	'1'

3.1   Generation of GF Elements

Here, we will illustrate the generation of elements of $GF(2^3)$ as an example. As each element in $GF(2^3)$ is a three tuple, the number of the columns in the DCM should either three or a multiple of three. For this purpose, we need DCM having 8 wordlines and 3 bitlines. Table 2 presents the intermediate state of the DCM and the inputs used for the generation of elements of GF. In Step 1, '1' is applied on 7th wordline and $\overline{a_{00}}$, $\overline{a_{01}}$, $\overline{a_{02}}$ are applied to the bitlines. Here, $(\overline{a_{00}}, \overline{a_{01}}, \overline{a_{02}})$ represent 1, 1 and 0 respectively (from the 3-tuple representation shown in Fig. 1b). Similarly, 0, 0 and 1 are loaded into the 7th row which basically represents α^0. In the next two steps, α and α^2 are loaded into the sixth and fifth row applying $(\overline{a_{10}}, \overline{a_{11}}, \overline{a_{12}})$ and $(\overline{a_{20}}, \overline{a_{21}}, \overline{a_{22}})$ to the bitlines respectively that represent $(1, 0, 1)$ and $(0, 1, 1)$.

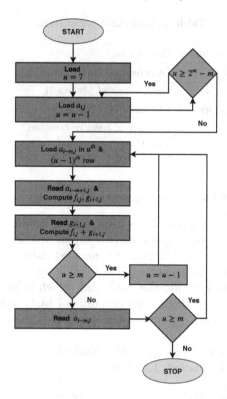

Fig. 5. Flowchart for the generation of elements of $GF(2^m)$.

Now α^3 will be calculated by modulo-2 addition of elements in 7th and 6th row. Modulo-2 addition between $a_{i,j}$ and $a_{(i+1),j}$ can be broken down into two operations.

$$a_{i,j} \oplus a_{(i+1),j} = a_{i,j} \cdot \overline{a_{(i+1),j}} + \overline{(a_{i,j} + \overline{a_{(i+1),j}})} \qquad (6)$$

$$= f_{i,j} + \overline{g_{i+1,j}} \qquad (7)$$

To compute $f_{i,j}$ and $g_{i+1,j}$, we require two copies of $a_{i,j}$. Here i represents power of α and j represents position of a bit when α^i is expressed in 3-tuple format. Hence, in Step 5 and Step 6, we have loaded a_{00}, a_{01} and a_{02} in 4th and 3rd row. $f_{0,j}$ and $g_{1,j}$ are calculated by applying '0' in 4th row, '1' in 3rd row and 0 along all the bitlines in Step 7 and Step 8 respectively. In order to do OR operation between $f_{0,j}$ and $\overline{g_{1,j}}$, $g_{1,j}$ is read from the 3rd row in Step 9 and then in Step 10, apply $g_{1,j}$ along all the bitlines and '1' in wordline of 4th row. Finally, 4th row will store the value α^3. Obeying the same procedure, α^4, α^5 and α^6 will be calculated and stored in the 3rd, 2nd and 1st row of the crossbar respectively. The flowchart shown in Fig. 5 describes the generation of elements for $GF(2^m)$ using DCM with u wordlines and m bitlines.

Table 3. BiBLAS-3 parameters.

Parameter	Description
m_1, n_1	Dimensions of Matrix A
m_2, n_2	Dimensions of Matrix B
m_1, n_2	Dimensions of Matrix C
r	Number of rows in crossbar
c	Number of columns in crossbar

3.2   Encoding and Decoding Operations

The encoding and decoding operations primarily involve binary matrix multiplications. During the encoding operation, the input data will be multiplied with
the generator matrix which will give the encoded data. Similarly, during the
decoding operation, the received data will be multiplied with the transpose of
parity check matrix to generate the syndromes which helps to locate the error
in the received data. Even though the decoding of BCH codes involve multiple
steps as presented in Sect. 2, we only require syndrome computation for achieving
single-bit error correction.

Suppose A and B are two matrices with dimensions 2×2 and C be the matrix
obtained after multiplication of A and B.

$$A = \begin{bmatrix} a_{11} & a_{12} \\ a_{21} & a_{22} \end{bmatrix} B = \begin{bmatrix} b_{11} & b_{12} \\ b_{21} & b_{22} \end{bmatrix} C = \begin{bmatrix} c_{11} & c_{12} \\ c_{21} & c_{22} \end{bmatrix} = \begin{bmatrix} a_{11}b_{11} \oplus a_{12}b_{21} & a_{11}b_{12} \oplus a_{12}b_{22} \\ a_{21}b_{11} \oplus a_{22}b_{21} & a_{21}b_{12} \oplus a_{22}b_{22} \end{bmatrix}$$

We will explain mapping of BiBLAS-3 on ReRAM crossbar using 2×2 matrix.
The parameters involved in the BiBLAS-3 implementation are described in
Table 3. We consider the following configuration for the BiBLAS-3 implemen-
tation.

- Matrices A, B are available in within the crossbar and the product matrix C
  is stored crossbar after computation.
- First five rows $(r_1, r_2, \ldots, r_5)$ are reserved for storage and last four rows
  (*reserve1*,...,*reserve4*) are used for computation.

The minimum dimensions of the matrix in mapping for BiBLAS-3 should
be 1×2. Algorithm 1 shows step by step mapping of BiBLAS-3. In step 1,
the elements of product matrix C is divided into a groups of size c. In this
example, C is of 2×2 size with a total of 4 product terms. As the column size of
choosen crossbar is 3, product terms are divided into two groups with elements
1, 3, 2 in group 1 and element 4 in group2. In step 2, the terms from matrices
A and B, responsible for the formation of each product term in a group, are
obtained. Each product constitutes a series of XORed dot products. The first
and second dot products of each element in group 1 is computed in *reserve1*
and *reserve2* rows respectively. Before computing third dot product if there are
reserve1, reserve2 they will be XORed first and followed by a clear operation

on *reserve2*. Likewise, the following dot products are computed in *reserve2* and accumulated to *reserve1* by XOR. This is repeated till all the dots products in the choosen group are completed. By the end of step 2, *reserve1* contains the products are of group 1. In step 3, the products from *reserve1* are copied to free memory and then *reserve1* is cleared. steps 2 and 3 are iterated till all the groups are computed on the crossbar. A detailed example is shown in Table 4.

Algorithm 1. BiBLAS-3

1: $groups \leftarrow$ GETGROUPS$(m1, n2, c)$ ▷ divides m1×n2 product terms into groups, with c being maximum size of each group
2: **for each** *groups* **do**
3:      $partialproducts \leftarrow$ GETPARTIALPRODUTS$(group)$
4:      **for each** *partialproducts* **do**
5:          **if** first partial product **then**
6:              LOADELEFROMA$(r1)$ ▷ load elements from matrix A present in partial product to row r1
7:              ANDELEFROMB$(r1)$ ▷ load elements from matrix B present in partial product and dot product with row r1
8:          **else**
9:              LOADELEFROMA$(r2)$
10:             ANDELEFROMB$(r2)$
11:             XOR$(r1, r2)$.   ▷ xor rows r1 and r2
12:             RESET$(r2)$ ▷ reset row r2
13:         **end if**
14:     **end for**
15:     COPY$(r1, x)$ ▷ copy r1 to an empty row x in crossbar
16:     RESET$(r1)$ ▷ reset row r1
17: **end for**

---

4   Experiment

In this section, we analyze the performance of in-memory computation of encoding and decoding operations of BCH code on GF for various order m and crossbar dimensions. The experiments were performed using Cadence Virtuoso, using device-accurate model of ReRAM devices [29]. The dimension of single bit error correcting BCH code varies with change in the order m of GF. Figures 6 and 7 show the delay in terms of number of clock cycles and area in terms of the number of ReRAM devices required to perform encoding and decoding operations, along with element generation of GF elements respectively using ReVAMP. The encoding operation involves generation of the generator matrix from parity check matrix and multiplication of the input data with the generator matrix whereas the decoding operation involves multiplication of the received data with the transpose of parity check matrix. Hence, the number of cycles required for encoding operation are more than the number of cycles required

Table 4. BiBLAS-3 computation with the input matrices A and B to compute the product matrix C.

step 1

Flag			
'1'	a_{11}	a_{21}	a_{12}
	a_{22}	0	0
	b_{11}	b_{12}	b_{21}
	b_{22}	0	0
	0	0	0
	0	0	0
	0	0	0
	0	0	0
	0	0	0
	0	0	0

step 2

Flag			
	a_{11}	a_{21}	a_{12}
	a_{22}	0	0
	b_{11}	b_{12}	b_{21}
	b_{22}	0	0
	0	0	0
	0	0	0
'1'	0	0	0
	0	0	0
	0	0	0
	a_{11}	a_{21}	a_{11}

step 3

Flag			
	a_{11}	a_{21}	a_{12}
	a_{22}	0	0
'1'	b_{11}	b_{12}	b_{21}
	b_{22}	0	0
	0	0	0
	0	0	0
	a_{11}	a_{21}	a_{11}
	0	0	0
	0	0	0
	b_{11}	b_{12}	b_{21}

step 4

Flag			
'1'	a_{11}	a_{21}	a_{12}
	a_{22}	0	0
	b_{11}	b_{12}	b_{21}
	b_{22}	0	0
	0	0	0
	0	0	0
'0'	a_{11}	a_{21}	a_{11}
	0	0	0
	0	0	0
	b_{11}	b_{11}	b_{12}

step 5

Flag			
'1'	a_{11}	a_{21}	a_{12}
	a_{22}	0	0
	b_{11}	b_{12}	b_{21}
	b_{22}	0	0
	0	0	0
	0	0	0
	$a_{11}\cdot b_{11}$	$a_{21}\cdot b_{11}$	$a_{11}\cdot b_{12}$
	0	0	0
	0	0	0
	0	0	0

step 6

Flag			
	a_{11}	a_{21}	a_{12}
	a_{22}	0	0
	b_{11}	b_{12}	b_{21}
	b_{22}	0	0
	0	0	0
	0	0	0
	$a_{11}\cdot b_{11}$	$a_{21}\cdot b_{11}$	$a_{11}\cdot b_{12}$
'1'	0	0	0
	0	0	0
	a_{12}		a_{12}

step 7

Flag			
'1'	a_{11}	a_{21}	a_{12}
	a_{22}	0	0
	b_{11}	b_{12}	b_{21}
	b_{22}	0	0
	0	0	0
	0	0	0
	$a_{11}.b_{11}$	$a_{21}.b_{11}$	$a_{11}.b_{12}$
	a_{12}	0	a_{12}
	0	0	0
	0	0	0

step 8

Flag			
	a_{11}	a_{21}	a_{12}
	a_{22}	0	0
'1'	b_{11}	b_{12}	b_{21}
	b_{22}	0	0
	0	0	0
	0	0	0
	$a_{11}.b_{11}$	$a_{21}.b_{11}$	$a_{11}.b_{12}$
'1'	a_{12}	0	a_{12}
	0	0	0
	0	0	0

step 9

Flag			
	a_{11}	a_{21}	a_{12}
	a_{22}	0	0
'1'	b_{11}	b_{12}	b_{21}
	b_{22}	0	0
	0	0	0
	0	0	0
	$a_{11}\text{-}b_{11}$	$a_{21}.b_{11}$	$a_{11}.b_{12}$
	a_{12}	a_{22}	a_{12}
	0	0	0
	0	0	0

step 10

Flag			
	a_{11}	a_{21}	a_{12}
	a_{22}	0	0
	b_{11}	b_{12}	b_{21}
	b_{22}	0	0
	0	0	0
	0	0	0
	$a_{11}.b_{11}$	$a_{21}.b_{11}$	$a_{11}.b_{12}$
'0'	a_{12}	a_{22}	a_{12}
	0	0	0
	b_{21}	b_{21}	

step 11

Flag			
	a_{11}	a_{21}	a_{12}
	a_{22}	0	0
	b_{11}	b_{12}	b_{21}
'1'	b_{22}	0	0
	0	0	0
	0	0	0
	$a_{11}.b_{11}$	$a_{21}.b_{11}$	$a_{11}.b_{12}$
	$a_{12}.b_{21}$	$a_{22}.b_{21}$	a_{12}
	0	0	0
	0	0	0

step 12...

Flag			
	a_{11}	a_{21}	a_{12}
	a_{22}	0	0
	b_{11}	b_{12}	b_{21}
	b_{22}	0	0
	0	0	0
	0	0	0
	$a_{11}.b_{11}$	$a_{21}.b_{11}$	$a_{11}.b_{12}$
'0'	$a_{12}.b_{21}$	$a_{22}.b_{21}$	a_{12}
	0	0	0
	b_{22}		

step 25

Flag			
	a_{11}	a_{21}	a_{12}
	a_{22}	0	0
	b_{11}	b_{12}	b_{21}
	b_{22}	0	0
	0	0	0
	0	0	0
	c_{11}	c_{21}	c_{12}
	0	0	0
	0	0	0
	0	0	0

step 26

Flag			
	a_{11}	a_{21}	a_{12}
	a_{22}	0	0
	b_{11}	b_{12}	b_{21}
	b_{22}	0	0
'1'	0	0	0
	0	0	0
	c_{11}	c_{21}	c_{12}
	0	0	0
	0	0	0
	c_{11}	c_{21}	c_{12}

step 27

Flag			
	a_{11}	a_{21}	a_{12}
	a_{22}	0	0
	b_{11}	b_{12}	b_{21}
	b_{22}	0	0
'0'	c_{11}	c_{21}	c_{12}
	0	0	0
	c_{11}	c_{21}	c_{12}
	0	0	0
	0	0	0
	'1'	'1'	'1'

step 28

Flag			
'1'	a_{11}	a_{21}	a_{12}
	a_{22}	0	0
	b_{11}	b_{12}	b_{21}
	b_{22}	0	0
	c_{11}	c_{21}	c_{12}
	0	0	0
'1'	0	0	0
	0	0	0
	0	0	0
	0	0	0

step 29

Flag			
	a_{11}	a_{21}	a_{12}
	a_{22}	0	0
	b_{11}	b_{12}	b_{21}
	b_{22}	0	0
	c_{11}	c_{21}	c_{12}
	0	0	0
	0	0	0
	0	0	0
	0	0	0
	a_{21}		

step 30

Flag			
	a_{11}	a_{21}	a_{12}
	a_{22}	0	0
'1'	b_{11}	b_{12}	b_{21}
	b_{22}	0	0
	c_{11}	c_{21}	c_{12}
	0	0	0
	a_{21}	0	0
	0	0	0
	0	0	0
	0	0	0

step 31

Flag			
	a_{11}	a_{21}	a_{12}
	a_{22}	0	0
	b_{11}	b_{12}	b_{21}
	b_{22}	0	0
	c_{11}	c_{21}	c_{12}
	0	0	0
'0'	a_{21}	0	0
	0	0	0
	0	0	0
	b_{12}		

step 32

Flag			
	a_{11}	a_{21}	a_{12}
'1'	a_{22}	0	0
	b_{11}	b_{12}	b_{21}
	b_{22}	0	0
	c_{11}	c_{21}	c_{12}
	0	0	0
	$a_{21}.b_{12}$	0	0
	0	0	0
	0	0	0
	0	0	0

step 33

Flag			
	a_{11}	a_{21}	a_{12}
	a_{22}	0	0
	b_{11}	b_{12}	b_{21}
	b_{22}	0	0
	c_{11}	c_{21}	c_{12}
	0	0	0
	$a_{21}.b_{12}$	0	0
'1'	0	0	0
	0	0	0
	a_{22}		

step 34

Flag			
	a_{11}	a_{21}	a_{12}
	a_{22}	0	0
	b_{11}	b_{12}	b_{21}
'1'	b_{22}	0	0
	c_{11}	c_{21}	c_{12}
	0	0	0
	$a_{21}.b_{12}$	0	0
	a_{22}	0	0
	0	0	0
	0	0	0

step 35.....

Flag			
	a_{11}	a_{21}	a_{12}
	a_{22}	0	0
	b_{11}	b_{12}	b_{21}
	b_{22}	0	0
	c_{11}	c_{21}	c_{12}
	0	0	0
	$a_{21}.b_{12}$	0	0
'0'	a_{22}	0	0
	0	0	0
	b_{22}		

step 48

Flag			
	a_{11}	a_{21}	a_{12}
	a_{22}	0	0
	b_{11}	b_{12}	b_{21}
	b_{22}	0	0
	c_{11}	c_{21}	c_{12}
'1'	0	0	0
	c_{22}	0	0
	0	0	0
	0	0	0
	0	0	0

step 49

Flag			
	a_{11}	a_{21}	a_{12}
	a_{22}	0	0
	b_{11}	b_{12}	b_{21}
	b_{22}	0	0
	c_{11}	c_{21}	c_{12}
	0	0	0
'0'	c_{22}	0	0
	0	0	0
	0	0	0
	c_{22}		

step 50

Flag			
	a_{11}	a_{21}	a_{12}
	a_{22}	0	0
	b_{11}	b_{12}	b_{21}
	b_{22}	0	0
	c_{11}	c_{21}	c_{12}
	c_{22}	0	0
	c_22	0	0
	0	0	0
	0	0	0
	'1'	'1'	'1'

for decoding operation, that can be verified from Fig. 6. Generation of generator matrix from the parity check matrix and multiplication of the input data with the generator matrix are sequential operations, so the same ReRAM devices will be used for both the operations. Thus, the area required for both encoding and decoding operations are basically ReRAM devices used for matrix multiplication. Hence, the area required for encoding and decoding operations are same as shown in Fig. 7.

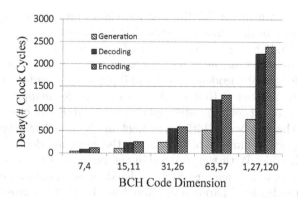

Fig. 6. Delay of mapping for various operations on different dimension of single bit error correcting BCH code.

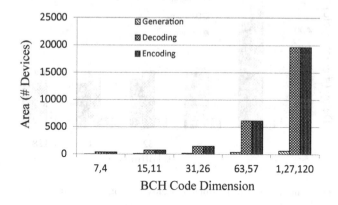

Fig. 7. Area or the number of ReRAM devices required for generation of the elements of GF, encoding and decoding operation of BCH code on that GF.

The increase in dimension of BCH code increases the order of GF, *i.e.*, the delay as well as area requirements for computation of BCH code grow exponentially. Specifically, the number of instructions I_m required for generating all the elements of $GF(2^m)$ can be expressed by Eq. (8).

$$I_m = m + 11(2^m - m - 1) \tag{8}$$

Similarly, the number of instructions required for encoding (I_{en}) and decoding operation (I_{de}) of BCH code can be calculated by Eqs. (9) and (10) respectively, where n and k are the length of encoded data and input data respectively.

$$I_{en} = 2n + (n-1)12 + (k*(n-k)) \tag{9}$$

$$I_{de} = 2n + (n-1)12 \tag{10}$$

Addition operation involves XORing the individual bits of the input operands, which is done in parallel using the rows of ReRAM crossbar. Hence, the delay of performing XOR between any number of elements in two rows of crossbar operation remain constant, even with increase in the number of bitlines. The change in the length of encoded data n and input data k leads to change in the delay as well the number of ReRAM devices required for mapping.

The number of bit-level parallel operations on ReRAM crossbar arrays is dependent on the number of bitlines present in the crossbar. Figure 8 demonstrates the impact of number of bitlines on the mapping delay for operations in (15,11) BCH code. With the increase in the number of bitlines, the delay of operations reduce, which demonstrate the effectiveness of the proposed mapping in harnessing the bit-level parallelism offered by the ReRAM crossbar array.

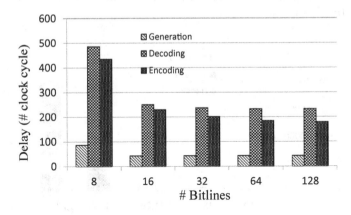

Fig. 8. Impact of the number of bitlines on delay for computation of (15,11) BCH code.

Figure 9 presents the mean energy required for element generation and encoding with decoding operation. Due to the large runtime of device-accurate simulations for all possible input combinations, we only report energy number for operations till BCH code with dimension (63,57). With the increase in dimension of BCH code, the dimensions of parity check and generator matrix also increases and hence, the total number of multiplications also increase. This drastically increases delay, area and energy consumption with the increase in dimension of BCH code.

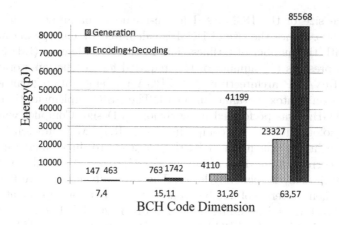

Fig. 9. Impact of BCH code dimensions on energy required for computation.

Table 5. Comparison of area and delay for BCH computation on ReVAMP, ASIC and FPGA.

Op.	BCH dimension	ReVAMP			ASIC		FPGA	
		Delay ns	DCM bits	IM bits	Delay ns	Area GE	Delay ns	Area #LUT
Generation	$(7, 4)$	36	8	154	4.975	2283	50	266
	$(15, 11)$	103	24	918	9.09	3260	90	316
	$(31, 26)$	239	64	2992	18.19	4619	170	341
	$(63, 57)$	519	160	10528	36.96	6883	330	390
	$(127, 120)$	768	384	20498	74.1	11028	650	456
Encoding	$(7, 4)$	118	400	531	6.88	3538	82	379
	$(15, 11)$	251	1600	33885	11.52	5126	91	421
	$(31, 26)$	590	3200	122130	22.36	8096	98	510
	$(63, 57)$	1310	5400	609150	40	9876	108	567
	$(127, 120)$	2391	6200	2418717	80	16078	119	625
Decoding	$(7, 4)$	81	400	3645	6.38	3050	77	377
	$(15, 11)$	230	1475	31050	10.83	5056	89	417
	$(31, 26)$	550	2890	113850	22.37	7820	97	510
	$(63, 57)$	1202	5400	558930	34.45	9201	106	568
	$(127, 120)$	2230	102	2325890	71.65	15890	117	627

Even though the contemporary technologies such as ASIC and FPGA cannot be directly compared with ReRAM based implementation, we report a coarse comparison for the sake of completeness in Table 5. For ReRAM, we assume mature ReRAM technology with 1 ns read/write times [32]. The DCM column presents the size of the DCM used for in-memory computation, in terms of number of bits. Hence the size of DCM is calculated by multiplying number of wordline with the number of bitlines. The Instruction Memory (IM) column in the Table 5 presents the number of bits required for instruction storage in the IM of the ReVAMP architecture. The FPGA implementation (synthesized at 100 MHz) is on Kintex-7 evaluation board. The ASIC implementation (synthesized at ≈1 GHz) was performed using Synopsys Design Compiler with TSMC 65 nm technology library. As computing using ReRAM is inherently sequential, increase in the dimension of BCH code leads to direct increase in delay, along with corresponding increase in area (DCM size). For ASIC and FPGA, the increase in delay is relatively lesser. The main advantage of ReRAM is low area requirement in terms of number of devices required for implementation. For example, encoding and decoding operation of (31,26) BCH code requires ≈8k GE for ASIC, 510 LUT for FPGA but only 590 devices for ReVAMP.

5   Conclusion

In this work, efficient mapping of encoding and decoding operation of single bit error correcting BCH code was proposed on state-of-the-art ReRAM based in-memory computing platform. Further, we have devised a technique for efficient in-memory realization of BiBLAS-3 operations using ReRAM crossbar array. We have explored multiple configurations for the crossbar dimensions and demonstrated performance trade-offs while varying the dimensions of BCH code. The proposed implementation has a low energy footprint and shows good improvements in terms of area requirements compared to traditional ASIC and FPGA based design. In future, the work can be extended for in-memory implementation of multi-bit error correcting BCH code.

References

1. Ibe, E., Taniguchi, H., Yahagi, Y., Shimbo, K., Toba, T.: Impact of scaling on neutron-induced soft error in srams from a 250 nm to a 22 nm design rule. IEEE Trans. Electron Devices **57**(7), 1527–1538 (2010)
2. Krasniewski, A.: Concurrent error detection in sequential circuits implemented using FPGAs with embedded memory blocks. In: Proceedings, 10th IEEE International On-Line Testing Symposium, pp. 67–72, July 2004
3. Asadi, G., Tahoori, M.B.: Soft error mitigation for SRAM-based FPGAs. In: 23rd IEEE VLSI Test Symposium (VTS 2005), pp. 207–212, May 2005
4. Reviriego, P., Argyrides, C., Maestro, J.A.: Efficient error detection in double error correction bch codes for memory applications. Microelectron. Reliab. **52**(7), 1528–1530 (2012). Special Section "Thermal, mechanical and multi-physics simulation and experiments in micro-electronics and micro-systems (EuroSimE 2011)"
5. Chen, B., Zhang, X., Wang, Z.: Error correction for multi-level NAND flash memory using reed-solomon codes. In: 2008 IEEE Workshop on Signal Processing Systems, pp. 94–99, October 2008

6. Park, S.P., Lee, D., Roy, K.: Soft-error-resilient FPGAs using built-in 2-D hamming product code. IEEE Trans. Very Large Scale Integr. (VLSI) Syst. **20**(2), 248–256 (2012)

7. Neuberger, G., de Lima, F., Carro, L., Reis, R.: A multiple bit upset tolerant SRAM memory. ACM Trans. Des. Autom. Electron. Syst. **8**(4), 577–590 (2003)

8. Poolakkaparambil, M., Mathew, J., Jabir, A.M., Mohanty, S.P.: Low complexity cross parity codes for multiple and random bit error correction. In: Thirteenth International Symposium on Quality Electronic Design (ISQED), pp. 57–62, March 2012

9. Jacobvitz, A.N., Calderbank, R., Sorin, D.J.: Writing cosets of a convolutional code to increase the lifetime of flash memory. In: 2012 50th Annual Allerton Conference on Communication, Control, and Computing (Allerton), pp. 308–318, October 2012

10. Chen, B., Cai, F., Zhou, J., Ma, W., Sheridan, P., Lu, W.D.: Efficient in-memory computing architecture based on crossbar arrays. In: 2015 IEEE International Electron Devices Meeting (IEDM), pp. 17.5.1–17.5.4, December 2015

11. Chen, Y., Petti, C.: Reram technology evolution for storage class memory application. In: 2016 46th European Solid-State Device Research Conference (ESSDERC), pp. 432–435, September 2016

12. Yu, S., Chen, P.: Emerging memory technologies: recent trends and prospects. IEEE Solid-State Circuits Mag. **8**(2), 43–56 (2016)

13. Zhu, L., Zhou, J., Guo, Z., Sun, Z.: An overview of materials issues in resistive random access memory. J. Materiomics **1**(4), 285–295 (2015)

14. Siemon, A., Menzel, S., Waser, R., Linn, E.: A complementary resistive switch-based crossbar array adder. IEEE J. Emerg. Sel. Top. Circuits Syst. **5**(1), 64–74 (2015)

15. Sah, M.P., Kim, H., Chua, L.O.: Brains are made of memristors. IEEE Circuits Syst. Mag. **14**(1), 12–36 (2014)

16. Gaillardon, P., et al.: The programmable logic-in-memory (PLiM) computer. In: 2016 Design, Automation Test in Europe Conference Exhibition (DATE), pp. 427–432, March 2016

17. Song, L., Qian, X., Li, H., Chen, Y.: Pipelayer: a pipelined ReRAM-based accelerator for deep learning. In: 2017 IEEE International Symposium on High Performance Computer Architecture (HPCA), pp. 541–552, February 2017

18. Wang, Z., Karpovsky, M.G., Kulikowski, K.J.: Replacing linear hamming codes by robust nonlinear codes results in a reliability improvement of memories. In: 2009 IEEE/IFIP International Conference on Dependable Systems Networks, pp. 514–523, June 2009

19. Bhattacharjee, D., Pudi, V., Chattopadhyay, A.: SHA-3 implementation using ReRAM based in-memory computing architecture. In: 2017 18th International Symposium on Quality Electronic Design (ISQED), pp. 325–330, March 2017

20. Bhattacharjee, D., Chattopadhyay, A.: In-memory data compression using ReRAMs. In: Chattopadhyay, A., Chang, C.H., Yu, H. (eds.) Emerging Technology and Architecture for Big-data Analytics, pp. 275–291. Springer, Cham (2017). https://doi.org/10.1007/978-3-319-54840-1_13

21. Haroussi, M.E., Chana, I., Belkasmi, M.: VHDL design and FPGA implementation of a fully parallel BCH SISO decoder. In: 2010 5th International Symposium On I/V Communications and Mobile Network, pp. 1–4, September 2010

22. Khan, M.A., Afzal, S., Manzoor, R.: Hardware implementation of shortened (48,38) Reed Solomon forward error correcting code. In: 7th International Multi Topic Conference, 2003, INMIC 2003, pp. 90–95, December 2003

23. Xie, J., Meher, P.K., Mao, Z.: High-throughput finite field multipliers using redundant basis for FPGA and asic implementations. IEEE Trans. Circuits Syst. I Regul. Pap. **62**(1), 110–119 (2015)
24. Mandal, S., Tavva, Y., Chattopadhyay, D.B.A.: ReRAM-based in-memory computation of galois field arithmetic. In: 2019 IFIP/IEEE International Conference on Very Large Scale Integration, VLSI-SoC 2019, pp. 1–6 (2019)
25. Couveignes, J.M., Edixhoven, B.: Computational Aspects of Modular Forms and Galois Representations. Princeton University Press, Princeton (2011)
26. Kyuregyan, M.K.: Recurrent methods for constructing irreducible polynomials over Fq of odd characteristics. Finite Fields Their Appl. **9**(1), 39–58 (2003)
27. Joiner, L.L., Komo, J.J.: Decoding binary BCH codes. In: Proceedings IEEE Southeastcon 1995, Visualize the Future, pp. 67–73, March 1995
28. Bhattacharjee, D., Devadoss, R., Chattopadhyay, A.: ReVAMP: ReRAM based VLIW architecture for in-memory computing. In: Design, Automation Test in Europe Conference Exhibition (DATE), 2017, pp. 782–787, March 2017
29. Siemon, A., Menzel, S., Marchewka, A., Nishi, Y., Waser, R., Linn, E.: Simulation of TaOx-based complementary resistive switches by a physics-based memristive model. In: 2014 IEEE International Symposium on Circuits and Systems (ISCAS), pp. 1420–1423, June 2014
30. Linn, E., Rosezin, R., Tappertzhofen, S., Böttger, U., Waser, R.: Beyond von neumann–logic operations in passive crossbar arrays alongside memory operations. Nanotechnology **23**(30), 305205 (2012)
31. Bhattacharjee, D., Merchant, F., Chattopadhyay, A.: Enabling in-memory computation of binary BLAS using ReRAM crossbar arrays. In: 2016 IFIP/IEEE International Conference on Very Large Scale Integration (VLSI-SoC), pp. 1–6, September 2016
32. Emerging research devices (ERD) report. In: International Technology Roadmap for Semiconductors (ITRS) (2013)

Optimizing Performance and Energy Overheads Due to Fanout in In-Memory Computing Systems

Md Adnan Zaman, Rajeev Joshi, and Srinivas Katkoori[✉]

Department of Computer Science and Engineering, University of South Florida,
Tampa, FL, USA
{mdadnanz,rajeevjoshi,katkoori}@mail.usf.edu

Abstract. For NOR-NOT based memristor crossbar architectures, we propose a novel approach to address the fanout overhead problem. Instead of copying the logic value as inputs to the driven memristors, we propose that the controller reads the logic value and then applies it in parallel to the driven memristors. We consider two different cases based on the initialization of the memristors to logic-1 at the locations where we want keep the first input memristor of the driven gates. If the memristors are initialized, it falls under case 1, otherwise case 2. In comparison to recently published works, experimental evaluation on ISCAS'85 benchmarks resulted in average performance improvements of 51.08%, 38.66%, and 63.18% for case 1 and 50.94%, 42.08%, and 60.65% for case 2 considering three different mapping scenarios (average, best, and worst). In regards to energy dissipation, we have also obtained average improvements of 91.30%, 88.53%, and 74.04% for case 1 and 86.03%, 78.97%, and 51.89% for case 2 considering the aforementioned scenarios.

Keywords: Memristor · In-memory computing · Fanout · MAGIC ·
Crossbar · Logic synthesis · Resistive memory

1 Introduction

Von Neumann architecture suffers from *memory wall* problem due to bandwidth mismatch between slower memory and faster CPU [1]. To overcome *memory wall* problem, non von-Neumann architecture is being actively considered where storage and computing can be performed in the same location. This computing inside memory is known as *in-memory computing*. Emerging non-volatile resistive memory technology such as memristor can enable such non von-Neumann computing paradigm. A Memory Processing Unit (MPU) has been proposed [2], where memristive memory is used as storage in conjunction with logical operations.

Due to high speed, low power consumption, scalability, data retention, endurance, and compatibility with conventional CMOS, many memristor based

© IFIP International Federation for Information Processing 2019
Published by Springer Nature Switzerland AG 2019
N. Bombieri et al. (Eds.): VLSI-SoC 2018, IFIP AICT 561, pp. 147–166, 2019.
https://doi.org/10.1007/978-3-030-23425-6_8

logic families and circuits have been proposed [3]. Based on logic state variable, memristor based logic families can be classified into stateful (logic value represented with memristor resistance) and non-stateful logic families [4]. In this work, we employ a stateful logic family, known as Memristor-Aided loGIC (MAGIC) [5]. In this logic style, for a given logic gate, input values and output value(s) are stored as memristor states. Memristors can be fabricated on a crossbar array, which offers high storage density and low power consumption [6]. With MAGIC, only NOR and NOT gates can be directly mapped to crossbar array.

In recent years, researchers have proposed a few in-memory logic synthesis approaches based on MAGIC logic style, where a given circuit netlist consisting of only NOR and NOT gates is mapped to a memristor crossbar. In [5], a detailed procedure to map NOR/NOT logic gates to crossbar has been discussed and also transpose crossbar concept has been introduced to allow gates to be mapped along the rows as well as columns in a crossbar architecture. In [7], a synthesis tool has been proposed that maps arbitrary logical functions within the memristive memory in an optimal manner. In [8], a scalable design flow for in-memory computing has been proposed that allows a given circuit netlist to be implemented in transpose crossbar. In both of these approaches, a given gate netlist is first converted into a netlist of NOR/NOT gates using an existing logic synthesis tool [9] and mapped to the crossbar architecture. While mapping, we come across fanout where a single output (driving) memristor of a logic gate has to be used as input (driven) memristors of multiple gates connected to it. For a fanout of two or more leaf memristors, current methods (previous approaches) perform the *copy* operation for a number of times equal to the number of driven memristors that are not on the same row or column as of the driving memristor. Such copy style requires two NOT operations which in turn requires two extra cycles. With the increment of fanouts in a given netlist, the number of extra cycles increases hence energy as well. To the best of our knowledge, no other previous works attempted to reduce the additional cycle count of a copy operation inherent to a fanout.

In this work, we propose a novel approach that will reduce the performance and energy overheads originated from fanout in a given circuit netlist. Instead of copying the value, the proposed controller can read the value and apply in parallel to the driven memristors. We consider two different cases based on the initialization of the memristors at the copy locations. The locations on the crossbar where we want to keep the first input memristors of the driven gates can be defined as the copy locations. In our prior work [10] which discusses case 1, like the previous works [7,8], we consider that the memristors at the copy locations are initilaized to logic-1 which provides an added advantage to decide whether to write the read value or not to the driven memristors. As proposed in MAGIC logic style, the output memristors are initialized to logic-1 prior to logic execution and it allows the controller to skip write cycle if the read value is one. We have compared our work with a recently published work [8] for three different mapping scenarios. We obtain average improvements of 51.08%, 38.66%, and 63.18% and 91.30%, 88.53%, and 74.04% in performance and energy dissipation respectively. For case 2, we consider that the memristors at the copy locations are not initialized to logic-1 which dictates the use of initialization cycles with the previous approach. We obtain average improvements of 50.94%, 42.08%, and 60.65% and 86.03%, 78.97%, and 51.89% in performance and energy dissipation respectively.

The rest of the chapter is organized as follows: Sect. 2 presents background and related work. Section 3 describes the proposed approach to reduce the number of cycles and energy dissipations related to fanout. Section 4 reports experimental results. Section 5 draws conclusions.

2   Background and Related Work

In this section, we discuss the basic working principle of a memristor, relevant logic design styles, crossbar architecture, and in-memory computing. We also review some of the recent works on memristor based in-memory logic synthesis for a given gate-level netlist with particular concentration on fanout.

2.1   Memristor

Memristor is a two terminal device that can remember its previous state and change its resistance based on a given potential across the device. Chua [11] first proposed memristor that links flux (ϕ) and charge (q) to its memristance (M) according to,

$$d\phi = Mdq \tag{1}$$

Structurally, memristor can be thought of as a thin semiconductor film with thickness (D) sandwiched between two contacts. We can change the overall resistance by changing its doped region width, w [12] (Fig. 1).

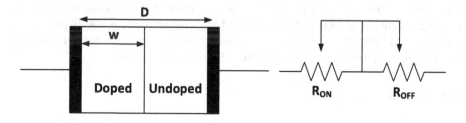

Fig. 1. Physical and circuit model of memristor [12].

2.2   Memristor Aided LoGIC (MAGIC)

Our proposed methodology is based on MAGIC logic style [5]. As shown in Fig. 2, memristors' resistances of the IN_1 and IN_2 are considered as input values and we can determine the output logic value by measuring OUT memristor resistance. An execution voltage V_G is applied to both input memristors and the output value is stored in the output memristor.

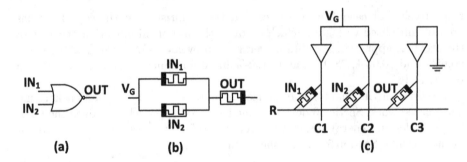

Fig. 2. NOR gate implementation using MAGIC on crossbar.

2.3 In-Memory Computation Using Memristor Crossbar

A Memory Processing Unit (MPU) based on *in-memory computing* architecture is as shown in Fig. 3 [2]. It consists of a controller, crossbar memory, and analog multiplexers. The analog multiplexers' outputs are connected to the bitlines and wordlines of the memristive memory and the voltage select lines of the multiplexers are connected to the controller. To carry out a regular read or write operation, controller sends suitable signals to the addressed memristor cells through multiplexers. We have also shown two signals, V_{SET} and V_{RESET} that can enable writing logic-1 and logic-0 to the memristor cells respectively.

The suitability of the crossbar architecture can be better explained by NOR operation as shown in Fig. 2. We, first, initialize the output memristor (OUT) to logic-1 and connect it to the ground (0V) and then we apply execution voltage V_G to the input memristors (IN_1 and IN_2). This voltage may corrupt data on other memristors on the same row/column, to avoid this, an isolation voltage V_{iso} needs to be applied to the columns and rows that we want to unselect. Parallel execution of NOR/NOT gates on the crossbar requires the alignment of the inputs and outputs of the respective gates. Since we are considering transpose memory here, gates can be aligned either by rows or columns.

2.4 Fanout

Fanout occurs when an output memristor at any circuit depth (excluding primary output) has to drive multiple memristors. It can degrade performance as circuit depth increases and incurs additional energy overheads by introduction of extra cycles. For a given gate-level netlist, a single memristor cell can only be used either as an input or output of a gate. Therefore, the value that is stored in the output memristor if needed can work as input to multiple following memristors. A naïve approach can perform this fanout operation by multiple copies of the logic value as equal to number of the driven memristors (on different rows or columns than driving memristor). This copy operation introduces additional cycles, as proposed in MAGIC logic style where each copy operation requires

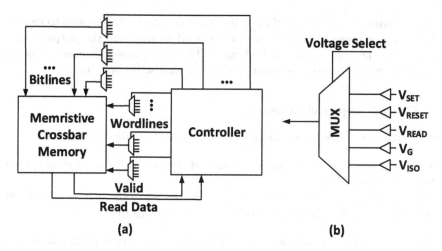

Fig. 3. (a) Memory processing unit (MPU), (b) Analog mux.

cascade of two NOT operations. Therefore, it will require two extra memristors as well as two extra cycles for a single copy operation. As the number of fanout increases for a specific gate output, the number of copy operations, hence additional cycles also increases linearly. Moreover, the energy dissipation also increases due to the extra NOT operations. Works [7,8] based in-memory logic synthesis did not address these performance related issues.

3   Proposed Approach

In this work, we propose a novel approach that will reduce the performance and energy overheads due to fanout in memristor based in-memory computing. The controller will apply relevant signals in proper sequence to the rows and columns in a crossbar architecture. Here, we consider two different cases based on the initialization of the output memristors at the copy locations.

- *Case 1:* Here, we maintain the same assumption as of works [8] and [12]. We consider that the output memristors at the copy locations are initialized to logic-1 which allows us to use a multiplexer through which controller can skip write cycle if the read value is one. With our approach, we have assumed on average 50% of the time, the sensed logic value is 1 which allows us to skip the write cycle. The equations for total cycle counts and energy consumption are formed considering this factor.
- *Case 2:* Here, we consider that the output memristors at the copy locations are not initialized to logic-1. With our proposed approach, we exclude the multiplexer circuit hence removing the ability to skip write cycle (cycle 2) on average 50% of the time. We calculate the total cycle counts and energy requirement and compare with the previous work [8]. Previous works rely on copy operation which requires cascade of two NOT executions which in

turn requires initialization of the output memristors of NOT gates to logic-1. Whereas with our approach, we do not need to initialize the output memristors at the copy locations to logic-1. This comparison demonstrates the trade-off between copy operation and direct read-write operation.

3.1 Overall Approach: Case 1

It will carry out the proposed method according to the following steps:

- *Cycle 1:* Controller reads the logic value of the output memristor which has fanout of two or more.
- *Cycle 2:* Controller writes the logic value as inputs to the driven memristors only if the sensed value is zero, otherwise, it can skip the cycle 2.

Previous works [7,8] utilized a controller that produces a similar state diagram as shown in Fig. 4(a). For regular memory read and write operations, it goes to the read and write states respectively and for executing a logic function, it goes to the execution state. Execution state consists of micro operations where the controller executes the logic function in multiple cycles.

With our proposed approach, the number of state transitions will increase as shown in the Fig. 4(b) but the number of states will remain the same. While executing the micro operations in the execution state, whenever there is a fanout event, the controller will go to the read state and depending on the read value, it will decide whether to go to the write state or not. We can achieve this by modifying the controller circuit. The sensed bit can act as selector for a 2:1 multiplexer and depending on the select bit, controller will determine whether to write to the memory or not. If the read value is 1, the multiplexer will pass the input signal r_{e1} to the controller to go the execution state skipping the write state, otherwise, it will go to the write state and then to the execution state. This allows us to avoid writing logic-1 if the sensed logic value is 1.

3.2 Mapping Scenario Analysis: Case 1

We have made the following assumptions for three different mapping scenarios of a logic function on a memristor crossbar.

We only assume that a single copy of primary input is stored in a single memristor cell and following a fanout scenario from this cell, one can do the copy operation on-demand. Previous works assume that multiple copies of primary inputs are already available depending on the number of gates they are driving. Hence, their assumptions underestimate the cycles required as they are able to eliminate the copy cycles produced from the fanouts of primary inputs.

Like the previous works [8,13], we have considered the output memristors are initialized to logic value one at the beginning of the execution process which is a requirement for MAGIC logic style.

The work [8] has also initialized the output memristors to logic-1 required for copy operations (which eventually become the first input memristors of the

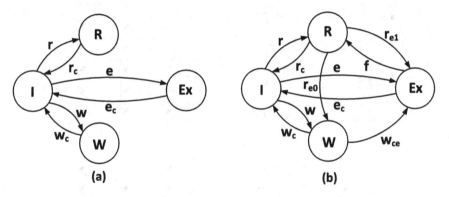

Fig. 4. Controller state diagram (Case 1). (a) Previous approach and (b) Proposed approach. The states are given as: I = Initial state, R = Read state, W = Write state, and Ex = Execution state; The different inputs denote the followings: r = read, r_c = read complete, w = write, w_c = write complete, e = execution, e_c = execution complete, f = fanout event, r_{e1} = read logic-1, r_{e0} = read logic-0, and w_{ce} = write complete and go to execution state.

driven gates). With our proposed approach, we are only considering fanout event related metrics not the whole synthesis procedure. Therefore, in our result analyses, we are not accounting the initialization cycles and energy consumption generated from initializing the output memristors. For fair comparison, we have maintained the same assumption while comparing with work [8]. In our work, the added consideration is, we can avoid writing logic value one. After reading the logic value of the driving memristor, if the controller finds the value as one, it can skip the write operation as the memristors are already initialized to one.

To demonstrate the efficacy of the approach, we have considered three different mapping scenarios (average, best, and worst) depending on the location of the second input memristors of the driven gates. To explain three scenarios, we consider the gate-level netlist shown in Fig. 5(a). We observe that there is a fanout of 4 from the node h. We also consider the logic value of h to be mapped on the location $(1, 1)$ in the memristor crossbar architecture.

Scenario 1. Here, we consider that all the second input memristors are aligned along the same row or same column. The mapped variable h in Fig. 5(b) needs to be copied 3 times to use as first input memristors of the driven gates and the variables a, i, j, and g are mapped as second input memristors on the second column of the crossbar. With the previous approach, it requires 4 cycles to copy logic value of h and now with all the input memristors of the driven gates in aligned position, it is possible to execute the gates in one cycle. The following equation can be used to estimate the total cycles required for copy operations with previous approach:

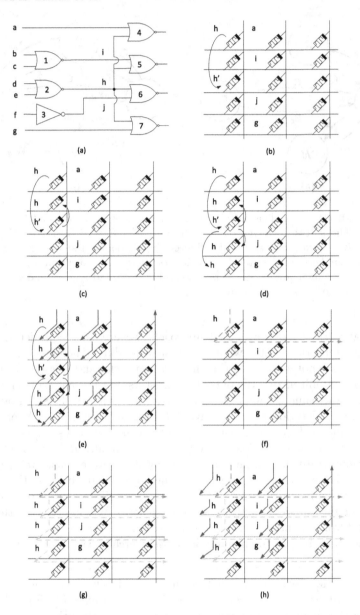

Fig. 5. Scenario 1 with Previous and Proposed Approach. (a) NOR/NOT based synthesized netlist. Regular Approach: (b) 1st cycle: 1st NOT execution to initiate the copy operation, (c) 2nd cycle: 2nd NOT execution to complete the first copy operation, (d) 3rd & 4th cycles: two NOT executions to complete all the copy operations, (e) execution of all the NOR gates in parallel. Proposed Approach: (f) 1st cycle: read operation to sense the logic variable h, (g) 2nd cycle: write operation to write h required number of times in one cycle, (h) 3rd cycle: execution of all NOR gates in parallel. Here, black arrows denote the NOT execution required for copy operation, blue arrow denotes the read operation, green arrows denote the write operations and red arrows denote the execution of NOR gates. (Color figure online)

$$\sum_{n=2}^{N}[n*freq(n)] \tag{2}$$

where, n denotes different fanouts (i.e., number of gates it is driving), N is maximum fanout degree, and $freq(n)$ is the number of times, a fanout of n is found in a netlist.

With the proposed approach, we need 1 cycle to read the logic value and one cycle to write multiple copies of h along the same row or column (given that the read value is logic-0). We consider that on average 50% of the time the read value is 0 which allows us to consider only half of the write cycles to the total cycle count. Therefore, we can estimate the total cycles required with the equation given below:

$$1.5\sum_{n=2}^{N}[freq(n)] \tag{3}$$

It should be noted that with our proposed approach, we require at most two cycles (read and write) for each fanout event and this is true for all scenarios considered here. Therefore, for all three scenarios, we can reuse Eq. 13 to estimate the total cycle counts.

We are providing a general formula to estimate the energy dissipation with both the previous and proposed approach due to the fanout only. According to the work [8], 52.49 fJ is the energy required for one NOT execution. Therefore, with previous approach, we can estimate the total energy dissipation by multiplying 52.49 fJ with the total cycle count (same as total NOT executions required for copy operations). The following equation gives us the total energy dissipation with this approach:

$$52.49\sum_{n=2}^{N}[n*freq(n)] \tag{4}$$

Whereas, for the proposed approach, the total energy required for a specific benchmark circuit can be estimated as:

$$\sum_{n=2}^{N}[\{(RE_m + (n-1)*WE)\}*freq(n)] \tag{5}$$

Where, RE_m denotes the total energy needed to read the variable and to decide (using multiplexer) whether to go to the write state or not. For fanout of n, we need to write $(n-1)$ memristors in a single cycle. Here, WE denotes the write energy required for writing a single memristor.

Scenario 2. We consider here some of the second input memristors are aligned on the same row as of the first input memristor (h) and some are scattered throughout the crossbar. Here, we divide different fanouts (n) according to the number of second input memristors residing on the same row. For example, for

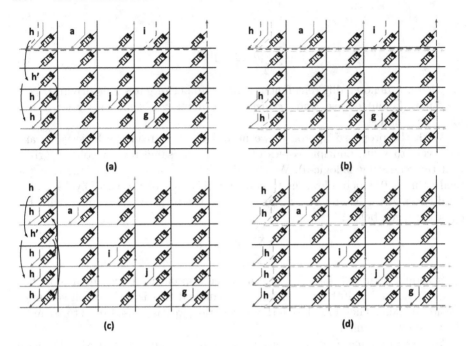

Fig. 6. Scenario 2: (a) previous approach, (b) proposed approach. Scenario 3: (c) regular approach, (d) proposed approach. Here, same color notation as Fig. 5 is maintained, the additional colors, orange, purple, and dark green represent different execution cycles and each composed of all the participating gates in that same cycle. (Color figure online)

fanout of 3, 4, 5, and 6, we have considered 2 second input memristors are on the same row as first input memristor. From Fig. 6(a), it can be seen that the logic variables a and i that are mapped to the second input memristors of the gates 4 and 5 are aligned on the same row and variables j and g are in random locations. With the previous approach, h needs to be copied two times (3 NOT executions) to use it as an inputs of gates 6 and 7. We can evaluate the following equation for the previous approach:

$$2 + \sum_{i=1}^{M} \sum_{n=4i-1}^{4i+2} [\{n - (2i - 1)\}freq(n)] \tag{6}$$

where, 2 cycles are required for fanout of 2. Here, i denotes the number of sub-divisions made on the different fanout and M denotes maximum degree of sub-division. For example, fanout of 4 falls under first sub-division ($i = 1$) which requires 3 cycles (given by the term $\{n - (2i - 1)\}$) to make two copies of the driving memristor. In this way, we find cycle count for each division and add together to get the total cycle counts. As discussed earlier, with the proposed approach, we will get the cycle counts from Eq. 13.

With the previous approach, as in Scenario 1, by simply multiplying the total cycle count with energy requirement of one NOT execution, we can estimate the total energy dissipation:

$$52.49 * [2 + \sum_{i=1}^{M} \sum_{n=4i-1}^{4i+2} [\{n - (2i - 1)\}freq(n)]] \tag{7}$$

and for the proposed approach:

$$(RE_m + WE) + \sum_{i=1}^{M} \sum_{n=4i-1}^{4i+2} [\{RE_m + (n - 2i) * WE\}freq(n)] \tag{8}$$

Where, first term $(RE_m + WE)$ is the energy required for fanout of 2. The term $(n - 2i)$ gives us the number of memristors that needs to be written in a single write cycle.

Scenario 3. For the third scenario, we consider that the second input memristors are scattered throughout the crossbar i.e., aligned neither horizontally nor vertically. From Fig. 6(c), we can see that variables a, i, j, and g are mapped on the memristors that are scattered on the crossbar. With the previous approach, it requires $(n + 1)$ copy cycles for a specific fanout of n and the total cycles required can be estimated as:

$$\sum_{n=2}^{N} [(n + 1)freq(n)] \tag{9}$$

For the proposed approach, we use Eq. 13 which gives us the same cycle counts as of scenario 1 and 2.

By maintaining the same procedure as of Scenarios 1 and 2, the total energy dissipation for the previous approach can be obtained. For the proposed approach, we need to write n memristors in a single write cycle for a fanout of n and the term $(n * WE)$ gives us the write energy required for this operation. For the previous and proposed approach, the energy dissipation can be estimated by the following two equations respectively:

$$52.49 * \sum_{n=2}^{N} [(n + 1)freq(n)] \tag{10}$$

$$\sum_{n=2}^{N} [\{RE_m + (n * WE)\}freq(n)] \tag{11}$$

3.3 Overall Approach: Case 2

It will carry out the proposed method according to the following steps:

- *Cycle 1:* Controller reads the logic value of the output memristor which has fanout of two or more.
- *Cycle 2:* Controller writes the logic value as inputs to the driven memristors without considering whether the sensed logic value is one or not.

Previous works [7,8] utilized a controller that produces a similar state diagram as shown in Fig. 7(a) and maintain the same operation as explained in Sect. 3.1.

With our proposed approach, While executing the micro operations in the execution state, whenever there is a fanout event, the controller will go to the read state and then go to the write state to write the value to the driven memristors without considering whether the read logic value is one or not. Here, we do not use the 2:1 multiplexer, so, controller does not have the capacity to determine whether to skip cycle 2 or not. Controller will always go to the read state and then to the write state irrespective of the read logic value. We do not initialize the output memristors at the copy locations to logic-1 which saves us the initialization cycles and energy required for this operation.

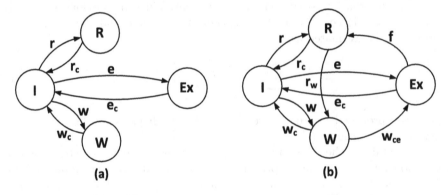

Fig. 7. Controller state diagram (Case 2). (a) Previous approach and (b) Proposed approach. The states are given as: I = Initial state, R = Read state, W = Write state, and Ex = Execution state; The different inputs denote the followings: r = read, r_c = read complete, w = write, w_c = write complete, e = execution, e_c = execution complete, f = fanout event, r_w = go to write state after reading logic value, and w_{ce} = write complete and go to execution state.

3.4 Mapping Scenario Analysis: Case 2

We maintain the same assumption as discussed in the Sect. 3.2 except the third assumption that assume the output memristors at the copy locations are initialized to logic-1. With the exclusion of this assumption, controller now does not have the ability to skip the write cycle as considered in case 1. Here, we discuss three different mapping scenarios of a logic function on a memristor crossbar.

Scenario 1. Here, we consider that all the second input memristors are aligned along the same row or same column. The mapped variable h in Fig. 5(b) needs to be copied 3 times to use as first input memristors of the driven gates and the variables a, i, j, and g are mapped as second input memristors on the second column of the crossbar. In case 2, we consider that output memristors at the copy locations are not initialized to logic-1. Hence, with the previous approach, it requires at least 1 cycle to initialize the memristors at the copy locations and 4 cycles to copy logic value of h. The following equation can be used to estimate the total cycles required for copy operations with previous approach:

$$\sum_{n=2}^{N} [(n+1) freq(n)] \tag{12}$$

where, n denotes different fanouts (i.e., number of gates it is driving), N is maximum fanout degree, and $freq(n)$ is the number of times, a fanout of n is found in a netlist.

With the proposed approach, we need one cycle to read the logic value and one cycle to write multiple copies of h along the same row or column. Therefore, we can estimate the total cycles required with the equation given below:

$$2 \sum_{n=2}^{N} [freq(n)] \tag{13}$$

It should be noted that with our proposed approach, we require two cycles (read and write) for each fanout event and this is true for all scenarios considered here. Therefore, for all three scenarios, we can reuse Eq. 13 to estimate the total cycle counts.

We are providing a general formula to estimate the energy dissipation with both the previous and proposed approach due to the fanout only. For case 2, we have to consider both the energy dissipation due to NOT execution and initialization of the output memristors at the copy locations. According to the work [8], 52.49 fJ is the energy required for one NOT execution, we can denote it by NEx and the energy required to set a memristor to logic 1 is 66.09 fJ, we can denote it by $init\_1$. For fanout of n, we need to initialize n number of memristors. The following equation gives us the total energy dissipation with this approach:

$$(NEx + init\_1) \sum_{n=2}^{N} [n * freq(n)] \tag{14}$$

Whereas, for the proposed approach, the total energy required for a specific benchmark circuit can be estimated as:

$$\sum_{n=2}^{N} [\{(RE + (n-1) * WE)\} * freq(n)] \tag{15}$$

Where, RE denotes the energy needed to read the variable. For fanout of n, we need to write $(n - 1)$ memristors in a single cycle. Here, WE denotes the write energy required for writing a single memristor.

Scenario 2. We consider here the same mapping scenario as discussed in Sect. 3.2, i.e. some of the second input memristors are aligned on the same row as of the first input memristor (h) and some are scattered throughout the crossbar. For details of this mapping scenario, we can refer to Sect. 3.2 (scenario 2). Referring to Fig. 6(a), with the previous approach, first, an initialization cycle is needed to initialize the three output memristors at the copy locations and then h needs to be copied two times (3 NOT executions) to use it as an inputs of gates 6 and 7. We can evaluate the following equation for the previous approach:

$$3 + \sum_{i=1}^{M} \sum_{n=4i-1}^{4i+2} [\{n - 2(i - 1)\} freq(n)] \tag{16}$$

where, 3 cycles are required for fanout of 2. Here, i denotes the number of sub-divisions made on the different fanout and M denotes maximum degree of sub-division. For a specific fanout of n, the term $\{n - 2(i-1)\}$ gives us the total cycle count which includes the copy cycles and the initialization cycle. In this way, we find cycle count for each division and add together to get the total cycle counts. As discussed earlier, with the proposed approach, we will get the cycle counts from Eq. 13.

With the previous approach, as in Scenario 1, we can estimate the total energy dissipation by the following equation:

$$(NEx + init\_1)[2 + \sum_{i=1}^{M} \sum_{n=4i-1}^{4i+2} [\{n - (2i - 1)\} freq(n)]] \tag{17}$$

and for the proposed approach:

$$(RE + WE) + \sum_{i=1}^{M} \sum_{n=4i-1}^{4i+2} [\{RE + (n - 2i) * WE\} freq(n)] \tag{18}$$

where, first term $(RE + WE)$ is the energy required for fanout of 2. The term $(n - 2i)$ gives us the number of memristors that needs to be written in a single write cycle.

Scenario 3. For the third scenario, we consider that the second input memristors are scattered throughout the crossbar i.e., aligned neither horizontally nor vertically. From Fig. 6(c), we can see that variables a, i, j, and g are mapped on the memristors that are scattered on the crossbar. With the previous approach, it requires 1 initialization cycle and $(n + 1)$ copy cycles for a specific fanout of n and the total cycles required can be estimated as:

$$\sum_{n=2}^{N} [(n + 2) freq(n)] \tag{19}$$

For the proposed approach, we use Eq. 13 which gives us the same cycle counts as of scenario 1 and 2.

By maintaining the same procedure as of Scenarios 1 and 2, the total energy dissipation for the previous approach can be obtained. For the proposed approach, we need to write n memristors in a single write cycle for a fanout of n and the term $(n * WE)$ gives us the write energy required for this operation. For the previous and proposed approach, the energy dissipation can be estimated by the following two equations respectively:

$$(NEx + init\_1) \sum_{n=2}^{N} [(n+1)freq(n)] \tag{20}$$

$$\sum_{n=2}^{N} [\{RE + (n * WE)\}freq(n)] \tag{21}$$

4   Experimental Results

To validate the proposed approach, we performed a set of experiments on ISCAS'85 benchmark circuits and compared our results with a recently published work [8]. While doing so, we maintained the assumptions as stated in Sect. 3. In a given NOR/NOT based synthesized netlist, total number of gate executions consist of regular execution of gates pertaining only to the netlist and the extra NOT executions required for copy operations produced by fanout. We estimated the total number of extra NOT executions over the total number of gate executions for a specific benchmark circuit and then averaged over all the benchmark circuits. An average of 47.41%, 41.82%, and 54.40% additional cycle count due to NOT operations has been measured for scenario 1, scenario 2, and scenario 3 respectively. With our proposed approach, we are able to reduce performance and energy overheads produced by these aforementioned additional cycles.

- *Case 1:* Previous works such as [7,8] have only considered energy dissipation due to gate executions, but as energy consumptions from read cycle, write cycle, and 2:1 multiplexer are inherent in our proposed approach, we have included these in our analysis. Performance and energy overheads for the multiplexer are obtained for a 45 nm CMOS process technology from PTM using HSPICE and our circuit level evaluation shows that the delay introduced by a multiplexer is in the picosecond range. The work [8] has used the VTEAM model [14] to find the maximum latency for MAGIC NOR operations (when either of the inputs is at logic-1) and also to find the read time. We consider these times as the cycle time and read time of the system respectively. According to [15], the latency introduced by MAGIC operations are much higher than that of read and write operations. Hence, the effective delay produced by the sense circuit and the multiplexer still stays below 1 cycle time. Therefore, in our analysis, we will not consider any performance overhead due to this added multiplexer.

– *Case 2:* In case 2, we do not initialize the output memristors at the copy locations to logic-1. This removes the 2:1 multiplexer from the system, as the controller is not aware of the logic value stored in the output memristors at the copy locations. In our result analysis, for the proposed approach, we exclude the energy consumed by the multiplexer and in case of previous approach, we add the energy required for initializing the memristor to logic-1. From [8], the energy required to write logic-1 to a memristor is 66.09 fJ. Therefore, with the previous approach, the total cycle count comes from the addition of initialization cycle and the copy cycles. With the proposed approach, we always need two cycles, one to read the logic value of the driving memristor and other to write the logic value to the driven memristors.

4.1   Experimental Setup

The experimental methodology we follow to validate our approach is as follows:

1. A given gate-level netlist is first synthesized with ABC tool [9] and target library of NOR and NOT gates.
2. For three different scenarios, number of fanout events has been found and cycle counts and energy dissipations estimation have been performed with the proposed method and compared with [8].

Table 1. Comparison of number of cycles (Average Scenario) with the regular and proposed approach.

Benchmark	Fanout events	Number of cycles due to fanout only					
		Case 1: Scenario 1 (Average)			Case 2: Scenario 1 (Average)		
		Approach [8]	Proposed	Improvement (%)	Approach [8]	Proposed	Improvement (%)
c432	80	260	120	53.85	340	160	52.94
c499	215	602	323	46.35	817	430	47.37
c880	159	448	239	46.65	607	318	47.61
c1355	215	602	323	46.35	817	430	47.37
c1908	215	610	323	47.05	825	430	47.87
c2670	328	1024	492	51.95	1352	656	51.48
c3540	352	1343	528	60.69	1695	704	58.47
c5315	596	2193	894	59.23	2789	1192	57.26
c6288	1223	3544	1835	48.22	4767	2446	48.69
c7552	966	2924	1449	50.44	3890	1932	50.33
Average improvements				51.08			50.94

4.2   Results and Analysis

Tables 1, 2, and 3 report the improvements over recently published work with respect to the number of cycles due to fanout in average, best, and worst scenarios respectively. For case 1, we observe average improvements of 51.08%, 38.66%, and 63.18% in cycle reduction considering three mapping scenarios.

In case 2, we consider that the memristors at the copy locations are not initialized to logic-1 which dictates the need of adding initialization cycle to the total cycle counts. With the proposed approach, we need two cycles to read the driving memristor and then write the logic variable to the driven memristors in parallel. We observe average improvements of 50.94%, 42.08%, and 60.65% in cycle reduction.

Table 2. Comparison of number of cycles (Best Scenario) with the regular and proposed approach.

Benchmark	Fanout events	Number of cycles due to fanout only					
		Case 1: Scenario 2 (Best)			Case 2: Scenario 2 (Best)		
		Approach [8]	Proposed	Improvement (%)	Approach [8]	Proposed	Improvement (%)
c432	80	207	120	42.03	287	160	44.25
c499	215	499	323	35.27	714	430	39.78
c880	159	357	239	33.05	516	318	38.37
c1355	215	499	323	35.27	714	430	39.78
c1908	215	492	323	34.35	707	430	39.18
c2670	328	832	492	40.87	1160	656	43.45
c3540	352	1015	528	47.98	1367	704	48.50
c5315	596	1703	894	47.50	2299	1192	48.15
c6288	1223	2672	1835	31.32	3895	2446	37.20
c7552	966	2373	1449	38.94	3339	1932	42.14
Average improvements				38.66			42.08

Tables 4, 5, and 6 report the improvements in energy consumption. For estimating the energy requirement, we have taken the same parameter values as discussed in [8]. The energy required for NOT execution is 52.49 fJ. The energy required to read logic-0 is 0.03 fJ, while that for logic-1 is 3.34 fJ. For our estimation purpose, we have averaged these two values and considered the read energy as 1.685 fJ. The energy required to write logic-1 to a memristor which is termed as SET operation is 66.09 fJ and through RESET operation, we can write logic-0 to a memristor and the energy required is 17.60 fJ. For case 1, as discussed in Sect. 3, we do not need to write logic-1 with our proposed approach, thus, no energy is consumed. Therefore, the average energy considered for SET and RESET operation is 8.8 fJ. For a specific benchmark circuit, we find all different fanout occurrences and add the energies required to estimate the total energy dissipation. We observe average improvements of 91.30%, 88.53%, and 74.04%

Table 3. Comparison of number of cycles (Worst Scenario) with the regular and proposed approach.

Benchmark	Fanout events	Number of cycles due to fanout only					
		Case 1: Scenario 3 (Worst)			Case 2: Scenario 3 (Worst)		
		Approach [8]	Proposed	Improvement (%)	Approach [8]	Proposed	Improvement (%)
c432	80	340	120	64.71	420	160	61.91
c499	215	817	323	60.47	1032	430	58.34
c880	159	607	239	60.63	766	318	58.49
c1355	215	817	323	60.47	1032	430	58.34
c1908	215	825	323	60.85	1040	430	58.65
c2670	328	1352	492	63.61	1680	656	60.95
c3540	352	1695	528	68.85	2047	704	65.61
c5315	596	2789	894	67.95	3385	1192	64.79
c6288	1223	4767	1835	61.51	5990	2446	59.17
c7552	966	3890	1449	62.75	4856	1932	60.22
Average improvements				63.18			60.65

Table 4. Comparison of energy dissipation (Average Scenario) with the regular and proposed approach.

Benchmark	Fanout events	Energy dissipation in pJ due to fanout only					
		Case 1: Scenario 1 (Average)			Case 2: Scenario 1 (Average)		
		Approach [8]	Proposed	Improvement (%)	Approach [8]	Proposed	Improvement (%)
c432	80	28.82	2.32	91.95	65.11	8.00	87.71
c499	215	52.60	4.63	91.20	118.83	16.90	85.78
c880	159	43.46	3.62	91.67	98.19	12.76	87.00
c1355	215	52.60	4.63	91.20	118.83	16.90	85.78
c1908	215	54.69	4.76	91.30	123.57	17.29	86.00
c2670	328	106.19	8.77	91.74	239.91	30.77	87.17
c3540	352	133.85	11.82	91.17	302.41	43.28	85.68
c5315	596	219.20	19.19	91.25	495.23	69.82	85.90
c6288	1223	265.02	25.86	90.24	598.761	99.76	83.34
c7552	966	268.38	23.51	91.24	606.351	85.59	85.88
Average improvements				91.30			86.03

by experimental evaluation on ISCAS'85 benchmark circuits. This improvement can be primarily attributed to the fact that we were able to eliminate the need for writing logic-1.

For case 2, with the previous approach, the memristors at the copy locations need to be initialized to logic-1. Therefore, this initialization energy needs to be accounted for in the total energy calculation. With the proposed approach, we exclude energy consumption produced by the multiplexer that is required in case 1. The only energies required are the energy to read the driving memristor and energy to write the driven memristors. We observe average improvements of 86.03%, 78.97%, and 51.89% in energy saving.

Table 5. Comparison of energy dissipation (Best Scenario) with the regular and proposed approach.

Benchmark	Fanout events	Energy dissipation in pJ due to fanout only					
		Case 1: Scenario 2 (Best)			Case 2: Scenario 2 (Best)		
		Approach [8]	Proposed	Improvement (%)	Approach [8]	Proposed	Improvement (%)
c432	80	10.87	1.28	88.22	24.55	5.34	78.25
c499	15	26.19	2.93	88.81	59.18	12.01	79.71
c880	159	18.74	2.06	89.01	42.34	8.39	80.18
c1355	215	26.19	2.93	88.81	59.18	12.01	79.71
c1908	215	25.83	2.87	88.89	58.35	11.72	79.92
c2670	328	43.67	5.09	88.34	98.67	21.22	78.49
c3540	352	53.28	6.54	87.73	120.37	27.78	76.92
c5315	596	89.39	10.93	87.77	201.96	46.39	77.03
c6288	1223	140.25	15.19	89.17	316.87	61.47	80.60
c7552	966	124.56	14.30	88.52	281.41	59.31	78.92
Average improvements				88.53			78.97

Table 6. Comparison of energy dissipation (Worst Scenario) with the regular and proposed approach.

Benchmark	Fanout events	Energy dissipation in pJ due to fanout only					
		Case 1: Scenario 3 (Worst)			Case 2: Scenario 3 (Worst)		
		Approach [8]	Proposed	Improvement (%)	Approach [8]	Proposed	Improvement (%)
c432	80	17.85	5.57	68.80	40.32	23.13	42.63
c499	215	42.88	10.04	76.59	96.89	42.12	56.53
c880	159	31.86	8.36	73.76	71.98	34.86	51.57
c1355	215	42.88	10.04	76.59	96.89	42.12	56.53
c1908	215	43.30	10.46	75.84	97.84	43.81	55.22
c2670	328	70.97	20.44	71.20	160.33	85.18	46.87
c3540	352	88.97	25.54	71.29	201.01	107.18	46.68
c5315	596	146.40	41.88	71.39	330.75	175.56	46.92
c6288	1223	250.22	49.86	80.07	565.32	211.61	62.57
c7552	966	204.19	51.28	74.89	461.32	214.95	53.41
Average improvements				74.04			51.89

5   Conclusions

In this work, we outline an effective approach that would significantly reduce the performance and energy overheads due to fanout while mapping a logic function in memristor based crossbar architecture. Comparison has been made with a recently published work and shows significant average improvements in average, best, and worst mapping scenarios in performance and energy dissipation. Future research direction would be to implement the entire logic synthesis process utilizing the fanout optimization discussed here.

References

1. Wulf, W.A., McKee, S.A.: Hitting the memory wall: implications of the obvious. ACM SIGARCH Comput. Arch. News **23**(1), 20–24 (1995)
2. Hur, R.B., Kvatinsky, S.: Memristive memory processing unit (MPU) controller for in-memory processing. In: 2016 IEEE International Conference on the Science of Electrical Engineering (ICSEE), pp. 1–5, November 2016
3. Kvatinsky, S., Friedman, E.G., Kolodny, A., Weiser, U.C.: The desired memristor for circuit designers. IEEE Circuits Syst. Mag. **12**(2), 17–22 (2013). Secondquarter
4. Lehtonen, E., Poikonen, J.H., Laiho, M.: Memristive stateful logic. In: Adamatzky, A., Chua, L. (eds.) Memristor Networks, pp. 603–623. Springer, Cham (2014). https://doi.org/10.1007/978-3-319-02630-5_27
5. Talati, N., Gupta, S., Mane, P., Kvatinsky, S.: Logic design within memristive memories using memristor-aided loGIC (MAGIC). IEEE Trans. Nanotechnol. **15**(4), 635–650 (2016)
6. Nair, R.: Evolution of Memory Architecture. Proc. IEEE **103**(8), 1331–1345 (2015)
7. Hur, R.B., Wald, N., Talati, N., Kvatinsky, S.: Simple magic: synthesis and in-memory mapping of logic execution for memristor-aided logic. In: 2017 IEEE/ACM International Conference on Computer-Aided Design (ICCAD), pp. 225–232, November 2017
8. Gharpinde, R., Thangkhiew, P.L., Datta, K., Sengupta, I.: A scalable in-memory logic synthesis approach using memristor crossbar. IEEE Trans. Very Large Scale Integr. (VLSI) Syst. **26**(2), 355–366 (2018)
9. Berkeley Logic Synthesis and Verification Group, ABC: A System for Sequential Synthesis and Verification, Release 90215. http://www.eecs.berkeley.edu/~alanmi/abc/
10. Zaman, M.A., Katkoori, S.: Minimizing performance and energy overheads due to fanout in memristor based logic implementations. In: 2018 IFIP/IEEE International Conference on Very Large Scale Integration (VLSI-SoC), pp. 7–12, October 2018
11. Chua, L.: Memristor-The missing circuit element. IEEE Trans. Circuit Theory **18**(5), 507–519 (1971)
12. Strukov, D.B., Snider, G.S., Stewart, D.R., Williams, R.S.: The missing memristor found. Nature **453**(7191), 80–83 (2008)
13. Ali, A.H., Hur, R.B., Wald, N., Kvatinsky, S.: Efficient algorithms for in-memory fixed point multiplication using MAGIC. In: 2018 IEEE International Symposium on Circuits and Systems (ISCAS), pp. 1–5, May 2018
14. Kvatinsky, S., Ramadan, M., Friedman, E.G., Kolodny, A.: VTEAM: a general model for voltage-controlled memristors. IEEE Trans. Circuits Syst. II: Express Briefs **62**(8), 786–790 (2015)
15. Talati, N., et al.: Practical challenges in delivering the promises of real processing-in-memory machines. In: 2018 Design, Automation Test in Europe Conference Exhibition (DATE), pp. 1628–1633, March 2018

Mapping Spiking Neural Networks on Multi-core Neuromorphic Platforms: Problem Formulation and Performance Analysis

Francesco Barchi[✉], Gianvito Urgese, Enrico Macii, and Andrea Acquaviva

DAUIN, Politecnico di Torino, Corso Duca degli Abruzzi, 24, 10129 Turin, Italy
{francesco.barchi,gianvito.urgese,enrico.macii,
andrea.acquaviva}@polito.it

Abstract. In this paper, we propose a methodology for efficiently mapping concurrent applications over a globally asynchronous locally synchronous (GALS) multi-core architecture designed for simulating a Spiking Neural Network (SNN) in real-time. The problem of neuron-to-core mapping is relevant as a non-efficient allocation may impact real-time and reliability of the SNN execution. We designed a task placement pipeline capable of analysing the network of neurons and producing a placement configuration that enables a reduction of communication between computational nodes. We compared four Placement techniques by evaluating the overall post-placement synaptic elongation that represents the cumulative distance that spikes generated by neurons running on a core have to travel to reach their destination core. Results point out that mapping solutions taking into account the directionality of the SNN application provide a better placement configuration.

Keywords: Graph mapping · Multicore neuromorphic architectures · Spiking neural networks

1 Introduction

Finding the best way to map tasks to processor cores in multi and many-core systems is a relevant optimisation problem, with significant impact on application reliability, performance, and energy consumption.

The solution of this particular problem in many cases can only be computed employing heuristic methodologies capable of providing approximated or suboptimal solutions.

The task placement problem is common in many fields of applications that go from the mapping of parallel applications on stream-oriented MPSoCs [24] to the placement of virtual machines in cloud data centres with parallel nodes [18]. Programming such architectures efficiently is a challenge because numerous

© IFIP International Federation for Information Processing 2019
Published by Springer Nature Switzerland AG 2019
N. Bombieri et al. (Eds.): VLSI-SoC 2018, IFIP AICT 561, pp. 167–186, 2019.
https://doi.org/10.1007/978-3-030-23425-6_9

hardware characteristics have to be taken into account, especially the memory hierarchy. One appealing idea to improve the performance of parallel applications is to decrease their communication costs by matching the communication pattern to the underlying hardware architecture. Such a method can be performed with the design of a strategy capable of partitioning the main application in several independent tasks with computation/communication load compatible with the capability of the parallel cores available on the architecture.

A good example of a solution for this problem has been proposed in [24] where they defined a placement system that split the original application in a directed acyclic task graph where each node is an independent atomic task that communicates with the other nodes in discrete time. Moreover, they considered the number and capability of available cores and the communication infrastructure of the targeted platform for reducing the placement problem on N tasks to M processors.

In the Neuromorphic domain, we explored the task placement problem in the case of a globally asynchronous locally synchronous (GALS) multicore architecture called SpiNNaker. However, the same type of analysis can be customised for Intel Loihi [5], IBM TrueNorth [2] and SpiNNaker2 [16], representing the future of the neuromorphic multi-core platforms, for discovery what are the best practices to be adopted for efficiently mapping running highly parallel tasks.

SpiNNaker has been designed mainly for running neuromorphic applications. Here, tasks to be executed are physical neuron models running in parallel on the platform and communicating through messages. These messages represent signals, called spikes, which biological neurons exchange through their physical (neural) connections inside the brain.

The overall purpose of this application is to execute a Spiking Neural Network (SNN) in real-time. In this case, real-time means that the timings of the spikes generated by the neurons should be compliant with the one of the real human brain. Thus opening the way for the use of neuromorphic platforms to interface external physical systems and elaborates their signals (e.g. images, sounds) in the same way as the brain does. Being the neurons executed as concurrent tasks by the general purpose cores, how to efficiently mapping neurons-to-cores is an issue that must be addressed for optimising the communication between cores.

Generalising, the problem we faced concerns the mapping of a large number of light parallel tasks with intensive communication to a many-core architecture. A non-efficient communication, in the specific case of SNN execution, may impact real-time capabilities as well as the reliability of the application. Indeed, spikes can be lost due to congestion problems. In general, a possible approach to face the mapping problem is to model the tasks and their communication as a graph to be mapped over the underlying hardware architecture, represented by another graph.

Sugiarto et al. [27] presented an approach for improving the overall performance of general-purpose applications running as a task graph on the same many-core neuromorphic supercomputer. Whereas in a recent paper, we have used the cortical microcircuit application as a test case for demonstrating that an enhanced partitioning and placement system studied for the SNN topology can produce a more reliable and stable configuration for the simulation on the SpiNNaker system [28,29].

In this document, we expand the work presented in [3] presenting a methodology for mapping a task graph representing the SNN computation on a multi-chip many-core architecture with communication awareness. To achieve this target, we designed a task mapping framework capable of analysing the network of neurons to find a configuration with the goal of reducing the communication between computational nodes. The neuron-to-core mapping problem has been formalised as a problem of minimisation of synaptic elongation. Intuitively, this metric represents the cumulative distance that spikes generated by neurons running on a specific core have to travel to reach their destination core.

The framework starts by extracting a graph of independent processes from a neural network description. In the case of SNN, the direction of a communication path is also to be represented using a directed graph. On the platform side, the interconnect structure is described as a graph where nodes represent on-chip cores while edges represent physical communication links between them. In this way, we formalised a neuron-to-core mapping as a graph-matching problem solvable through the exploitation of various algorithms available in the literature. The specific formulation we devised for SNN mapping takes into account the typical organisation of these type of neural networks into neuron populations, sharing similar characteristics as well as the neuron model.

The results obtained by comparing four mapping algorithms points out and quantify the relevance of the communication direction information to achieve a better mapping if compared with non-directional algorithms.

2 Background

In this section, we will introduce the application and the MCSoC board selected as a target for demonstrating the advantages of adopting our task-placement communication aware framework.

2.1 Target Application: Neural Network Simulation

Spiking Neural Network (SNN) is a particular neural model used by neuro-scientist for simulating biologically plausible brain activity. Two of the most adopted neuron models are the *Leaky Integrate-and-Fire* (LIF) [1] and *Izhikevich* (IZK) [11], because they can ensure a plausible picture of the biological behaviours with reduced computational costs. During SNN simulations neurons and their synapses are modelled as differential equations capable of emulating the behaviours observed in biological networks [17]. An SNN can be described as a graph where each vertex is called *Population* containing a homogeneous group of neurons sharing the same model and parameters. Whereas, each edge (*Projection*) represents the rule used to generate synaptic connections between the neurons of two *Populations*. Using PyNN [6] scientist can describe many neurons/synapses models and configurations that can be exploited on different backends such as software simulators and neuromorphic platforms.

Using this SNN description system, Van Albada et al. [30] designed an SNN application implementing the cell-type specific cortical microcircuit (CM) model created by Potjans et al. [21]. Then they simulated this SNN on a neuromorphic multi-chip many-core platform called SpiNNaker [8] using the standard application partitioning and placement system for setting up the simulation on the board.

2.2   Target Architecture: Neuromorphic MPSoCs Board

For validating our placement methodology framework we took as target a GALS Neuromorphic many-core architecture and used its native application such as an example case. We used the SpiNNaker architecture which is a many-core platform that follows an event-driven computational approach, mainly used for simulating neural networks in real-time [8]. This system mimics the features of a biological neural network through the implementation of several features:

- Native parallelism: Each biological neuron is a fundamental computational element within a massively parallel system. Likewise, SpiNNaker uses parallel computation.
- Spiking communications: In biology, neurons communicate through spikes. The SpiNNaker architecture uses source-based Address Event Representation (AER) packets to transmit the equivalent of neural signals (i.e. action potentials) [22]. Each AER packet identifies the event source through an addressing scheme.
- Event-driven behaviour: Neurons are very power efficient, and consume much less power than other modern hardware, in fact to reduce power consumption, the hardware is put into "idle" state until an interrupt event doesn't trigger an action [12].
- Distributed memory: In biology, neurons use only local information to process incoming stimuli. The SpiNNaker architecture features a hierarchy of memories: memory local to each of the cores and an SDRAM local to each chip.

The SpiNNaker chip (Fig. 1) has 18 ARM 968 cores running at 200 MHz with no floating point units[1], a full customized router for intra/inter-chip communications, and an SDRAM external to the chip and accessible through the PL340 interface [9]. Each core of a chip can access three four memory levels: (i) a 96 kB Tightly Coupled Memory (TCM) that is part of each ARM core. It is divided into ITCM containing instructions (32 kB) and DTCM containing application data (64 kB). (ii) a 32 kB System RAM integrated into the chip and shared between all the cores. (iii) a 32 kB System ROM shared between all processors that contains the bootstrap software. (iv) a 128 MB SDRAM shared between all cores of a chip.

---

[1] The SpiNNaker simulator applies a mechanism of rescaling that allows working with only integers, even if in the equations of the neural models are in the domains of real numbers.

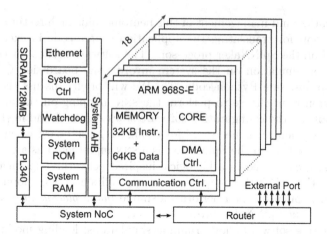

Fig. 1. The SpiNNaker chip is a system-on-chip with 18 compute-units based on ARM processors. Each compute-unit, in addition to the processor, is equipped with two TCM (for instructions and data), a DMA controller and it interacts with other components of the SoC (System RAM, System ROM, External SDRAM) through a communication controller.

The SpiNNaker system is built with boards of 48 chips interconnected to form a toroidal shaped triangular mesh where each chip is connected to six nearby chips. Each router is in charge to dispatch packets along intra-chip and inter-chip cores, and it can manage transmission of four types of packets:

- Multi-Cast (MC) packets are used for reaching many cores across the board. They are widely used during neural simulations for spreading neural potentials to multiple destinations (emulating synapses potential transmission). These packets are routed using a routing table of 1024 entries, stored in a ternary CAM with three values per entry: routing key, routing mask and routing rule. The routing header of a multicast packet is compared with all the table entries and then redirected following the selected rule. The length of those packets could be up to 72 bits.
- Point-to-Point (PP) packets are used for reaching an exact core of the board uniquely identified by the coordinates of the belonging chip and its relative number (from 0 to 17). These packets are routed using a dedicate routing table. If the destination is within the local chip, the packet is delivered to the monitor processor. This type of packet can transport a payload of 32 bits over the available 72 bits.
- Nearest Neighbour (NN) packets are used for initialising the board and for implementing a keep-alive mechanism useful for understanding if there are broken links and, in this case, calculate a different path.
- Fixed Route (FR) packets are used for reaching a fixed destination (by default, the chip attached to the ethernet controller). The advantage of this type of packet is that it provides 64 bits of payload.

Configuration and management of this neuromorphic architecture need a set of software tools for translating the application source code in executables to be processed on the SpiNNaker processors. The software needed for configuring and running a simulation on the system involves the board-side C/Assembly code and the host-side Python code [23]. We will briefly discuss the host-side modules currently in charge to perform the SNN mapping on the architecture. Further details on the configuration software stack can be found in [13].

A mapping manager is necessary for configuring the board when the application to be executed on the SpiNNaker is a SNN represented as a graph of sets of neurons interconnected in a biological-inspired network. The current implementation of the SpiNNaker mapping manager splits each SNN population in a set of partial populations and performs a simple *radial placement* of the partial populations on the SpiNNaker processors.

The host-side software allows running simulations, loading modules and to managing connections and data transfer. It is made of five modules:

- sPyNNaker: a module that provides a wrapper of the PyNN [6] neural network software simulator implementing the neural models (implemented by both Python and C/Assembly code), synapse models, populations and projections. The tool parses all the parameters from the configuration files and translates the PyNN representation into executables and configuration data to be loaded into SpiNNaker.
- SpiNNMachine: implements a set of classes that represents at a high level all the SpiNNaker components (e.g. *Processor, SDRAM, Router*). The main class, *Machine*, is the representation of the whole architecture.
- PACMAN: The *Partition and Control Manager* performs the partitioning of the SNN graph splitting each Population in a set of vertices (partial-populations) and performs the placement of the partial-populations on the SpiNNaker processors.
- SpiNNMan: is a tool that implements at a lower level the communication between the computer host end the SpiNNaker board allowing to send and receive messages (SDP packets, SCP commands, EIEIO Packets) using the UDP protocol. It is widely used by the other modules for load executables and data.
- DataSpecification: contains a tool that allows specifying data (synaptic matrices, data structures and configuration rules) for the application running on a processor.

This full software stack can be combined with a new protocol [26] designed for simplifying configuration and execution of applications by enabling: (i) A more efficient generation of data structures during the configuration phase, (ii) An on-the-fly reconfiguration of specific parameters, avoiding the re-load of simulation data, and (iii) The possibility of embedding alternative computational flows in the applications, allowing users to switch between predefined tasks.

3   Problem Formulation

The SNN placement into the neuromorphic architecture can be view as an optimisation problem that involves two graphs: $\mathcal{G}_\mathcal{N}$ and $\mathcal{G}_{\text{CPU}}$.

A graph $\mathcal{G} = (V, E, \mathcal{W})$ is a mathematical representation for describing a set of elements V and a set of relations $E \subseteq \{(v_i, v_j) : v_i, v_j \in V\}$ among them. The elements are called *nodes* of the graph and the relations are called *edges* of the graph. An edge $e_{ij} \in E$ binds two nodes $v_i, v_j \in V$ to each other. A graph can have a $\mathcal{W} : E \to W$ function that associates an edge $e_{ij} \in E$ to a value $w_{ij} \in W$. The value $w_{ij} = \mathcal{W}(e_{ij})$ is called edge weight. A graph can be categorised according to two properties: (i) If the nodes on edges form unordered pairs $e_{ij} : \{v_i, v_j\}$ the graph is said *undirected* otherwise it is said *directed* and the nodes on edges form ordered pairs $e_{ij} : (v_i, v_j)$. (ii) If the weight set W is empty the graph is said *unweighted*, otherwise it is said *weighed*.

A Spiking Neural Network (SNN) can be represented using a directed and weighted graph called *neuron graph* $\mathcal{G}_\mathcal{N}$. In $\mathcal{G}_\mathcal{N}$ the nodes are the SNN neurons and the edges are the SNN synapses. Taking into account a synapse $e_{ij} : (v_i, v_j)$, the neuron v_i is called pre-synaptic neuron and the neuron v_j is called post-synaptic neuron. The edge weight w_{ij} (called synaptic weight) represents the synapse contribution to injected current into the post-synaptic neuron after a stimulus received by the pre-synaptic neuron.

The neuromorphic architecture can be represented using an undirected and weighed graph, called *target graph* $\mathcal{G}_\mathcal{T}$.

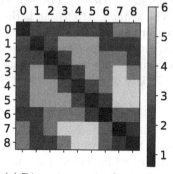

(a) Distance matrix obtained using a coarse-grain target graph

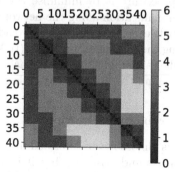

(b) Distance matrix obtained using a fine-grain target graph

Fig. 2. The distance matrix of a placement area using a coarse-grain and a fine-grain target graph.

The *target graph* can be more or less detailed. If the nodes of the graph are the SpiNNaker Chips, we define $\mathcal{G}_\mathcal{T}$ as *coarse-grain*. If the nodes of the graph are the SpiNNaker Processors, we define $\mathcal{G}_\mathcal{T}$ as *fine-grain*.

If the *target graph* is coarse-grain, all edges represent the inter-chip communication links. If the *target graph* is fine-grain, all edges between two processors located on the same chip have a weight of one, while all edges between two processors belonging to adjacent chips have a weight of two.

This choice is determined by the structure of the arbiter which feeds the SpiN-Naker Routers. A SpiNNaker Router has two branches for introducing packets according to their origin: the 18 internal processors and the six nearby chips. It has been demonstrated in [28] that the arbiter does not correctly manage some traffic configurations coming from the external links. It was therefore decided to disadvantage all inter-chip communications with twice the weight of intra-chip communications. The Fig. 2 shows the differences between the coarse-grain model and the fine-grain model through the distance matrices obtained from the graphs of the target nodes.

We can define the placement problem $\Pi : \mathcal{G}_\mathcal{N} \to \mathcal{G}_T$ as a minimization problem (1).

$$\underset{f(\pi)}{\text{minimize}} \qquad f : \sum_{e_{ij} \in E_\mathcal{N}} d(\pi(v_i), \pi(v_j)) \tag{1a}$$

$$\text{subject to} \qquad \pi(i) = \pi(j) \to \mathcal{M}(i) = \mathcal{M}(j), \ i, j \in V_\mathcal{N} \tag{1b}$$

$$|\pi(i) = p| \leq \mathcal{S}(\mathcal{M}(i)), \ i \in V_\mathcal{N}, p \in V_T \tag{1c}$$

Where $\pi : V_\mathcal{N} \to V_T$ is the placement rule, $\mathcal{M} : V_\mathcal{N} \to M$ is the neuron-model association rule and, $\mathcal{S} : M \to \mathbb{N}$ is the association rule between a neuron model and the maximum number of neurons per node. The goal of the placement procedure is to minimise the *overall synaptic stretching* (1a) to reduce the communication along the network nodes. The *synaptic stretching* is the distance between the nodes where two adjacent neurons are placed. Two constraints affecting the placement problem: (i) All neurons mapped into a target node must be of the same model (1b). (ii) Each node can simulate only a certain number of neurons, and the quantity depends on the complexity of the neuron model (1c).

3.1   Problem Relaxation

A SNN is almost never described in $\mathcal{G}_\mathcal{N}$ form, due the high complexity in manage all neurons and synapses, but it is normally described in terms of Populations and Projections. A Population $\mathcal{P}$ is a set of neurons that share the same model and the same properties. A Projection between two Population $\mathcal{P}^{(a)}$ and $\mathcal{P}^{(b)}$ defines the rule in charge to generate a set of synapses where the pre-synaptic neurons are in $\mathcal{P}^{(a)}$ and the post-synaptic neurons are in $\mathcal{P}^{(b)}$. We will refer to the *Population-Projection graph* using the notation $\mathrm{G}_\mathcal{P}$.

We can eliminate the two constrains (1b, 1c) redefining the problem Π working with $\mathcal{G}_\mathcal{P}$ and splitting each population $\mathcal{P}^{(i)}$ into a set of partial populations $\left\{ \mathcal{P}_1^{(i)}, \mathcal{P}_2^{(i)}, \ldots, \mathcal{P}_z^{(i)} \right\}$. All partial populations must contains at most a number of neurons equal to the maximum number of neurons allowed to be simulated in a target node: $|\mathcal{P}_j^{(i)}| \leq n^{(i)} \ \forall j = 1, \ldots, z$, with $n^{(i)} = \mathcal{S}(\mathcal{M}(\mathcal{P}^{(i)}))$.

In this way we obtain the *partial population graph* $\mathcal{G}_{\mathrm{pp}}$. The edges of the partial population graph are weighed and ordered. Given an edge $e_{ij} \in E_{\mathrm{pp}}$ between two partial population, its weight w_{ij} is equal to the number of synapses shared between the neurons belonging to the two partial populations.

We can redefine (1) using the placement rule $\pi : V_{\mathrm{pp}} \to V_{\mathcal{T}}$ that map a partial population into a processor (2).

$$\underset{f(\pi)}{\text{minimize}} \qquad \sum_{e_{ij} \in E_{\mathrm{pp}}} d(\pi(v_i), \pi(v_j)) * w_{ij} \qquad (2a)$$

$$\text{subject to} \qquad |\pi(i) = p| \leq 1, \ i \in V_{\mathrm{pp}}, p \in V_{\mathcal{T}} \qquad (2b)$$

In (2a) we modify the cost function to take into account the number of synapses shared between the target nodes. The rule in (2b) describes the single constraint of the problem: a target node can only contain one partial population.

3.2 Graph Partitioning

The partition problem of $\mathcal{G}_{\mathcal{P}}$ can be solved in different ways. In [29] it was treated as a problem of clustering. The provided solution was divided into three step:

- Graph expansion: $\mathcal{G}_{\mathcal{P}} \to \mathcal{G}_{\mathcal{N}}$
- Spectral embedding: $\mathcal{G}_{\mathcal{N}} \to \mathbf{L}$
- Clustering and legalisation: $\mathbf{L} \to \mathcal{G}_{\mathrm{pp}}$.

In the first step the neuron graph $\mathcal{G}_{\mathcal{N}}$ is created by applying the synaptic generation rules defined in $\mathcal{G}_{\mathcal{P}}$ (the populations graph). In the second step, a spectral embedding procedure is applied to the neuron graph.

The spectral embedding involves the eigendecomposition of a representative matrix of the graph. In the case of $\mathcal{G}_{\mathcal{N}}$ (a directed graph) it was used a Laplacian Matrix (3) obtained throught a transition matrix induced by a random walk [4].

$$L = I - \frac{(\Phi^{\frac{1}{2}} P \Phi^{-\frac{1}{2}} + \Phi^{-\frac{1}{2}} P^T \Phi^{\frac{1}{2}})}{2} \qquad (3)$$

The results of the spectral embeddings is the representation of $\mathcal{G}_{\mathcal{N}}$ in the eigenspace $\mathbf{L}$, a space belonging to $\mathbb{R}^{|V_{\mathcal{N}}|}$. The neurons can be clustered in the eigenspace using the *KMeans* algorithm. After the clustering, a legalisation phase gathers in groups all neurons belonging to the same cluster and the same population. Finally, a second legalisation phase, called *fusion*, builds the partial populations putting together the nearby groups of neurons until reach the maximum number of neurons that a processor can simulate.

Other techniques of graph clustering are *Multilevel Graph Partitioning* and *Markov Cluster Algorithm* [14,31]. These techniques, like the Spectral Clustering, was born for undirected graph and their usage should be analysed using different symmetrisation techniques if applied to a directed graph.

4 Placement

As seen in Sect. 3 our goal is placing $\mathcal{G}_\mathcal{N}$ into a set of nodes $\mathcal{G}_T$. In Subsect. 3.1 we have relaxed the constraints of the problem separating it into two subproblems: (i) Clustering $\mathcal{G}_\mathcal{N}$ (or partitioning if consider $\mathcal{G}_P$ as a starting point) into the partial population graph. (ii) Placement of $\mathcal{G}_{pp}$ into $\mathcal{G}_T$. We have briefly described the clustering (or partitioning problem) in the Sect. 3.2. In this section, we independently explore the placement problem (2) by comparing different techniques: Naïve, Spectral Embedding, Scotch and Simulated Annealing.

4.1 Naïve Placement

The Naïve approach is the standard mapping procedure adopted in the SpiN-Naker toolchain for assigning populations of neurons to be simulated on the cores available in the SpiNNaker Platform. It is a computationally light method to perform the graph placement without taking into account neither the connectivity of the source graph and the connectivity of the target graph.

The target graph was ordered following a polar coordinate system (ρ, φ) starting from a chip of choice. The radius $\rho = \max(|x|, |y|, |x - y|)$ has been calculated using the hexagonal distance. The angle $\varphi \in [0, 2\pi)$ is expressed in radians. The procedure starts to place a partial population into each processor and change the chip when all processors inside a chip are used. As the ρ increases, the sub-populations will be distributed along chips separated by a greater and greater distance.

4.2 Spectral Embedding

The Spectral Embedding placement was partially used in a previous work described in [29]. The procedure involves the spectral analysis of the graph and a dimension reduction procedure to obtain a planar representation of it. By doing so, the target graph can be directly superimposed on the graph of the partial populations. Contrary to previous work, in which the association of partial populations with processors was performed through a greedy heuristic, in this work the mapping was performed through an *Integer Linear Programming* (ILP) problem.

This procedure requires the extraction of the first five eigenvalues, and the relative eigenvectors, from the matrix **L**. The eigenvectors form a matrix Λ that represents the partial populations in a $\mathbb{R}^5$ space. We apply a non-linear dimension reduction procedure using *Sammon Mapping* obtaining a space in $\mathbb{R}^2$.

The Sammon Mapping algorithm minimise the error function in (4) where d_{ij} is the distance in the high-dimensional space (eigenspace) and d_{ij}^* is the distance in the low-dimensional space (placement space) [25].

$$E = \frac{1}{\sum_{i<j} d_{ij}} \sum_{i<j} \frac{(d_{ij} - d_{ij}^*)^2}{d_{ij}} \tag{4}$$

Each chip is represented as a point (x, y) using an axial coordinate system on an hexagonal grid (the chip mesh). We superimpose the graph $\mathcal{G}_T$ on $\mathcal{G}_{pp}$ projecting the chip mesh in the placement space (5).

$$\begin{pmatrix} x^* \\ y^* \end{pmatrix} = \sqrt{\frac{2A_h}{3\sqrt{3}}} \begin{pmatrix} \sqrt{3} & -\frac{\sqrt{3}}{2} \\ 0 & \frac{3}{2} \end{pmatrix} \begin{pmatrix} x \\ y \end{pmatrix} \tag{5}$$

Where (x, y) is the chip coordinate in the hexagonal grid, and (x^*, y^*) is the chip coordinate in the placement space. The side length of the hex is used as a normalising factor and calculated using the area $A_h = \frac{A}{m}$ occupied by each chip (with m the number of chips). The normalising factor allows scaling the chip mesh making it compatible with the area A occupied by the partial populations.

In the case where the target graph is fine-grain, we need to introduce the processors in the placement space. To ensuring spatial coherence, it was decided to place them equidistant along a circumference centred on the chip coordinate. The radius is chosen in such a way that it is smaller than the distance between two processors belonging to different chips.

After projecting the points into the placement space, they are translated to centre them on the median of the points representing the partial populations. Now we can describe the placement problem using the ILP formulation (6).

$$\begin{array}{ll} \underset{f(\mathbf{X})}{\text{minimize}} & f : \sum_{i=1}^{n} \sum_{j=1}^{m} x_{i,j} d_{i,j} \tag{6a} \\ \\ \text{subject to} & \sum_{i=1}^{n} x_{i,j} \leq k \quad \forall j \in \{1, \ldots, m\} \tag{6b} \\ \\ & \sum_{j=1}^{m} x_{i,j} = 1 \quad \forall i \in \{1, \ldots, n\} \tag{6c} \end{array}$$

Where the matrix $\mathbf{X} = (x_{ij})$, $x_{ij} \in \{0, 1\}$ is the *placement matrix*. An entry $x_{ij} = 1$ means that a partial population i is mapped on a target node j. Two constraints affecting this ILP formulation: (i) Each target node can host at most k partial populations (6b). (ii) Each partial population can be associated to only one target node (6c).

The ILP problem was modelled using PuLP Python library and solved with *COIN-OR branch and cut* (CBC) solver.

4.3   Scotch

The Scotch mapping procedure makes use of the programs available in the homonym software suite (SCOTCH). The Dual Recursive Bipartitioning (DRB) is the primary procedure used by this tool [19]. The DRB can use a plethora of other bi-partitioning methods according to a strategy defined by the user or deducted by graph properties. The main available methods are: Gibbs-Poole-Stockmeyer [10], Fiduccia-Mattheyses [7], Greedy Graph Growing [14] and Diffusion [20].

The mapping workflow with SCOTCH plans to pre-partition the target graph through the *amk_grf* program. The *amk_grf* program take in input a graph (*grf* format) and create a target file (*tgt* format) which contains a decomposition-defined target architecture of same topology as the input graph.

Once a decomposition of the target graph has been obtained, the graph of the partial populations is placed on the target graph using the *gmap* program. The program *gmap* take in input the partial population graph in *grf* format and the target graph in *tgt* format and perform the DRB procedure minimising the communication cost function[2]. The *gmap* output file is a mapping file (*map* format) that contains the association between the Source and the Target nodes.

We had developed a Python module able to exporting a NetworkX graph to a file according to the *grf* format used by SCOTCH and capable of automating the procedures described above.

4.4   Simulated Annealing

The Simulated Annealing is a well know procedure used to find a good solution to an optimisation problem [15]. Given the problem in (2a), it is convenient to express the overall synaptic stretching in a matrix form and define a cost function to minimise. Given the partial population graph $\mathcal{G}_{pp}$ we build its Adjacency matrix $\mathbf{A} = (a_{ij})$ as described in (7).

$$a_{ij} = \begin{cases} w_{ij} & \text{if } \exists (v_i, v_j) \in E_{pp} \\ 0 & \text{otherwise} \end{cases} \quad \forall i, j \in \{1, \ldots, n\} \tag{7}$$

Given the target graph $\mathcal{G}_T$ we build its distance matrix $\mathbf{D} = (d_{ij})$ where each entry d_{ij} is the length of the mimimum path between two target nodes cpu_i and cpu_j. The distance matrix can be build using the Floyd–Warshall algorithms or repeating Dijkstra's algorithms if $|E_T| \ll |V_T|^2$.

Assuming to have as many partial populations as target nodes and a placement rule $\Pi : \{v_1, \ldots, v_n\} \rightarrow \{cpu_1, \ldots, cpu_n\}$ we construct the *permutation vector* $\pi : (\Pi(v_1), \ldots, \Pi(v_n))$ and the *permutation matrix* $\mathbf{P}_\pi = (p_{ij})$ in row form (8).

$$p_{ij} = \begin{cases} 1 & \text{if } i = \pi_j \\ 0 & \text{otherwise} \end{cases} \quad \forall i, j \in \{1, \ldots, n\} \tag{8}$$

The permutation matrix is applied to $\mathbf{D}$ to permutate its rows and columns. We obtain the matrix $\mathbf{D}_\pi = \mathbf{P}_\pi \mathbf{D} \mathbf{P}_\pi$. The overall synaptic stretching can be expressed in a matrix form and used as the cost function for the simulated annealing algorithm (9).

$$f : \mathbf{e}^T (\mathbf{A} \odot \mathbf{D}_\pi) \mathbf{e} = \sum_{i,j} a_{ij} * d_{ij}^{(\pi)} \tag{9}$$

---

[2] The SCOTCH cost function is similar to our Synaptic Stretching.

Where $\odot$ is an element-wise multiplication and $\mathbf{e}$ is a column vector whose all elements are equal to one. In the case of a fine-grain $\mathcal{G}_\mathcal{T}$, before perform the synaptic stretching evaluation, the matrix $\mathbf{A} \odot \mathbf{D}_\pi$ should be collapsed in order to aggregate the processors belonging to the same chip. We used the Simulated Annealing implementation provided in the SciPy ecosystem using the *temperature* to decide how many elements of the permutation vector π are to be swapped.

5   Results

In this section, we present the exploration experiments using the methods described in Sect. 4.

We use the Cortical Microcircuit (CM) as benchmark network [21]. This network represents the connectivity of neurons inside a slice of the cerebral cortex with an area of $1\,\text{mm}^2$. The CM has been chosen because it is a representative biological model with a relatively high global connectivity (5%) and natural clusters defined by the four cerebral cortex layers $\{L_{23}, L_4, L_5, L_6\}$. The CM is described in terms of Populations and Projections with two populations for each layer, for a total of 8 Populations and 64 Projections.

The network is composed of *Leaky Integrate-and-Fire* (LIF) and *Spike Source* (SRC) neuron models. The LIF neurons are models that mimic the biological neurons behaviour. The SRC neurons are simple programmable applications for outputting signals when desired. In this network, the SRC neurons are used to simulate the background activity of cortical neurons not in the model. Each SRC neuron is connected to only one LIF neuron, so they can be excluded by the $\mathcal{G}_N$ provided that processors are reserved for their execution.

The CM model has 7.72e+4 LIF neurons and 2.99e+8 synapses. A network CM_p is a down-scaled CM to a percentage p:

- $CM_{5\%}$ has 3.86e+3 neurons and 7.47e+5 synapses.
- $CM_{10\%}$ has 7.72e+3 neurons and 2.99e+6 synapses.
- $CM_{50\%}$ has 3.86e+4 neurons and 7.47e+7 synapses.

For each processor in charge of simulating a LIF partial population, we must reserve two further processors. A processor is reserved for the simulation of SRC neurons and a further processor is reserved to host a special application necessary to manage synapses with delays greater than $10\,\text{ms}$, as described in [28]. Taking into account a set of 16 processors belonging to the same chip, we can place five partial populations per chip for a total of a thousand neurons per chip.

For simplifying the problem we perform a sequential slicing of each population in order to obtain partial populations with at most $1\,000$ neurons. In this way, we can use a coarse-grain target graph where the nodes are the spinnaker chips (each chip with 5 processors and 200 LIF neurons per processor).

The experiment environment is composed of four different mapping procedures: Naïve, Spectral, Scotch and Simulated Annealing. We had generated 5 CM networks for 10 different scale factors, from 5% to 50%, for a total of 50

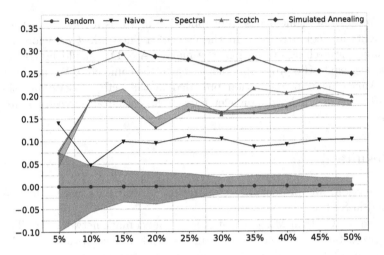

Fig. 3. The graph represents the improvement of a mapping technique compared to the median of the results obtained with a random placement using a constraint of 1000 neurons per chip. The x-axis shows the CM scale factor. The areas represent the first and third quartile of the results obtained on 100 samples.

networks. For each network, we applied all mapping procedures 20 times. We evaluate the performance of each mapping procedure for each scale factor, using the fitness function (9). As a result, we obtain a distribution of 100 different placement results concerning overall synaptic stretching.

The performance of mapping procedures is compared to the performance of random placement. The median value of the results obtained with the Random procedure is used to compute the percentage improvement of the results obtained with other techniques.

In Fig. 3 is depicted a chart that summarize all the experiments. On the x-axis, there are the network scale factors, on the y-axis the percentage placement improvements versus random. The data series are represented by polylines of different colours representing the medians of the results set. Each polyline is drawn within an area whose extremes delimit the first and third quartile of the results set.

In Fig. 4 are depicted the mapping results of a $CM_{20\%}$ into a target graph of 19 chip using the four placement techniques. Each hex represents a SpiNNaker chip connected with six neighbours. The colour of the hex area points out the belonging of the neurons, mapped on the chip, to one of the eight populations of the CM. The number of synapses shared between two partial populations is highlighted with the colour intensity of the edge that connects them. The different concentration of the connections with more synapses can be appreciated qualitatively from the Figs. 4a to f and quantitatively from the Figs. 4c to h. In Fig. 4a can be seen how the Näive method does not consider the connectivity but place each partial population sequentially following the polar ordering of

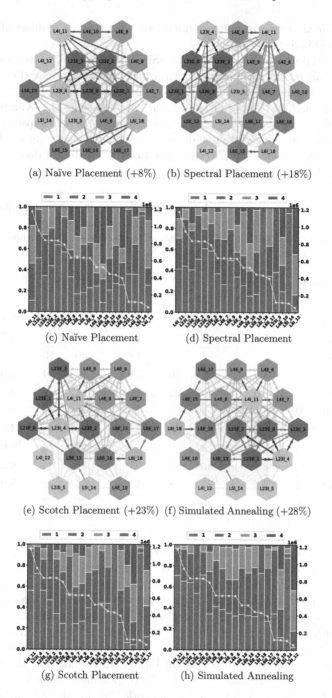

(a) Naïve Placement (+8%)   (b) Spectral Placement (+18%)

(c) Naïve Placement   (d) Spectral Placement

(e) Scotch Placement (+23%)   (f) Simulated Annealing (+28%)

(g) Scotch Placement   (h) Simulated Annealing

Fig. 4. The figures in the first row represent the placement of the partial population graph build from a $CM_{20\%}$ with 1000 neurons per chip on 19 chip (5 processors per chip). The figures in the second-row represent for each partial population the number of synapses (white line) and the percentage of synapse stretching. (Color figure online)

the chip. Indeed there are many connections with a large number of synapses directed towards distant chips.

This not happens in Fig. 4f where the Simulated Annealing can localise in a defined area all partial populations with a high number of shared synapses. In Fig. 4c and h the same information can be appreciated quantitatively. The chart has a bar for each partial population. Each bar represents the overall outgoing synapses of a partial population and shows the percentage of synapses at different levels of elongation. The white line depicts the number of synapses belonging to each partial population. The partial populations are sorted in descending order according to the total number of synapses.

Table 1. The size of the target graph in terms of number of cores and number of chips. We have always tried to keep five processors per chip using different constraints for the number of neurons per chip. Configurations marked with (*) can not be mapped on five processors per chip.

| | Neurons per node | | | | | | | | |
| | 200 | | | 150 | | | 100 | | |
CM	Core	Chips	Core/Chips	Core	Chips	Core/Chips	Core	Chips	Core/Chips
5%	24	5	4.8	28	6	4.7	42	9	4.7
10%	42	9	4.7	54	11	4.9	80	16	5.0
15%	62	13	4.8	80	16	5.0	120	24	5.0
20%	80	16	5.0	107	22	4.9	157	32	4.9
25%	100	20	5.0	132	27	4.9	196	40	4.9
30%	120	24	5.0	157	32	4.9	236	48	4.9
35%	140	28	5.0	184	37	5.0	274	46	6.0*
40%	157	32	4.9	209	42	5.0	312	45	6.9*
45%	178	36	4.9	236	48	4.9	351	44	8.0*
50%	196	40	4.9	261	44	5.9*	390	44	8.9*

We can see how better methods improve the percentage of synapses at a distance of one chip (Green) and decrease the percentage of synapses at a distance of four chips (Red).

While the results of the coarse-grain model were obtained by imposing a maximum of 1000 neurons per chip belonging to the same population, the results obtained with the fine-grain model were evaluated using three different values that limit the neurons per processor: 100, 150, 200. The results obtained using 200 neurons per processor are shown in Fig. 5a. In the Table 1, the results are shown in terms of processors involved. Where possible, a maximum of 5 processors per chip was used, because the network CM, in addition to the *lif* neurons considered there, makes use of other applications including a manager for synapses for high delays and a manager of external stimuli [src]. For each processor that simulates *lif* neurons, two other processors are required for a total

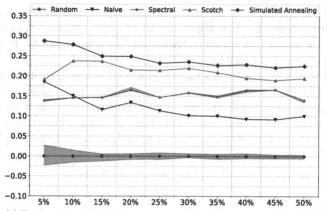

(a) Exploration with 200 neurons per node and fine-grain target graph

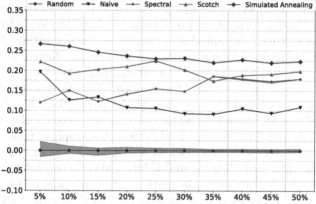

(b) Exploration with 150 neurons per node and fine-grain target graph

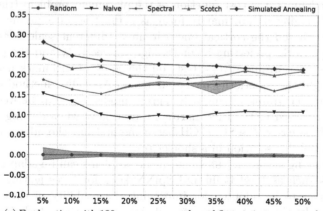

(c) Exploration with 100 neurons per node and fine-grain target graph

Fig. 5. The three graphs represent the improvement of a mapping technique compared to the median of the results obtained with a random placement using three different constraints for the number of neurons in a processor.

of 15 processors per chip. In any case, in this exploration some configurations required more processors than theoretically available, so we ignored this constraint where necessary. Each chip, therefore, hosts from 500 to 1000 neurons belonging to different populations.

As the Fig. 5 shows, the results show a profile similar to the one obtained with the coarse-grain model. However, it is noted, mainly for problems with many processors are involved, that the use of the methodology based on SCOTCH obtains results slightly inferior to Simulated Annealing. Considering the high efficiency of the solution offered by the SCOTCH suite and the simple $A + A_T$ symmetrisation necessary to use the tool, it is possible to renounce to the 2% of improvement but obtain a fast and acceptable solution.

6   Conclusions

In this paper, we described a mapping problem that involves a complex directed graph to be placed in a mesh of processors. We have modelled the mapping problem of an SNN into the SpiNNaker processors-mesh splitting the problem into 3 phases: population graph expansion, neuron graph clustering, and partial populations graph mapping. Focusing on the mapping phase, we have identified and tested 4 methodologies to solve the problem. The *Naïve* method (a simple heuristics) tries to maintain the location of the populations by placing them according to the order of creation without taking into account the real connectivity of the network. The *Spectral* method uses the graph eigendecomposition to obtain a planar representation of the SNN graph and performs the node association with the chip mesh through an ILP formulation. The *Scotch* method uses the *Dual Recursive Bipartitioning* heuristic for fast mapping of a source graph into a target graph. The *Simulated Annealing* method uses the well-known *SA* procedure to minimise a cost function, the synaptic elongation.

We are redefining the cost function of the placement problem (the synaptic elongation) bringing it into matrix form as a function of a permutation vector. We have chosen the cortical microcircuit at different scale factors as our benchmark network, preferring it for its high connectivity and the presence of clusters. After performing several tests on the chosen benchmark network, the results highlight the superiority of the Simulated Annealing method that works natively on direct graphs. Using a fine-grain model, the gap between the SA and SCOTCH based method has narrowed, especially when dealing with large graphs. In these cases, the SCOTCH-based method has the advantage of providing an acceptable solution in a shorter time.

This modelling system for SNN placement problems can be adapted to other architectures such as Intel Loihi and SpiNNaker 2 for investigating new mapping techniques to be adopted for improving the usability of these emerging architectures. In the next works, we will implement these techniques within the placement pipeline of the SpiNNaker neuromorphic architecture, to offer an alternative to the currently implemented method (Naïve) and evaluating experimentally the reduction of communications between the chips involved.

References

1. Abbott, L.F.: Lapicque's introduction of the integrate-and-fire model neuron (1907). Brain Res. Bull. **50**(5), 303–304 (1999)
2. Cassidy, A.S., et al.: Real-time scalable cortical computing at 46 giga-synaptic OPS/watt with 100x speedup in time-to-solution and 100,000x reduction in energy-to-solution. In: SC14: International Conference for High Performance Computing, Networking, Storage and Analysis, pp. 27–38, November 2014
3. Barchi, F., Urgese, G., Acquaviva, A., Macii, E.: Directed graph placement for SNN simulation into a multi-core GALS architecture. In: 2018 IFIP/IEEE International Conference on Very Large Scale Integration (VLSI-SoC), pp. 19–24. IEEE (2018)
4. Chung, F.: Laplacians and the cheeger inequality for directed graphs. Ann. Comb. **9**(1), 1–19 (2005)
5. Davies, M., et al.: Loihi: a neuromorphic manycore processor with on-chip learning. IEEE Micro **38**(1), 82–99 (2018)
6. Davison, A.P., et al.: PyNN: a common interface for neuronal network simulators. Front. Neuroinf. **2** (2008)
7. Fiduccia, C.M., Mattheyses, R.M.: A linear-time heuristic for improving network partitions. In: Papers on Twenty-Five Years of Electronic Design Automation, pp. 241–247. ACM (1988)
8. Furber, S.B., et al.: The spinnaker project. Proc. IEEE **102**(5), 652–665 (2014)
9. Furber, S., et al.: On-chip and inter-chip networks for modeling large-scale neural systems. In: 2006 IEEE International Symposium on Circuits and Systems, ISCAS 2006, Proceedings, p. 4. IEEE (2006)
10. Gibbs, N.E., et al.: A comparison of several bandwidth and profile reduction algorithms. ACM Trans. Math. Softw. (TOMS) **2**(4), 322–330 (1976)
11. Izhikevich, E.M.: Simple model of spiking neurons. IEEE Trans. Neural Netw. **14**(6), 1569–1572 (2003)
12. Jin, X., Furber, S., Woods, J.: Efficient modelling of spiking neural networks on a scalable chip multiprocessor. In: IEEE International Joint Conference on Neural Networks, IEEE World Congress on Computational Intelligence, IJCNN 2008, pp. 2812–2819, June 2008
13. Jin, X., et al.: Algorithm and software for simulation of spiking neural networks on the multi-chip spinnaker system. In: The 2010 International Joint Conference on Neural Networks (IJCNN), pp. 1–8. IEEE (2010)
14. Karypis, G., Kumar, V.: A fast and high quality multilevel scheme for partitioning irregular graphs. SIAM J. Sci. Comput. **20**(1), 359–392 (1998)
15. Kirkpatrick, S., et al.: Optimization by simulated annealing. Science **220**(4598), 671–680 (1983)
16. Liu, C., et al.: Memory-efficient deep learning on a spinnaker 2 prototype. Front. Neurosci. **12** (2018)
17. Maass, W.: Networks of spiking neurons: the third generation of neural network models. Neural Netw. **10**(9), 1659–1671 (1997)
18. Mann, Z.Á.: Multicore-aware virtual machine placement in cloud data centers. IEEE Trans. Comput. **65**(11), 3357–3369 (2016)
19. Pellegrini, F.: Static mapping by dual recursive bipartitioning of process architecture graphs. In: Proceedings of the Scalable High-Performance Computing Conference, pp. 486–493. IEEE (1994)

20. Pellegrini, F.: A parallelisable multi-level banded diffusion scheme for computing balanced partitions with smooth boundaries. In: Kermarrec, A.-M., Bougé, L., Priol, T. (eds.) Euro-Par 2007. LNCS, vol. 4641, pp. 195–204. Springer, Heidelberg (2007). https://doi.org/10.1007/978-3-540-74466-5_22

21. Potjans, T.C., et al.: The cell-type specific cortical microcircuit: relating structure and activity in a full-scale spiking network model. Cereb. Cortex **24**(3), 785–806 (2014)

22. Rast, A., et al.: AERIE-P: AER intersystem exchange protocol (2015)

23. Rhodes, O., et al.: sPyNNaker: a software package for running PyNN simulations on spinnaker. Front. Neurosci. **12** (2018)

24. Ruggiero, M., et al.: A fast and accurate technique for mapping parallel applications on stream-oriented MPSoC platforms with communication awareness. Int. J. Parallel Program. **36**(1), 3–36 (2008)

25. Sammon, J.W.: A nonlinear mapping for data structure analysis. IEEE Trans. Comput. **100**(5), 401–409 (1969)

26. Siino, A., Barchi, F., Davies, S., Urgese, G., Acquaviva, A.: Data and commands communication protocol for neuromorphic platform configuration. In: 2016 IEEE 10th International Symposium on Embedded Multicore/Many-Core Systems-on-Chip (MCSOC), pp. 23–30, September 2016

27. Sugiarto, I., et al.: Optimized task graph mapping on a many-core neuromorphic supercomputer. In: High Performance Extreme Computing Conference (HPEC), 2017 IEEE, pp. 1–7. IEEE (2017)

28. Urgese, G., Barchi, F., Macii, E.: Top-down profiling of application specific many-core neuromorphic platforms. In: IEEE 9th International Symposium on Embedded Multicore/Many-core Systems-on-Chip (MCSoC-15) (IEEE MCSoC-15), Turin, Italy, September 2015

29. Urgese, G., Barchi, F., Macii, E., Acquaviva, A.: Optimizing network traffic for spiking neural network simulations on densely interconnected many-core neuromorphic platforms. IEEE Trans. Emerg. Top. Comput. **pp**(99) (2016)

30. Van Albada, S.J., et al.: Full-scale simulation of a cortical microcircuit on SpiNNaker. In: Frontiers in Neuroinformatics Conference Abstract: Neuroinformatics, vol. 10 (2016)

31. Van Dongen, S.: Graph clustering via a discrete uncoupling process. SIAM J. Matrix Anal. Appl. **30**(1), 121–141 (2008)

Improved Test Solutions for COTS-Based Systems in Space Applications

Riccardo Cantoro[1], Sara Carbonara[1], Andrea Floridia[1(✉)],
Ernesto Sanchez[1], Matteo Sonza Reorda[1], and Jan-Gerd Mess[2]

[1] Politecnico di Torino, Turin, Italy
{riccardo.cantoro, sara.carbonara, andrea.floridia,
ernesto.sanchez, matteo.sonzareorda}@polito.it
[2] DLR, Bremen, Germany
Jan-gerd.Mess@dlr.de

Abstract. In order to widen the spectrum of available products, companies involved in space electronics are exploring the possible adoption of COTS components instead of space-qualified ones. However, the adoption of COTS devices and boards requires suitable solutions able to guarantee the same level of dependability. A mix of different solutions can be considered for this purpose. Test techniques play a major role, since they must guarantee that a high percentage of permanent faults can be detected (both at the end of the manufacturing and during the mission) while matching several constraints in terms of system accessibility and hardware complexity. In this paper we focus on the test of the electronics used within launchers, and outline an approach based on Software-based Self-test. The proposed solutions are currently being adopted within the MaMMoTH-Up project, targeting the development of an innovative COTS-based system to be used on the Ariane5 launcher. The approach aims at testing both the OR1200 processor and the different peripheral modules adopted in the system, while providing new techniques for the identification of safe faults. The results show the effectiveness and current limitations of the method, also including a comparison between functional and structural test approaches.

1 Introduction

Space applications are known to be extremely challenging from a dependability point of view, since they are supposed to work in a harsh environment (not only in terms of radiation but also from the point of view of stresses coming from extreme temperature, pressure, vibration, etc.) with strong requirements in terms of reliability. In order to reduce cost and especially to increase device availability, there is a trend towards the adoption of Commercial Off-The-Shelf (COTS) components instead of the space qualified ones. Obviously, this trend requires evaluating the costs and efforts for guaranteeing that the resulting reliability still reaches the target threshold [2]. A special niche within the general domain of space applications relates to launchers. In this case, the mission time is more reduced, while the radiation environment corresponds to all the layers from ground up to the geostationary orbit (GEO). The MaMMoTH-Up project [3], funded by the European Commission within the frame of the Horizon 2020

The original version of this chapter was revised: The spelling of the third author's name was corrected. The correction to this chapter is available at https://doi.org/10.1007/978-3-030-23425-6_14

research and innovation program, aims at developing and evaluating a COTS-based system to be used in the telemetry unit of the Ariane5 (A5) launcher. More in details, the MaMMoTH-Up system is composed of several boards targeting data acquisition and processing, power management, and data transmission. All these boards use COTS components, including a flash-based FPGA where several IPs are mapped, including an OpenRISC1200 (OR1200) processor [4] whose design has been properly modified to harden it with respect to radiation effects. The adoption of such processor allows the MaMMoTH-Up system to perform significantly more powerful functions than the system it is going to substitute, e.g., in terms of data analysis and compression [1]. In order to match the strict reliability targets of A5, the MaMMoTH-Up system must be protected not only from the radiation effects, which are mainly responsible for Latch-up and transient fault effects, but also from possible permanent faults arising during both the manufacturing process and the following system life. To target permanent faults several test steps have been identified, which are performed during and at the end of the manufacturing process, at the end of the assembly step, and after the system is mounted in the final position. Some test is also performed during the mission. The fault coverage which can be achieved by these test steps is important, since it directly impacts the achieved reliability level. To estimate the Fault Rate of the different components, we followed the FIDES guidelines [5], taking into account the stress conditions which are applied to the system before and during the mission. The Failure Rate is then derived by applying an FMECA (Failure Mode, Effects, and Criticality Analysis) procedure [11] which identifies the fault effects (and their criticality) and takes into account the timing and effectiveness (i.e., the fault coverage) of the different test steps. Remarkably, some of them have to be performed while the system is already mounted in its final position. Hence, they must basically correspond to a self-test, during which some command is sent to the system, the system performs a test of the hardware, and then results are sent outside. In the previous versions of the target system, which was based on much simpler space qualified hardware, a *functional test* was used for this purpose, where the system was asked to perform some basic operations, and a check on the computed results was sufficient to identify possible faults. Due to the much higher complexity of the MaMMoTH-Up system, this approach can hardly guarantee the achievement of the required fault coverage, especially on the OR1200 core. Hence, a *structural test* has been developed, based on a set of self-test procedures in charge of checking the possible presence of permanent faults affecting the processor core. The key difference between the two approaches lies in the fact that the functional one checks whether the system is able to deliver the expected functions, while the structural one identifies first some fault model related to the implementation of the underlying circuit, and then tries to detect the resulting faults. A major advantage of the structural approach clearly lies in the fact that the adopted fault coverage metric can be more deterministically and quantitatively evaluated than for the functional approach. Moreover, while for simple systems the functional approach (if suitably implemented) can achieve a sufficient testing quality, for more complex systems (e.g., including a CPU, some memory, and peripheral modules) the same is not true, as we will experimentally show in the paper. When dealing with a CPU-based system, the self-test procedures implementing the structural approach follow the Software-based Self-test (SBST) paradigm [6]. Their code is integrated in the application software and, when activated, forces the processor to execute a proper sequence of instructions. The produced results are compacted into a signature which is returned to the calling program, which can thus check the possible presence of a fault by comparing it with the expected one.

The contribution of this paper lies first in describing a case of study (corresponding to a subsystem including the OR1200 core, some memories, and an I/O peripheral) where the characteristics of a functional and structural approach can be compared (not only in terms of achieved fault coverage, but also of memory footprint and duration). Secondly, it describes a scenario, where SBST can be effectively adopted, matching the several requirements of the qualification, acceptance and in-fly test of a space application. Finally, the target system is expected to perform a well-defined set of functions and in a very specific configuration (e.g., in terms of memory address space). Therefore, the FMECA is in charge of identifying which faults within the considered cores can produce any failure, and which faults will never be able to do so, e.g., because they relate to some hardware part which is not used by the application. While a few techniques have been proposed to automatically identify some categories of untestable faults, we focus here on those faults called *Safe faults*. These faults cannot produce any failure due to the specific (hardware or software) constraints the system matches during its normal operation. The paper shows that the number of safe faults is far from being negligible and uses an improved version of the method proposed in [7] to partly automate their identification, both within the CPU and the serial interface core. Due to the impact of the considered scenario, the fault coverage results reported in this paper are not directly comparable with those in [8], which focus on end-of-manufacturing test, although they refer to the same processor. A preliminary version of this paper appeared in [23], where only faults within the CPU core were considered, while in this paper we extend the analysis to an I/O peripheral core, too. The paper is organized as follows. Section 2 summarizes the main characteristics of the MaMMoTH-Up system, both in terms of underlying hardware and performed functions. Section 3 compares the functional and structural approaches, while Sect. 4 focuses on the identification of safe faults. Section 5 finally draws some conclusions.

2   The MaMMoTH-Up System

2.1   General Architecture and Functions

The MaMMoTH-Up system shall provide an experiment and data acquisition opportunity on board the Ariane5 upper stage [3]. It is designed to offer the following functionalities:

1. Acquire measurement data
2. Configure and control the experiment
3. Provide a power supply
4. Perform self-testing and fault management.

To meet these functional requirements, a COTS-based system including one experiment controller (TCM-S), two computing nodes (OBC-S), two data acquisition boards

(AQB) and a power supply unit (PSU) was developed. The system is housed in a pressurized and foam-cushioned container to protect it from the harsh environment on board the launch vehicle. In order to collect sensor data and communicate with the Ariane5 upper stage, the system offers analogue acquisition channels for temperature, acceleration, vibration, shock as well as a CAN-interface for digital sensors and pressure sensors and a RS422 interface for data down-link. Synchronization with the launcher timeline and direct status reporting is done using three closed-current loops as inputs and eight discrete output pins. During the mission, the system steps through a number of different acquisition schemes according to the specific mission profile. An acquisition scheme determines which sensors are activated at which sampling rates up to 10 kHz. The data is collected and preprocessed by the computing nodes and then sent to the experiment controller using the internal SpaceWire bus. On the experiment controller, the data is analyzed, compressed and stored on a flash-based mass memory before it is sent to the Ariane5 and downlinked using the launcher's telemetry chain. The complete data flow including its allocation to the different boards is depicted in Fig. 1.

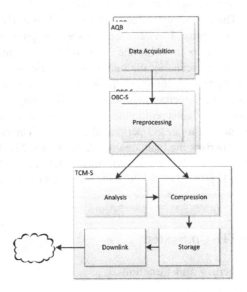

Fig. 1. Data flow

Each OBC-S board as well as the TCM-S board include a flash-based IGLOO2 FPGA. Each of these is holding an OR1200 soft core as well as accompanying IP cores, e.g. for SpaceWire communication amongst the boards. The required software images (three updatable images and three write-protected golden images) are kept in a two gigabyte NAND-flash memory that is implemented on each board. For data storage, the TCM-S is equipped with an additional sixteen gigabyte NAND-flash. The data acquisition is performed by a custom IP core that samples ADC channels and returns a block of samples to the software. Preprocessing, analysis and compression are then performed by software run by the OR1200 processors. The data compression algorithm consists of two steps whose computational load is divided between the OBC-S and the TCM-S. The OBC-S boards perform a wavelet transform. The transformed data is then sent to the TCM-S. From the received wavelet transform, certain characteristics of the underlying data (e.g., value range and maximum gradient) are deduced. The transformed coefficients are then encoded into an embedded bitstream. According to the deduced characteristics of a given block, a certain number of bytes in the downstream are allocated for this bitstream. All other bits are cut to save downlink budget. The complete compression scheme is described in [9]. From a reliability point of view, although the OR1200 processors on the FPGAs and especially their memories and registers are hardened by duplication or triplication of some of the underlying flip-flops, there is no redundancy at the unit or system level. If a detected failure is not permanent, the system is able to recover by performing a software reset or power-cycle on the affected board. Should this not be successful because the failure proves to be permanent, the board has to be deactivated, inevitably resulting in a loss of the connected sensor channels. In this case, the MaMMoTH-Up system follows the concept of graceful degradation: although parts of the sensors cannot be acquired anymore, the remaining transfer budget can be reallocated to use it as efficiently as possible.

2.2   The OR1200 Processor

The OR1200 is the only major RTL implementation of the OR1K architecture spec. The OR1200 is a 32-bit scalar RISC with Harvard micro-architecture and 5 stage integer pipeline. The OR1200 core is mainly intended for embedded, portable and networking applications. Figure 2 shows its architecture.

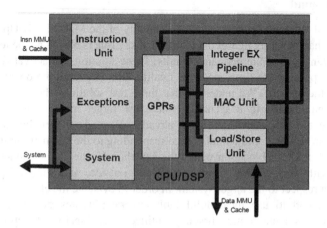

Fig. 2. OR1200 CPU architecture

2.3 The UART Core

The UART 16550 core provides serial communication capabilities, which allow communication with a modem or other external devices, using a serial cable. The peripheral core is designed to be maximally compatible with the industry standard National Semiconductors' 16550 A device. It offers an 8-bit-wide Wishbone interface, FIFO only operation and a debug interface. Figure 3 depicts the most relevant modules composing it. FIFOs are not explicitly represented since they are deeply embedded in the transmitter and receiver logic.

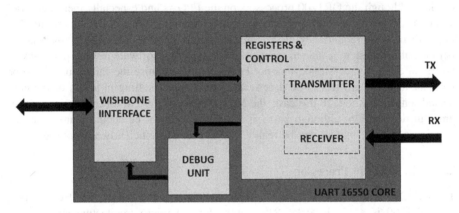

Fig. 3. UART 16550 internal architecture.

3 Comparing the Functional and the Structural Approaches

3.1 Background

In the frame of the actions to evaluate the reliability of the MaMMoTH-Up system and to guarantee that the target figures are matched, a key role is played by the test solutions adopted to identify possible permanent faults. These solutions are activated in different phases of the product life time, since the qualification step until the operational phase (i.e., during the launch). We underline that these test solutions should be usable and effective when applied in a scenario, where the target modules (e.g., the FPGA implementing the processor) have been already mounted on their boards, and each board has been included in the final box corresponding to the telemetry unit, which has been installed in its final location within the launcher. Hence, the whole test should be performed with very limited support from the outside, and should be minimally invasive with respect to the target system. In order to evaluate the effectiveness of these test solutions and to use meaningful fault coverage figures during the reliability evaluation process, a metric must first be identified. Traditionally, a functional metric is adopted. Since the early specification phases, the list of functions that the system must support is defined. For each of them, a *functional test* is then developed, aimed at verifying that the target function is correctly performed by the system. Hence, in this scenario a qualitative metric is adopted, which guarantees that the system is not affected by any fault if all the functional tests for all the functions are successful. When moving to more complex systems including COTS components, a different metric can be considered, which first identifies a structural fault model which is supposed to represent the possible permanent faults in the target device, and then computes the percentage of structural faults which are detected by the considered test solution. One of the goals of the MaMMoTH-Up project is to define new procedures for reliability evaluation, able to match the characteristics of COTS-based systems. Given their complexity, the project partners decided to assess the effectiveness of the functional approach when a structural fault model was adopted. Since the detailed information about the structure of the adopted FPGA were missed, we decided to perform such an assessment resorting to the popular stuck-at fault model, computing first the fault coverage achieved by the functional test when the CPU circuitry mapped on the FPGA was synthesized with a generic gate-level library. This approach is partly sup-ported by the results of [20], showing that the stuck-at fault model, when applied to FPGAs, provides Fault Coverage results which are not far from those which can be obtained resorting to more accurate fault models, based on the knowledge of the internal implementation of the device (which is not available in our case). Moreover, we developed a set of SBST test procedures targeting the stuck-at faults inside the system. These procedures (that we cumulatively call *structural test* in the following) are integrated within the application software of the system and can be easily launched from the outside or by the system itself when required. Each of them returns a signature compacting the results produced by the test code, which can be compared with the expected one. A mismatch means that a permanent fault exists in the CPU core. In the following, we first report some information and figures (Tables 1 and 2) about the functional test and the structural one (based on SBST procedures) we developed for both the OR1200 processor and the UART peripheral core. We will then report the experimental results aimed at comparing the effectiveness of the two test approaches (Tables 3 and 4).

3.2   The Functional Test

The functional test for the OR1200 processor is composed of a compression algorithm that imposes a high workload on the arithmetic units of the processors. It is essential that the processor is fault-free, because even small changes in single bits of the output stream can result in a completely different set of data after decompression. Since it is impossible to predict the exact sensor readings, the processor cannot be checked using live data. Instead, precompiled blocks of sensor data together with expected values for the resulting transformation coefficients and bitstream are used. By comparing the output of the compression algorithm with the expected values, it is checked whether the calculations can be executed as planned. However, in case of an error, no diagnostic conclusions about the affected units within the processor can be drawn. The second line of Table 1 reports the size and duration of the functional test in terms of amount of memory to store the code and test time execution.

Table 1. Characteristics of the test programs for the OR1200.

	Size [Byte]	Duration [#clock cycles]
Functional test	17,360	379,815
Structural test	25,676	74,761
genpc-if	2,896	41,635
ctrl	980	980
rf	10,076	7,281
opmux	544	508
alu	3,184	10,497
multmac	2,996	9,962
lsu	4,244	3,224
wbmux	756	674

Concerning the UART core, the functional test is in charge of verifying whether the peripheral functionalities are fully operational. It is made of three main parts: first, the peripheral is configured, selecting the appropriate operational mode and BAUD rate; then, a sequence of characters is transmitted out; finally, at the end of the transmission, it reads a sequence of characters. Such sequence is compared with the expected one, checking whether they match or not. It is important to underline that the initial configuration of the peripheral should reflect the one used in field. As for the functional test of the OR1200 processor, in Table 2 the most relevant characteristics of the functional test are shown.

Table 2. Characteristics of the test programs for the UART core.

	Size [Byte]	Duration [#clock cycles]
Functional test	212	17,760
Structural test	2,996	651,687

3.3 The Structural Test

The structural test for the OR1200 core is based on a suite of test procedures that target the different modules of the processor: program counter generator (*genpc*), instruction fetch (*if*), control unit (*ctrl*), register file (*rf*), operand muxes (*opmux*), arithmetic logic unit (*alu*), multiply and accumulate unit (*multmac*), load and store unit (*lsu*) and write back multiplexer (*wbmux*). Each test program executes a sequence of instructions aimed at stimulating as much as possible the target unit. At the end of the test, a signature is stored in memory: if the produced result is different than the expected one, it means that the CPU module is affected by a fault. All the test procedures have been written manually following the guidelines provided in [8]. In the following, we provide the most important characteristics of every one of the developed test programs.

The *genpc* and *if* modules are tested together using a single program. Any type of instruction from the Instruction Set must be tested. The program is written in such a way, that each type of instruction is followed by an unconditional jump to a procedure to the bottom of the code that updates the value of the signature and then it jumps back again to the top. In this way, the program counter adder inside the *genpc* is well tested, since it continuously jumps backward and forward, so performing additions and sub-tractions. In order to test the *ctrl* module, it is necessary to give it as inputs all the possible instructions from the Instruction Set: arithmetic, logic, branch, jump, compare, multiply, load and store, immediate or register-to-register. Since the *ctrl* module also generates signals to freeze some selected stages of the pipeline or to activate the forwarding when data hazards occur, it is important to include some instruction sequences with suitable data dependency in order to stimulate those signals. The values of the operands are not so important in this case, so random values are chosen for the operations. The *rf* module is tested using register to register operations. Basically, the test consists in writing a value into a register and then reading it. The test is divided into four parts. In the first part of the test, the stack pointer and the link registers are tested. In the second part, the first half of the registers (r2–r15) is tested, assuming the other part is not faulty and using one among these registers to hold the signature. In the third part of the test, the second half is considered in turn, assuming the first part is not faulty. The values written in the registers are 0x55555555 and 0xAAAAAAAA. To protect the CPU core against temporary faults the register file has been duplicated and the first operand is read from one register, while the second operand is read from the second register; the write back operation updates both registers. Hence, it is necessary to perform each instruction twice, swap-ping the two operands, in order to read the values from both registers. The *opmux* module selects the operands for the execution units, choosing between values coming from the register file or from the various pipeline registers when forwarding is needed. The idea to test this module is to choose arithmetic, logic, load/store and multiply instructions in such a sequence that causes data dependencies in different stages of the pipeline. The *alu* module test addresses all the possible arithmetic/logic instructions of the instruction set. Some special values generated resorting to an Automatic Test Pattern Generation (ATPG) tool launched on the combinational part are chosen as operands to better test its functionalities and all the operations are performed choosing as operands all the possible combinations between the values above. The test of the *mult_mac* module depends significantly on the values chosen for the operands. Therefore, an ATPG tool has been used again to generate proper input values. The test program consists in a series of multiplications (also with immediate, signed and unsigned operands), multiply-accumulate and multiply-subtract instructions of the computed random operands. Division instructions also involve the *mult_mac* module to operate and it has also been tested. Since the mac instruction uses special purpose registers to accumulate, it is necessary to read the values written in these registers after each multiply-accumulate instruction. For testing the *lsu* module, all kinds of load and store instructions are considered: load/store byte or word, extended to zero or signed. The program is constituted of a sequence of instructions to write and read contiguous locations in memory; each block is composed of instructions performing the following three steps: a) Storing a value in a memory location, b) Reading the value from the same location, c) Updating the signature. The values chosen to be written in memory are random and the offset to be added to the base address is a large value (from 16,380 to 17,380). The *wbmux* module chooses the value to be written back into the register file, whether it comes from the memory system (for a load instruction) or from the execution units. Since this module basically corresponds to a mux, the program is very similar to that developed for the *opmux* module. Table 1 summarizes the characteristics of the Functional and Structural tests for the OR1200 processor in terms of size and duration. For the Structural test, we detailed these figures for each test procedure.

The structural test of the UART consists of a unique test program, which was developed following the guidelines presented in [22]. Differently than in the afore-mentioned work, the UART was exclusively configured in one operational mode, namely the very same that the application software is using within the MaMMoTH-Up system. In fact, there is no reason to test the peripheral in all the possible operational modes: the only operational mode that matters is the one used when the device is in mission mode. After a first initialization phase, a loopback connection is activated. This feature is normally available in most serial communication protocols, and it is essential for devising any in-field testing strategy. The structural test can be split in different phases as well, each of them targeting the test of a specific module.

First the transmitter and receiver FIFOs are tested. FIFOs can be tested resorting to any test algorithm developed for a register file, as the one proposed in [21]. The two FIFOs can be considered as a unique register file, since whenever an entry is written in the transmitter FIFO, the same entry is written in the receiver FIFO as well. The significant difference with respect to a register file lies in the fact that the entries are not randomly addressable, since the access to the FIFO is performed through specific pointers. As specified in [21], first the entries are grouped into two groups (group 0 and 1), depending on the hamming distance of their encodings. Then, the patterns 0x55 and 0xAA are applied (that is, written and then read) to the FIFO. Patterns are written to the transmitter FIFO by initiating a transmission, and read out when the transmission ends. On the transmission, the same patterns are also applied to the receiver FIFO. It is worth noting that since the entries are not randomly addressable, the sequence of write operations to the FIFO should be fixed and carefully constructed, in order to write the intended pattern to the specific entry. Specifically, the algorithm requires that the value 0x55 is written to group 0 and 0xAA to group 1. Then, the test is repeated, but with the patterns inverted.

The second part of the test focuses on the circuitry embedded in the receiver, in charge of detecting possible transmission errors. For some error types (e.g. break indicator error, overrun error), it is required to simply force the error during the transmission and then check whether it was acknowledged by reading out the peripheral register that keeps track of such events. For example, the overrun error is tested by simply transmitting a number of characters higher than the number of entries in the receiving FIFO. For other types of error (namely, parity and frame error), they are caused by physical faults (e.g., noise) in the communication channel. Hence, it is required to deactivate the loopback connection for emulating these errors. A trans-mission of a certain number of characters is first initiated. While the transmission is still ongoing, the loopback connection is disabled. Depending on how long the connection is interrupted it is possible to emulate both parity and frame (i.e., missing STOP bit in the received frame) errors, and consequently excite the logic that checks incoming data for these types of errors. Short periods of interruption cause parity errors, while longer one can trigger the frame ones. The characteristics of the functional and structural test procedures of the UART are reported in Table 2. It is noteworthy that the structural test requires a considerable higher number of clock cycles than the functional one due to the higher complexity of the latter. Specifically, they originate from the fact that the structural test fully tests the FIFOs and the error detection logic, which require several transactions to be completed and (for the error detection test) interruption of the transmission. Moreover, it is important to underline that the peripheral transmits data at lower frequency (i.e., the BAUD rate) compared to the one used by the CPU.

3.4   Results

For the purpose of our experiments, we created a simulation setup where both the OR1200 processor and the UART cores lie in a system composed also of a 64 MB RAM, as in the MaMMoTH-Up OBC-S boards. They were synthesized and mapped to the CMOS NanGate 45 nm Open Cell Library. The obtained netlists are used to perform the fault simulation experiments with a commercial EDA tool. Using this setup, we evaluated the stuck-at Fault Coverage obtained by both the functional and the structural test described above.

Results are reported in Table 3 for the CPU core, detailing also the results achieved on each component module. As the reader can notice, the Fault Coverage achieved by the Functional test on the CPU core is far lower than the one of the Structural test. This supports the claim that a Functional test cannot be effectively used when complex COTS-based systems are used. It is also worth underlining that the comparison between the two tests provides very different results depending on the considered module. For some of them (e.g., genpc) the fault coverage achieved by the Functional test is slightly higher than by the Structural test. This is basically due to the fact that some modules can be tested in a good way by executing long programs, and the Functional test is much longer than the Structural one. However, for modules that include large combinational parts (e.g., alu and mult-mac) or require a specific sequence of operations to be tested (e.g., rf) the Structural approach is far more effective.

Table 3. Stuck-at (SA) fault coverage of functional and structural test on OR1200.

Module	Total SA faults	Functional test	Structural test
Whole CPU	124,612	32.09%	81.89%
genpc	4,906	60.80%	57.97%
if	2,268	50.57%	71.12%
ctrl	4,320	71.53%	80.25%
rf	39,056	33.97%	90.93%
opmux	2,530	90.51%	96.05%
alu	14,532	46.04%	78.50%
mult_mac	39,398	13.91%	95.77%
sprs	5,522	8.31%	37.61%
lsu	2,708	67.61%	65.99%
wbmux	2,286	69.29%	78.83%
freeze	126	75.40%	76.98%
except	6,716	15.86%	18.92%
cfgr	232	0.00%	0.00%

Table 4 reports the results of the fault simulation campaigns concerning the UART. By comparing columns three and four of such table, it can be noticed that the fault coverage follows the same trend as for the OR1200, i.e., the functional test achieves a significantly lower fault coverage than the structural one. In particular, the structural test clearly outperforms the functional test for all the modules composing the UART. Indeed, for most of the units (e.g., the circuitry of receiver and transmitter) composing the peripherals the structural test at least doubles the fault coverage of the functional one.

This is a further evidence that strengthens our claim for the necessity of a more complex and detailed structural test when dealing with these systems. Specifically to this case study, it is evidently not enough verifying whether the peripheral is actually able to deliver the intended functionalities. Considering for example the transmitter and receiver FIFOs (*Tx_fifo* and *Rx_fifo*, respectively), if one would rely on the result of the functional test solely, 80% of the faults for each FIFO would be missed.

Table 4. Stuck-at (SA) fault coverage of functional and structural test on the UART core.

Module	Total SA faults	Functional test	Structural test
Whole UART	17,876	36.38%	68.00%
wb_interface	1,400	53.36%	63.36%
regs	15,962	35.38%	69.83%
transmitter	3,956	41.86%	94.08%
Tx_fifo	2,196	20.40%	99.73%
receiver	7,794	32.13%	70.45%
Rx_fifo	2,196	20.17%	99.36%
dbg	338	0.00%	0.00%

4   Safe Faults

We denote as *Safe Faults* those faults that can never produce a failure in the considered system[1]. One of the goals of the FMECA process is their identification, since they do not contribute to the Failure Rate, and should thus be removed from the Fault List to be considered when evaluating the Fault Coverage achieved by the test procedures.

Moving from the space domain to the automotive one, we could mention that the ISO 26262 standard for automotive applications also considers Safe Faults, and defines them as "application dependent". Clearly, Safe Faults include untestable faults, i.e., faults for which no test exists. Hence, it can be useful to review the different categories included in the set of Safe Faults for a given system:

---

[1] When performing FMECA, it is common to also categorize faults depending on the criticality of the resulting failures, i.e., on how serious their effects are. Reliability figures typically depend only on critical safe faults. For the purpose of this paper we ignore any distinction within the set of safe faults.

- *Structurally (or combinationally) untestable faults,* i.e., faults for which a test does not exist even if the combinational block where the fault is located is fully controllable and observable (e.g., via scan test). Examples of faults belonging to this category include faults that cannot be tested due to some redundancy in the combinational logic. Structurally untestable faults identification is a by-product of the combinational ATPG process, for which very effective algorithms are known [24]. Hence, if a gate-level description of the block is available, an ATPG tool can identify these faults.
- *Sequentially untestable faults,* i.e., faults that do not belong to the previous group, but cannot be tested due to the sequential behavior of the circuit, for example, because the circuit cannot reach any of the states required for their test. Several works proposed techniques to automatically identify these faults, either in a generic circuit [12–14, 17, 18] or specifically in a CPU [15]. Sequentially untestable faults identification is a sub-problem of sequential ATPG, which is known not to be a practically solvable problem for generic real circuits. Design for Testability techniques (e.g., scan) have been introduced to circumvent this problem reconfiguring the circuit under test at test time.
- *On-line functionally untestable faults,* [10], i.e., faults that do not belong to the previous groups, but cannot be tested in a functional manner (i.e., without resorting to Design for Testability) in the operational conditions the target device works in. On-line functionally untestable faults can be related for example to the specific memory configuration adopted by the system [16]. Several bits in the processor Program Counter or in the registers storing the addresses in the Load-Store Units become untestable if the memory area storing the code and the data is less than the maximum one.

Safe faults include and extend the previous categories. In the following we report some examples of safe faults:

- The debug circuitry possibly existing in a processor generates safe faults, since debug facilities are not used during the normal behavior, and most faults within it cannot impact the system behavior and produce any failure.
- Several faults in the Design for Testability hardware (e.g., the scan chains) used for end-of-manufacturing test also correspond to safe faults: for example, faults on the scan-in input of the scan flip-flops are safe faults.

In [7], we reported some results concerning the identification of safe faults in the openMSP430 processor. In that paper, we also considered those safe faults that cannot produce any failure due to the specific application code executed by the CPU. As a simple example, if the system application only uses integer arithmetic, faults in the Floating-Point Unit become untestable.

4.1 Safe Faults Identification

The typical approach for safe faults identification is based on manual analysis. In many project teams, the designers, test engineers, and reliability/functional safety experts systematically cooperate to categorize faults and (based on their effects) identify safe faults. Clearly, this process is extremely time consuming (and hence expensive), as well as prone to possible errors. For this reason, in [7] we proposed an approach, which aims at partly automating the safe faults identification process taking into account all the constraints coming from the application scenario, including the application software to be run by the CPU. Some preliminary results coming from the application of the same method to the OR1200 CPU have been reported in [19]. In this paper, we improve the procedure used in [7, 19] and extend the work reported in [23] to peripheral modules, not necessarily CPU only. The improved method is now able to identify a larger number of safe faults, thanks to a mechanism allowing to exploit the power of a commercial ATPG tool. In the following, the proposed method for safe faults identi- fication is detailed. For sake of generality, it is presented assuming a generic sequential circuit as Device Under Analysis (hereinafter, DUA). However, as it is explained further in this section, the applicability of the proposed method spans DUAs of dif- ferent kinds, namely from CPUs (as in the above-mentioned works) to peripheral cores (as described in this paper). Our method for safe faults identification operates on the gate-level netlist of the DUA, and it is based on the following steps:

1. We identify the set of all inputs of the DUA which will remain at a fixed value during the system operation (e.g., the Normal/Test signal). Let us call PI_{fixed} this set.
2. We perform several simulation experiments on the DUA running the actual workload that the circuit will experience in the operating conditions and with different but realistic data input sequences. Then, we use the toggle activity to identify the set $FF_{possibly-fixed}$ of flip-flops which never toggle.
3. We focus on $FF_{possibly-fixed}$, and manually check whether any of the flip-flops in this set may possibly toggle if a different sequence of input data and events is consid- ered. The remaining set of flip-flops, called FF_{fixed} is composed of those flip-flops that will never toggle in the operating conditions.
4. We resort to an ATPG tool to identify the faults in the combinational logic of the DUA that become untestable once the constraints coming from the fixed values of the PI_{fixed} and FF_{fixed} signals are applied. In other words, the combinational logic is extracted from the whole gate-level netlist and then we specify the inputs of such portion of circuit whose values always remain fixed during the operational phase (i.e., connecting the inputs either to ground or to V_{DD}). Finally, given these con- ditions on the inputs, the ATPG tool is asked to generate test patterns for all the possible faults within the combinational logic. At the end of the generation process, the ATPG tools identifies a certain number of untestable faults due to the constraints on the combinational logic inputs. These faults correspond to safe faults for the system.

The method is also applicable to combinational circuits. In this case, the procedure described above can be simplified since it is not necessary to consider the values of flip- flops. Moreover, the reader should note that in [7, 19] the last step was performed resorting to a simple topological analysis of the effects of the fixed values in the combinational logic: the analysis identified for each gate the possible safe faults caused by any fixed value on the inputs of the fault. To perform the same step, in this paper we resort to an ATPG tool, so that a larger number of safe faults can be identified, taking into account the constraints on the input signals of the combinational logic. The reasoning behind the usage of an ATPG tool originates from the test pattern generation process itself. As an example, let us consider the portion of combinational logic shown in Fig. 4, where I_0 to I_4 represent the inputs of the logic cone for the output Out. Let us assume that as a result of the analysis in steps 1 to 3, we realize that I_4 always remains to a fixed value (i.e., zero, therefore connected to ground). We can now force the ATPG tool to derive a test pattern for the fault stuck-at-0 on the output of gate U3. For testing the stuck-at-0 on that signal, the ATPG tool has to force U3 inputs both to 1 and then propagate up to the Out signal. The only input pattern that satisfies these requirements would be 01111. However, I_4 is connected to ground. Therefore, the value of U3 is always at 0 *independently from the other inputs* of the logic cone. If the ATPG tool is not able to derive a test pattern given the constraints on the inputs, it means that the fault can be marked as untestable. Since the constraints on the inputs derive from a workload that mimics the operating condition of the DUA, the occurrence of that fault will never cause a failure and can be labeled as safe.

Leveraging an ATPG tool allowed us to increase by about 3% the number of safe faults identified by this step with respect to the results presented in [19]. Moreover, the usage of a commercial tool also makes the applicability of the proposed method easier. It is important to underline *that our method cannot identify all safe faults in the system.* However, we claim that it can identify a significant number of them and represents a first step towards the automation of the whole safe fault identification procedure, thus contributing *to significantly reducing its cost.*

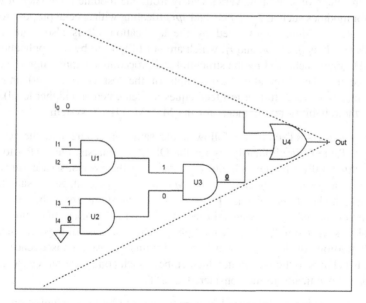

Fig. 4. Safe fault identification process with an ATPG tool.

4.2   Results

We implemented a tool based on a set of TCL scripts interacting with a logic simulator and an ATPG to implement the procedure described in the previous sub-section. The required time to run the simulation campaign to gather the data for the Toggle analysis and to process them to extract the list of Safe Faults (including the ATPG step) is in the order of a few hours. In the following we will present and discuss the experimental results for the same setup used in Subsect. 3.4, including the OR1200 CPU and the UART.

By using the same commercial ATPG tool we also identified the number of structurally untestable faults in the OR1200, which amounts to 80. Following the proposed procedure and referring to the environment and application code of the OBC-S board, we identified a set of safe faults in the OR1200 processor, as reported in the second column of Table 5. We also computed the Safe Fault Coverage (*SFC*) for the Functional and Structural tests (columns 4 and 5), defined as:

$$SFC = \frac{\#detected\ faults}{\#faults - \#safe\ faults}$$

The reported results show that:

- The number of safe faults is relevant, accounting for about 13% of the whole stuck-at fault list.
- The percentage of safe faults varies widely from one module to another. It is about 20% for modules such as *mult_mac* and *sprs* (dealing with special purpose registers, which are not significantly used by the application). It is also significant for modules such as *if*, *genpc* and *rf*, which are not fully used by the application code.
- The SFC figure achieved by the structural test procedures is quite high (taking also into account the observability constraints of the test environment) and allows (combined with some further test techniques implemented at a higher level) to fully match the reliability requirements for the MaMMoTH-Up system.

Concerning the UART core, we followed the same procedure and the results are gathered in Table 6. Preliminarily, as for the OR1200 analysis, the ATPG tool identified 13 structurally untestable faults. Compared to the previous case study, when dealing with a peripheral it can be observed that the percentage of safe faults is considerably higher (29% against 13%). This mainly stems from the fact that the functionalities offered by a peripheral often depend on a set of configuration registers whose value is written in the initialization phase. Thus, because of these registers, non-negligible portions of the design can be actually unused. As a consequence, most of these faults belongs to the *regs* unit, which embeds such configuration registers and the control part. Specifically to the considered UART:

- The *receiver* is the module which is directly affected by the configuration registers. Among the other duties, this unit is in charge of generating interrupts as response to several events. In our application, the UART was used in polling solely. As a consequence, the interrupt facilities are not used at all. The same reasoning applies also to the Modem configuration. The peripheral can be connected to an external

Table 5. Safe stuck-at fault coverage (SFC) of functional and structural tests for the OR1200.

Module	Safe faults	Safe faults w.r.t. total faults	SFC	
			Functional Test	Structural Test
CPU	16,183	12.98%	36.88%	84.41%
genpc	425	8.66%	66.57%	63.24%
if	204	9.00%	55.57%	76.74%
ctrl	13	0.30%	71.74%	80.42%
rf	5,550	14.21%	39.60%	92.89%
opmux	41	1.62%	92.00%	96.47%
alu	75	0.51%	46.28%	78.54%
mult_mac	7,861	19.95%	17.38%	97.04%
sprs	1,070	19.38%	10.31%	44.41%
lsu	7	0.26%	67.79%	66.16%
wbmux	0	0.00%	69.29%	78.83%
freeze	7	5.55%	79.83%	79.51%
except	912	13.58%	18.35%	21.85%
cfgr	18	7.76%	0.00%	0.00%

model through a dedicated interface, which is not needed by the application. Finally, depending on the format of the transmission format, some portions of the circuit become inactive as well. All these factors affect partially the FIFO as well, for which some safe faults were identified.

- Safe faults can be found also in the *transmitter*, although their number is significantly smaller compared to the receiver. These faults mainly originates from: (1) modem not being used and (2) the configuration of the transmission format (e.g., the selected BAUD rate).
- The debug unit (*dbg*) is not used at all, since this unit is mainly intended for checking the correctness of the operation during the development phase and clearly not for the in-field operations.
- The remaining safe faults are part of the control circuitry, included in the *regs* module.

By comparing the fourth column of Table 6 with the fourth of Table 4, it is possible to observe that removing the safe faults significantly increases the fault coverage achieved by the structural test, reaching quite high SFC figures. Furthermore, removing safe faults considerably reduces the effort for the development of the self-test procedures. Indeed, the test engineer should not target all the possible faults affecting the UART, but instead exclusively the ones considered critical for the application (i.e., not safe) However, it is worth noting that 16% of the remaining undetected faults might still include safe faults. From the experiments, it emerged that most of them could be linked to the interrupt circuitry. However, they cannot be clearly identified with the current methodology, thus we decided not to include them in the set of safe faults.

Table 6. Safe stuck-at fault coverage (SFC) of functional and structural tests for the UART 16550.

Module	Safe faults	Safe faults w.r.t. Total SA faults	SFC	
			Functional test	Structural test
UART	5,192	29.04%	49.96%	84.02%
wb_interface	340	24.29%	69.62%	74.81%
regs	4,484	28.09%	47.85%	84.99%
transmitter	217	5.49%	43.89%	97.17%
Tx_fifo	0	0.00%	20.40%	99.68%
receiver	2,213	28.39%	42.36%	81.04%
Rx_fifo	288	13.11%	20.89%	99.42%
dbg	338	100.00%	100.00%	100.00%

5   Conclusions

This paper deals with the adoption of COTS components in the design and manufacturing of electronic systems to be used on a launcher. We focused on the MaMMoTH-Up system to be used on board the Ariane5 launcher, which represents a testbench for developing a suitable design and manufacturing flow compatible with the adoption of COTS components. In particular, we focused on the test of a couple of modules within the whole system (i.e., the CPU core and a serial peripheral core), showing first that a functional test is not able to achieve a sufficient test quality, while structural SBST test procedures can be much more effective. We also focused on the identification of safe faults, i.e., those faults that cannot produce any failure due the hardware and software constraints provided by the application environment. We proposed a semi-automated method able to significantly reduce the cost and effort for safe faults identification, showing that the method can identify a significant number of safe faults. We reported experimental results on the OR1200 processor core used within the MaMMoTH-Up system. The same experiments were also performed on a peripheral for serial communication embedded in the system (namely the UART 16550). Although the proposed method has been experimentally evaluated referring to stuck-at faults, only, the same approach can be adopted to deal with other fault models (e.g., transition delay faults, or bridges), if required. We are currently working towards the development of improved techniques for safe faults identification and towards a new and more effective release of our SBST procedures.

Acknowledgments. This work has been supported by the European Commission through the Horizon 2020 Project No. 637616 (MaMMoTH-Up).

References

1. Avramenko, S., Sonza Reorda, M., Violante, M., Fey, G., Mess, J.-G., Schmidt, R.: On the robustness of DCT-based compression algorithms for space applications. In: 2016 IEEE 22nd International Symposium on On-Line Testing and Robust System Design (IOLTS) (2016)
2. Pignol, M.: COTS-based applications in space avionics. In: 2010 Design, Automation & Test in Europe Conference & Exhibition (DATE 2010) (2010)
3. http://www.mammoth-up.eu/
4. https://openrisc.io/
5. UTE FIDES guide 2009, Edition A, September 2010
6. Psarakis, M., et al.: Microprocessor software-based self-testing. IEEE Des. Test Comput. 27(3), 4–19 (2010)
7. Cantoro, R., Firrincieli, A., Piumatti, D., Sanchez, E., Sonza Reorda, M., Restifo, M.: About functionally untestable fault identification in microprocessor cores for safety-critical applications. In: IEEE Latin-American Test Symposium (LATS) (2018)
8. Kranitis, N., Merentitis, A., Theodorou, G., Paschalis, A., Gizopoulos, D.: Hybrid-SBST methodology for efficient testing of processor cores. IEEE Des. Test Comput. 25(1), 64–75 (2008)
9. Mess, J.-G., Schmidt, R., Fey, G.: Adaptive compression schemes for housekeeping data. In: 2017 IEEE Aerospace Conference (2017)
10. Bernardi, P., Bonazza, M., Sanchez, E., Sonza Reorda, M., Ballan, O.: On-line functionally untestable fault identification in embedded processor cores. In: Proceedings of the 2015 Design, Automation & Test in Europe Conference & Exhibition, pp. 1462–1467, March 2013
11. Globe, W.M.: Control Systems Safety Evaluation and Reliability, 3rd edn. ISA, Durham (2010). ISBN 978-1-934394-80-9
12. Raik, J., Fujiwara, H., Ubar, R., Krivenko, A.: Untestable fault identification in sequential circuits using model-checking. In: Proceedings of IEEE Asian Test Symposium, pp. 21–26 (2008)
13. Syal, M., Hsiao, M.S.: New techniques for untestable fault identification in sequential circuits. IEEE Trans. Comput. Aided Des. Integr. Circuits Syst. 5(6), 1117–1131 (2006)
14. Liang, H.-C., Lee, C.L., Chen, J.E.: Identifying untestable faults in sequential circuits. IEEE Des. Test Comput. 12(3), 14–23 (1995)
15. Lai, W.-C., Krstic, A., Cheng, K.-T.: Functionally testable path delay faults on a microprocessor. IEEE Des. Test Comput. 17(4), 6–14 (2000)
16. Riefert, A., Cantoro, R., Sauer, M., Sonza Reorda, M., Becker, B.: A flexible framework for the automatic generation of SBST programs. IEEE Trans. Very Large Scale Integr. (VLSI) Syst. 24(10), 3055–3066 (2016)
17. Long, D.E., Iyer, M.A., Abramovici, M.: FILL and FUNI: algorithms to identify illegal states and sequentially untestable faults. ACM Trans. Des. Autom. Electron. Syst. (TODAES) 5(3), 631–657 (2000)
18. Tille, D., Drechsler, R.: A fast untestability proof for SAT-based ATPG. In: 12th International Symposium on Design and Diagnostics of Electronic Circuits and Systems, pp. 38–43, 15–17 April 2009
19. Carbonara, S., Firrincieli, A., Sonza Reorda, M., Mess, J.-G.: On the test of a COTS-based system for space applications. In: 24th IEEE International Symposium on On-Line Testing and Robust System Design, Poster Session (2018)

20. Borecky, J., Kohlik, M., Kubalik, P., Kubatova, H.: Fault models usability study for on-line tested FPGA. In: 14th Euromicro Conference on Digital System Design, pp. 287–290 (2011)
21. Sabena, D., Sonza Reorda, M., Sterpone, L.: A new SBST algorithm for testing the register file of VLIW processors. In: 2012 Design, Automation & Test in Europe Conference & Exhibition (DATE), Dresden, pp. 412–417 (2012)
22. Apostolakis, A., Psarakis, M., Gizopoulos, D., Paschalis, A.: Functional processor-based testing of communication peripherals in Systems-on-Chip. IEEE Trans. Very Large Scale Integr. (VLSI) Syst. 15(8), 971–975 (2007)
23. Cantoro, R., Carbonara, S., Floridia, A., Sanchez, E., Sonza Reorda, M., Mess, J.: An analysis of test solutions for COTS-based systems in space applications. In: 2018 IFIP/IEEE International Conference on Very Large Scale Integration (VLSI-SoC), Verona, Italy, pp. 59–64 (2018)
24. Bushnell, M., Agrawal, V.: Essentials of Electronic Testing for Digital, Memory, and Mixed-Signal VLSI Circuits. Kluwer Academic Publisher, Boston (2000)

Analysis of Bridge Defects in STT-MRAM Cells Under Process Variations and a Robust DFT Technique for Their Detection

Victor Champac[1]([✉]), Andres Gomez[1]([✉]), Freddy Forero[1]([✉]),
and Kaushik Roy[2]([✉])

[1] National Institute for Astrophysics, Optics and Electronics,
Tonanzintla, Mexico
{champac,fgomez,freddy.alexforero}@inaoep.mx
[2] Purdue University, West Lafayette, USA
kaushik@ecn.purdue.edu

Abstract. Spin-Transfer-Torque Magnetic RAM (STT-MRAM) is a promising non-volatile memory technology due to its ultra-integration density capability, nanosecond speeds for reading and writing operations and CMOS/FinFET fabrication process compatibility. STT-MRAMs may be affected by manufacturing defects, which may be challenging to detect under process variations in deeply scaled semiconductor technologies. Because of this, the importance of test techniques to target defects in this emerging memory technology. In this work, an STT-MRAM bit-cell is presented with its states due to the magnetic orientation of the ferromagnetic layers. The read and write operations of an STT-MRAM cell, including the read and write circuits, are revised in the scope of this work. The write time definition for an STT-MRAM cell is also revised. A defect model is used to analyze the STT-MRAM cell under short defects in the presence of process variations. A Design-For-Test (DFT) circuit to detect short defects in the STT-MRAM cells is proposed. The proposed methodology is based on the observation that a short defect modifies the amplitude of the currents entering and leaving the memory cell. Hence, the current difference between the currents entering and leaving the memory cell is used to discriminate between good cells and defective cells. The proposed DFT circuitry is robust to process-induced parameters variations in the memory cell. In such a way, defects detection probabilities are increased, and a high-quality product can be guaranteed.

Keywords: STT-MRAM · Short defect · Test · Design-For-Test · FinFET

N. Bombieri et al. (Eds.): VLSI-SoC 2018, IFIP AICT 561, pp. 207–231, 2019.
https://doi.org/10.1007/978-3-030-23425-6_11

1   Introduction

Spin-Transfer-Torque Magnetic RAM (STT-MRAM) is an emerging non-volatile memory technology with high endurance and CMOS/FinFET compatibility [1]. STT-MRAM has attractive features such as non-volatility, which means that the stored information remains when the power supply is turned off, and high endurance, which means it is possible to write data for an unlimited number of times. STT-MRAM also provides zero standby leakage. The International Technology Roadmap for Semiconductor (ITRS) highlighted STT-MRAM as a promising candidate for future on-chip memory applications [2].

Like in other types of memories, the main operations carried out in STT-MRAM are the writing and reading operations. The correct behavior of an STT-MRAM may be impacted by manufacturing defects, which may affect the access transistor, the MTJ and the interconnections of the STT-MRAM cell. If the access transistor is fabricated with FinFET technology new defects like stuck-open fin or single open gate in multi-fin structures may affect it [3–5]. The MTJ device may be affected by different types of defects like a short on the insulator oxide [6], an open defect in any terminal and a stuck-at-AP/stuck-at-P faults [7]. Resistive shorts/opens may affect the interconnections in the STT-MRAM memory [8,9]. Fault models based on defective memory behavior are usually developed for test purposes [9]. Fault models may be used for test pattern generation. Memory fault models are usually classified depending on the operation they affect, reading or writing operation, as shown in Fig. 1.

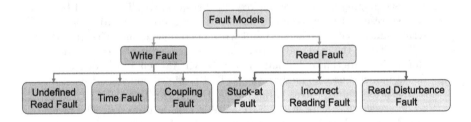

Fig. 1. STT-MRAM cell fault models

In a writing operation, an open resistive defect may reduce the current applied to the cell memory, and the cell may not change state. However, in an STT-RAM memory, the writing process has a probabilistic nature, so write failure also has the same nature, and it can not be known with certainty if the failure occurs always occur [10]. This fault is known as Undefined Write Fault (UWF) [11]. It is said that a Time Fault (TF) [9] occurs if the open resistive defect allows the current to be large enough to ensure that the desired state is written in the STT-MRAM cell, but it does not allow the memory cell to perform the writing process in a particular time. A short resistive defect may affect the gates of the access transistors in two STT-MRAM cells. The short defect is sensitized when trying to write a cell, and the access transistor is not completely turned on. As a consequence, the writing operation is not correctly performed. This fault is known as Coupling Fault (CF) [9]. An incorrect Reading Fault (IRF) [11] is said to occur when a resistive defect changes the measured voltage value of the cell in a read operation. A Read Disturbance Fault (RDF) [9] occurs when a short defect increases the current in a reading operation and change the value stored in STT-MRAM memory. In the Stuck-at Fault (SaF) a resistive short defect connects the internal node of the STT-MRAM cell with the power rails electrically, which causes malfunctions in both writing and reading operations [11]. Recently, a novel generic defect modeling methodology that captures the non-linear behavior of the STT-MRAM has been proposed [12].

Efficient defect test and diagnosis are critical to assure high-quality memory arrays, but this is a challenging task due to process-induced parameters variations, which may mask the impact of a defect on the functionality of the cell. The test approaches for digital integrated circuits can be categorized as fault-oriented or defect-oriented tests. In a fault-oriented test, the obtained logic result at the primary outputs is compared against the expected result. In a defect-oriented test approach, a parameter of the tested circuit (i.e., current consumption) is monitored to detect the presence of a defect. There is not required to observe the faulty logic behavior at main circuit outputs, which is a significant advantage. Thus, a defect-oriented test is more adequate for the detection of both strong and weak defects. In [13], a circuit-level approach to detect read disturbs faults was proposed. The circuit detects the change in the current through a cell when a read disturb fault occurs.

In this work, we propose a modified Design-For-Test (DFT) read circuit to detect resistive-short defects between an internal node of an STT-MRAM and an external node [14]. The proposed test circuit performs a defect-oriented test, which is adequate for the detection of weak defects that may escape to conventional logic test and degrade the memory block reliability [15]. The proposed test circuit is based on the observation that a short defect makes different the amplitude of the currents entering and leaving a memory cell. The DFT read circuitry can measure both the currents entering and leaving a memory cell. The proposed test technique provides higher defect detection and diagnosis capabilities. The capability of the proposed test circuit to detect resistive-short defects that can escape conventional logic test is validated under process variations effects, and it is shown that the defect detectability is improved. This chapter extends the analysis of the previous work and performs a comparative analysis between the conventional test techniques and the proposed DFT technique.

The rest of this chapter is organized as follows: Sect. 2 presents the operating principles of an STT-MRAM cell. Section 3 describes the read and write operation of the STT-MRAM cell with the read and write circuits used. In Sect. 4, the writing time definition of an STT-MRAM cell is analyzed closely. Section 5 presents an analysis of the electrical behavior of the memory cell under the presence of resistive short defects. Section 6 presents the proposed test technique. Section 7 analyzes the cost of the proposed test technique, and a comparison between the proposed test technique and a conventional logic based test is made. Finally, Sect. 8 presents the conclusions of this work.

2 Memories Based on STT-MRAM

A single STT-MRAM memory is formed by a Magnetic Tunneling Junction (MTJ), which is a spintronic storage device, and an access transistor as illustrated in Fig. 2(a). The MTJ has two ferromagnetic layers separated by a very thin insulator [16]. The use of a FinFET transistor as the access device is preferred over a CMOS planar transistor due to its superior gate controllability, larger "ON" current, and lower variability. The magnetic orientation of the bottom layer, called Pinned Layer (PL), is fixed. However, the magnetic orientation of the top layer, called Free Layer (FL), is allowed to switch its magnetic orientation concerning the PL using a spin-polarized current through the MTJ. The electrical resistance of the device depends on the magnetic orientation of the two ferromagnetic layers (See Fig. 2(b)). A larger electrical resistance is observed when the magnetic orientations of the layers point in opposite directions (known as Anti-parallel state) compared to the state when the magnetic orientations of the layers point in the same direction (known as Parallel state) [17,18]. This phenomenon is known as Giant Magneto Resistance [19,20]. The low and high MTJ resistance states correspond to the logic 0 and 1 states, respectively.

A data can be written into and read from the cell by applying appropriate voltages to bit-line (BL), source-line (SL) and Word-Line (WL) terminals of the cell (See Table 1). A current needs to flow from the BL to the SL terminals for writing a Parallel (P) state, which is accomplished by applying BL = VDD, and SL = 0. On the other hand, a current needs to flow from the SL to the BL terminals for writing an Anti-Parallel (AP) state, which is accomplished by applying BL = 0, and SL = VDD. The current that flows through the MTJ has to be large enough to switch the magnetization orientation of the free-layer [21] during a write operation successfully. In this way, the memory can change from anti-parallel state to parallel state $(AP \rightarrow P)$ or vice-versa $(P \rightarrow AP)$. It is important to mention that this current must be bidirectional to perform the change of state in both cases.

The read operation is performed by sensing the resistance of the MTJ. This is done by applying a small read current to the cell and comparing the voltage drop with a reference voltage. Unlike write operation that requires bi-directional current, the read operation only requires current flowing from BL to SL termi-

Table 1. Signal conditions for write and read operations.

Node	Write		Read
	$AP \rightarrow P$	$P \rightarrow AP$	
WL	V_{DD}	V_{DD}	V_{DD}
BL	0	V_{DD}	V_{DD}
SL	V_{DD}	0	0

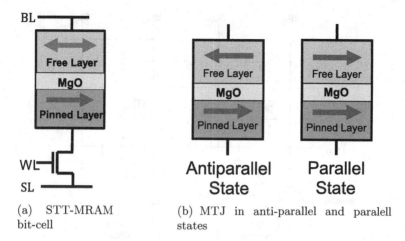

(a)   STT-MRAM bit-cell

(b) MTJ in anti-parallel and paralell states

Fig. 2. STT-MRAM bit-cell and its states due to the magnetic orientation of the ferromagnetic layers.

Table 2. MTJ parameters

Parameter	Value
MTJ size	$30\,\mathrm{nm} \times 30\,\mathrm{nm} \times 1.5\,\mathrm{nm}$
Saturation magnetization	$850\,\mathrm{emu/cm^3}$
Energy barrier	$56\,\mathrm{k_B T}$
MgO thickness	$1\,\mathrm{nm}$

nals. In the reading procedure, a lower current than the write current is applied at the cell, and the voltage at the cell is measured to identify its state [22].

Table 2 shows some of the main MTJ parameters used in this work. Other parameters were settled as default in [23].

3   Read and Write Operations of STT-MRAM Cells

Figure 3 illustrates a memory array architecture using the STT-MRAM cell. Memory cells are accessed by activating a word line (WL_i) and the pass transistors of the desired column. The access to the cells is defined by the word and column decoder circuitries. It should be noted that the number of selected columns depend on the required application. Figure 4 shows a single STT-MRAM cell with the used read and write circuits. The access transistor of the cell, which is driven by the word-line (WL) signal, controls whether current can flow through the MTJ to perform write and read operations.

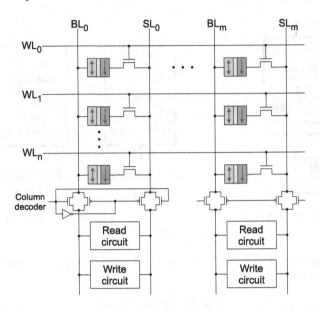

Fig. 3. Memory array using the STT-MRAM bit-cell.

3.1   Read Operation

The read circuit (See Fig. 4) is activated when the Read Enable signal is set at a high logic state (RE = 1). A current I_{REF} is generated using a reference cell whose resistance is designed to be the average between the parallel (R_P) and anti-parallel (R_{AP}) resistances of the STT-MRAM cell ($R_P + R_{AP}$)/2). This current is copied and applied to the memory cell to be read. The current I_{REF} generates a voltage V_{REF} at one end of the terminals of the current mirror, and the current I_{cell} generates a voltage V_{cell} at the other end terminal of the current mirror. The voltages generated at the current mirror terminals (V_{REF}, V_{cell}) are not the same since the resistances of the STT-MRAM cell, and the reference cell are different. The voltage difference between V_{REF} and V_{cell} is measured using a sense amplifier to determine whether the STT-MRAM cell is in the P or AP state. The clamp voltage (CLP) is used to limit the amount of reading current (I_{REF}), so that unintentional writes do not occur.

3.2   Write Operation

The write circuit is activated when the Write Enable signal is set at a high logic state (WE = 1). The direction of the current applied to the memory cell depends on the Data Input (DI) to be written. The AP state is written if $DI = 1$ while the parallel state is written if $DI = 0$. A current flows from SL to BL for $DI = 1$, and thus, an AP state is written in the MTJ. A current flows from BL to SL for $DI = 0$, and thus, a P state is written in the MTJ. The transistors of the writing circuit were made large enough to provide sufficient current capability for a correct write operation.

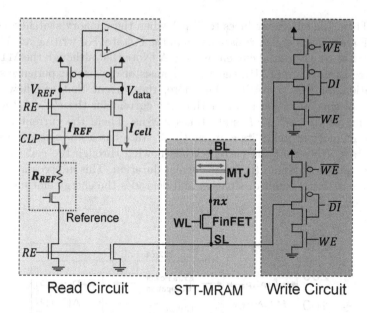

Fig. 4. STT-MRAM bit-cell with read and write circuits.

4   Write Time Definition for an STT-MRAM Cell

One of the major issues for proper operation of the STT-MRAM cell is that a sufficiently large current has to flow through the cell for a long enough time to perform a successful write operation. The required large current leads to a high write energy consumption. Energy efficiency is further degraded due to the required current asymmetry in the write operations [24]. Energy efficiency of the STT-MRAM has been addressed by carefully size optimization of the access transistor in [25]. The size of the access transistor is iteratively increased until the desired write time performance for the slow process corner is achieved. This Section closely analyzes the write time behavior when writing P and AP states.

In a conventional STT-MRAM cell, the latency time for each writing transition ($P \rightarrow AP$ or $AP \rightarrow P$) is different. This asymmetry is caused due to the different spin-transfer efficiency of each MTJ layer, which makes the current to switch the MTJ magnetization state different depending on the state to be written. Write time asymmetry also occurs due to source-degeneration of the access transistor during the $P \rightarrow AP$ write operation, which reduces the effective gate to source voltage of the NFET, and consequently, its current driving capability, resulting in larger write latency. Figure 5 shows the current waveform for the two write operations in an STT-MRAM cell. A FinFET access transistor with 2 Fins and 2 Fingers ($W_{eff} \sim 224\,\text{nm}$) was used. As can be observed, the write latency is determined by the $P \rightarrow AP$ operation where source degeneration occurs.

For writing a $P \rightarrow AP$ state (See Fig. 5), the current that initially flows through the cell is $130\,\mu\text{A}$, which makes the MTJ flip its magnetic orientation in

7.28 ns. Then, the current reduces to 76 μA when the memory switches its state as the AP state has a higher resistance than the P state. For writing an $AP \rightarrow P$ state (See Fig. 5), the initial current is 142 μA. Note that although the MTJ is at the high resistance state (AP), the access transistor does not experience source-degeneration for this transition. Therefore, the current that can flow at the beginning of this operation is larger than the current for the $P \rightarrow AP$ writing. The writing of the $AP \rightarrow P$ state takes 2.98 ns. Then, the current increases when the memory switches its state as the P state has a lower resistance than the AP state. Note that the current keeps flowing through the cell the slower $P \rightarrow AP$ transition defines the pulse current duration. This unnecessary current contributes to extra power dissipation and degrades the energy efficiency of the memory cell.

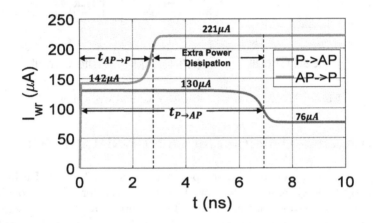

Fig. 5. Current waveforms for both $P \rightarrow AP$ and $AP \rightarrow P$ write operation.

STT-MRAM suffers from process variations on the access transistor and the MTJ. Process variations lead to variations in the write time of the cell because they affect the current drive capability of the access transistor as well as the magnetic and electric properties of the MTJ (i.e., MTJ resistance and critical switching currents). Due to process variations, the write delay distribution of the STT-MRAM cell has a long tail, which may degrade the memory yield [26,27]. The size of the access transistor must be selected to compensate for the impact of process variations with an acceptable write failure probability.

5   Analysis of STT-MRAM Behavior Under Short Defects

Correct STT-MRAM behavior may be affected by manufacturing defects. A comprehensive analysis of all the possible defects in an STT-MRAM was presented in [9]. It was shown that due to the fundamental differences between classic SRAM and STT-MRAM, some fault models and test techniques used in

SRAM are not extendable to STT-MRAM technology. Resistive short defects may alter the correct functionality of the cell. However, when the defects are not strong enough, its detection becomes very difficult, and they may escape the post-manufacturing test, especially under the effect of process variations.

An STT-MRAM cell including the read and write circuits has been simulated. The design characteristics of the single memory and the set-up conditions for Spice simulations used from now on are given. The MTJ has dimensions of $60\,nm \times 40\,nm \times 1.4\,nm$. A stability factor of $\Delta = 70$ is considered. Other MTJ parameters are set as in [23]. A FinFET access transistor with 6 *fins* was used to provide enough current capability to perform a successful write operation in $3.5\,ns$. A Predictive $20\,nm$ FinFET technology [28] is used along with the SPICE-compatible MTJ model proposed in [23]. Variations in the MTJ were assumed of 15% for the cross-sectional area (A_t) and 5% for the oxide barrier thickness (t_{ox}). For the access transistor, 30% of threshold voltage (V_{th}) variation due to the work function variation was assumed. For simplicity purposes, process parameters variations were only considered for the single memory cell.

5.1   Defect Model for Short Defects in the STT-MRAM

Figure 6 shows the used general defect model to analyze the behavior of the STT-MRAM under short defects. The resistance R_{VDD} considers those possible resistive-short defects between the internal node of the STT-MRAM cell and the power supply terminal, and the resistance R_{GND} considers those possible resistive-short defects between the internal node of the STT-MRAM cell and the ground terminal. R_{VDD} and R_{GND} represent the behavior of realistic short defects that occur between the internal node of the cell and power/ground terminals. However, the proposed methodology is also valid to detect other types of short defects as explained later in Sect. 7.4.

5.2   Impact of Short Defects on Write Operation

The nominal current that flows through the MTJ (I_{MTJ}) during the writing process of a P and an AP states is shown in Figs. 7(a) and (b), respectively. The writing time (t_{wr}) to switch the magnetization orientation of the MTJ depends on the amplitude of the current that initially flows through the MTJ. For writing a parallel state (See Fig. 7(a)), the current that initially flows through a *"good"* cell is close to $145\,\mu A$. When a resistive defect R_{VDD} exists, the write time increases because this defect reduces the current that can flow through the MTJ since the access transistor has to drive both the MTJ current and the defect current. On the other hand, defect R_{GND} slightly reduces the write time because more current flows through the MTJ due to an additional conducting path to ground. For writing an anti-parallel state (See Fig. 7(b)), the current that flows through a *"good"* cell is close to $139\,\mu A$. A resistive defect R_{VDD} increases the current that flows through the MTJ, which reduces the write time. A resistive defect R_{GND} reduces the current that flows through the MTJ, which increases the write time.

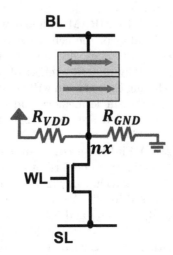

Fig. 6. STT-MRAM cell with resistive short defects.

Impact of Process Variations

The write pulse duration constraint for the designed cell was of 3.5 ns. This write time value corresponds to the largest write time that the defect-free cell can take under process variations. 1000 Monte-Carlo simulations were made. Note that this write time value corresponds to the $P \rightarrow AP$ operation, which is slower than the $AP \rightarrow P$ operation due to source degeneration of the access transistor [24]. If the cell's write time becomes larger than 3.5 ns due to a short defect, an incorrect write operation is performed, and the defect presence can be detected using a conventional logic-based test. A resistive defect value 2 kΩ has been considered for R_{VDD} and R_{GND}.

Write time histograms for the $AP \rightarrow P$ write operation for good and defective cells are shown in Fig. 8(a). R_{GND} moves the write time distribution to the left, and therefore, it does not cause a logic fault. R_{VDD} moves the write time distribution to the right, but most of the write time values does not cause a logic fault. It can be observed that most of the write time values are within the designed write time margin of the cell ($t_{wr} = 3.5$ ns), and hence, they represent test escapes.

Write time histograms for the $P \rightarrow AP$ write operation for good, and defective cells are shown in Fig. 8(b). R_{VDD} moves the write time distribution to the left, and consequently, it does not trigger a logic fault. On the other hand, defect R_{GND} moves the write time distribution to the right. In this case, most of the write time values of the defective cell are larger than the designed write time margin of the cell ($t_{wr} = 3.5$ ns), and hence, they can be detected using a logic-based test. However, some defective cells with write times smaller than the designed write time margin of the cell are not detected using a logic based test.

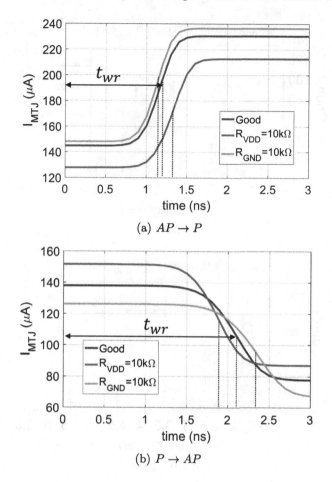

(a) $AP \rightarrow P$

(b) $P \rightarrow AP$

Fig. 7. Current waveforms for both $P \rightarrow AP$ and $AP \rightarrow P$ write transitions.

Figures 8(a) and (b) suggest that a conventional logic-base test using the write operation may fail to detect short defects related to R_{VDD}. Moreover, some short defects related to R_{GND} also may not be detected.

5.3   Impact of Short Defects on the Read Operation

Figure 9 shows the voltage V_{cell} generated at the current mirror terminals in the read circuit (See Fig. 4) as a function of the short defect resistance for both R_{GND} and R_{VDD} defects. The black dashed lines correspond to the case of V_{cell} of a defect-free cell, where V_{cell} is 0.30 V and 0.85 V for the MTJ at the P and AP state, respectively. The voltage V_{REF} generated by the reference cell is 0.66 V.

A read error of the AP state is assumed for the following condition:

$$V_{cell} < V_{REF} \tag{1}$$

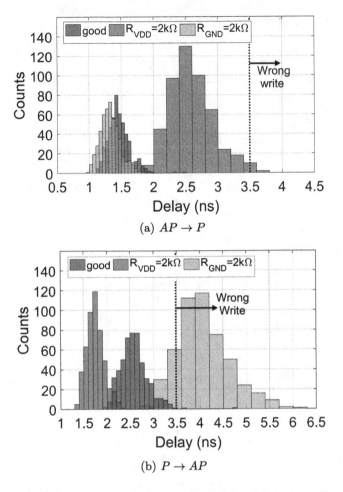

Fig. 8. Write time histograms for the good and defective cells.

A read error of the P state is assumed for the following condition:

$$V_{cell} > V_{REF} \qquad (2)$$

Resistive defect R_{VDD} injects extra current to the internal node of the cell, which has to be driven by the access transistor. Because of this, the resistance seen from the BL node increases, and hence, the generated voltage V_{cell} increases. Figure 9 shows that no logic error appears for reading an AP state for the defect R_{VDD}. However, a logic error occurs in a small range of defect resistance values for reading a P state.

Defect R_{GND} is placed in parallel with the access transistor. When the resistance of the short defect is large, its effect on the overall cell resistance is negligible. When the resistance of the short defect is small, the equivalent resistance reduces until it becomes closer to the pure resistance of the MTJ. The gen-

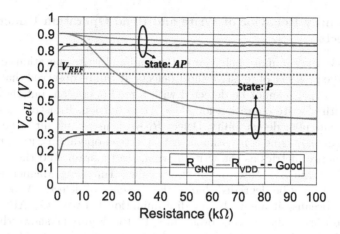

Fig. 9. Voltage generated by the memory cell (V_{cell} in Fig. 4) in a read operation as a function of the short defect resistance.

erated voltage V_{cell} reduces as R_{GND} becomes smaller (See Fig. 9). Resistive defect R_{GND} defect does not trigger any incorrect read operations. Therefore, this defect can not be detected by a read operation using conventional logic test.

Impact of Process Variations

Figure 10 shows the histograms of the voltage V_{cell} for good and defective cells. A resistive shorts defect of $20\,k\Omega$ has been considered for R_{GND} and R_{VDD}. As expected, the defect R_{GND} does not trigger an incorrect read. Some of the defective cells with R_{VDD} may not cause an incorrect read (logic fault) and may escape the logic test.

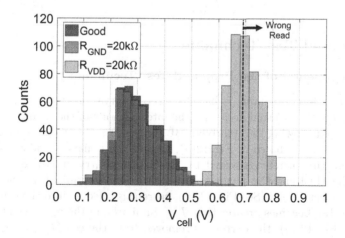

Fig. 10. Histogram of the voltage generated by the memory cell (V_{cell} in Fig. 4) in a P state read operation.

5.4   Summary Behavior of Write and Read Operation Under Short Defects

Table 3 shows the summary behavior of the read and write operations of a memory cell in the presence of resistive short defects. It can be observed that resistive short defect R_{GND} cannot be detected with a read operation, but they may be detected with a write operation for $P \rightarrow AP$ condition. Resistive short defect R_{VDD} presents poor detectability. Defect R_{VDD} is more difficult to be detected than defect R_{GND} using conventional write and read operations. Even more, the cell performance metrics as the write margin, read margin, and the MTJ resistance between the AP state and P state, called Tunneling Magnetoresistance Ratio (TMR), may be degraded due to the presence of defects. A higher TMR is desirable because it allows better discrimination between the AP state and the P state during the reading procedure [12,18]. Figure 11 shows the behavior of the high-resistance state (R_{AP}), the low-resistance state (R_P) and cell TMR (CTMR) as a function of the resistance value of the short defect. It can be observed that the resistive defect modifies the values of R_{AP} and R_P, and as a consequence, the cell TMR. Lower TMR values affect sense margin, and they may pose a reliability concern.

Table 3. Summary behavior of write and read operation under short defects

Defect	Write		Read	
	$AP \rightarrow P$	$P \rightarrow AP$	AP	P
R_{GND}	NO	YES	NO	NO
R_{VDD}	Poor	NO	NO	Poor

6   Proposed Test Technique

6.1   Fundamental of the Proposed Test Technique

The proposed test technique is based on the observation that a resistive-short defect between an external node and the internal node of the memory cell modifies the current flowing into (through BL terminal) and out (through SL terminal) of the cell. As shown in Fig. 12(a), a good cell behaves as a single current path, where the current provided by the read circuitry at BL terminal flows through the MTJ and the access transistor to the SL terminal. In the presence of a short defect R_{VDD} (See Fig. 12(b)), current is injected into the cell (I_{short}), and hence, I_{SL} becomes greater than I_{BL}. Similarly, in the presence of a R_{GND} short (See Fig. 12(c)), the current is removed from the cell (I_{short}), and hence, I_{BL} becomes greater than I_{SL}.

Figures 13(a) and (b) show the currents flowing through BL (I_{BL}) and SL (I_{SL}) terminals and also the current flowing through the short defect (I_{short}).

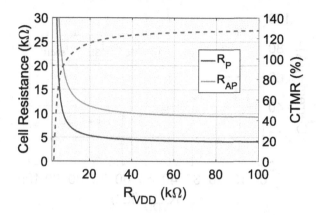

Fig. 11. Impact of the resistance value of the short defect on the Cell TMR.

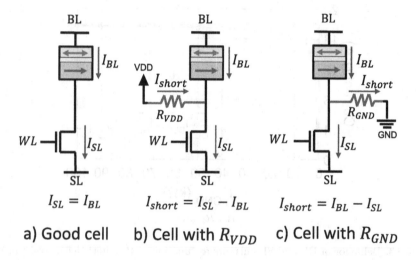

a) Good cell   b) Cell with R_{VDD} c) Cell with R_{GND}

Fig. 12. Current paths in defect-free and defective STT-MRAM cells.

These currents are plotted as a function of the resistance values of R_{VDD} and R_{GND} for a read operation. It can be observed that the currents in the terminals SL (I_{SL}) and BL (I_{BL}) have different behavior. This is due to the existence of an alternative conducting in the presence of the resistive short defect. Another important observation is that the current difference between I_{SL} and I_{BL} is more significant for lower resistance values of the short defect. The current difference between I_{SL} and I_{BL} indicates that monitoring the current difference between I_{SL} and I_{BL} is more effective than monitoring only a single current value. Resistive defect R_{VDD} causes a more significant current difference than the defect R_{GND} (See Figs. 13(a) and (b)). Hence, defect R_{VDD} would present better detectability than defect R_{GND} with our proposed test methodology.

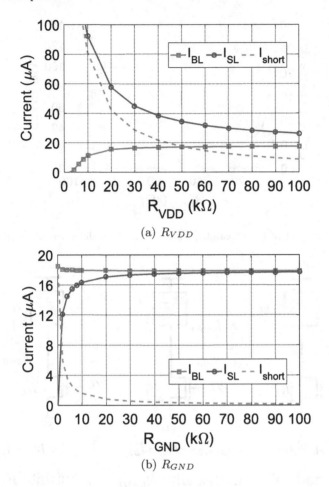

(a) R_{VDD}

(b) R_{GND}

Fig. 13. Behavior of BL and SL currents as function of the short defect resistance.

Figure 14 illustrates the benefits of our proposal under the effect of process variations for resistive defect R_{GND}, which present lower current values. Figure 14(a) shows the single values of the currents I_{BL} and I_{SL} under process variations. It can be observed that the single current values go up and down from the nominal value, which makes difficult to discriminate good circuits from bad circuits sensing only one of these currents. Figure 14(b) shows the current difference values between the currents I_{BL} and I_{SL} under process variations. It can be observed that the current difference values increase following a monotonic trend as the resistive defect values decreases. This behavior of the current difference allows distinguishing good circuits from bad circuits.

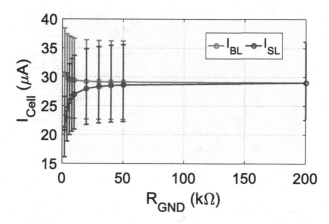

(a) Single current monitoring under process variations

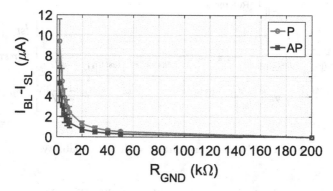

(b) Difference current monitoring under process variations

Fig. 14. Comparison between monitoring single and current difference under process variations.

6.2 Proposed Test Circuitry

In this Section, a DFT circuit oriented to defect detection without observability capability of the logic faulty behavior at main circuit outputs is proposed. This approach is adequate for the detection of weak defects, which are difficult to detect with a test based on classic logic fault observation. The benefit of the proposed test circuit to detect short defects sizes that can escape conventional logic test is validated under process variations effects. Therefore, the proposed test technique is able to detect those weak short defects that do not cause a faulty behavior, but limiting the quality and lifetime of the entire memory block.

Figure 15 shows the proposed modified readout circuit with test capability based on the previous observation that a resistive short defect between an external node and the internal node of the memory cell modifies the current flowing into and out of the cell. The modified read circuit measures the difference

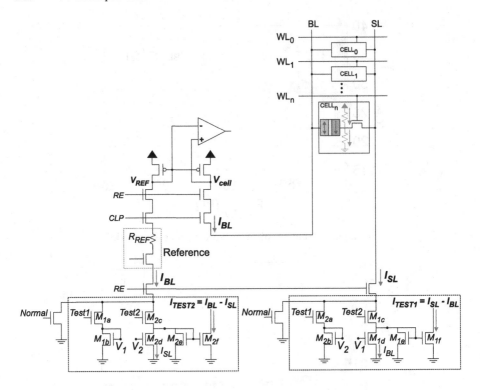

Fig. 15. Modified read circuit with test capability.

between the current flowing into and out of the cell in the column. A significant current difference indicates the presence of a defect. Differential current amplifiers are introduced at both sides of the column (BL and SL). The modified read circuit has three possible operation modes: (1) Normal mode, (2) Test 1, and (3) Test 2 (See Fig. 15).

The mode Normal is activated by setting the signals $Normal = 1$ and $Test$ $1=Test\ 2=0$. Under these conditions, the normal functionality of the read circuit is obtained. The mode Test 1 is activated by setting the signals *"Test 1=1"* and $Normal=Test\ 2=0$. In mode Test 1, the reference current (I_{REF}) passes through transistors M_{1a} and M_{1b} generating a voltage $V1$, which is used to copy I_{REF} to transistor M_{1d}. Note that $I_{REF} \approx I_{BL}$, thus the copied current represents I_{BL}. Since I_{SL} flows through M_{1c}, the current difference $I_{TEST,1} = I_{SL} - I_{BL}$ flows through transistor M_{1e}. This current is copied to M_{1f} which is the output transistor of the differential current amplifier. In other words, in mode Test 1 the operation $I_{TEST,1} = I_{SL} - I_{BL}$ is performed to generate an output current when I_{SL} is bigger than I_{BL}. Hence, possible resistive R_{GND} shorts defects are tested in mode Test 1. The mode Test 2 is activated by setting the signals *"Test 2=1"* and $Normal=Test\ 1=0$. The operation of mode Test 2 is very similar to mode Test 1, but in this case, the operation $I_{TEST,2} = I_{BL} - I_{SL}$ is performed to generate an output current at M_{2f} when I_{BL} is greater than I_{SL}. Hence, possible resistive R_{VDD} shorts defects are tested in mode Test 2.

The detection capability of the proposed circuit has been analyzed under the effect of process variations. Figures 16(a) and (b) show histograms of the current difference between BL and SL at the output of the proposed test circuit for both operation modes Test 1 and Test 2, respectively. 1000 Montecarlo simulations were run. Figure 16(a) shows that for strong resistive defects (smaller resistance), the test output current difference is more significant making easier the detection of the defect. Defective cells with weak short R_{VDD} as large as 100 kΩ can be fully distinguished from good cells as there is no overlap between the distribution of the defective cell and the good one. Defect R_{GND} is more difficult to detect. For defect $R_{GND} = 100$ kΩ, there is still a significant overlap between the current distribution of a good cell and the defective cell. However, resistive short defects of 20 kΩ can be fully detectable, which is still a significant improvement of the detection capability compared to the logic test.

The obtained results show that the proposed DFT test circuit is capable of detected the resistive short defects with sizes that are not detectable using a conventional logic test. Moreover, the proposed test circuit could be used to diagnose the severity of a short defect by defining thresholds in the current difference.

7   Cost and Comparison of Our Proposal with Logic Test

7.1   Detection Probability Comparison

Figures 17 and 18 shows the value of the detection probability (P_{det}) of short defects as a function of its resistance value for conventional test techniques (write and read operations test) and the proposed current difference test technique. 500 Monte Carlo simulations are done for each resistance value of the short defect. The Detection Probability (P_{det}) is computed with (3), where N_f is the number of runs presenting a fault and N_{MC} is the total number of Monte Carlo simulations.

$$P_{det} = \frac{N_f}{M_{MC}} \tag{3}$$

The largest write time ($P \rightarrow AP$) including process variations has been considered for a write fault to occur. A write fault occurs when the write time of the defective cell is greater than 3.5 ns. A read fault occurs when the V_{cell} is lower (higher) than $V_{ref} = 0.66$ V for P state (AP state). The detection thresholds of the proposed test technique are obtained from the histograms of the defect-free currents. A resistive short defect is assumed detectable when the current difference is higher than the maximum defect-free current from the histogram. The detection threshold current is 4.6 μA for $I_{TEST,1}$ and 4.0 μA for $I_{TEST,2}$.

For the R_{VDD} defect (See Fig. 17), a conventional write test detects the defect in the range from 0 to 1 kΩ. The defect is not detectable using a conventional

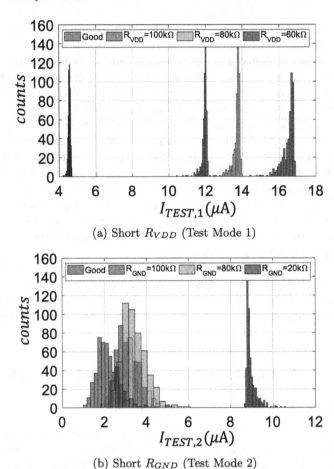

(a) Short R_{VDD} (Test Mode 1)

(b) Short R_{GND} (Test Mode 2)

Fig. 16. Current difference histograms for good and defective cells.

read operation when the cell has stored an AP state ($P_{det} = 0$), but when the cell has stored a P state the defect is detectable in the range from 0 to 200 kΩ. The proposed test technique increases the detection range of this defect in two orders of magnitude concerning the test based in the read operation when the cell has stored at P state. With the proposed DFT technique the R_{VDD} defects with values up to 1 MΩ are fully detectable and partially detectable at the range from 1 MΩ to 10 MΩ.

On the other hand, the R_{GND} defect presents a lower detection range than the R_{VDD} defect (See Fig. 18). This defect can not be detected with a test based in the cell read operation, ($P_{det} = 0$ for both states). However, with a conventional test during the write operation, R_{GND} defects with values up to 1 kΩ are fully detectable and partially detectable in the range from 1 kΩ to 10 kΩ. The proposed DFT technique fully detect the R_{GND} defect in a range from 0 Ω to 40 kΩ and partially detects this defect in a range from 40 kΩ and 100 kΩ.

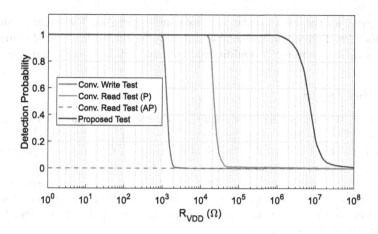

Fig. 17. Detection probability for R_{VDD} short.

7.2 Hardware Comparison

A conventional test based in write and read operation does not present area overhead. Our proposal requires to include additional transistors and test control signals. The total area of the channels of all the transistors is used as an estimation on the area overhead of the proposed DFT technique. The area of the access transistor of each memory cell is taken into account. It is assumed that the MTJ does not impact the area as is located above the access transistor. It is important to emphasize that the transistors used to copy currents in the DFT circuit have a longer channel length to ensure a correct copy of the currents. For a column composed of 2k bit, the DFT read circuit adds an approximated area overhead of 5% for the column. It should be noted that modern memories are

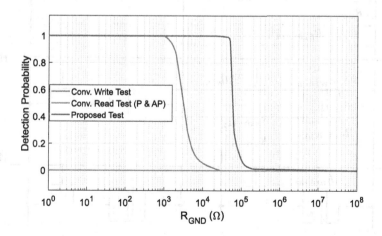

Fig. 18. Detection probability for R_{GND} short.

much bigger, so the area overhead significantly decreases for larger memories. Even more, read circuit in memory arrays may be shared for several columns.

Our proposal requires two additional control signals $I_{TEST,1}$ and $I_{TEST,2}$.

7.3   Other Issues

Regarding test time, a logic test requires to perform multiple writes and reads operations. The test time of our proposal depends on the actual method to measure the currents (built-in or external). Our proposal does not add performance degradation because the transistors connected to BL and SL have the same sizes in the DFT read circuit and the original read circuit. Even more, our proposal presents robustness against process variations. The differential current amplifier cancels most of the variations in the memory, as they impact the current flowing into and out of the cell similarly.

7.4   Short Defects that Can Be Detected

The analysis above is based on assuming a defect modeling of short defects between supply rails (VDD and GND) and the internal node (nx) of the STT-MRAM cell. The proposed technique is valid to detect all those short defects that create an unbalanced current between BL and SL nodes. Note that resistive-open defects cannot be detected with the proposed approach, as these defects do not make different the current flowing through BL and SL terminals. Figure 19 shows a memory array, where some short defects that can be detected using the proposed approach are highlighted. The probability of occurrence of the short defects depends on the memory array architecture and how its layout is made.

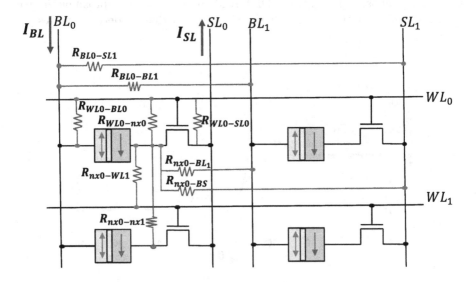

Fig. 19. Resistive shorts that can be detected using the proposed approach.

Typically, wider lines placed closer to other lines are more likely to present bridge defects [29]. The defects that are shown in Fig. 19 exhibit similar behavior to defects R_{VDD} and the R_{GND} in the defect model used in this work. Gate short defects between the W_{L0} and either B_{L0}, nx0, or S_{L0} behave as R_{VDD} because WL signal is settled to V_{DD} during a read operation to activate the access to the cell. Similarly, inter-cell shorts could be detected by previously setting the voltages of the adjacent cell at adequate values. For example, $R_{BL0-SL1}$ behaves as R_{VDD} is S_{L1} terminal is set to V_{DD}. Therefore, the proposed test technique can cover a wide variety of manufacturing short defects.

8   Conclusions

The behavior of an STT-MRAM cell under short defects in the presence of process variations has been analyzed. A DFT circuit for a defect-oriented test of resistive-shorts in an STT-MRAM cell was proposed. The proposed test technique is based on the observation that a short defect modifies the amplitude of the currents entering (I_{BL}) and leaving (I_{SL}) the memory cell. Thus, the DFT circuit senses the current difference between the currents I_{BL} and I_{SL}. The proposed approach is robust to process variations and significantly improves the detectability of resistive short defects that otherwise could escape to the conventional logic test. Detection probabilities of the resistive short defects are increased leading to high-quality electronic products.

Acknowledgments. This work was supported by CONACYT (Mexico) through the PhD scholarship number 434673/294398.

References

1. Bhattacharya, A., Pal, S., Islam, A.: Implementation of FinFET based STT-MRAM bitcell. In: 2014 IEEE International Conference on Advanced Communications. Control and Computing Technologies, pp. 435–439 (2014)
2. ITRS International Technology Roadmap for Semiconductor. http://www.itrs2.net/
3. Liu, Y., Xu, Q.: On modeling faults in FinFET logic circuits. In: 2012 IEEE International Test Conference, pp. 1–9 (2012)
4. Harutyunyan, G., Tshagharyan, G., Vardanian, V., Zorian, Y.: Fault modeling and test algorithm creation strategy for FinFET-based memories. In: 2014 IEEE 32nd VLSI Test Symposium (VTS), pp. 1–6 (2014)
5. Mesalles, F., Villacorta, H., Renovell, M., Champac, V.: Behavior and test of open-gate defects in FinFET based cells. In: 2016 21th IEEE European Test Symposium (ETS), pp. 1–6 (2016)
6. Panagopoulos, G., Augustine, C., Roy, K.: Modeling of dielectric breakdown-induced time-dependent STT-MRAM performance degradation. In: Proceedings of DRC, pp. 125–126 (2011)
7. Bishnoi, R., Oboril, F., Tahoori, M.B.: Design of defect and fault-tolerant non-volatile spintronic flip-flops. IEEE Trans. Very Large Scale Integr. (VLSI) Syst. **25**, 1421–1432 (2017)

8. Chintaluri, A., Parihar, A., Natarajan, S., Naeimi, H., Raychowdhury, A.: A model study of defects and faults in embedded spin transfer torque (STT) MRAM arrays. In: 2015 IEEE 24th Asian Test Symposium (ATS), pp. 187–192 (2015)
9. Chintaluri, A., Naeimi, H., Natarajan, S., Raychowdhury, A.: Analysis of defects and variations in embedded spin transfer torque (STT) MRAM arrays. IEEE J. Emerg. Sel. Top. Circuits Syst. **6**(3), 319–329 (2016)
10. Diao, Z., et al.: Spin-transfer torque switching in magnetic tunnel junctions and spin-transfer torque random access memory. J. Phys. Condens. Matter **19**(16), 165209 (2007)
11. Vatajelu, E.I., Prinetto, P., Taouil, M., Hamdioui, S.: Challenges and solutions in emerging memory testing. IEEE Trans. Emerg. Top. Comput. (2017). https://doi.org/10.1109/TETC.2017.2691263
12. Wu, L., Taouil, M., Rao, S., Marinissen, E.J., Hamdioui, S.: Electrical modeling of STT-MRAM defects. In: 2018 IEEE International Test Conference (ITC), pp. 1–10 (2018)
13. Bishnoi, R., Ebrahimi, M., Oboril, F., Tahoori, M.B.: Read disturb fault detection in STT-MRAM. In: 2014 International Test Conference, Seattle, pp. 1–7 (2014)
14. Gomez, A.F., Forero, F., Roy, K., Champac, V.: Robust detection of bridge defects in STT-MRAM cells under process variations. In: 2018 IFIP/IEEE International Conference on Very Large Scale Integration (VLSI-SoC), pp. 65–70 (2018)
15. Gomez, A.F., et al.: Effectiveness of a hardware-based approach to detect resistive-open defects in SRAM cells under process variations. Microelectron. Reliab. **67**, 150–158 (2016)
16. Hosomi, M., et al.: A novel nonvolatile memory with spin torque transfer magnetization switching: spin-RAM. In: IEEE International Electron Devices Meeting. IEDM Technical Digest, pp. 459–462 (2005)
17. Andre, T., et al.: ST-MRAM fundamentals, challenges, and applications, In: Proceedings of the IEEE 2013 Custom Integrated Circuits Conference, pp. 1–8 (2013)
18. Fong, X., Kim, Y., Venkatesan, R., Choday, S.H., Raghunathan, A., Roy, K.: Spin-transfer torque memories: devices, circuits, and systems. Proc. IEEE **104**, 1449–1488 (2016)
19. Baibich, M.N., et al.: Giant magnetoresistance of (001) Fe/(001) Cr magnetic superlattices. Phys. Rev. Lett. **61**, 2472 (1988)
20. Yuasa, S., Nagahama, T., Fukushima, A., Suzuki, Y., Ando, K.: Giant room-temperature magnetoresistance in single-crystal Fe/MgO/Fe magnetic tunnel junctions. Nat. Mater. **3**(12), 868 (2004)
21. Fong, X., Choday, S.H., Roy, K.: Bit-cell level optimization for non-volatile memories using magnetic tunnel junctions and spin-transfer torque switching. IEEE Trans. Nanotechnol. **11**(1), 172–181 (2012)
22. Hosomi, M., et al.: A novel nonvolatile memory with spin torque transfer magnetization switching: spin-RAM. In: IEEE International Electron Devices Meeting, pp. 459–462 (2005)
23. Fong, X., Choday, S.H., Georgios, P., Augustine, C., Roy, K.: Spice models for magnetic tunnel junctions based on monodomain approximation (2013)
24. Zhang, Y., Wang, X., Li, Y., Jones, A.K., Chen, Y.: Asymmetry of MTJ switching and its implication to STT-RAM designs. In: 2012 Design, Automation Test in Europe Conference Exhibition (DATE), pp. 1313–1318 (2012)
25. Zhang, Y., Wang, X., Li, H., Chen, Y.: STT-RAM cell optimization considering MTJ and CMOS variations. IEEE Trans. Magn. **41**, 2962–2965 (2011)

26. Emre, Y., Yang, C., Sutaria, K., Cao, Y., Chakrabarti, C.: Enhancing the reliability of STT-RAM through circuit and system level techniques. In: 2012 IEEE Workshop on Signal Processing Systems, pp. 125–130 (2012)
27. Motaman, S., Ghosh, S., Rathi, N.: Impact of process-variations in STTRAM and adaptive boosting for robustness. In: Proceedings of the 2015 Design, Automation & Test in Europe Conference & Exhibition, pp. 1431–1436 (2015)
28. Predictive technology models. http://ptm.asu.edu/
29. Forero, F., Galliere, J.-M., Renovell, M., Champac, V.: Detectability challenges of bridge defects in finfet based logic cells. J. Electron. Test. **34**(2), 123–134 (2018)

Assessment of Low-Budget Targeted Cyberattacks Against Power Systems

XiaoRui Liu[1], Anastasis Keliris[2], Charalambos Konstantinou[1(✉)],
Marios Sazos[3], and Michail Maniatakos[3]

[1] FAMU-FSU College of Engineering, Center for Advanced Power Systems,
Florida State University, Tallahassee, FL, USA
{xliu9,ckonstantinou}@fsu.edu
[2] New York University Tandon School of Engineering, Brooklyn, NY, USA
apk5@nyu.edu
[3] Center for Cyber Security, New York University Abu Dhabi, Abu Dhabi, UAE
{mks5,mm6446}@nyu.edu

Abstract. The security and well-being of societies and economies are tied to the reliable and resilient operation of power systems. In the next decades, power systems are expected to become more heavily loaded and operate closer to their stability limits and operating constraints. On top of that, in recent years, cyberattacks against computing systems and networks integrated in the power grid infrastructure are a real and growing threat. Such actions, especially in industrial environments such as power systems, are generally deemed feasible only by resource-wealthy nation state actors. This chapter challenges this perception and presents a methodology, named Open Source Exploitation (OSEXP), which utilizes information from public infrastructure to assess an advanced attack vector on power systems. The attack targets Phasor Measurement Units (PMUs) which depend on Global Positioning System (GPS) signals to provide time-stamped circuit quantities of power lines. Specifically, we present a GPS time spoofing attack using low-cost commercial devices and open source software. The necessary information for the instantiation of the OSEXP attack is extracted by developing a test case model of the power system in a digital real-time simulator (DRTS). DRTS is also employed to evaluate the effectiveness and impact of the developed OSEXP attack methodology. The presented targeted attack demonstrates that an actor with limited budget has the ability to cause significant disruption to a nation.

1 Introduction

Since the first public electric power system was established in the 1880's for providing street lighting [1], power systems have significantly evolved and grew to become essential in our everyday life. This is evident by the global demand

© IFIP International Federation for Information Processing 2019
Published by Springer Nature Switzerland AG 2019
N. Bombieri et al. (Eds.): VLSI-SoC 2018, IFIP AICT 561, pp. 232–256, 2019.
https://doi.org/10.1007/978-3-030-23425-6_12

for energy which is increasing at an accelerating rate [2]. The energy demand is driven with the increasing human population, economic growth, as well as technological advances. As the "backbone" of critical infrastructure on which other sectors (including transportation networks, military defense systems, water treatment and desalination, telecommunications) rely on, electric power systems need to have sufficient capacity to meet peak demand, flexibility to deal with uncertainty and variability in regards to the desired load demand and generation sources, and be able to maintain voltage and frequency stability criteria [3].

The normal operation of all infrastructures dependent on power systems is maintained only if supply of electrical energy is steady. Power outages (also known as *blackouts*), however, cause large-scale disruptions of electric power supply and can lead to loss of power in parts of a power system's network due to the activation of protection equipment. Typical causes of blackouts include extreme weather and natural phenomena, misoperation, human errors, equipment failures, and animals [4]. Examples of power outages due to extreme weather events include *(i)* the nor'easter during March 2018 that caused major impacts across the Northeast US where over 2.2 million customers left without power [5], and *(ii)* hurricane Michael which made landfall near Mexico Beach, Florida, on October 10, 2018, leaving approximately 2.5 million electricity customers in the southeast without power [6]. The 2011 Southwest blackout, the largest in California history, was initiated due to a mistake by a technician that caused a 500 kV line to shut down between two Arizona substations [7]. In 2017, 1205 utility outages lasted eight hours or longer. The financial impact for the 274 of the events was more than $27 million [8].

In power systems, the stable operation could be disrupted not only by natural hazards, operators errors, or failures at production units, but also by software vulnerabilities and errors, malware or intentional criminal cyberattacks [9–11]. The financial loss in 2016 to the US economy caused by malicious cyberattacks is estimated between $57 and $109 billion [12]. One of the first indications that power systems can be vulnerable to cyberattacks was demonstrated in 2007 by the Idaho National Laboratory with the "Aurora Generator Test", showcasing how cyberattacks can transcend the virtual world and cause physical damage on power systems equipment [13]. The test showed how an attacker able to access the control network of a diesel generator could install a malicious program that rapidly opened and closed the relay controllers of a generator. The out-of-sync closing of the relays caused the generator to slip out of synchronism and as a result create a frequency difference between the machine and the grid, maximizing the stress, provoking immoderate torque, and finally causing the generator to spin out of control. Besides proof-of-concept cases, real-world incidents demonstrate that cyberattacks could be disastrous and affect the lives of millions of people [14]. For instance, in December 2015, attackers were able to cause a blackout in Ukraine. The attackers compromised supervisory control and data acquisition (SCADA) systems and infected software with malicious code that tripped breakers, causing a power outage and preventing the utility from detecting the attack [15,16]. Particularly, the attack initiated with scheduled disconnects for uninterruptible power supply (UPS) systems and telephonic

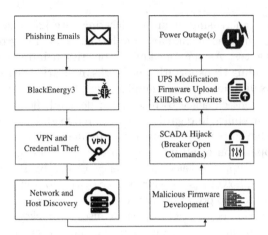

Fig. 1. Cyber kill chain of 2015 cyberattack on the Ukrainian power grid.

floods against customer supported lines. The primary attack vector hijacked SCADA with malicious commands to open breakers. The amplifying stage of the attack wiped using KillDisk[1] workstations, servers, and human machine interface (HMI) cards while overwriting the legitimate firmware on critical devices at distribution substations, leaving them unresponsive to any remote commands from operators [17]. Figure 1 graphically depicts the main steps of the kill chain of the 2015 cyberattack on the Ukrainian power grid. One year later (December, 2016), Ukraine suffered another sophisticated attack against the Pivnichna substation near the capital, Kiev [18]. The attack against this transmission facility resulted in power outages across the Kiev wider area for an hour. The adversaries employed the CrashOverride malware, which enables direct control of circuit breakers and switches [19].

Taking into account inadvertent and deliberate incidents, power utilities are taking steps to establish better protective functions against attacks on the grid infrastructure. These systems often incorporate advanced sensing and measurement technologies that include, among others, smart meters, advanced protective relaying systems, asset condition monitors, and Wide Area Monitoring Systems (WAMS). Specifically, WAMS highly rely on Global Positioning System (GPS) or similar time references for substation clock synchronization. WAMS can be utilized to analyze dynamic system events able to augment monitoring, control, and protection functions as shown in Fig. 2 (e.g., state estimation, dynamic monitoring, relay protection schemes, islanding strategies, etc.). Phasor measurements form the cornerstone of WAMS infrastructure. The phasor network consists of Phasor Measurement Units (PMUs) able to provide synchronized voltage and current phasors, as well as frequency measurements. PMUs synchronize phasor measurements across a wide geographical area by leveraging absolute timestamps provided by GPS signals [20,21]. In particular, PMUs receive and

---

[1] KillDisk is a malware variant designed to wipe data from hard drives.

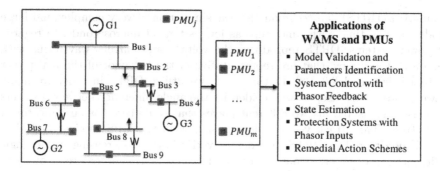

Fig. 2. Applications of Phasor Measurement Units (PMUs) and Wide Area Monitoring Systems (WAMS).

decode the GPS data in order to estimate their clock position offset with respect to the GPS time measured by the on-board satellite clocks. They then leverage GPS data to achieve clock synchronization and derive a Coordinated Universal Time (UTC) time-stamp reference for their measurements (typically reported at 30–120 samples/second [22]).

Despite the transition towards grid modernization and the inclusion of monitoring systems across the power infrastructure, WAMS, control, and protection schemes can be exposed to malicious interference. For example, GPS signals are vulnerable to jamming, spoofing, and accidental receiver malfunctions [23]. The vulnerability of time synchronization protocols of PMU devices to such attacks is a potential risk factor that may lead to falsified data measurements, and at a larger scale, may lead to inaccurate monitoring and trigger unnecessary, and possibly destabilizing, remedial control actions which can become hazardous for system safety [24]. Oftentimes, such attack scenarios are considered to only be within the reach of well-funded organizations or nation states, and require substantial technical education [25]. However, given the plethora of publicly available information regarding power systems and the dependency of these systems on public infrastructure, we argue that it is feasible for actors with lower budgets to also develop and instantiate disrupting attacks. To that end, we introduce a low-budget methodology capable of causing wide area blackouts, solely relying on public information and public infrastructure.

Similar to Open Source Reconnaissance[2], where meaningful information is extracted from public sources [26], we introduce Open Source Exploitation (OSEXP) in which the information required to deploy an attack is extracted from public resources and infrastructure [27]. Low budget attack vectors are constructed against judiciously GPS time spoofing, that exploits the reliance of power systems and specifically PMU devices on GPS for time synchronization.

Furthermore, in order to verify the feasibility of the proposed method, we run real-time test simulations based on the OPAL-RT platform. Digital real-time

---

[2] The term open source is not related to open source software throughout this work, unless explicitly stated.

simulation (DRTS) is a technique for the simulation of very complex and large models in real-time with time steps as low as tens of microseconds. In regards to power systems, DRTS reproduces the voltage and current waveforms with the desired accuracy, that are representative of the behavior of the real power system being modeled [28]. In this work, we utilize DRTS in order to model power system test case, as well as identify the angle difference between two sets of phasors measured at two different places that could serve as an indicator of grid stress. The attack vector – forged signals in the GPS receiver of PMUs – is demonstrated in DRTS in order to verify how an increasing phase angle difference can cause erroneous protection decisions by triggering circuit breakers to trip.

Our main contribution in this work is the characterization and experimental verification of GPS time spoofing attacks against carefully selected power grid devices using *low-cost Commercial-Off-The-Shelf (COTS) equipment and open source software*. Prior literature has demonstrated the potential of GPS spoofing attacks to affect power system measurements but required specialized, expensive equipment and extended technical knowledge [24,29]. Our approach significantly reduces the cost and complexity of GPS time spoofing, "open sourcing" the exploitation phase of campaigns targeting power systems. Furthermore, it enables a one-time design of an exploitation vector and reuse of the same vector worldwide, as GPS is employed for time synchronization purposes in systems across the globe. The effectiveness of the developed low-budget attack vector is validated using DRTS on the IEEE 9-bus system. In particular, the real-time model streams phasor data using the standard IEEE C37.118 protocol mimicking the behavior of an actual transmission network employed with PMUs, i.e., the test case of the grid is monitored by modelled PMUs across the network resembling their placement in a real network.

This chapter challenges the perception that extensive damage and/or disruption of a nation's computers and networks are feasible only by resource-wealthy nation state actors. To that end, we introduce a methodology dubbed OSEXP, which leverages public infrastructure to execute an advanced cyberattack on critical infrastructure. The first section of this chapter provides preliminaries on power systems along with the background information about PMU and GPS systems. The next section discusses our proposed end-to-end open source approach for constructing attack vectors against power systems, introduces OSEXP, and elaborates on a specific OSEXP attack, GPS time spoofing. Next, we experimentally verify the feasibility of this attack using low-cost equipment and open source software. In addition, we provide simulation results and verify the feasibility of the attack vector in DRTS. The last section concludes the chapter.

2   Background

2.1   Power Systems

Electrical power systems consist of a variety of generation plants, substations, transmission lines, distribution lines, and loads. In general, power systems are

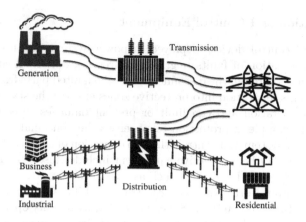

Fig. 3. Power grid architecture.

comprised of four stages, namely generation, transmission, distribution, and consumption. As seen in Fig. 3, all the components are interconnected in a large scale network, also known as power grid.

The *generation* part is the first stage of a power system. It is the procedure of generating electric power from sources of primary energy. The three major categories of energy for electricity generation are fossil fuels (coal, natural gas, and petroleum), nuclear energy, and renewable energy sources. Most electricity is generated with steam turbines using fossil fuels, nuclear, biomass, geothermal, and solar thermal energy. Other electricity generation technologies include gas turbines, hydro turbines, wind turbines, and solar photovoltaics.

The power is then transferred through high-voltage lines and substations via the *transmission* network. Specifically, high-voltage transmission lines span across large geographical regions and carry electricity over long distances to where consumers need it. In the U.S. 97% of transmission lines are overhead [30]. Electric power can also be transmitted by underground power cables instead of overhead power lines. However, underground transmission systems have higher initial construction costs due to the requirement of insulated cables and excavation. For example, the estimated cost for constructing underground transmission lines ranges from 4 to 14 times more expensive than overhead lines of the same voltage and same distance [31].

The energy is then distributed via the *distribution* stage to end consumers. Distribution lines span in smaller distances and operate at lower voltages compared to transmission lines. Step down transformers are used to reduce the voltage levels to ranges that match the operational voltages of end consumers. Finally, electricity is utilized in the *consumption* stage. Electric utilities typically distinguish between consumers based on the type of activity they perform: residential, commercial, and industrial.

2.2   Protection and Control Equipment

Protection and control devices deployed in power systems are used to ensure the automatic isolation of faults (e.g., short circuits), abnormal conditions, or equipment failures through the disconnection of the faulted parts from the rest of the network. This separation into protective zones ensures the stable and secure power system operation and can limit or prevent damages to equipment and personnel. For example, a protection relay senses the abnormal conditions in a part of the power system and controls the trip operation of a circuit breaker when a fault is detected. Other protective equipment includes fuses, sectionalizers, as well as automatic operation devices such as auto-reclosers.

As reported from North American Electric Reliability Council (NERC), 70% of the major disturbances in the U.S. are associated with faulty operation of relay controllers [32]. Optimal attack strategies may require changing the breaker status signal at only one transmission line [33]. Furthermore, traditionally, power systems are designed to sustain a single component outage ($N-1$ criterion). Due to the growing complexity of modern power systems (e.g., significant generation uncertainty, malicious cyber-threats, distributed generations, etc.) regulatory agencies also require operators to ensure system stability in the event of multiple (two or more) contingencies k: either k (near-)simultaneous losses [$N-k$ ($k \geq 2$) contingency] or consecutive losses [$N-1-1$ contingency] [34]. The above highlight the necessity of constant and reliable operation of circuit breakers and relay controllers for avoiding catastrophic to the power grid consequences (e.g., cascading failures leading to blackouts).

2.3   Grid Modernization

An important step towards grid modernization is the integration of Operational Technology (OT) and Information Technology (IT). Components in power grid are being upgraded with "smart" counterparts that enable fine-grain control, faster incident response times, and decision-making strategies. In addition, the incorporation of such units in control systems within the grid contributes in having increased efficiency, reliability and lower production and maintenance costs. The enabler of grid modernization four decades ago was the inclusion of microprocessor-based devices with communication capabilities in control processes. Nowadays, the enablers of grid modernization are the advanced computation and networking abilities of these "smart" comprising components. To achieve these goals while keeping development costs low, vendors of power equipment typically leverage COTS technology, use common general-purpose microprocessor architectures (e.g., ARM, Intel x86) and real-time versions of commercial operating systems (e.g., Windows and Linux) [35].

The driving factors of grid modernization contribute to the development of grid systems equipped with embedded devices and communication protocols. The main grid components (generation, transmission, distribution, and consumption) are equipped with various embedded systems including communication networks, control automation systems, and Intelligent Electronic Devices (IEDs). In general, IEDs deployed in power systems gather data from sensors across the grid, observe the variables and state of the system, store necessary data, make decisions, and take protection and control actions towards preserving performance and stability. For example, WAMS highly rely on IEDs to gather system information from multiple sources. WAMS are mainly enabled by PMUs that take synchronized snapshots of electrical quantities across the system, and use the comparative measurements to estimate the health and power quality of the grid.

Phase Measurement Units (PMUs): PMUs are deployed primarily in the transmission stage and provide synchronized phasor (synchrophasor) measurements of voltage and current levels as well as frequency data at several locations in order to provide time-aligned information of the system's state. Due to their ability to monitor and analyze power system behavior, NERC's CEO Rick Sergel has said in 2008 that synchrophasors are "like the MRI of the bulk power system" [36].

Given the dispersed topology of the power grid, accurate time synchronization between such devices is essential for their operation. To that end the 50/60 Hz analog AC waveforms of the collected measurements are digitized via analog to digital converters and the majority of PMUs rely on timing provided by GPS modules for capturing synchronized snapshots of the system across geographically dispersed locations. In contrast with traditional SCADA systems that collect data every 2−4 s, the collection of PMUs' synchronized measurements at rates of 30 to 120 samples/second enable real-time situational awareness [37]. Current uses of synchrophasor technology for power grid situational awareness include wide-area visualization, oscillation detection, voltage stability and phase angle monitoring, state estimation, fault location, etc. In addition, PMU data can be utilized for offline analysis such as identification of equipment problems and misoperations, model validation (e.g., equipment, generation), forensic event analysis, NERC standard compliance, field equipment commissioning, etc [38].

A major limitation to large-scale deployment of PMUs is their high capital cost. The average overall cost per PMU (cost for procurement, installation, and commissioning) often ranges from \$40,000 to \$180,000 [39]. Due to the significant costs related with PMU installation, utilities often follow two major site selection methods. The first method follows a *(i) function-dominant approach* in which the location meet utilities' needs relative to the desired synchrophasor data applications (e.g., placement of PMUs for power system observability [40–42]), including location choices driven by regional or NERC criteria. The power utility then upgrades its communication infrastructure to support the PMU-based applications being deployed. The second selection strategy follows a *(ii) site-dominant approach* in which locations are identified based on the existing communication infrastructure and the utility stations that are sufficient to support the applications being deployed. The locations are then selected based on the utility's needs as driven by regional and/or NERC disturbance recorder placement criteria.

2.4 Global Positioning System

Global Navigation Satellite Systems (GNSS), an example of which is GPS, is an earth-orbiting satellite system where receivers on or near the Earth could collect the geolocation and time information from GNSS transmitters. The time measurements are based on atomic clocks on the satellites which are synchronized to the UTC. The geolocation information of the transmitters is assumed known at all times, as the satellites follow predetermined trajectories. As of December 2018, there were a total of 31 operational satellites in the GPS constellation, not including the decommissioned, on-orbit spares [43]. The constellation requires a minimum of 24 operational satellites. The U.S. is committed to maintaining the availability of at least 24 operational GPS satellites, 95% of the time. The U.S. Air Force normally flies more than 24 GPS satellites to maintain coverage whenever the baseline satellites are serviced or decommissioned.

Each satellite is broadcasting a navigation signal with time stamp data and the deviation from its predetermined trajectory. The GPS space segment consists of a constellation of satellites transmitting radio signals to users. It ensures that users have, at least, four simultaneous satellites in view from any point at the Earth surface at any time. Receivers obtain such signals from satellites within their field of view, and use the signal propagation delays to calculate their three-dimensional location data and time [44]. Each GPS satellite simultaneously transmits on two L-band frequencies denoted by L1 and L2, which are 1575.42 and 1227.60 MHz and are utilized in civilian and military applications (encrypted restricted signals), respectively. Additional GPS signals are used or being proposed as summarized below [45]:

- L1 - 1575.42 MHz: this GPS signal is used to provide the course-acquisition (C/A) and encrypted precision P(Y) codes. It is also used for the L1 civilian (L1C) and military (M) codes on the Block III satellites.
- L2 - 1227.60 MHz: this signal is used to carry the P(Y) code, as well as the L2C and military codes on the Block IIR-M and later satellites.
- L3 - 1381.05 MHz: this frequency is used to carry information regarding any nuclear detonation and high-energy infrared events.
- L4 - 1379.913 MHz: this signal is being studied for use with additional ionospheric correction.
- L5 - 1176.45 MHz: this GPS signal is being proposed for use as a civilian safety-of-life signal.

In this work, we focus on L1 signals, as PMUs utilize these signals for time synchronization.

3 Open Sourcing Power System Cyberattacks

Adversaries can utilize a plethora of tools and approaches for disrupting national power grids. In this section, we focus on how malicious campaigns could adopt end-to-end open source approaches (i.e., cyberattacks based solely on public information and infrastructure). Retracing the steps of a malicious actor whose objective is causing a wide area blackout, we identify three main requirements for achieving this goal. These are:

1. Formulate and construct an as accurate as possible model of the target system. This model is necessary for understanding the system, its dependencies, and also identifying weak spots.
2. Analyze the model to identify and evaluate critical targets. By carrying out analytical, data-driven studies of the system model, adversaries can identify critical locations, which could lead to cascading failures.
3. Instantiate attack vectors that target the critical locations identified in the previous step, materializing the attack towards achieving its objectives.

3.1   Threat Model

The increased complexity and the modernization of power systems expose them to several vulnerabilities that one can use to gain access to the control network of the power systems. For example, COTS-based designs, including IEDs like PMUs, integrated in various parts of the grid are plagued by the same vulnerabilities present in processors and microcontrollers. In our scenario, the threat actors are considered to have the technical expertise to operate power systems. Moreover, they should have the knowledge of leveraging public resources and infrastructure to achieve their goals. The ultimate goal is to interrupt the normal operation of the power system and cause a large scale power blackout.

The threat model adopted in this analysis considers adversaries whose aim to cause power system disruption that would result in large scale power outages. We assume that the adversaries are proficient in power system operations, have sufficient technical expertise, and can, if required, be in physical proximity to power grid assets. However, we do not consider them to possess confidential information, or have network access to the equipment and control center of the target power system (e.g., phishing power system administrator credentials is outside the scope of this chapter).

In addition, we assume that the malicious actors can leverage publicly available information and infrastructure at scale to achieve their objectives. An immediate and noteworthy implication of this assumption is that adversaries are not limited to resource-wealthy nation states. Their motivation falls outside the scope of this paper, but it can for example be political, financial or to divert national resources in restoring the power while they pursue another primary objective.

3.2   Open Source Intelligence for Modeling Power Systems

Comparing the several incidents that have led to power outages to date, most of them are the result of faults occurring on the transmission stage. Thus, adversaries are most likely to focus on this stage to cause power outages. To that end, a target model could be constructed that includes the network topology of all the transmission substations, transmission lines, loads and their interconnections to enable further studies of the target system.

To the aid of adversaries, there exists a plethora of public information regarding power systems available, concerning system parameters, energy generation, power consumption, network topology, etc. From such sources it is possible for adversaries to reconstruct a model. Evidently, this form of "open source reconnaissance" or Open Source Intelligence (OSINT) is employed in an ongoing campaign against U.S. systems [46].

Some examples of sources include: (a) public reports, such as blackout reports, regional expansion planning reports, load forecast reports, (b) power system databases, such as Enipedia [47] and Open Energy Information [48], and (c) press releases and success stories from power utilities and power grid equipment vendors. By combining and fusing information from such sources, a model of a target power system can be constructed for carrying out subsequent analyses. For example, detailed information regarding the construction of a power system model using public information can be found in [49,50].

3.3 Identifying Critical Locations with Contingency Analysis

Identification of the critical locations for a given model is crucial for an attacker because it provides information both on the particular locations and also on the complexity of the final attack vector. To achieve this, power studies on the constructed model can enable judicious selection of optimal target locations for materializing an attack.

Contingency analysis is one of the most important studies for a security assessment of a power system, and one of particular usefulness to malicious actors. Contingency studies aim to analyze unscheduled events (e.g., generator, transformer, and/or transmission line failures) in a power system, and provide details on the stability of the system in case of any component failure within the power grid. In general, power systems are designed to sustain a single component failure, which is $N - 1$ criterion. For example, North America Electric Reliability Corporation (NERC) power security standards require system operators to maintain continuous and reliable operation power systems under the $N - 1$ constraint. Due to the computational overhead of contingency analysis, most research currently focuses on $N - 2$ contingency analyses. Further information can be found in [51].

Nevertheless, for all systems there exists a number of contingencies that can lead to non-sustainable scenarios and cause cascading failures and ultimately a power outage. By applying contingency analysis techniques on the model constructed in the previous step, adversaries can identify the critical transmission lines and interconnections of a system, and focus their attacks against these particular locations to maximize disruption.

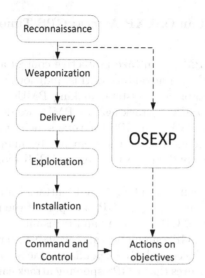

Fig. 4. Conventional Cyber Kill Chain with our proposed OSEXP step.

3.4   Open Source Exploitation - OSEXP

With knowledge of the critical points of a power system, adversaries need to construct attack vectors against the system. More specifically, they need to devise ways to disconnect critical transmission lines capable of a nonsustained contingency scenario. In this work, we focus on the exploitation of *public infrastructure*, and propose an open source methodology, which we call Open Source Exploitation (OSEXP). OSEXP techniques can be used both standalone, or in conjunction with conventional cyberattack techniques (e.g., phishing, credential harvesting, lateral movement, etc.), depending on the campaign objectives and resources available to the malicious actors. For a campaign whose target is to cause large scale power outages rather than just get information and leverage on a target system, we argue that OSEXP techniques can be advantageous.

In general, the Cyber Kill Chain (CKC) model can be used to describe the structure of a cyberattack [52]. The seven steps of the conventional CKC model are: (1) reconnaissance, where information is gathered, (2) weaponization, where a payload is designed, (3) delivery of the payload, 4) exploitation, where a vulnerability of the target system is exploited, (5) installation, where the payload is installed and executed on the target system, (6) command and control, where adversaries remotely tweak and instruct the payload and finally (7) actions on objectives, where adversaries fulfill the objectives of their campaign. By exploiting public infrastructure using OSEXP, steps 2 to 6 are replaced with an OSEXP step leading to an alternative path in the CKC, depicted in Fig. 4. The resulting CKC using OSEXP attacks has fewer steps, is reusable and leaves less evidence behind, making forensic studies and attribution harder.

3.5 Instantiation of an OSEXP Attack: GPS Time Spoofing Against PMUs

As outlined in Sect. 2, PMUs can take protective control actions in addition to their monitoring role. Taking advantage of this, judicious manipulation of PMU measurements can destabilize a system, making PMUs attractive targets for malicious actors. The OSEXP attack against PMUs we describe in this section exploits the reliance of PMUs on GPS for time synchronization. Our OSEXP attack introduces erroneous PMU measurements by manipulating the timing source of PMUs, effectively disconnecting selected PMU-controlled transmission links.

Corroborating the feasibility of OSEXP GPS attacks, information, implementation details, and software regarding GPS are part of the public domain. Open source implementations of GPS receivers and transmitters for Software Defined Radios (SDRs), software GPS simulators and available literature lower the technical requirements for successful GPS spoofing attacks [53]. Furthermore, the global nature of GPS ensures that a GPS spoofing attack can be reused in diverse systems employing different hardware across the globe. In contrast, techniques that require identifying and exploiting deployed devices, software, and network channels are system-specific and require undertaking laborious research for each system. These observations render GPS time spoofing an effective attack vector that can be developed once and reused several times against disparate systems.

GPS receivers inherently trust the signals they receive, assuming the signals have not been tampered with. In most countries in the world, any transmission in the frequency band of GPS is illegal, addressing the risk with policy safeguards. However, from a technical standpoint L1 GPS signals do not have any built-in integrity protection mechanisms. With OSEXP GPS spoofing attacks, we challenge the inherent trust in the integrity of these signals, arguing that adversaries with far-reaching agendas, such as causing blackouts, will not be bound by ethical and legal concerns.

Given the reliance of PMUs on GPS for capturing the state of a power system in a synchronized manner, we describe the process of introducing errors in PMU measurements by manipulating GPS signals in their vicinity. This can cause desynchronized snapshots of the system state from PMUs in different geographical locations, leading to system destabilization and even cascading failures. In particular, GPS time spoofing attacks can introduce errors in the absolute time perceived by the affected PMUs. For an f-Hz signal the relationship between the clock offset error $\tilde{t}_\delta - t_\delta$ and the phase angle measurement error ϵ are described by the following equation [54]:

$$\epsilon = [f \times (\tilde{t}_\delta - t_\delta) \times 360°] \ (\mathrm{mod}\ 360°) \tag{1}$$

PMUs with control capabilities have a preconfigured threshold for allowed phase angle difference, that is dependent on the specifics of the system they are deployed in. Phase differences larger than this threshold cause connected CBs to open for avoiding fault propagation and protecting the equipment. However, introducing timing errors with GPS spoofing to instantly change the perceived

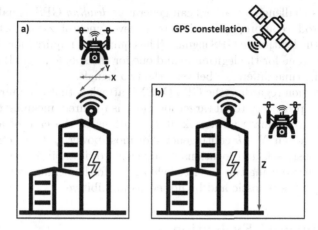

Fig. 5. Estimation of 3D location of a static GPS receiver using a drone. (a) x, y coordinates. (b) z coordinate.

state of the system for a PMU to exceed this threshold is not possible, because of the standards that govern PMUs. In particular, the IEEE standard for Synchrophasor Measurements for Power Systems (C37.118) dictates that clock synchronization errors between any two measurements from different PMUs should not exceed 31(26) µs for 50(60) Hz systems [55]. For a successful attack, it is thus necessary to slowly drift angle measurements, without exceeding these limits.

Another requirement for a successful GPS spoofing attack is knowledge of the legitimate GPS signal as it is perceived by the target receiver, including location information. This requirement can be fulfilled by co-locating the spoofing equipment in the physical vicinity of the target. The location information of a receiver is static, as the antenna is mounted on a building. Towards measuring the receiver location, attackers can measure their relative distance from the receiving antennas and calculate the offset, for example by employing drones equipped with cameras and GPS receivers. By flying directly over the target antenna, adversaries can capture the x, y location using the drone mounted GPS receiver. Subsequently, the z coordinate can be measured independently. Figure 5 illustrates this scenario.

In addition to identifying receiver location, generation of appropriate synthetic GPS signals requires that the spoofed and legitimate GPS signals are time-synchronized [56]. This enables attackers to concurrently transmit a spoofed signal that is synchronized with the legitimate signal, gradually increase the transmitting power overtaking the GPS receivers in the affected vicinity, and then introduce time delays that will cause erroneous PMU measurements. The naive approach of recording legitimate GPS signals and replaying them after introducing the necessary time delays is not possible due to non-deterministic delays introduced by the retransmitting equipment's hardware components and the strict timing requirements of the IEEE C37.118 synchrophasor standard. To overcome this challenge, attackers can generate a *leading* GPS signal, and then gradually introduce appropriate delays to achieve synchronization between their spoofed and the legitimate GPS signals. The equipment required for this are two GPS receivers (one for the legitimate and one for the spoofed signal) and means to measure the time difference between the two signals.

An observation regarding the GPS OSEXP attack is that it requires simultaneous physical proximity to all target locations is required, meaning that adversaries need to coordinate an attack at k locations in the case of attacking a system to trigger an $N - k$ contingency. For most power systems, opening CBs at two judiciously selected locations is sufficient to destabilize the system. We argue here that requiring two to three field agents for launching an attack of this scale and impact is realistic and by no means prohibitive.

4   Experimental Evaluation

In this section we evaluate the feasibility of the proposed GPS time spoofing OSEXP attack. To that end, we present two experimental setups. The first one utilizes DRTS and specifically the OPAL-RT platform in order to perform a real-time simulation of a test case power system. From an attacker's standpoint, this step will verify the developed power grid model using OSINT as well as extract required information to be utilized for the instantiation of the OSEXP attack vector. In the second experimental setup, we verify that open source software and SDR platforms are capable of launching GPS time spoofing attacks with the necessary granularity as this is defined by IEEE C37.118.

4.1   Power System Modeling

The model of a power system is developed in RT-LAB, the software platform of OPAL-RT's simulation systems. It can communicate with hardware equipment through FPGA I/O interfaces and is used for the execution of the MATLAB/Simulink blocks, including those in the SimPowerSystems (SPS) blockset, in real-time on a PC-based cluster. Time domain simulation method is used in this work to assess the stability of the power system. The time step, Δt, for the simulations is set at 0.02 s. The model is developed in the RT-LAB/Simulink environment offline, and then, compiled and downloaded to the OPAL-RT simulator that performs a real-time simulation with a cluster of processors.

The power system used in this study is the IEEE 9-bus case which represents a simple approximation of the Western System Coordinating Council (WSCC) to an equivalent system with three generators and nine buses [57]. The single line diagram of the WSCC 9-bus system is presented in Fig. 6. The system was slightly modified for simulation purposes: circuit breakers are included at each line and after each generator before connected to the grid. Also, the power system is monitored by modelled PMUs (available in OPAL-RT) across the network resembling their placement in a real power grid network. PMUs are added to three of the system buses to monitor the real-time phasors of both voltages and

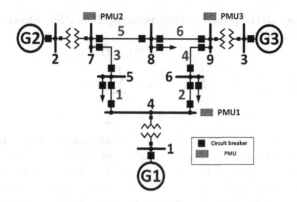

Fig. 6. Modified WSCC 9-bus system.

currents. The simulation model consists of 3 subsystems: a master subsystem (SM), a slave subsystem (SS), and a console subsystem (SC). The SM is the main subsystem of the model which includes all computational and measurements elements. The SS includes the PMU models distributed across multiple nodes of the grid. The SC is the interface module available during execution in order to interact with the system while it is running. Our objective is to collect phase angle measurements from the PMUs before and after a set of events (e.g., faults, breaker tripping, etc.). The angle difference between two sets of phasors measured at two different locations can serve as an indicator of the grid stress [24]. Thus, an attacker able to manipulate GPS signals in the receiver of PMUs could trigger protection and control schemes.

As mentioned in Sect. 2, a major drawback to large-scale deployment of PMUs is the cost related with their installation. In our work, the minimum number as well as the optimal locations of the PMUs in the system follows a *function-dominant approach* from literature which aims to make the system topologically observable [40,41]. An integer linear programming (ILP) method that generates all possible candidate PMU placement solutions to guarantee topological observability is as follows [40]:

$$N_{PMU} = min \sum_{i=1}^{n} y_i$$

$$s.t. \ T_{PMU} Y \geq b$$

(2)

where T_{PMU} is a binary connectivity matrix [40], $b = [1, 1, ..., 1]_{n \times 1}^{T}$, $Y = [y_1, y_2, ..., y_n]^{T}$, where $y_i \in \{0, 1\}$ is the PMU placement variable on the i_{th} bus, with 1 indication a placement and 0 indicating no placement. This method gives only one possible solution for the minimum number of PMUs N_{PMU}. Adding an auxiliary parameter $D = [d_1, d_2, ..., d_n]$, $d_i = rand(0, 1)$, $i = 1, 2, ..., n$ to the cost function of the above equation and when the number of realizations of D is sufficiently large, all the possible of candidate optimal PMU placement solutions can be generated [41]:

$$min \ DY$$

$$N_{PMU} = min \sum_{i=1}^{n} y_i \tag{3}$$

$$s.t. \ T_{PMU}Y \geq b$$

The outcome of the placement modified algorithm using (3) allows for more than one optimal solution to exist. For the implemented 9-bus test case, four sets of three buses are determined to place PMUs. The four solutions are $\{2, 4, 9\}$, $\{3, 7, 4\}$, $\{1, 7, 9\}$ and $\{4, 7, 9\}$. The optimal solution considered for this work, places PMUs in the following set of 9-system buses $\{4, 7, 9\}$, as shown in Fig. 6. Based on our threat model, the locations of those installed PMUs can be identified using OSINT methods such as using satellite images to identify the GPS antennas at the grid substations [50].

In the developed model of the power system, three-phase (3-ϕ) faults are created at different locations of the system at any one time. In power systems, faults could occur as a result of eventful conditions such as natural events and accidents in which phase(s) establish a connection with other phase(s), the ground, or both in some circumstances. This results in a rapid and massive flow of current via an improper path which could cause injuries and death, interruption of power, as well as equipment damage. Faults in power systems are classified into open and short circuit faults which can either symmetrical or unsymmetrical [58]. During a fault, the power system goes through pre-fault, fault-on, and post-fault stages [59]. In our model, we simulate 3-ϕ faults at the lines of the system; when a fault occurs, a breaker operates and disconnects the corresponding line at the fault clearing time (FCT) which is set at the 4 cycles (4×16.7 ms). The protection system clears the fault instantaneously without intentional time delay. We consider a normal clearing time of 4 cycles: 2 cycles for relay/PMU time and 2 cycles for breaker time [60].

Modeling Results: After constructing the IEEE 9-bus simulation model and adding the three required PMUs in the system at buses $\{4, 7, 9\}$, we run simulations for different fault scenarios and we observe the differences on the PMU phase angle measurements. Specifically, for each case we introduce a 3-ϕ to ground fault at the transmission line ij between bus i and bus j, and measure the phase angle difference from the, simulated in OPAL-RT, PMU before and after (2 cycles) the fault has been triggered. The simulation results are shown in Table 1. For example, in case 5 where a $3-\phi$ fault is applied to line between buses 7–8, the phase angle difference $\Delta\theta = \theta_{PMU2} - \theta_{PMU3}$, i.e., between the PMUs installed at buses 7 and 9 respectively, changes from $1.8°$ in normal operating conditions to $-72.2307°$ 2 cycles after the fault. Figure 7 presents the difference in the positive-sequence voltage phase angle between the two PMUs before, during, and after the clearing time of the fault at line 5 (buses 7–8). The data are obtained in real-time using the simulated PMUs of OPAL-RT. As shown in

Table 1. Positive-sequence voltage phase angle difference ($\Delta\theta$) between PMU-supported buses of modified WSCC 9-bus system. $\Delta\theta_0$ indicates normal operation and each presented scenario is $\Delta\theta$ 2 cycles after the $3-\phi$ fault at the lines between buses $i - j$.

A/A	Line $(i - j)$	$\Delta\theta^{\circ}_{(PMU_1 - PMU_2)}$ $\Delta\theta_0 = -5.841^{\circ}$	$\Delta\theta^{\circ}_{(PMU_2 - PMU_3)}$ $\Delta\theta_0 = 1.8^{\circ}$	$\Delta\theta^{\circ}_{(PMU_1 - PMU_3)}$ $\Delta\theta_0 = -4.0414^{\circ}$
1	4–5	−15.9893	5.2364	−10.7530
2	4–6	−15.1038	2.0563	−13.0475
3	5–7	−15.9932	5.2271	−10.7661
4	6–9	−18.4971	80.1049	61.6078
5	7–8	59.0539	−72.2307	−13.1768
6	8–9	−18.4997	85.3294	66.8297

Table 1, phase angle difference can serve as an effective indicator of the performance of a power system. Monitoring and protective schemes often utilize such data to detect reliably, among others, instantaneous changes in the transmission lines' impedance and thus contingency conditions. In our presented results, an angle difference threshold of 70° can detect, for example, the occurrence of the presented case 5 for PMU_2 and PMU_3. System operators can utilize this information to set the PMU-based protective configuration accordingly in order to trip the breaker once this phase angle difference occurs between PMU at bus 7 (PMU_2) and bus 9 (PMU_3). However, such schemes can be leveraged by the presented spoofer attacker who may target one or both PMUs as the target of the OSEXP attack. The timing error introduced by spoofing the GPS receiver of the PMU(s) will cause a corresponding phase error in the reported synchrophasor data, and therefore trigger the presented scheme unnecessarily (without any actual fault in the system). A series of such attacks has the potential to cause cascading effects in the system leading to instability conditions and power outages.

4.2   GPS Experimental Setup

In this part, we evaluate the feasibility of a low cost GPS time spoofing attack. For our GPS spoofing experiments we assume that attackers have synchronized their synthetic signals to legitimate GPS signals and have taken over control of the GPS receiver. These are realistic assumptions if an attacker can introduce *arbitrary delays* to a GPS signal, as arbitrary delays can be leveraged to achieve synchronization of leading signals with the legitimate ones. After the two signals are synchronized, attackers can gradually increase the spoofed signal power, overtaking control of receivers within their vicinity [29].

The hardware in our experimental setup consists of a GPS receiver, an Arduino board, a SDR, a logic analyzer and a host computer. The GPS receiver employs the Venus638FLPx chip, which is a commercial, high performance

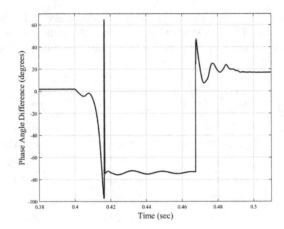

Fig. 7. Positive-sequence voltage phase angle difference between PMU_2 and PMU_3 at buses 7 and 9 respectively before, during, and after the clearing time of a three-phase (3-ϕ) fault at line 5 (buses 7–8) applied at $0.4\,s$ for $0.1\,s$.

receiver with 29 s cold start time-to-first-fix, up to 20 Hz update rate, and built-in jamming detection and mitigation. The GPS receiver is powered by an Arduino UNO board, which is also connected to the host computer for receiving and outputting the decoded NMEA messages. We utilize a Saleae Logic Pro 8 logic analyzer for sampling the Pulse-Per-Second (PPS) output pin of the receiver at a sampling rate of 10 MHz, which is satisfactory given the GPS receiver's PPS measured accuracy of 2 µs. For transmitting GPS signals we use an Ettus USRP N210 SDR, equipped with a GPSDO kit and a 40 MHz SBX 400–4400 MHz Rx/Tx. Respecting the legal framework concerning GPS signal transmission over-the-air, we conduct all of our experiments using cable connections and never transmit signals over-the-air, without loss of generality. To further ensure no side-effects we attenuate the USRP output to −140 dBm, which is close to the minimum required signal by our GPS receiver for a fix (−148 dBm). Finally, we enclose the experimental setup in RF shielding fabric to avoid leakage. Our experimental setup is depicted in Fig. 8.

In terms of software, we rely solely on open source software. For generating synthetic GPS data we use the Software-Defined GPS Signal Simulator (`gps-sdr-sim`) [61]. We download the required ephemerides data that indicate the current state of the satellite constellation from the Crustal Dynamics Data Information System [62]. Using `gps-sdr-sim` and the current ephemerides we create a raw synthetic static L1 GPS signal with a 2.5 MHz sampling rate, that is leading the current wall time by a few seconds. We input this signal to GNU Radio to perform the necessary type conversions, and add a delay block of user-specified duration between the file source and the USRP sink. This entire process is automated.

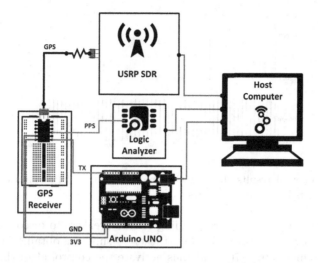

Fig. 8. Experimental setup for GPS spoofing attack.

GPS Spoofing Results: Since the maximum clock offset error required by the IEEE C37.118 protocol is 31 μs for a 50 Hz system, we aim to introduce approximately 30 μs delay to the targeted PMU in order for the attack to remain undetected. To that end, we select 30 μs as the user-specified delay duration in our GNU Radio flowchart and launch the automated script. We present the experimental results regarding time as it is perceived by the receiver in Fig. 9. In particular, the figure presents the absolute duration of PPS signals as it is perceived by the GPS receiver and measured by the logic analyzer. We observe that up to $t = 16$ s (which is when the attack is launched), each PPS signal is received exactly every one second, as expected. After the attack is launched, the particular pulse duration at $t = 16$ s becomes 1.0000289 s, indicating a shift in the perceived time by the GPS receiver as a result of our GPS signal manipulation. The introduced delay of 28.9 μs is below the 31 μs threshold, verifying the feasibility of using COTS equipment and open source software to launch fine-grain GPS time spoofing attacks.

The introduced time delay of the GPS spoofing attack introduces errors in the absolute time perceived by the targeted PMUs which can be calculated using (1). This allows to examine the impact of the spoofing scenario on the power system. In particular, the 28.9 μs time delay results in a shift of 0.54° in the measured angle by the corresponding PMU. *Delays of arbitrary duration* can be introduced by repeatedly applying the same time-shifting technique. Accumulation of such delays can gradually increase the phase difference between actual and measured angles, reaching the pre-programmed threshold at which the respective circuit breakers are tripped, leading to sectionalization and cascading failures. Note that in addition to introducing erroneous measurements to PMUs, the same time-shifting technique can be employed to synchronize leading synthetic signals and legitimate GPS signals. In the presented case 5 of Sect. 4.1, the protection scheme

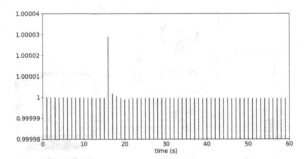

Fig. 9. Experimental results showing GPS receiver output PPS duration. The GPS spoofing attack is launched at $t = 16\,\text{s}$.

automatically triggers the corresponding circuit breakers to disconnect the line after a fault occurs. In order for an attacker to shift the obtained PMU phase angle measurements by $\geq 70°$ and thus activate the control algorithm resulting in falsified protection actions, she is required to repeat the above step 130 times $(130 \times 0.54 = 70.2°)$.

4.3   Budget

Our first experimental setup utilizes a DRTS to model the power grid. The reason is twofold: verify the developed power system model and identify the synchronized phase angle difference measurements by PMUs which are utilized to detect topology changes. The cost of acquiring and utilizing the described DRTS and its functions is in the order of a few tens of thousands of dollars. However, this can be additionally reduced by using newer versions of DRTS equipment which can a substantial lower cost.

The cost of the equipment we utilize for GPS time spoofing mainly consists of the Ettus USRP SDR (and its respective add-on modules) and the Saleae Pro 8 logic analyzer. Their costs are $3529 USD and $699 USD respectively, for a total of $4228 USD. Launching a concurrent attack against k locations to materialize an $N - k$ contingency would require $k \times$ $4228 USD (typically $k = 2$ or $k = 3$ locations are sufficient), which is low given the attack's far-reaching impact.

Our equipment costs in the GPS spoofing attack are dominated by the Ettus USRP SDR and they can be further reduced by replacing it with cheaper hardware, such as the bladeRF ($420 USD), or HackRF ($295 USD). An inherent limitation of these lower-cost devices is the reduced accuracy of their built-in oscillator, which is not adequate for transmitting GPS signals. However, this problem can be alleviated with OSEXP by leveraging another public infrastructure; *GSM base stations* [63]. As cell towers must be accurate within 0.5 parts-per-million (which is sufficient for GPS transmission), we can initially configure SDRs as GSM receivers. Using GSM signals, we can calculate the internal clock drift of our SDR with reference to the GSM base station clock, and then reconfigure the SDR as a GPS spoofer to carry out the spoofing technique as described above.

5   Conclusions

In this work, we introduce OSEXP, a technique that utilizes public infrastructure towards constructing an attack vector against power systems. We experimentally verify a specific OSEXP vector, GPS time spoofing, that can cause inaccuracies and errors in the measurements of PMUs deployed in WAMS applications. As a result, the GPS spoofing attack can desynchronize phase angle measurements of judiciously selected PMUs and can further cause deterioration to the system or even cause wide-area blackouts. The demonstrated OSEXP vector employs COTS hardware and open source software, enabling reusable low-budget high-impact attacks against power systems. For simulating the power system as well as determining the angle which an attacker needs to shift in order to trigger protective schemes, we use real-time data from simulated PMUs in a DRTS. With this study we aim to challenge the perception these attacks are feasible only by resource-wealthy nation state actors, and assist stakeholders and regulators take informed decisions to secure power grids around the world.

References

1. Lobenstein, R., Sulzberger, C.: Eyewitness to DC history. IEEE Power Energy Mag. **6**(3), 84–90 (2008)
2. Enerdata: Electricity domestic consumption. https://yearbook.enerdata.net/electricity/electricity-domestic-consumption-data.html
3. U.S. Department of Energy: Maintaining reliability in the modern power system. https://www.energy.gov/sites/prod/files/2017/01/f34/Maintaining%20Reliability%20in%20the%20Modern%20Power%20System.pdf
4. Eaton: Blackout tracker: United States annual report 2017 (2017)
5. Strange, P.: Monster nor'easter pummels east coast, vol. 126, no. 9, pp. 863–868 (1979)
6. Wikipedia: Hurricane michael (2018). https://en.wikipedia.org/wiki/Hurricane_Michael
7. Ditler, J.: The great coronado blackout of 2011 (2011)
8. Department of Defense: Annual Energy Management and Resilience Report (AEMRR) (2018). https://www.acq.osd.mil/eie/Downloads/IE/FY%202017%20AEMR.pdf
9. Kaspersky: Cyperthreats to ICS systems (2014). http://media.kaspersky.com/en/business-security/critical-infrastructure-protection/Cyber_A4_Leaflet_eng_web.pdf
10. McLaughlin, S., et al.: The cybersecurity landscape in industrial control systems. Proc. IEEE **104**(5), 1039–1057 (2016)
11. Konstantinou, C., Maniatakos, M.: Security analysis of smart grid. Commun. Control. Secur. Chall. Smart Grid **2**, 451 (2017)
12. The Council of Economic Advisers. The cost of malicious cyber activity to the U.S. economy (2018). https://www.whitehouse.gov/wp-content/uploads/2018/03/The-Cost-of-Malicious-Cyber-Activity-to-the-U.S.-Economy.pdf
13. CNN: Mouse click could plunge city into darkness, experts say (2007). http://www.cnn.com/2007/US/09/27/power.at.risk/index.html

14. Yamashita, K., Joo, S.-K., Li, J., Zhang, P., Liu, C.-C.: Analysis, control, and economic impact assessment of major blackout events. Eur. Trans. Electr. Power **18**(8), 854–871 (2008)

15. Trivellato, D., Murphy, D.: Lights out! who's next? how to anticipate the next "cyber-blackout" (2016)

16. Defense Use Case: Analysis of the cyber attack on the Ukrainian power grid. Electricity Information Sharing and Analysis Center (E-ISAC) (2016)

17. Zetter, K.: Inside the cunning, unprecedented hack of Ukraine's power grid. http://www.wired.com/2016/03/inside-cunning-unprecedented-hack-ukraines-power-grid/

18. Goodin, D.: Hackers trigger yet another power outage in Ukraine (2017). https://arstechnica.com/information-technology/2017/01/the-new-normal-yet-another-hacker-caused-power-outage-hits-ukraine/

19. Dragos Inc., Crashoverride: Analysis of the threat to electric grid operations (2017). https://dragos.com/blog/crashoverride/CrashOverride-01.pdf

20. Steinmetz, C.P.: Complex quantities and their use in electrical engineering. In: Proceedings of the International Electrical Congress, pp. 33–74 (1893)

21. Phadke, A.G.: Synchronized phasor measurements-a historical overview. In: Transmission and Distribution Conference and Exhibition 2002: AsiaPacific, IEEE/PES, vol. 1, pp. 476–479. IEEE (2012)

22. North American Synchrophasor Initiative (NASPI): Time synchronization in the electric power system (2017). https://www.naspi.org/sites/default/files/reference_documents/tstf_electric_power_system_report_pnnl_26331_march_2017_0.pdf

23. Humphreys, T.E., Ledvina, B.M., Psiaki, M.L. O'Hanlon, B.W., Kintner, P.M.: Assessing the spoofing threat: development of a portable GPS civilian spoofer. In: Radionavigation Laboratory Conference Proceedings (2008)

24. Konstantinou, C., Sazos, M., Musleh, A.S., Keliris, A., Al-Durra, A., Maniatakos, M.: GPS spoofing effect on phase angle monitoring and control in a real-time digital simulator-based hardware-in-the-loop environment. IET Cyber-Phys. Syst.: Theory Appl. **2**(4), 180–187 (2017)

25. Konstantinou, C., Maniatakos, M.: Hardware-layer intelligence collection for smart grid embedded systems. J. Hardw. Syst. Secur. **3**(2), 132–146 (2019)

26. Steele, R.D.: Open source intelligence. In: Handbook of Intelligence Studies, pp. 129–147 (2007)

27. Keliris, A., Konstantinou, C., Sazos, M., Maniatakos, M.: Low-budget energy sector cyberattacks via open source exploitation. In: 2018 IFIP/IEEE International Conference on Very Large Scale Integration (VLSI-SoC), pp. 101–106. IEEE (2018)

28. Faruque, M.O., et al.: Real-time simulation technologies for power systems design, testing, and analysis. IEEE Power Energy Technol. Syst. J. **2**(2), 63–73 (2015)

29. Shepard, D.P., Humphreys, T.E., Fansler, A.A.: Evaluation of the vulnerability of phasor measurement units to GPS spoofing attacks. Int. J. Crit. Infrastruct. Prot. **5**(3–4), 146–153 (2012)

30. Alonso, F., Greenwell, C.: Underground vs. overhead: Power line installation-cost comparison and mitigation (2013). https://www.elp.com/articles/powergrid_international/print/volume-18/issue-2/features/underground-vs-overhead-power-line-installation-cost-comparison-.html

31. Public Service Commission of Wisconsin: Underground electric transmission lines (2011). https://psc.wi.gov/Documents/Brochures/Under%20Ground%20Transmission.pdf

32. North American Electric Reliability Council: New Jersey, NERC Disturbance Reports 1992–2009

33. Deka, D., Baldick, R., Vishwanath, S.: One breaker is enough: hidden topology attacks on power grids. In: 2015 Power & Energy Society General Meeting, pp. 1–5. IEEE (2015)
34. NERC: Standard TPL-001-1. https://www.nerc.com/files/TPL-003-0.pdf
35. Stouffer, K., Falco, J., Scarfone, K.: Guide to industrial control systems security. NIST special publication SP 800–82 (2011)
36. Schweitzer, E.O., Whitehead, D., Zweigle, G., Ravikumar, K.G., Rzepka, G.: Synchrophasor-based power system protection and control applications. In: 2010 Proceedings of the International Symposium on Modern Electric Power Systems (MEPS), pp. 1–10. IEEE (2010)
37. Kim, Y.-J., Lee, J., Atkinson, G., Thottan, M.: Griddatabus: information-centric platform for scalable secure resilient phasor-data sharing. In: 2012 IEEE Conference on Computer Communications Workshops (INFOCOM WKSHPS), pp. 115–120. IEEE (2012)
38. Silverstein, A.: Synchrophasors & the grid. https://www.naspi.org/sites/default/files/reference_documents/naspi_naruc_silverstein_20170714.pdf
39. U.S. Department of Energy: Factors affecting PMU installation costs. https://www.smartgrid.gov/files/PMU-cost-study-final-10162014_1.pdf
40. Gou, B.: Optimal placement of PMUS by integer linear programming. IEEE Trans. Power Syst. **23**(3), 1525–1526 (2008)
41. Tai, X., Marelli, D., Rohr, E., Fu, M.: Optimal pmu placement for power system state estimation with random component outages. Int. J. Electr. Power Energy Syst. **51**, 35–42 (2013)
42. Chakrabarti, S., Kyriakides, E.: Optimal placement of phasor measurement units for power system observability. IEEE Trans. Power Syst. **23**(3), 1433–1440 (2008)
43. U.S. Government: GPS.gov. https://www.gps.gov/support/faq/#gap1
44. Kaplan, E., Hegarty, C.: Understanding GPS: Principles and Applications. Artech house, London (2005)
45. El-Rabbany, A.: Introduction to GPS: The Global Positioning System. Artech house, London (2002)
46. U.S. DHS and FBI: Russian government cyber activity targeting energy and other critical infrastructure sectors. https://www.us-cert.gov/ncas/alerts/TA18-074A
47. Davis, C., Chmieliauskas, A., Nikolic, I.: Enipedia. Energy & Industry group, TU Delft (2015)
48. Open energy information. http://openei.org
49. Konstantinou, C., Sazos, M., Maniatakos, M.: Attacking the smart grid using public information. In: IEEE Latin-American Test Symposium, pp. 105–110 (2016)
50. Keliris, A., Konstantinou, C., Sazos, M., Maniatakos, M.: Open source intelligence for energy sector cyberattacks. In: Gritzalis, D., Theocharidou, M., Stergiopoulos, G. (eds.) Critical Infrastructure Security and Resilience. ASTSA, pp. 261–281. Springer, Cham (2019). https://doi.org/10.1007/978-3-030-00024-0_14
51. Pajic, S.: Power system state estimation and contingency constrained optimal power flow: A numerically robust implementation (2007)
52. Martin, L.: Cyber Kill Chain (2014). https://www.lockheedmartin.com
53. Blossom, E.: GNU radio: tools for exploring the radio frequency spectrum. Linux J. **2004**(122), 4 (2004)
54. Jiang, X.: Spoofing GPS receiver clock offset of phasor measurement units. Master's thesis, UIUC (2012)
55. PSR Committee: IEEE Standards for synchrophasor measurements for power systems C37.118, New York, USA (2011)

56. Tippenhauer, N.O., Pöpper, C., Rasmussen, K.B., Capkun, S.: On the requirements for successful GPS spoofing attacks. In: Proceedings of the 18th ACM conference on Computer and communications security, pp. 75–86. ACM (2011)

57. Illinois Center for a Smarter Electric Grid (ICSEG), WSCC 9-Bus System. Information Trust Institute (ITI) (2017)

58. Anderson, P.M., Fouad, A.A.: Power System Control and Stability. Wiley, Hoboken (2008)

59. Amjady, N., Majedi, S.F.: Transient stability prediction by a hybrid intelligent system. IEEE Trans. Power Syst. 22(3), 1275–1283 (2007)

60. North American Electric Reliability Corporation: Protection system reliability redundancy of protection system elements. https://www.nerc.com/docs/pc/spctf/Redundancy_Tech_Ref_1-14-09.pdf

61. Ebinuma, T.: Software-Defined GPS signal simulator. https://github.com/osqzss/gps-sdr-sim

62. Noll, C.E.: The crustal dynamics data information system: a resource to support scientific analysis using space geodesy. Adv. Space Res. 45(12), 1421–1440 (2010)

63. Varma, G.N., Sahu, U., Charan, G.P.: Robust frequency burst detection algorithm for GSM/GPRS. In: 2004 IEEE 60th Vehicular Technology Conference, VTC 2004-Fall, vol. 6, pp. 3843–3846. IEEE (2004)

Efficient Hardware/Software Co-design
for NTRU

Tim Fritzmann[(✉)] [iD], Thomas Schamberger, Christoph Frisch,
Konstantin Braun, Georg Maringer, and Johanna Sepúlveda[iD]

Technical University of Munich, Munich, Germany
{tim.fritzmann,t.schamberger,chris.frisch,konstantin.braun,
georg.maringer,johanna.sepulveda}@tum.de

Abstract. The fast development of quantum computers represents a
risk for secure communications. Current traditional public-key cryptography will not withstand attacks performed on quantum computers. In
order to prepare for such a quantum threat, electronic systems must integrate efficient and secure post-quantum cryptography which is able to
meet the different application requirements and to resist implementation
attacks. The NTRU cryptosystem is one of the main candidates for practical implementations of post-quantum public-key cryptography. The
standardized version of NTRU (IEEE-1363.1) provides security against
a large range of attacks through a special padding scheme. So far, NTRU
hardware and software solutions have been proposed. However, the hardware solutions do not include the padding scheme or they use optimized
architectures that lead to a degradation of the security level. In addition,
NTRU software implementations are flexible but most of the time present
a low performance when compared to hardware solutions. In this work,
for the first time, we present a hardware/software co-design approach
compliant with the IEEE-1363.1 standard. Our solution takes advantage
of the flexibility of the software NTRU implementation and the speedup
due to the hardware accelerator specially designed in this work. Furthermore, we provide a refined security reduction analysis of an optimized
NTRU hardware implementation presented in a previous work.

Keywords: Lattice-based cryptography · NTRU ·
HW/SW co-design · Side-Channel Attack

1   Introduction

Public-key cryptography (PKC) provides the basis for establishing secured communication channels between multiple parties. It supports the confidentiality,
authenticity and non-repudiation of electronic communications and data storage. Internet-of-Things (IoT) and Cloud computing are some of the technologies
that use PKC to secure channels. Traditional PKC such as the Rivest-Shamir-
Adleman (RSA) cryptosystem, which is based on the factorization of larger numbers, or Elliptic Curve Cryptography (ECC), which is based on the discrete

ⓒ IFIP International Federation for Information Processing 2019
Published by Springer Nature Switzerland AG 2019
N. Bombieri et al. (Eds.): VLSI-SoC 2018, IFIP AICT 561, pp. 257–280, 2019.
https://doi.org/10.1007/978-3-030-23425-6_13

logarithm problem, are considered insecure to attacks performed by a quantum computer. The foreseeable breakthrough of quantum computers therefore represents a risk for all communication systems. By executing Shor's [22] and Grover's [16] quantum algorithms, these computers will be able to solve the problems, on which classical PKC (RSA, ECC) relies, in polynomial time and to decrease the security level of symmetric cryptosystems, respectively. While symmetric cryptosystems can be easily secured against quantum computers by choosing larger key sizes, securing PKC requires new hard mathematical problems. To ensure long-term communication security, quantum-resistant (also called post-quantum) cryptography must be adopted. Post-quantum cryptography relies on mathematical problems that are secure against attacks from both traditional and quantum computers.

The skyrocketing evolution of quantum computers in particular poses a significant threat for applications with long life-cycles (e.g., cars, airplanes and satellites), where deployed devices are hard to update. As a reaction, the National Institute of Standards and Technology (NIST) started the process for post-quantum standardization in 2017 [18]. The goal is to select a set of appropriate post-quantum solutions which are able to meet the security, performance, cost, and adaptability requirements of current and future applications. Lattice-based cryptography is among the most promising post-quantum solutions. The lattice-based cryptosystem NTRU is one of the main alternatives for practical implementations of post-quantum PKC. NTRU is characterized by small key sizes (low memory footprint) and computational efficiency when compared to other post-quantum approaches [5,6,21]. NTRU has been standardized in the IEEE Standard Specification for Public Key Cryptographic Techniques Based on Hard Problems over Lattices (IEEE-1363.1) [10].

Empowering electronic devices with strong security poses several challenges due to limited resources, strict performance requirements, a tight time-to-market window, and the vulnerability to implementation attacks. To cope with the ever-increasing complexity when designing an embedded system both hardware and software solutions are usually explored. Embedded system design is based on powerful design strategies, such as co-design, where the algorithm tasks are split and implemented through hardware and software elements, resulting in high-speed and flexible implementations. In addition, security solutions do not only rely on efficient implementations, but they should be resistant to attacks, such as Chosen-Ciphertext Attacks (CCA) or Side-Channel Attacks (SCA). Adversaries can recover the secret key by gathering information obtained through the decryption of fabricated ciphertexts or by the physical information leakage during the cryptographic operation due to, e.g., timing, power consumption, and electromagnetic radiation. CCA can be avoided by adopting a padding scheme such as the Short Vector Encryption Scheme (SVES) which is defined by the NTRU standard (IEEE-1361.1). SCA on the other hand requires a careful implementation of the cryptographic algorithm.

NTRU hardware implementations have been demonstrated in [1,2,12,14,15, 24]. While current hardware solutions focus on efficient convolution techniques, a complete hardware implementation of the standardized NTRU is still missing. Moreover, security aspects of the implementation are still largely unexplored. The works presented in [1,2,12,14,15,24] do not implement the SVES padding scheme and have no protection against CCA. Furthermore, the NTRU optimization presented in [15] reduces the security of NTRU by leaking information regarding the secret key as the execution time of this implementation depends on the value of the secret key. This makes an implementation impractical for real applications.

NTRU software implementations have been demonstrated in [2,4,13,17]. Despite showing good results, all of the aforementioned works present at least one of the following drawbacks: (i) NTRU parameters are already deprecated; (ii) Protection against CCA is not considered; and (iii) the implementations are based on outdated microprocessor/microcontroller architectures. Only the works of [5,20,23] present a complete NTRU software solution. The software solution proposed in [23] is the official NTRU implementation and [5,20] are implementations tailor-made for ARM Cortex M0 and protected against timing as well as cache attacks.

While NTRU hardware implementations present better performance, software implementations are easier to develop and to maintain. The exploration of complete hardware solutions and co-design techniques are essential for practically implementing NTRU on embedded devices.

This work extends our previous contribution presented in [3], where we demonstrate the first complete, compact, and secure NTRU hardware implementation and show that the optimized NTRU implementation in [15] exhibits a timing side-channel by giving a bounded security reduction analysis. In this extended work, we present the first HW/SW co-design NTRU solution compliant with the IEEE 1363.1 standard. It takes advantage of the flexibility of the software implementation and the speedup through the design of a specific hardware accelerator. In addition, we present the refinement of our previous security reduction analysis and we state the exact result instead of a bound. In summary, the contributions of the paper are:

- First complete NTRU hardware implementation which includes the SVES padding scheme;
- A compact NTRU implementation able to execute encryption and decryption operations;
- HW/SW co-design of NTRU by outsourcing polynomial multiplication and modulo reduction to hardware;
- A security analysis of the previous NTRU implementation presented in [15] and demonstration of the exact security reduction;
- Performance and cost evaluation of our NTRU implementations.

The remainder of this article is organized as follows: Sect. 2 gives an overview of the previous works on NTRU hardware implementations. Section 3 describes the instantiation of NTRU with the SVES padding scheme. Sections 4 and 5 present our complete NTRU hardware and HW/SW co-design implementations.

Section 6 describes the security analysis of the optimized NTRU presented in [15]. The experimental results are provided in Sect. 7. A conclusion is given in Sect. 8.

2   Related Works

The probably first NTRU encryption hardware implementation was proposed by Bailey *et al.* in 2001 [2]. To speed up the polynomial multiplication, which is usually the performance bottleneck of NTRU, the authors propose to scan the coefficients of the blinding polynomial r. For each non-zero coefficient, the public key h is added to a temporary result. Atıcı proposed the first encryption and decryption NTRU hardware implementation. The architecture includes power saving methods such as clock gating and partially rotating registers [1]. The implementation of Kamal *et al.* uses the special structure of the public key, which has a large number of zero coefficients to optimize the performance [12]. In [14], Liu *et al.* use the fact that the polynomial multiplication in the truncated polynomial ring of NTRU can be modeled with a Linear Feedback Shift Register (LFSR) to implement the polynomial multiplication. In [15], they speed up their implementation by skipping the multiplication operation when two consecutive zero coefficients in the ternary polynomial are detected. Thus, the multiplication time depends on the number of double zeros contained in the polynomial. This information decreases the NTRU security level as discussed in [3] and now refined in Sect. 6.

Moreover, so far none of the existing works has proposed a full hardware implementation of NTRU with the SVES padding scheme as defined in the IEEE-1363.1 standard. The work of [9] discusses different hardware design strategies for NTRU. However, it presents neither implementation results nor a detailed description of their approach that would allow to reproduce their architecture. Furthermore, the polynomial multiplication suggested in this work requires N^2 operations whereas recent works only require N clock cycles. Hardware design strategies required for the SVES padding scheme were not discussed. As the integration of SVES is mandatory to inhibit CCA, implementations that only integrate polynomial multiplication in hardware show a misleading picture of the implementation costs. A commonly used tool for transforming cryptographic algorithms into CCA secured schemes is the NAEP transformation [8]. SVES is a concrete instantiation of the NAEP transform, which was specifically designed for NTRU. The first iterations, SVES-1 and SVES-2, are vulnerable to attacks exploiting decryption errors [7]. The latest iteration, SVES-3, which is sometimes only referred to as SVES, does not show this vulnerability. It is standardized in IEEE-1363.1 [10]. In contrast to previous works, we present a complete CCA-secure NTRU hardware implementation compliant with the standard.

Regarding the NTRU software implementations, many of them are not compliant with the standard, use outdated parameter sets or are tailored for a specific platform. The NTRUOpenSourceProject provides the official software reference implementation for NTRU that is fully compliant with the standard [23]. This implementation builds the basis for our HW/SW co-design. We accelerate the performance critical multiplications during the encryption and decryption routines by outsourcing them to hardware. Our proposal combines the efficiency of a hardware design with the flexibility of a software design.

3 NTRU

3.1 Notation

The main elements of NTRU are the polynomials in the following integer rings:

$$R_{N,p} = \frac{(\mathbb{Z}/p\mathbb{Z})[x]}{(x^N - 1)}, \quad R_{N,q} = \frac{(\mathbb{Z}/q\mathbb{Z})[x]}{(x^N - 1)}. \tag{1}$$

These rings define each polynomial to be at most of degree $N - 1$ and to have integer coefficients. For $R_{N,p}$ and $R_{N,q}$ these coefficients are reduced modulo p and modulo q, respectively. Unless otherwise noted, all polynomials are elements of the ring $R_{N,q}$.

For the standardized parameter sets of NTRU the modulus p is fixed to a small prime $p = 3$. In this case, the elements of the ring $R_{N,p}$ are called ternary polynomials. A ternary polynomial $\mathcal{T}_N(d_1, d_2)$ has d_1 coefficients equal to one and d_2 coefficients equal to minus one, while the remaining coefficients are set to zero. Ternary polynomials in NTRU are sparse, that is, the majority of coefficients are set to zero. The values d_1 and d_2 are part of the parameter set and can be changed to achieve different security levels.

Additionally, the parameter q is fixed to $q = 2048$, which simplifies the implementation of the algorithm. By choosing the modulus to be a power of two, the modulo operation can be performed without additional costs by considering only the corresponding least significant bits.

3.2 Short Vector Encryption Scheme (SVES)

In order to provide a CCA-secure encryption algorithm, NTRU is instantiated with the SVES. SVES defines a general padding scheme for the message which prevents CCA by identifying invalid ciphertexts using two auxiliary methods: (i) Blinding Polynomial Generation Method (BPGM); and (ii) Mask Generation Function (MGF). The general description of these two methods is presented in the next paragraphs. Implementation-specific details are given in Subsects. 4.2 and 4.3.

Blinding Polynomial Generation Method (BPGM). This method generates an ephemeral blinding polynomial r in a deterministic way with the use of a Pseudo-Random Number Generator (PRNG). This PRNG is based on a hash function **G** and is initialized by a seed consisting of four values:

$$r = BPGM(OID, m, b, h_{trunc}). \tag{2}$$

The identifier OID is an unique three-byte value which depends on the parameter set. The parameter b is a random number and m the message to be encrypted. Finally, h_{trunc} is a pre-defined part of the public key in binary representation.

Mask Generation Function (MGF). Similar to the BPGM module, the MGF module uses a hash function **G** to generate a mask. The input of **G** is the result of the polynomial multiplication of the ephemeral blinding polynomial r and the public key h:

$$m_{mask} = MFG(r * h). \tag{3}$$

The resulting mask m_{mask} is added to the message m.

3.3 NTRU with SVES

The NTRU scheme instantiated with SVES consists of the three cryptographic operations: key generation, encryption and decryption.

The key generation step creates a key pair, consisting of the public key h with its corresponding secret key f, through three steps. The first step generates two random ternary polynomials, $F \in R_{N,p}$ and $g \in R_{N,p}$. The positions of the polynomial coefficients with value one and minus one are selected based on an uniform distribution. The second step calculates the private key f as $f = 1 + pF$ together with its inverse f^{-1} modulo q. Not all the polynomials have an inverse in the corresponding ring. Therefore, it is possible that the inverse f^{-1} cannot be found. In this case, the key generation is restarted until a key with a valid inverse is found. The third step computes the public key h as $h = pf^{-1} * g$.

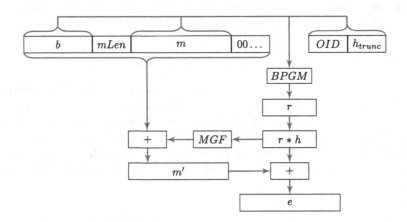

Fig. 1. NTRU encryption with SVES

The NTRU encryption is shown in Fig. 1. It transforms a message m into a ciphertext e through four steps. The first step encodes m into a ternary polynomial representation and concatenates this polynomial together with the random number b, the identifier OID, and h_{trunc} as input to the BPGM. Then the ephemeral polynomial r is created as $r = BPGM(OID \| m \| b \| h_{trunc})$. The second step multiplies r with the public key polynomial h. This result is used as an input to the MGF in order to obtain a mask as $m_{mask} = MFG(r * h)$. The third step adds the mask to the padded message $m_{pad} = (b \| mLen \| m \| 00 \dots)$ to produce $m' = m_{pad} + m_{mask}$. The final step computes the ciphertext as $e = m' + r * h$.

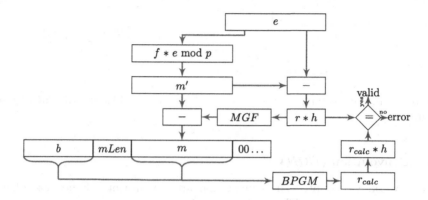

Fig. 2. NTRU decryption with SVES

The NTRU decryption is shown in Fig. 2. It retrieves the original message m from the ciphertext e through four steps. The first step extracts m' by multiplying the ciphertext e with the private key f as $m' = f * e \pmod{p}$. In the second step, $r * h$ can be retrieved by subtracting m' from the ciphertext e, as the equation $r * h = e - m'$ holds. The third step uses the resulting product as an input to the MGF to retrieve the padded message as $m = m' - MGF(r * h)$. The fourth step checks the validity of the ciphertext by applying the BPGM to the corresponding elements of m to produce the value r_{calc}. The multiplication result of $r_{calc} * h$ is now compared with the polynomial $r * h$ from the second decryption step. If both polynomials are equal, the algorithm outputs the padded message m. Otherwise an invalid ciphertext input is detected and the algorithm outputs an error message.

4   NTRU Full Hardware Architecture

Our proposed NTRU hardware architecture is illustrated in Fig. 3. The encryption and decryption flows are highlighted in green and red, respectively. To keep the area costs low, the encryption and decryption operation share common hardware modules. The resource sharing is managed by a small controller that sets the data selector values of all multiplexers. The NTRU architecture is composed of four main hardware modules: $CONV$, $BPGM$, MGF and $MOD\,p$. Their implementation is described in the following subsections.

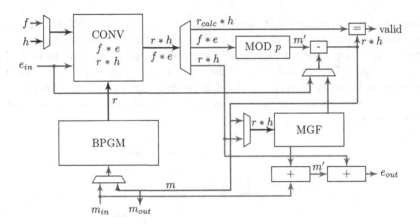

Fig. 3. NTRU architecture, green encryption, red decryption, blue shared (Color figure online)

4.1 Convolution (*CONV*)

In this work, we adopted the convolution architecture of [14] because of its efficiency and simplicity. This architecture is able to multiply a ternary polynomial with a regular polynomial in $R_{N,q}$. However, in order to support the encryption and decryption operations, the following modifications are required: (i) integration of the *control unit* to manage the convolution during encryption and decryption operations; and (ii) support for the multiplication of two regular polynomials ($f * e$). The enhanced convolution circuit (*CONV*) is shown in Fig. 4.

CONV multiplies a ternary polynomial $A \in \mathcal{T}_N$ with coefficients $\{-1, 0, 1\}$ and a regular polynomial $B \in R_{N,q}$. The circularity of the convolution is realized by shifting the resulting polynomial C in an LFSR. Depending on the sequentially inputted coefficient of A, each Modular Arithmetic Unit (*MAU*) respec-

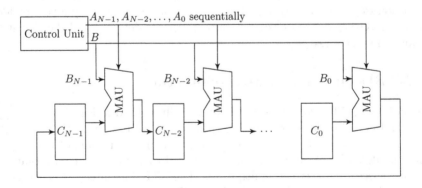

Fig. 4. Circular convolution model

tively either adds B_i to C_i, subtracts B_i from C_i or keeps C_i unchanged, where $i = 0, 1, \ldots N - 1$. The result of each MAU is forwarded to the next register. A more in-depth explanation of the functionality is given in the following: During the first clock cycle, the control logic outputs coefficient A_0, which is either -1, 0 or 1. The value of A_0 determines the operation mode of all MAU instances. In case of a -1 a subtraction is performed, in case of a 0 the value of the previous register is forwarded, and in case of a 1 an addition is performed. The first input of the i-th MAU is the coefficient B_i, which remains fixed for all clock cycles. The second input is the value of the previous register C_i. As $q = 2048$ each value of B_i and C_i has 11 bits. In the next cycle, the coefficient A_1 selects the operation mode of the $MAUs$. After n clock cycles the result of $A * B$ is stored in the registers.

During encryption, the ternary polynomial r and a regular polynomial h are multiplied through $CONV$, thus generating $r * h$. However, the decryption requires a multiplication of two regular polynomials f and e. In order to use $CONV$ for this multiplication, we use the definition of f given in the standard, such that $f = 1 + pF$, where F is a ternary polynomial. As a result, $f * e = (1 + pF) * e = e + pF * e$. To obtain $pF * e$, we repeat the convolution of $F * e$ two more times ($p = 3$) without resetting the registers after each round. Thus, after n clock cycles the registers have the value $F * e$, after $2n$ cycles $F * e + F * e$, and after $3n$ cycles $F * e + F * e + F * e = 3(F * e)$. At the end of this operation, the *control unit* inputs a ternary polynomial such that the value of the first coefficient is 1 and 0 otherwise. The second input will remain with the polynomial e. This procedure for calculating the addition of $pF * e$ with e takes one round (n cycles). It is also possible to skip this round if the registers are preloaded with e at the beginning of the decryption process. In addition to the calculation of $f * e$, the decryption has to calculate $r_{calc} * h$, which requires one additional round. The proposed process increases the convolution processing time during the decryption operation by a factor of four. However, it avoids the integration of additional multipliers, thus decreasing the required area for the decryption.

4.2   Blinding Polynomial Generation Method ($BPGM$)

Hash functions are the core of the $BPGM$ and MGF modules. The IEEE-1363.1 standard suggests the use of SHA-1 or SHA-256, depending on the chosen parameter set. SHA-1 and SHA-256 have a 512 bit input and 160 or 256 bit output, respectively. The seed varies in each hash call by using the four values described in Subsect. 3.2 (OID, m, b, h_{trunc}) concatenated with a *counter* value, which is increased after each hash call. The counter ensures that the hash output changes in each call. Our SHA cores use parts of the open core modules from [19].

The concrete generation of the ternary polynomial r, which is the output of the $BPGM$, is described in the following paragraph. Figure 5 shows the generation of the hash output. The *Control Unit* is responsible for managing the counter, setting the seed and writing the hash output to a buffer. The size of the buffer depends on the *minCallsR* variable defined in the standard. The buffer output is used for determining the indexes of ones and minus ones in r. In total, the polynomial r has d_r ones and d_r minus ones. The BPGM uses c-bits (a variable in the standard) from the buffer output and calculates this value modulo N. This modulo operation is currently done in a naive way by subtracting N from the value until it is smaller than N. Unfortunately, the algorithm used in Sect. 4.4 cannot be used because N is not a Mersenne prime number. However, Barrett and Montgomery reduction can be considered in future works. The result of the c-bit hash value modulo N determines the position of the corresponding one or minus one in the polynomial. If the position was already set, the next c-bits are used to create a new random position. The described process is repeated with new bits from the buffer until all indexes are found.

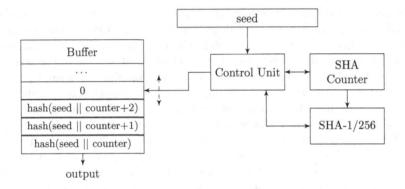

Fig. 5. Buffer generation

4.3   Mask Generation Function *(MGF)*

The *MGF* shares the buffer generation module presented in Fig. 5 with the *BPGM*. However, instead of using the buffer output for finding the value of the indexes of r, the *MGF* transforms the output from a binary into a ternary representation. More specifically, repetitively eight bits are taken from the buffer and converted to five ternary values if the value of these eight bits is smaller than $3^5 = 243$. Otherwise, it is rejected and the next byte of the buffer is used. In contrast to the algorithm defined in the standard, we use an efficient Lookup Table (LUT) for this conversion.

4.4   Modulo Reduction *(MOD P)*

The naive way to compute the modulo reduction of polynomials is to repeatedly subtract the modulus p from each coefficient of the polynomial until the coefficient is smaller than p. However, as $p = 3$ is a Mersenne prime number, a faster method to calculate the modulo reduction can be employed, as shown in [11] and optimized in [5]. Algorithm 1 presents the modulo reduction used in our NTRU architecture. To improve the throughput, the *MOD p* block is instantiated twice.

Algorithm 1: Mersenne prime modulo division ($p = 3$)

Input: Integer a
Result: Integer a mod 3
additional_reduction $= \{0, 1, 2, 0, 1, 2\}$
// reduce a
$a = (a \gg 8) + (a~\&~0xFF)$
$a = (a \gg 4) + (a~\&~0xF)$
$a = (a \gg 2) + (a~\&~0x3)$
$a = (a \gg 2) + (a~\&~0x3)$
// at this point a < 6
a = additional_reduction$[a]$

---

5 NTRU HW/SW Co-design

While "pure" hardware implementations offer high performance solutions they also have several disadvantages such as the loss in flexibility, portability, and the increasing area overhead. In contrast, a "pure" software solution is easier to develop and maintain. It offers a high flexibility and portability, but provides a lower performance. Hybrid solutions that aim to profit from the individual benefits of hardware and software are the basis of the powerful co-design techniques.

Previous works [5,20] identify the multiplication as the performance bottleneck of a NTRU software implementation. Therefore, in this work we propose and analyze a HW/SW co-design approach. In our proposal, the NTRU software implementation is accelerated by outsourcing performance-critical multiplications to hardware. This approach can speed up the software implementation while decreasing the hardware costs. As the NTRU key generation must be executed only once in a Public-Key Encryption (PKE) setting, in this work we focus on accelerating the encryption and decryption routines.

System-on-Chip (SoC) FPGAs have become very attractive due to their flexibility and fast development capabilities. They combine one or multiple processors with the programmable logic and are therefore well suited for prototyping the NTRU HW/SW co-design approach. Figure 6 shows the block diagram of our developed architecture. It is composed of three main blocks. The first one is the *Processing System*, which executes the software application. It is linked to the remaining components of the system through the High Performance (HP) and General Purpose (GP) ports, used for high-bandwidth and low-bandwidth data transfers, respectively. The second block is the *Accelerator*, which performs the polynomial multiplication. Finally, the *Direct Memory Access (DMA)* module is used as a high throughput interface between *Processing System* and *Accelerator* for the data transfer of the polynomial coefficients. These three modules are interconnected through the AXI bus.

In our setting, the *Processing System* is responsible for configuring the *DMA* module. It sets the memory region (start/end address), configures the direction and triggers the data transfer. The configuration is realized by writing to specific registers located in the *DMA* module via the GP0 port. The *Accelerator* has two AXI4-Stream interfaces, which are the optimal solutions to transport arbitrary unidirectional data streams. In order to perform efficient data transfers through the 32-bit data AXI bus structure, one packet contains a value of four coefficients, which are stored in a 32 bit memory line according to $(000 \,\|\, A_{i+1} \,\|\, B_{i+1} \,\|\, 000 \,\|\, A_i \,\|\, B_i)$, where $A \in \mathcal{T}_N$, $B \in R_{N,q}$ and $q = 2048$.

The *Accelerator* has five different states: *idle*, *read*, *conv_enc*, *conv_dec* and *write*. The state switches from *idle* to *read* when the *DMA* sends a valid input packet. The state machine remains in the *read* state until the signal that identifies the last packet is set to one. Depending on the *config* signal, the state machine switches to the *conv_enc* or *conv_dec* state. After n cycles (encryption) or $4n$ cycles (decryption), the *Accelerator* writes the coefficients via the *DMA* back to the memory. If the *Accelerator* was in the *conv_dec* state, a modulo reduction is performed on the coefficients of B before sending the result. The *Accelerator* uses the same sub-modules for the convolution and modulo reduction as described in Subsects. 4.1 and 4.4. More specifically, it uses one *CONV* module and two *MOD p* modules: one for the reduction of B_i and one for the reduction of B_{i+1}.

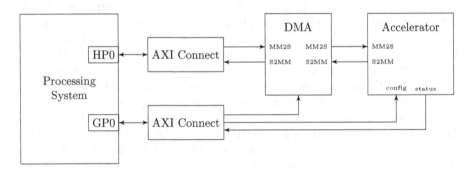

Fig. 6. HW/SW co-design architecture with NTRU executed on the 'Processing System' and hardware accelerator connected via DMA module. Abbreviation MM2S indicates memory mapped to stream ports and S2MM stream to memory mapped ports.

5.1   Software Implementation

Among the existent NTRU software implementations, for the sake of simplicity and reproducibility, we decided to use the NTRU software implementation presented in the open-source library of NTRUOpenSourceProject [23]. This software solution corresponds to the official NTRU implementation compliant with the IEEE-1363.1 standard and is designed by the NTRU authors.

In our NTRU HW/SW co-design solution, it is possible to switch between software and hardware polynomial multiplication during compile time through define directives.

The software-based multiplication algorithm uses the fact that one of the NTRU multiplication factors always consists of a ternary polynomial, which is characterized by its sparsity (most of the values of the polynomial are zero) and the fact that its coefficients only take the values minus one, zero and one. This allows the substitution of the NTRU multiplication by additions and subtractions of polynomials in $R_{N,q}$. The algorithm iterates over all non-zero coefficients of the ternary polynomial and applies operations according to the coefficient's value, i.e. addition in case of a one and subtraction in case of a minus one. The respective index of a coefficient defines the location where these additions/subtractions onto a result array are performed. As coefficients equal to zero are skipped, the overall execution time of the multiplication is decreased.

In addition to the previous single coefficient implementation, the NTRUOpenSourceProject library also provides two multiplication alternatives that are able to perform simultaneously either two (32 bit architecture) or four (64 bit architecture) coefficient addition/subtractions. This modification was introduced by the authors with the aim to support different bit width processing architectures. However, by examining the required clock cycles to perform a multiplication, we observed that on our target architecture Cortex-A53 (with optimization "-O3"), the single coefficient implementation outperforms the other alternatives. As the Cortex-A53 is the core of our platform, we have chosen the single coefficient implementation as the reference implementation used for comparison with our NTRU HW/SW solution.

6   Security Analysis

In [15], the authors show an optimization of their NTRU hardware implementation presented in [14]. It is based on scanning the coefficients of the ternary polynomial during the multiplication. When two consecutive zeros are detected, the two corresponding multiplications can be reduced to one, thus speeding up the execution. In the following subsections, we describe the optimized architecture and present the security vulnerability caused by this optimization.

6.1   Optimized Architecture

The optimized architecture is able to detect two consecutive zeros in the ternary input polynomial A (Fig. 4). The processing of a zero coefficient during the convolution can be seen as a single circular shift of the coefficients C_i. Therefore, two zeros can be substituted by a single shift of two places within one clock cycle. This results in a reduction of one cycle in the total multiplication time for each pair of consecutive zeros. The implementation of Liu *et al.* [15] requires an additional multiplexer for the MAU, which is connected to the preceding register output of the result coefficient C_i. In comparison to their original and non-optimized implementation in [14], the authors report a reduction of 36.7 % of the execution time for the convolution with the parameter set *ees541ep1*.

6.2   Vulnerabilities

In the conference version of this paper [3], it was shown that the optimized implementation of [15] leaks information about the secret key through a timing side-channel because the convolution time depends on the structure of the key, i.e. the amount of double zeros in the secret key polynomial. The term double zero is used in the following to express that two subsequent coefficients of the secret polynomial are zero. Three consecutive zeros are processed as one double zero (the first two) and one single zero (the third coefficient) as opposed to a single zero and then a double zero. This corresponds to the actual optimization in [15]. The vulnerability to a timing side-channel is inherent to the design as the optimization is solely based on exploiting the occurrence of double zeros: The overall reduced processing time is a clear indicator of how many double zeros are present in the secret polynomial F. Based on this knowledge, part of the key space can be discarded by an attacker. This reduces the effective length of the private key polynomial and hence the security level.

Whereas, the previous conference version [3] provided a bound for the number of possible secret polynomials given an observed amount of double zeros, now the result has been sharpened. The following theorem provides the exact amount of these polynomials, such that the precise complexity reduction of the exhaustive search space can be computed.

Theorem 1. *The number of valid ternary polynomials for a given number of double zeros d_z is given by*

$$u_r(n, d_f, d_z) = \frac{(2d_f + d_z)!}{d_z! \cdot d_f! \cdot d_f!} \cdot \binom{2d_f + 1}{d_s}, \tag{4}$$

where n is the number of coefficients of the polynomial, d_f the number of 1's and also of the -1's in the private key F, and d_s is the amount of single zeros, i.e. $d_s = n - 2d_z - 2d_f$. Note that $2d_f$ is for d_f 1's and the additional d_f -1's.

Proof. The proof of this theorem consists of two steps as visualized in Fig. 7. It is derived how many possibilities exist to build a polynomial given the amount of 1's, -1's, and double zeros.

Step I: First all the 1's, -1's, and double zeros are placed. A double zero is not to be handled as two numbers, but as one symbol, because both zeros are placed at once. Overall there are $2d_f + d_z$ spots for these symbols (the grey squares in Fig. 7). This results in

$$\frac{(2d_f + d_z)!}{d_z! \cdot d_f! \cdot d_f!} \tag{5}$$

possibilities to arrange all the 1's, -1's and double zeros according to the multiset permutation formula. The denominator is needed to exclude configurations which cannot be distinguished. For example, interchanging the 1's does not change the overall sequence.

Step II: Given any configuration of Step I, now the single zeros are placed among the sequence of 1's, −1's, and double zeros. However, two conditions have to be satisfied in Step II:

(a) No two single zeros are allowed next to each other, because they would then count as one double zero.
(b) A single zero followed by a double zero (0 00) is not valid as this would in fact be considered as a double zero followed by a single zero (00 0). This corresponds to the definition of double zeros and matches how zeros are processed in the optimized architecture.

If only condition (a) is considered, there are $2d_f + d_z + 1$ positions to place the single zeros. This is depicted in Fig. 7 Step II (a) by the white squares: Each of the d_f 1's, the d_f −1's, and the d_z double zeros (i.e. each grey square) has exactly one empty spot to its left $(d_f + d_f + d_z)$. Exactly one spot is necessary to ensure that no two single zeros can be placed directly next to each other, that is: no two white squares are next to each other, as there is always a grey square in between. Furthermore, an empty spot is merely a possible position for a single zero. Hence, it is not necessary to actually put a single zero there. Finally, there is an empty spot on the very right (+1), i.e. the white box with +1.

Under condition (b) however, the amount of valid spots for a single zero is limited as the spots left to a double zero are not allowed. In Fig. 7 Step II (a)+(b), they are represented by a crossed-out spot left of every double zero position (grey box with 00). (0 00 is by definition not valid and would be understood as 00 0). Thus, in fact there are only $2d_f + 1$ free and valid spots (white boxes) for a single zero. There are exactly d_z double zeros and wherever they are placed, they have got exactly one possible free spot as left neighbour which has to be crossed out. Out of the remaining $2d_f + 1$ possible positions now d_s spots are chosen for the d_s single zeros:

$$\binom{2d_f + 1}{d_s} \qquad (6)$$

Because the amount of possibilities in Step (II) holds for any possible configuration in Step (I), multiplying the two intermediate results proves Theorem 1.

□

Based on this result, one can compute by which factor the search complexity is reduced given a certain amount of observed double zeros and different parameter sets. Figure 8 illustrates the complexity reduction factor α for the parameter sets in [10]. This factor can be computed by

$$\alpha = \frac{u_r(n, d_f, d_z)}{K_c}, \text{ with } K_c = \frac{n!}{(d_f!)^2 (n - 2d_f)!}, \qquad (7)$$

where K_c denotes the cardinality of the key space. Overall, for any of the parameter sets as given in [10], the greatest loss of security is given for the minimum amount of double zeros for the respective parameter set. Note that this minimum

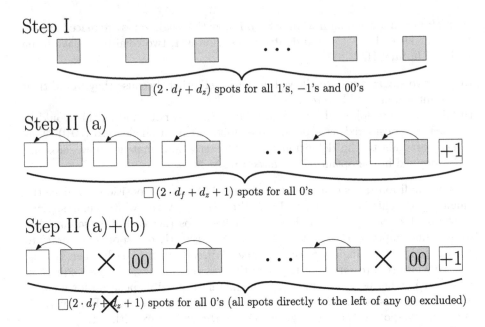

Fig. 7. Visualization of the proof

number of double zeros $d_{z,min}$ is not necessarily 0, but

$$d_{z,min} = \max\left(\left\lfloor \frac{n - 4d_f}{2} \right\rfloor, 0 \right).$$ (8)

The worst case complexity reduction for every parameter set can be computed given $d_{z,min}$ by means of Eq. 7. The parameter set with the greatest loss in security when exploiting double zeros as in [15] is *ees677ep1* with a complexity reduction factor up to 10^{-160}. This means that if the secret polynomial has the minimum amount of double zeros, then an attacker can discard most of the key space and only focus on a subset of polynomials which is 10^{160} times smaller than the original key space. Additionally, the enlarged part of Fig. 8 illustrates that a minimum leakage regardless of the amount of double zeros exists. Even for a configuration with the most likely amount of double zeros, part of the key space can be excluded by the attacker. E.g. for *ees659ep1*, 276 double zeros result in an effective key space with a size that is roughly 17.8% of the whole key space. Consequently, in the best case from a legitimate user's point of view still 82.2% of the possible secret keys can be neglected by an attacker. In case of every other parameter set, even more keys are discarded in the best case scenario.

Yet, it could be argued that despite the possibility for an attacker to disregard a certain part of the key space, the remaining key space still might be large enough to withstand an exhaustive search. However, this vulnerability only considers brute-force attacks. If by means of a more sophisticated attack the key space shrinks further, security might no longer be guaranteed. This shows that

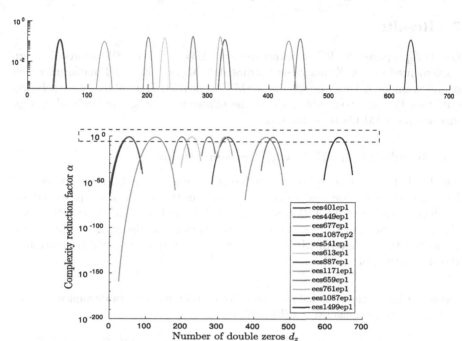

Fig. 8. Complexity reduction of the exhaustive search space of the private key F for a known amount of double-zeros and the parameter sets in [10]. The top part of the figure is an excerpt of the whole graph to illustrate complexity reduction in the best case scenario.

leaking the exact amount of double zeros by a timing side-channel reduces the security. As a final remark, one could consider exploiting exactly the minimum amount of double zeros for a given parameter set. Because given a parameter set there are at least $d_{z,min}$ double zeros, the attacker gains no information if for any d_z exactly $d_{z,min}$ double zeros are used to speed up the computations. Consequently, a counter could keep track of how many double zeros have been exploited by processing them as double zero. If $d_{z,min}$ double zeros have been used for a speed-up, the zeros to come are processed normally. For most of the parameter sets, the amount of clock cycles can be reduced. However, the usage of a counter introduces a new side-channel. If an attacker can detect the point in time when the implementation stops processing double zeros, the key space once again can be reduced. Furthermore, an attacker might be able to detect which coefficients are double zeros, resulting in an additional complexity reduction. Overall, saving few clock cycles in such a way is not worth the overhead and especially the leakage through this side-channel.

7   Results

Our two proposed NTRU architectures (full HW and HW/SW approach) were implemented on the Xilinx Zynq UltraScale+ MPSoC ZCU102 platform, which contains among others a quad-core ARM Cortex-A53. The full hardware solution only uses the programmable logic of the platform whereas the HW/SW design utilizes the ARM Cortex-A53, too.

7.1   Results of Full Hardware Implementation

The IEEE-1363.1 standard defines different parameter sets for different security levels and optimization goals. Table 1 summarizes the results of our proposed full hardware implementation. It contains the total number of LUTs, registers, and the required number of clock cycles for encryption and decryption. The results show that the number of LUTs scales with the parameter n, which determines the size of the polynomials.

Table 1. Clock cycle count and resource utilization of the full hardware implementation with parameter sets defined in IEEE-1363.1

Security level	Parameter set	n	LUT	Register	#CC Enc.	#CC Dec.
Low	ees401ep1	401	29,119	25,445	3,423	5,430
	ees541ep1	541	36,990	27,617	2,409	5,116
	ees659ep1	659	45,685	31,540	2,413	5,711
Middle	ees449ep1	449	32,851	27,263	3,642	5,890
	ees613ep1	613	44,168	30,555	2,675	5,743
	ees761ep1	761	52,208	35,586	2,799	6,606
High	ees677ep1	677	50,441	38,819	4,020	7,407
	ees887ep1	887	64,539	42,636	3,113	7,551
	ees1087ep1	1,087	74,774	50,000	3,760	9,197
Highest	ees1087ep2	1,087	75,393	53,740	4,723	10,159
	ees1171ep1	1,171	74,730	52,497	4,345	10,202
	ees1499ep1	1,499	98,774	66,200	4,715	12,212

Figure 9 provides a more detailed view of the required clock cycles for the encryption. The time required for the convolution depends directly on the value of n because n clock cycles are required for the circular shift within the LFSR. Results show that the impact of the padding scheme on the cost and performance of NTRU is not negligible. For some NTRU configurations, in hardware the convolution has a minor influence on the computation cost when compared to the SVES padding scheme. For the parameter set ees401ep1, the padding scheme takes nearly 90 % of the encryption time.

The main bottleneck of the padding scheme are the repetitive calls of the hash function. The number of clock cycles spent by the BPGM mainly depends on the parameter d_r, which determines the number of ones and minus ones in r and thus the number of hash calls. Please note that the amount of clock cycles for the BPGM slightly depends on the seed of the hash function. As described in Subsect. 4.2, the c-bits of the hash value must be discarded if the generated index is already set. Moreover, the runtime of the reduction modulo N varies. For these two reasons, a variation in the execution time of the BPGM in the lower double-digit range was observed. As the differences are small, the determined values remain meaningful.

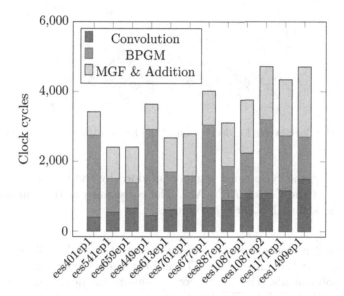

Fig. 9. Clock cycles for encryption of the full hardware implementation

Figure 10 illustrates the computation costs for the decryption. Whereas the decryption requires $4n$ clock cycles for the convolution, the encryption only requires n clock cycles. Both, the convolution and the modulo p operation directly scale with n. Note that the execution time of the MGF can also slightly vary when the fetched byte is not smaller than 243. In practice, this has only a marginal influence on the performance.

7.2   Results of HW/SW Co-design

In this subsection, the resource utilization and runtime of the HW/SW co-design is described. For all clock cycle measurements, the Cortex ARM-A53 ran at a target frequency of 1,200 MHz (real 1,199.880 MHz) and the hardware accelerator at a target frequency of 200 MHz (real 187.481 MHz). The runtime was

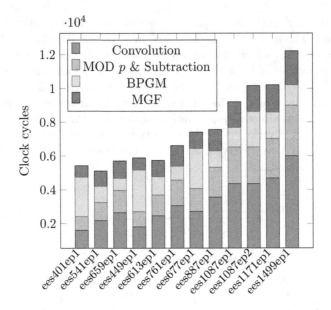

Fig. 10. Clock cycles for decryption of the full hardware implementation

measured using the cycle count register provided by the Performance Monitor Unit (PMU) of the Cortex ARM-A53. The correctness of these measurements was cross-checked with a hardware counter.

Area. Table 2 presents the resource utilization of our HW/SW solution. The results show that the amount of LUTs and registers depends on the size of the processed polynomials. The largest components in the design are the *Accelerator* and the *DMA* module. The *DMA* module requires, in addition to the listed LUTs and registers, two Block RAM (BRAM) instances. Its resource utilization remains constant for all parameter sets. Within the *Accelerator*, the *CONV* module is the largest component. The results also show that the required amount of LUTs and registers is lower for the HW/SW solution when compared to the full hardware design.

Performance. Tables 3 and 4 present the clock cycle counts for the NTRU software implementation with and without hardware accelerator. For the software implementation, the open-source library discussed in Sect. 5.1 is used. Two different compiler optimization levels were tested: '-O1' for small optimizations (Table 3) and '-O3' for the highest speed optimization (Table 4). The results with the hardware accelerator include the communication overhead. The measured clock cycles are related to the clock of the *Processing System*, i.e. one clock cycle in hardware corresponds to roughly six cycles in the *Processing System*.

Table 2. HW/SW co-design resource utilization

Parameter set	Total LUT/ Register	Accelerator LUT/Register	Convolution LUT/Register	DMA LUT/ Register
ees401ep1	19,582/16,104	15,572/10,710	11,378/5,342	1,263/1,759
ees541ep1	25,108/19,729	21,090/14,335	15,167/7,074	1,273/1,759
ees659ep1	29,181/22,787	25,169/17,393	18,454/8,614	1,270/1,759
ees449ep1	21,463/17,375	17,440/11,981	12,763/5,980	1,272/1,759
ees613ep1	27,547/21,583	23,533/16,189	17,169/8,013	1,265/1,759
ees761ep1	32,615/25,449	28,602/20,055	21,303/9,944	1,267/1,759
ees677ep1	29,891/23,249	25,880/17,855	18,956/8,848	1,267/1,759
ees887ep1	38,670/28,752	34,659/23,358	24,832/11,590	1,268/1,759
ees1087ep1	46,788/33,966	42,773/28,572	30,423/14,199	1,271/1,759
ees1087ep2	46,788/33,966	42,773/28,572	30,423/14,199	1,271/1,759
ees1171ep1	50,402/36,183	46,384/30,789	32,757/15,296	1,272/1,759
ees1499ep1	63,221/44,766	59,197/39,372	41,912/19,574	1,276/1,759

The defined parameter sets have different optimization goals. The parameter sets $ees401ep1$, $ees449ep1$, $ees677ep1$ and $ees1087ep2$ are optimized for size and have the smallest polynomials in their respective security category. The sets $ees541ep1$, $ees613ep1$, $ees887ep1$ and $ees1171ep1$ are cost-optimized and have the lowest value of '(operation time)$^2\times$ size'. Obviously, $ees659ep1$, $ees761ep1$, $ees1087ep1$ and $ees1499ep1$ are optimized for speed. They have the lowest amount of clock cycles in their security category. This classification does not apply for the HW/SW co-design anymore. Similar to the area consumption, the required amount of clock cycles for the polynomial multiplication depends on the parameter n.

With the optimization level '-O1' and the fastest parameter set of the highest security category—parameter set $ees1499ep1$—a speedup factor of 44.38 can be achieved for calculating $h * r$ and a factor of 17.74 for calculating $peF + e$ mod p. By setting the optimization flag to '-O3', the speedup decreases to 9.87 and 4.77, respectively. However, this is still a considerable improvement because the Cortex-A53 is already a very powerful processor running at a higher clock frequency when compared to the frequency of the hardware accelerator. The runtime of the whole encryption function is improved by the factor 5.55 ('-O1') and 1.99 ('-O3'), the runtime for decryption is improved by a factor of 7.94 ('-O1') and 2.60 ('-O3'). Other parameter sets even have a higher improvement because the mentioned parameter set belongs to the fastest in software.

Table 3. HW/SW co-design cycle count (kilo cycles) when optimization -O1 is used ('yes' and 'no' for usage of hardware accelerator)

Parameter set	$h * r$	$peF + e$	Encryption	Decryption
	no/yes	no/yes	no/yes	no/yes
ees401ep1	557.7/13.6	572.1/27.2	690.6/145.8	1,278.2/188.5
ees541ep1	329.2/14.4	348.9/32.9	440.8/125.6	809.3/178.1
ees659ep1	312.3/16.0	336.4/39.3	433.2/136.0	772.6/178.7
ees449ep1	738.0/15.5	754.3/30.8	889.3/166.6	1,662.1/214.0
ees613ep1	417.0/15.5	439.2/36.8	541.9/140.6	1,004.1/199.4
ees761ep1	397.0/18.0	424.4/44.3	537.5/157.7	966.4/207.2
ees677ep1	1,296.2/20.1	1,320.9/43.0	1,494.8/218.8	2,844.0/289.3
ees887ep1	879.0/21.5	911.3/52.2	1,065.5/207.6	2,007.6/289.0
ees1087ep1	841.0/24.6	880.4/62.4	1,049.8/232.5	1,937.7/303.2
ees1087ep2	1,588.6/26.3	1,628.1/64.0	1,830.0/268.0	3,499.9/372.7
ees1171ep1	1,513.0/27.3	1,555.0/67.9	1,761.0/276.0	3,360.9/388.5
ees1499ep1	1,446.8/32.6	1,500.8/84.6	1,725.3/310.6	3,238.3/407.8

Table 4. HW/SW co-design cycle count (kilo cycles) when optimization -O3 is used ('yes' and 'no' for usage of hardware accelerator)

Parameter set	$h * r$	$peF + e$	Encryption	Decryption
	no/yes	no/yes	no/yes	no/yes
ees401ep1	141.6/13.0	153.3/24.3	257.3/131.5	421.5/164.0
ees541ep1	81.1/14.0	97.0/29.2	180.1/114.8	289.1/154.3
ees659ep1	73.4/16.0	92.8/34.7	181.2/124.8	273.6/156.0
ees449ep1	183.7/14.6	196.3/27.2	316.5/149.9	524.5/186.5
ees613ep1	100.5/15.3	118.1/32.8	211.8/128.4	343.2/171.8
ees761ep1	90.6/17.6	113.7/39.3	215.3/144.8	329.6/182.7
ees677ep1	307.1/19.6	327.7/38.5	482.0/194.7	824.5/247.9
ees887ep1	201.7/21.2	229.1/47.0	365.9/187.5	613.1/249.8
ees1087ep1	189.5/24.5	221.4/55.2	374.8/212.1	593.9/263.9
ees1087ep2	357.1/25.6	389.4/56.8	567.8/239.5	980.8/318.5
ees1171ep1	335.1/26.5	369.3/60.2	553.0/247.8	947.1/330.6
ees1499ep1	314.8/31.9	358.8/75.2	559.2/280.7	919.7/353.8

8   Conclusion

Efficient and secure post-quantum cryptography is mandatory to ensure long-term security. The lattice-based cryptographic scheme NTRU is a promising candidate to replace traditional PKC. Previous works in NTRU hardware implementations focused on the development of a fast polynomial multiplication architecture. In this work, for the first time, we propose a full hardware/software implementation that is compliant with the IEEE-1363.1 standard. By including the SVES scheme, our NTRU solution is secure against CCA. The results show that for the full NTRU hardware implementation, the costs of the SVES scheme cannot be neglected. For some parameters it requires nearly 90 % of the total encryption time. In order to increase the flexibility, the HW/SW co-design NTRU solution can be used. By outsourcing the polynomial multiplication and modulo operation to hardware, we achieve significant performance improvements. Moreover, we show that an efficient NTRU implementation is not enough. We have demonstrated that a state-of-the-art hardware optimized NTRU [15] presents a leakage that reduces the security level of NTRU. Their polynomial multiplication introduces a timing side-channel that reduces the private key search space. Thus an attacker can exploit this weakness to recover the secret key.

References

1. Atici, A.C., Batina, L., Fan, J., Verbauwhede, I., Örs, S.B.: Low-cost implementations of NTRU for pervasive security. In: 19th IEEE International Conference on Application-Specific Systems, Architectures and Processors, ASAP 2008, July 2–4, 2008, Leuven, Belgium, pp. 79–84 (2008)
2. Bailey, D.V., Coffin, D., Elbirt, A., Silverman, J.H., Woodbury, A.D.: NTRU in constrained devices. In: Koç, Ç.K., Naccache, D., Paar, C. (eds.) CHES 2001. LNCS, vol. 2162, pp. 262–272. Springer, Heidelberg (2001). https://doi.org/10.1007/3-540-44709-1_22
3. Braun, K., Fritzmann, T., Maringer, G., Schamberger, T., Sepúlveda, J.: Secure and compact full NTRU hardware implementation. In: 2018 IFIP/IEEE International Conference on Very Large Scale Integration (VLSI-SoC), pp. 89–94. IEEE (2018)
4. Collen Marie, O.: Efficient NTRU implementation. Master's thesis, Worcester Polytechnic Institute (2002). https://www.wpi.edu/Pubs/ETD/Available/etd-0430102-111906/unrestricted/corourke.pdf
5. Guillen, O.M., Pöppelmann, T., Mera, J.M.B., Bongenaar, E.F., Sigl, G., Sepulveda, J.: Towards post-quantum security for IoT endpoints with NTRU. In: Design, Automation Test in Europe Conference Exhibition (DATE), pp. 698–703, March 2017. https://doi.org/10.23919/DATE.2017.7927079
6. Hoffstein, J., Pipher, J., Schanck, J.M., Silverman, J.H., Whyte, W., Zhang, Z.: Choosing parameters for NTRUEncrypt. IACR ePrint 2015, 708 (2015). http://eprint.iacr.org/2015/708
7. Howgrave-Graham, N., Nguyen, P.Q., Pointcheval, D., Proos, J., Silverman, J.H., Singer, A., Whyte, W.: The impact of decryption failures on the security of NTRU encryption. In: Boneh, D. (ed.) CRYPTO 2003. LNCS, vol. 2729, pp. 226–246. Springer, Heidelberg (2003). https://doi.org/10.1007/978-3-540-45146-4_14

8. Howgrave-Graham, N., Silverman, J.H., Singer, A., Whyte, W.: NAEP: provable security in the presence of decryption failures. IACR Cryptology ePrint Archive 2003, 172 (2003)
9. Hu, F., Wilhelm, K., Schab, M., Lukowiak, M., Radziszowski, S., Xiao, Y.: NTRU-based sensor network security: a low-power hardware implementation perspective. Secur. Commun. Netw. **2**(1), 71–81 (2009)
10. IEEE: IEEE Standard Specification for Public Key Cryptographic Techniques Based on Hard Problems over Lattices. IEEE Std 1363.1-2008, pp. C1–69, March 2009. https://doi.org/10.1109/IEEESTD.2009.4800404
11. Jones, D.W.: Modulus without division, a tutorial (2001). http://homepage.cs.uiowa.edu/~jones/bcd/mod.shtml
12. Kamal, A.A., Youssef, A.M.: An FPGA implementation of the NTRUEncrypt cryptosystem. In: 2009 International Conference on Microelectronics (ICM), pp. 209–212. IEEE (2009)
13. Lee, M.-K., Kim, J.W., Song, J.E., Park, K.: Sliding window method for NTRU. In: Katz, J., Yung, M. (eds.) ACNS 2007. LNCS, vol. 4521, pp. 432–442. Springer, Heidelberg (2007). https://doi.org/10.1007/978-3-540-72738-5_28
14. Liu, B., Wu, H.: Efficient architecture and implementation for NTRUEncrypt system. In: 2015 IEEE 58th International Midwest Symposium on Circuits and Systems (MWSCAS), pp. 1–4. IEEE (2015)
15. Liu, B., Wu, H.: Efficient multiplication architecture over truncated polynomial ring for NTRUEncrypt system. In: IEEE International Symposium on Circuits and Systems, ISCAS 2016, Montréal, QC, Canada, May 22–25, 2016, pp. 1174–1177 (2016)
16. Grover, L.K.: A fast quantum mechanical algorithm for database search. In: 28th Annual ACM Symposium on the Theory of Computing, p. 212, May 1996
17. Monteverde, M.: NTRU software implementation for constrained devices. Master's thesis, Katholieke Universiteit Leuven (2008)
18. National Institute of Standards and Technology: Announcing request for nominations for public-key post-quantum cryptographic algorithms (2016). https://csrc.nist.gov/news/2016/public-key-post-quantum-cryptographic-algorithms
19. de la Piedra, A.: SHA-256 Core (2013). https://opencores.org/project/sha256core/
20. Sepulveda, J., Zankl, A., Mischke, O.: Cache attacks and countermeasures for NTRUEncrypt on MPSoCs: post-quantum resistance for the IoT. In: 2017 30th IEEE International System-on-Chip Conference (SOCC), pp. 120–125, September 2017. https://doi.org/10.1109/SOCC.2017.8226020
21. Sepulveda, J., Liu, S., Mera, J.M.B.: Post-quantum enabled cyber physical systems. In: IEEE Embedded Systems Letters, pp. 1–4 (2019)
22. Shor, P.W.: Algorithms for quantum computation: discrete logarithms and factoring. In: 1994 Proceedings of the 35th Annual Symposium on Foundations of Computer Science, pp. 124–134. IEEE (1994)
23. Whyte, W.: NTRU Open Source Project (2017). https://github.com/NTRUOpenSourceProject/NTRUEncrypt
24. Zhan, X., Zhang, R., Xiong, Z., Zheng, Z., Liu, Z.: Efficient implementations of NTRU in wireless network. Commun. Netw. **5**(03), 485 (2013)

Correction to: Improved Test Solutions for COTS-Based Systems in Space Applications

Riccardo Cantoro, Sara Carbonara, Andrea Floridia, Ernesto Sanchez, Matteo Sonza Reorda, and Jan-Gerd Mess

Correction to:
Chapter "Improved Test Solutions for COTS-Based Systems in Space Applications" in: N. Bombieri et al. (Eds.): *VLSI-SoC: Design and Engineering of Electronics Systems Based on New Computing Paradigms*, IFIP AICT 561, https://doi.org/10.1007/978-3-030-23425-6_10

The original version of this chapter contained an error in the third author's name. The spelling of Andrea Floridia's name was incorrect in the header of the paper. The author's name has been corrected.

The updated version of this chapter can be found at
https://doi.org/10.1007/978-3-030-23425-6_10

Author Index